# DEFENSES IN CONTEMPORARY INTERNATIONAL CRIMINAL LAW

## GEERT-JAN G.J. KNOOPS

Transnational Publishers, Inc.
Ardsley, New York

Library of Congress Cataloging-in-Publication Data

Knoops, Geert-Jan G.J.
    Defenses in contemporary international criminal law / Geert-Jan G.J. Knoops.
        p.cm.— (International & comparative criminal law series)
    Includes bibliographical references and index.
    ISBN 1–57105–151–1
        1. Defenses (criminal procedure) 2. International offenses. I. Title. II. Series.

    K5455.K59 2001
    595.78′092—dc21
    [B]                                                  2001023081

Manufactured in the United States of America

# INTERNATIONAL AND COMPARATIVE CRIMINAL LAW SERIES

"I pray that the world will have taken even greater steps toward democracy and the guarantee of human rights, and that dignity will have become the universally accepted value of mankind."

(Chaim Herzog, in Living History at XIII).

"... and they shall judge the people a righteous judgment."

(Deut. 16:18)

"Ultimately, if the ICC (and the system of ICL; GJK) saves but one life, as it is said in the Talmud, it will be as if it saved the whole of humanity."

(M. Cherif Bassiouni, in Preface to Commentary on the Rome Statute of the International Criminal Court (Otto Triffterer, ed.)

*To my beloved wife Carry: "Far beyond pearls is her value* (Proverbs 31: 10–31).

*To my beloved family.*

*To peace.*

# TABLE OF CONTENTS

# TABLE OF ABBREVIATIONS

| | |
|---|---|
| Add. Prot. | Additional Protocol to the four Geneva Conventions |
| ALL ER | All England Reports |
| AM. J. INT'L.L. | American Journal of International Law |
| BRIT.Y.B. INT'L.L | British Yearbook of International Law |
| Crim. L. Rev. | Criminal Law Review |
| Conf. | Conference |
| ECRM | European Court of Human Rights |
| ed. | Editor |
| eds. | Editors |
| e.g. | for example |
| et al. | and others |
| et seq. | et sequitur ("and what follows") |
| dd | de dato |
| Doc. | Document |
| 1988 Drug Convention | United Nations Convention Against Illicit Traffic in Narcotic Drugs and Psychotropic Substances opened for signature at Vienna 20 Dec. 1988, U.N. Doc. E/CONF. 82/15, reprinted in 28 I.L.M. 493 (1989) |
| G.A. Res. | (U.N.) General Assembly Resolution |
| G.A. | (U.N.) General Assembly |
| GAOR | (U.N.) General Assembly Official Records |
| ibid | ibidem ("same as previous") |
| ICC | International Criminal Court |
| ICCPR | International Covenant on Civil and Political Rights |
| ICC Statute | Rome Statute of the International Criminal Court, A/Conf.183/9, 17 July 1998 |
| ICJ | International Court of Justice |
| ICJ Reports | International Court of Justice Reports |
| ICL | International Criminal Law |

| | |
|---|---|
| ICRC | International Commission of the Red Cross |
| ICTR | International Criminal Tribunal for Rwanda |
| ICTY | International Criminal Tribunal for the Former Yugoslavia |
| ICDAA | International Criminal Defence Attorneys Association |
| id | idem ("the same") |
| IHL | International Humanitarian Law |
| ILC | International Law Commission |
| I.L.M. | International Legal Materials |
| I.L.R. | International Law Reports |
| IMT | International Military Tribunal; see also: Nuremberg War Crimes Tribunal |
| LJIL | Leiden Journal of International Law |
| Mil. L. Rev. | Military Law Review |
| Nuremberg War Crimes Tribunal | The International Military Tribunal at Nuremberg, created by the Agreement for the Prosecution and Punishment of Major War Criminals of the European Axis, Aug. 8, 1945 (see also IMT) |
| NGO | Non-Governmental Organization |
| NILR | Netherlands International Law Review |
| NJ | Nederlandse Jurisprudentie (Dutch jurisprudence) |
| No. | number |
| Nos. | numbers |
| para | paragraph |
| paras. | paragraphs |
| PCIJ Statute | Statute of the Permanent Court of International Justice |
| Preparatory Committee Report | Report of the Preparatory Committee on the Establishment of an International Criminal Court, Vols. I. U.N. GAOR, 51st Sess. Supp. No. 22, 212–93 U.N. Doc A/51/22 (1996) |
| Res. | Resolution |
| RNLMC | Royal Netherlands Marine Corps |
| Rules | Rules of Procedure and Evidence |
| ROE | Rules of Engagement |
| seq. | sequentis |
| sess. | session |
| Soc. Sci. Med. | Social Science Medicine |

| Supp. | Supplement |
|---|---|
| Torture Convention | Convention Against Torture and Other Cruel, Inhuman or Degrading Treatment or Punishment, Dec. 10 1984, G.A. Res. 39/46 |
| U.N./UN | United Nations |
| U.N. Doc. | United Nations Document |
| U.S. | United States |
| v. | versus |
| Vol. | Volume |
| Vols. | Volumes |

# TABLE OF AUTHORITIES

ABIEW, FRANCIS K., THE EVOLUTION OF THE DOCTRINE AND PRACTICE OF HUMANITARIAN INTERVENTION (1999).

Albert, D.J., M.L. Walsh, & R.H. Jerik, *Aggression in Humans: What is its Biological Foundation?*, 17 NEUROSCIENCE AND BEHAVIORAL REVIEWS 405–425 (1993).

ALKEMA, E.A., THE ROLE AND INDEPENDENCE OF THE JUDICIARY AND THE ADMINISTRATION OF JUSTICE IN THE PERSPECTIVE OF THE RULE OF LAW 1.1 (1997).

ALLEN, FRANCIS A., THE HABITS OF LEGALITY, CRIMINAL JUSTICE AND THE RULE OF LAW 14 (1996).

Alper, Joseph S., *Genes, Free Will and Criminal Responsibility*, 46 SOCIAL SCIENCES MEDICINE 1599–1611 (1998).

Ambos, Kai, *Article 25, Margin No. 1* in COMMENTARY ON THE ROME STATUTE (Otto Triffterer ed., 1999).

Arbour, Louise, Chief Prosecutor of the ICTY and ICTR to the ISISC meeting on Comparative Criminal Justice Systems: Diversity and Approachment, 18 December 1997: *"The development of a coherent system of Rules of International Criminal Procedure and Evidence before the ad hoc International Tribunals for the Former Yugoslavia and Rwanda."*

Ascepsio, H., *The Rules of Procedure and Evidence of the ICTY*, 9 LJIL 478 (1996).

Bakker, J.L., *The Defense of Obedience to Superior Orders: The Mens Rea Requirement*, 17 AMERICAN JOURNAL OF CRIMINAL LAW 72–73.

Bantekas, Ilias, *The contemporary law of superior responsibility*, 93 THE AMERICAN JOURNAL OF INTERNATIONAL LAW 594–595 (1999).

BASSIOUNI, M. CHERIF, 1 INTERNATIONAL CRIMINAL LAW 13 (1999).

Bassiouni, M. Cherif, *Human Rights in the Context of Criminal Justice: Identifying International Procedural Protections and Equivalent Protections in National Constitutions*, 3 DUKE JOURNAL OF COMPARATIVE & INTERNATIONAL LAW, 242–243 (1993).

BASSIOUNI, M. CHERIF, & PETER MANIKAS, THE LAW OF THE ICTY 953 (1996).

BASSIOUNI, M. CHERIF, 1 INTERNATIONAL CRIMINAL LAW 4 (1999).

Bassiouni, M. Cherif, *A Functional Approach to General Principles of International Law*, 11 MICHIGAN JOURNAL OF INTERNATIONAL LAW 775–776 (1990).

Bassiouni, M. Cherif, *Combating Impunity in International Crimes*, 71 UNIVERSITY OF COLORADO LAW REVIEW 414 (2000).

BASSIOUNI, M. CHERIF, CRIMES AGAINST HUMANITY IN INTERNATIONAL CRIMINAL LAW 483 (1999).

Bassiouni, M. Cherif, *The Normative Framework of IHL: Overlaps, Gaps and Ambiguities*, in *International Criminal Law*, in 1 INTERNATIONAL CRIMINAL LAW 619 (M. Cherif Bassiouni, ed., 1999).

Bassiouni, M. Cherif, *The Penal Characteristics of Conventional International Crimes Law* in 15 CASE WESTERN RESERVE JOURNAL OF INTERNATIONAL LAW 27 at 30.

BASSIOUNI, M. CHERIF, THE PROTECTION OF HUMAN RIGHTS IN THE ADMINISTRATION OF CRIMINAL JUSTICE (1994).

Bassiouni, M.Cherif, *The Sources and Content of International Criminal Law*, in 1 INTERNATIONAL CRIMINAL LAW 20–21 (M. Cherif Bassiouni, ed., 1999).

Bergsma, M., & M. Keegan, *A note on case preparation for the ICTY*, at 5.

Blakesley, Christopher L. *Atrocity and its Prosecution: The ad hoc Tribunals for the former Yugoslavia and Rwanda*, in THE LAW OF WAR CRIMES 204 (Timothy L.H. McCormack & Gerry J. Simpson, eds., 1997).

Bohlander, Michael, *International Criminal Defence Ethics: The Law of Professional Conduct for Defence Counsel Appearing Before International Criminal Tribunals*, 1 SAN DIEGO INTERNATIONAL LAW JOURNAL 98 (2000).

Bonnie, Richard J., *The Moral Basis of the Insanity Defense*, in LAW AND PSYCHOLOGY 283 (Martin Lyon Levine, ed., 1995).

BROWNLIE, IAN, BASIC DOCUMENTS ON HUMAN RIGHTS 391 (1992).

BROWNLIE, IAN, PRINCIPLES OF PUBLIC INTERNATIONAL LAW 588–590 (1990).

BROWNLIE, IAN, THE RULE OF LAW IN INTERNATIONAL AFFAIRS 65 (1998).

Brunner, Han G., et al., *Borderline Mental Retardation with Prominent Behavioral Disturbance: Phenotype Genetic Cocalization and Evidence for Disturbed Monoamine Metabolism*, 52 AMERICAN JOURNAL HUMAN GENETICS 1032–1039 (1998).

Cadoret, Remi J., Leslie D. Leve, & Eric Devor, *Genetics of Aggressive and Violent Behaviour*, 20 THE PSYCHIATRIC CLINICS OF NORTH AMERICA 301–322 (1997).

CARDOZO, BENJAMIN N., THE NATURE OF THE JUDICIAL PROCESS 23 (1921).

Casesse, Antonio, *The Statute of the ICC: Some Preliminary Reflections*, EUROPEAN JOURNAL OF INTERNATIONAL LAW 154–155 (1999), also 144–171.

Cassese, Antonio, *Ex Iniuria ius oritur: Are We Moving Towards International Legitimation of Forcible Humanitarian Countermeasures in The World Community*, 10 EUROPEAN JOURNAL OF INTERNATIONAL LAW 3 (1998).

Charney, Jonathan I., *Anticipatory Humanitarian Intervention in Kosovo*, in Editorial Comments: NATO's Kosovo Intervention, 93 THE AMERICAN JOURNAL OF INTERNATIONAL LAW 841 (1999).

Coccaro, E.F., *Impulsive aggression and central serotonergic system function in humans: an example of a dimensional brain-behavior relationship*, 7 INTERNATIONAL CLINICAL PSYCHOPHARMACOLOGY 3–12 (1992).

Coccaro, Emil F., C.S. Bergeman, R.J. Kavoussi, & A.D. Seroczynski, *Heritability of aggression and irritability: A twin study of the Buss-Durkee aggression scales in adult male subjects*, 1 BIOL PSYCHIATRY 273–284 (1997).

COHEN, E.A., HET DUITSE CONCENTRATIEKAMP, EEN MEDISCHE EN PSYCHOLOGISCHE STUDIE (1956).

Comings, D.E., *The Molecular Genetics of Pathological Gambling*, 3 THE INTERNATIONAL JOURNAL OF NEUROPSYCHIATRIC MEDICINE 20–37 (1998).

CRAIG, PAUL, & GRAINNE DE BURCA, EU LAW 3 (1998).

deGuzman, Margaret McAuliffe, *Article 21, Margin No. 15* in COMMENTARY ON THE ROME STATUTE (Otto Triffterer, ed., 1999).

DERSHOWITZ, ALAN M., REASONABLE DOUBTS: THE O.J. SIMPSON CASE AND THE CRIMINAL JUSTICE SYSTEM 157 (1996).

Dinstein, Yoram, *International Criminal Law*, 20 ISRAEL LAW REVIEW 235 (1985).

DINSTEIN, YORAM, THE DEFENSE OF OBEDIENCE TO SUPERIOR ORDERS IN INTERNATIONAL LAW 253 (1965).

DINSTEIN, YORAM, WAR, AGGRESSION AND SELF-DEFENSE 202–212 and 221–229 (1988).

Dinwiddle, Simon H., *Genetics, Antisocial Personality and Criminal Responsibility*, 24 BULLETIN OF THE AMERICAN ACADEMY OF PSYCHIATRIC LAW 95–108 (1996), especially at 98.

Dugard, C.J.R., *Een Internationale balie bij het Internationale Strafhof*, 1 ADVOCATENBLAD 17–18 (2000).

Dugard, John, *Independent Defence Before the ICC: The Role of Lawyers Before International Courts*, in AN INDEPENDENT DEFENCE BEFORE THE INTERNATIONAL CRIMINAL COURT 22 (Hans Bevers & Chantal Joubert, eds., 2000).

DUGARD, JOHN, INTERNATIONAL LAW, A SOUTH AFRICAN PERSPECTIVE (2000).

Dugard, John, *The Criminal Responsibility of States*, in 1 INTERNATIONAL CRIMINAL LAW 239–253 (M. Cherif Bassiouni, ed., 1999).

Duursma, Jorrie, *Justifying Nato's Use of Force in Kosovo?* 12 LJIL 287–295 (1999).

DWORKIN, RONALD, TAKING RIGHTS SERIOUSLY 184 (1977).

Eser, Albin, *Article 31, Margin Nos. 2–3* in COMMENTARY ON THE ROME STATUTE (O. Triffterer ed., 1999).

Evans, Malcolm D., *International Wrongs and National Jurisdiction* in REMEDIES IN INTERNATIONAL LAW: THE INSTITUTIONAL DILEMMA 173 (Malcolm D. Evans, ed., 1998).

Fenrick, William J., *Article 28, Margin No. 6.*, in COMMENTARY ON THE ROME STATUTE (Otto Triffterer, ed., 1999).

Fenrick, William J., *Attacking the Enemy Civilian as a Punishable Offence*, 7 DUKE JOURNAL OF COMPARATIVE & INTERNATIONAL LAW 542–544 (1999).

Kandel, Eric R., *Brain and Behaviour*, in PRINCIPLES OF NEURAL SCIENCE 5–17 (E.R.Kandel, J.H. Swartz & Th.M. Jessell, eds., 1993).

KANDEL, ERIC, PRINCIPLES OF NEURAL SCIENCE 5 (1993).

Kavoussi, Richard, Ph. Armstead & Emil F. Coccaro, *The neurobiology of impulsive aggression*, 20 THE PSYCHIATRIC CLINICS OF NORTH AMERICA 395–403 (1997).

Keijzer, Nico, *Self-defence in the Statute of Rome*, at 4 (unpublished).

KELSEN, HANS, HAUPTPROBLEME DER STAATSRECHTSLEHRE 108 (1945).

Knoops, Gerardus G.J., *De Lockerbie Affaire: transponering van internationalrechtelijke staatsaanspraeklijkheid naar nationale jurisdictie: No hiding place for the state?* 29 DELIKT EN DELINKWENT 601–613 (1999).

Knoops, Gerardus G.J., *Het EVRM en de internationale overdracht van gevonniste personen*, 79 ADVOCATENBLAD 137–138 (1999).

Knoops, Gerardus G.J., *Interstatelijk Noodweerrecht: disculpatiegrond voor internationaal-rechtelijke onrechtmatige daad*, 43 NEDERLANDS JURISTENBLAD 2013 et.seq (1999).

Knoops, Gerardus G.J., *Nieuwe visie op opzet en toerekeningsvatbaarheid*, 22 ADVOCATENBLAD 1125–1127 (1999).

KNOOPS, GERARDUS G.J., PSYCHISCHE OVERMACHT EN RECHTSVINDING (Transl.: Duress and Law-Finding) (1998).

Kremnitzer, Mordechai, *The World Community as an International Legislator in Competition with National Legislators*, in PRINCIPLES AND PROCEDURES FOR A NEW TRANSNATIONAL CRIMINAL LAW 345 (Albin Eser and Otto Lagodny, eds., 1992.

Lauterpacht, Hersch, *The Law of Nations and the Punishment of War Criminals*, 21 BRITISH YEARBOOK OF INTERNATIONAL LAW 58, 87 (1944).

LAWSON, RICK, OUT OF CONTROL: STATE RESPONSIBILITY AND HUMAN RIGHTS 1 (1998).

Lee, G.P., A. Bechara, R. Adolphs J. Arena, K.J. Meador, D.W. Loring, & J.R. Smith, *Clinical and Physiological Effects of Stereotaxic Bilateral Amygdalotomy for Intractable Aggression*, 10 JOURNAL OF NEUROPSYCHIATRY 413–420 (1998).

Leigh, Marian N., *The Yugoslav Tribunal: Use of unnamed witnesses against accused, Editorial Comments*, 90 AM. J. INT'L L 238 (1996).

LENSING, JOHANNES A.W., AMERIKAANS STRAFRECHT, EEN VERGELIJKENDE INLEIDING 236–239 (1996).

Levine, Martin Lyon, *Introduction*, in LAW AND PSYCHOLOGY XVIII (Martin Lyon Levine, ed., 1995).

Loftus, Elisabeth F., *Ten Years in the Life of an Expert Witness*, 10 LAW AND HUMAN BEHAVIOR 245 (1986).

MACPHAIL, EUAN M., THE EVOLUTION OF CONSCIOUSNESS 212–213 (1998).

Malekian, Farhad, *International Criminal Responsibility*, in 1 INTERNATIONAL CRIMINAL LAW 168 (M. Cherif Bassiouni, ed., 1999).

Manuck, Stephen B., et al., *Aggression and Anger-related Traits Associated with Polymorphism of the Tryptophan Hydroxylase Gene*, 45 SOCIETY OF BIOLOGICAL PSYCHIATRY 603–614 (1999).

Marschik, Axel, *The Politics of Prosecution: European National Approaches to War Crimes*, in THE LAW OF WAR CRIMES 84–85 (Timothy L.H. McCormack & Gerry J. Simpson, eds., 1997).

Matscher, F., *Methods of Interpretation of the Convention*, in THE EUROPEAN SYSTEM FOR THE PROTECTION OF HUMAN RIGHTS 70 (MacDonald et al eds., 1993).

McCormack Timothy L.H., & Gerry J. Simpson, *Preface* in THE LAW OF WAR CRIMES XXII (Timothy L.H. McCormack & Gerry J. Simpson, eds., 1997).

McCORMACK, TIMOTHY L.H., SELF-DEFENSE IN INTERNATIONAL LAW: THE ISRAELI RAID ON THE IRAQI NUCLEAR REACTOR 276–277 (1996).

Meron, Theodor, *Crimes and Accountability in Shakespeare* in WAR CRIMES LAW COMES OF AGE 82, 87 (Theodor Meron, ed., 1998).

Meron, Theodor, *Geneva Conventions as Customary Law* in WAR CRIMES LAW COMES OF AGE 156 (Theodor Meron, ed., 1998).

Meron, Theodor, *International Criminalization of Internal Atrocities*, in WAR CRIMES LAW COMES OF AGE 224 (Theodor Meron, ed., 1998)

Meron, Theodor, *The Case for War Crimes Trials in Yugoslavia*, in WAR CRIMES LAW COMES OF AGE 187, 197 (Theodor Meron, ed., 1998).

Meron, Theodor, *The Normative Impact on International Law of the International Tribunal for Former Yugoslavia* in WAR CRIMES LAW COMES OF AGE 224 (Theodor Meron, ed., 1998).

Miles, D.R., & G. Carey, *Genetic and Environmental Architecture of Human Aggression*, 72 JOURNAL OF PERSONALITY AND SOCIAL PSYCHOLOGY 207–217 (1997).

Mout, P., *Korte Notities over de Raadsman in Strafzaken*, in NAAR EER EN GEWETEN 388, 383–391 (Liber Amicorum J. Remmelink, 1987).

Mueller, Gerhard.O.W., & Douglas J. Besharov, *Evolution and Enforcement of ICL*, in 1 INTER-NATIONAL CRIMINAL LAW 258 (M. Cherif Bassiouni, ed., 1999).

Nelkin, D., & L. Tancredi, *Dangerous Diagnostics: The Social Power of Personality*, 72 SOCIAL PSYCHOLOGY 207–217 (1994).

Neugebauer, R., H.W. Hoek & E. Susser, *Prenatal Exposure to Wartime Famine and Development of Antisocial Personality Disorder in Early Adulthood*, 282 JAMA 455–462 (1999).

NILL-THEOBALD, C., DEFENSES BEI KRIEGSVERBRECHEN 197, 363 (1998).

Ntanda Nsereko, Daniel D., *Rules of Procedure and Evidence of the ICTY*, 5 CRIMINAL LAW FORUM 554 (1994).

O'Brien, C., *The International Tribunal for Violations of International Humanitarian Law in the Former Yugoslavia*, 87 AMERICAN JOURNAL OF INTERNATIONAL LAW 654, 693 (1993).

Paust, Jordan J., *My Lai and Vietnam: Norms, myths and leader responsibility*, 57 MILITARY LAW REVIEW 171 (1972).

Paust, Jordan J., *Superior Orders and Command Responsibility*, in 1 INTERNATIONAL CRIMINAL LAW 225 (M. Cherif Bassiouni, ed., 1999).

PERKINS, ROLLIN M., & RONALD N. BOYCE, CRIMINAL LAW 1062 (1982).

Piragoff, Donald K., *Article 30, Margin No. 3* in COMMENTARY ON THE ROME STATUTE (Otto Triffterer, ed., 1999).

Pruitt, Renee C., *Guilt by Majority in the ICTY: Does this meet the standard of Beyond Reasonable Doubt?*, 10 LJIL 557–578 (1997).

Raine, Adrian, J.Reid Melog, Susan Bihrle, Jackie Stoddard, Lori LaCasse, and Monte S. Buchsbaum, *Reduced Prefrontal and Increased Subcortical Brain Functioning Assessed Using Position Emission Tomography in Predatory and Affective Murderers*, 16 BEHAVIOURAL SCIENCE AND THE LAW 319–332 (1998).

Raine, Adrian, Peter Brennan, B. Mednick, and S.A. Mednick, *High rates of violence, crime, academic problems and behavioral problems in males with both early neuromotor deficits and unstable family environment*, 53 ARCHIVES OF GENERAL PSYCHIATRY 544–549 (1996).

Reinisch, J.M., *Prenatal Exposure to Synthetic Progestins Increases Potential for Aggression in Humans*, 211 SCIENCE 1171–1173 (1981).

Robinson, F.R., *The Bioscientist as an expert witness*, 37 VETERINARY AND HUMAN TOXICOLOGY 5 (1995).

ROBINSON, P.H., CRIMINAL LAW DEFENSES 350, 353–355, 366 (1986).

ROSE, STEVEN, LIFELINES, BIOLOGY, FREEDOM DETERMINISM (1992).

Schabas, William A., *International Sentencing: From Leipzig (1923) to Arusha (1996)*, in III INTERNATIONAL CRIMINAL LAW 171–193 (M. Cherif Bassiouni, ed., 1999).

Schabas, William A., *Article 66, Margin No. 13*, in COMMENTARY ON THE ROME STATUTE (Otto Triffterer, ed., 1999).

SCHACHTER, OSCAR, INTERNATIONAL LAW IN THEORY AND PRACTICE IN 178 GENERAL COURSE IN PUBLIC INTERNATIONAL LAW 124 (1982–V).

SCHERMERS, HENRI G., & NIELS M. BLOKKER, INTERNATIONAL INSTITUTIONAL LAW 1338 (1999).

SCHNEERSON, MENACHEM M., TOWARD A MEANINGFUL LIFE 189 (1995).

Shahabuddeen, M., *The World Court at the Turn of the Century*, in THE INTERNATIONAL COURT OF JUSTICE 8 (A.S. Muller et al., eds., 1997).

Shaw, Malcolm N., *A practical look at the International Court of Justice*, in REMEDIES IN INTERNATIONAL LAW: THE INSTITUTIONAL DILEMMA 41 (M.D. Evans, ed., 1998).

SHAW, MALCOLM N., INTERNATIONAL LAW 103 (1997).

SIMMA, BRUNO, ed., THE CHARTER OF THE UNITED NATIONS: A COMMENTARY 597.

Simpson, Gerry J., *War Crimes: A Critical Introduction*, in THE LAW OF WAR CRIMES 16 (Timothy L.H McCormack and Gerry J. Simpson, eds., 1997).

Sjöcrona, Jan M., *The ICTY: Some Introductory Remarks from a Defense Point of View*, 8 LJIL 468 (1995).

Sluyter, Goran K., *Recht op aanwezigheid van raadsman tijdens politieverhoor*, 23 NJCM-BULLETIN 80–87 (1998).

SMITH, JOHN, & BRIAN HOGAN, CRIMINAL LAW 193 (1996).

Swift, R.G., M.H. Polymerpoulos, R. Torres, & M. Swift, *Predisposition of Wolfram Syndrome heterozygotes to psychiatric illness*, 3 MOLECULAR PSYCHIATRY 68–91 (1998).

Tochilovsky, Vladimir, *Rules of Procedure for the International Criminal Court: Problems to address in light of the experience of the Ad hoc Tribunals*, 46 NILR 345 (1999).

Triffterer, Otto, *Article 33, Margin No. 12* in COMMENTARY ON THE ROME STATUTE (Otto Triffterer, ed., 1999).

van der Wilt, Harmen, in 1 ANNOTATED LEADING CASES OF INTERNATIONAL CRIMINAL TRIBUNALS 535 (1999).

VAN EIKEMA HOMMES, H.J., DE ELEMENTAIRE GRONDBEGRIPPEN DER RECHTSWETENSCHAP 239 (1983).

van Hegelsom, Gert-Jan F., *The Law of Armed Conflict and UN Peace-keeping and Peace-enforcing Operations*, 6 HAGUE YEARBOOK OF INTERNATIONAL LAW 47 and 57 (1993).

van Kampen, Petra, *Confronting Expert Evidence under the European Convention*, in HARMONISATION IN FORENSIC EXPERTISE 201 (Johannes F. Nijboer & Wim J.J.M Sprangers, eds., 2000).

Verwey, W.D., *Humanitarian Intervention*, in THE CURRENT LEGAL REGULATION OF THE USE OF FORCE 57–78 (Antonio Cassese, ed., 1986).

Weinberger, D.R., *Implications of normal brain development for the pathogenesis of schizophrenia*, 44 ARCHIVES GENERAL PSYCHIATRY 660–669 (1987)

Wenig, Jonathan M., *Enforcing the Lessons of History: Israel Judges the Holocaust* in THE LAW OF WAR CRIMES 121 (Timothy L.H. McCormack & Gerry J. Simpson, eds., 1997).

White, Robin M., and Jeremy J.D. Greenwood, *DNA Fingerprinting and the Law*, 51 THE MODERN LAW REVIEW 149 (1988).

Williams, Sharon A., *Laudable Principles Lacking Application: The Prosecution of War Criminals in Canada*, in THE LAW OF WAR CRIMES 164–170 (Timothy L.H. McCormack & Gerry J. Simpson, eds., 1997).

Wladimiroff, Michail, *Position of the Defence: The Role of Defence Counsel before the ICTY and the ICTR*, in AN INDEPENDENT DEFENCE BEFORE THE INTERNATIONAL CRIMINAL COURT 35–42 (Hans Bevers & Chantal Joubert, eds., 2000).

Wladimiroff, Michail, *The Assignment of Defense Counsel before the ICTR*, 12 LJIL 2 (1999).

Zwanenburg, Martin, *The Secretary-General's Bulletin on Observance by United Nations Forces of IHL: Some Preliminary Observations*, at 3; also Reparations for Injuries suffered in the Service of the UN, Advisory Opinion of 11 april 1949, ICJ Reports 1949, at 174.

# PREFACE

The origins of international criminal law can be traced through its enforcement mechanisms and substantive prescriptive norms. The former are rooted in the practice of international extradition, which was first referred to in the Old Testament in connection with an event that occurred in 1350 B.C., while the first extradition treaty provision appeared in the 1268 B.C. Treaty of Peace between Ramses II of Egypt and Hatusilli of the Hittites. The latter, substantive prescriptive norms first emerged in the 1600s with the customary international law prohibition of piracy. This was followed in the late 1800s by the codification of the customary international law regulating armed conflicts, as well as treaties prohibiting the international traffic in slaves. Since then substantive international criminal law has come to encompass 25 categories of crimes about which some 280 international treaties have been elaborated between 1815 and 2000.

The enforcement of international criminal law developed contemporaneously with the prescriptive development of substantive international criminal law at the end of the 19th century. This body of law, which is also referred to as interstate cooperation in penal matters, is evidenced by an extensive web of specialized multilateral and bilateral treaties, as well as through specific provisions in substantive international criminal law conventions. It presently encompasses several modalities, which are relied upon by states to enforce violations of substantive international and domestic criminal law.

The essence of international criminal law enforcement is embodied in the shorthand maxim *aut dedere aut judicare*. That maxim is predicated on the assumption that states have an obligation to either prosecute or extradite those individuals who commit international crimes and to assist states investigating such crimes for eventual prosecution. In order to carry out their duty to prosecute, states must domesticate international criminal law obligations by incorporating international crimes and enforcement obligations into their national legislation. Furthermore, states have the duty to see to it that those who are found guilty in accordance with a fair legal process also receive their just punishment. This reliance on states to enforce international criminal law is referred to as the "indirect enforcement system," which is embodied in substantive international criminal law conventions and reflected in customary international law.

Parallel to the "indirect enforcement system" which relies on national legal systems, is the "direct enforcement system" whereby the international community establishes international investigatory and adjudicatory bodies to enforce international criminal law. The "direct enforcement system" avoids the intermediation of national legal systems, but neither necessarily supplants nor replaces them. The relationship between such internationally established bodies and national legal systems is best expressed in the Statute of the International Criminal Court (ICC) as a "complementary" one.

The first instances of a "direct enforcement system" were the International Military Tribunal at Nuremberg (IMT) and the International Military Tribunal for the Far East at Tokyo (IMTFE), respectively established in 1945 and 1946. In these two historical manifestations of a "direct enforcement system" substantive international criminal law was applied directly to individuals by two international judicial bodies that were established by some members of the international community. Well over half a century later two international criminal tribunals were established by the United Nations Security Council, respectively: the International Criminal Tribunal for the Former Yugoslavia (ICTY) in 1993 and the International Criminal Tribunal for Rwanda (ICTR) in 1994. Thereafter, it became apparent that the international community would soon establish a permanent international criminal court and that occurred with the signing of the Rome Statute for the Establishment of an International Criminal Court on July 17, 1998.

With the advent of these institutions, starting with the IMT and IMTFE, international criminal law required a "general part" consisting *inter alia*, of principles of criminal responsibility and conditions of exonerations or defenses. Resort to the "direct enforcement system" also required international criminal law to have rules of procedure and evidence by which to conduct international proceedings. These dimensions were not contained in international criminal law because they were not needed in the context of the "indirect enforcement system." Indeed, the national laws of enforcing states usually contain the necessary substantive norms, penalties and procedural rules and thus have no need to rely on international criminal law. Consequently, international criminal law did not at first develop these aspects of its legal discipline. But these *lacunae* became evident when, in application of the "direct enforcement system," international criminal tribunals were established, in the aftermath of certain conflicts. Thus, these *lacunae* had to be filled.

The IMT and the IMTFE Charters contained only a few norms relative to the "general part," and they had even fewer rules of procedure and evidence applicable to these proceedings. The needed "general part" norms and the "procedural part" rules were developed by these tribunals in the course of ongoing proceedings or as jurisprudential pronouncements. For obvious reasons such practice violates contemporary due process standards.

The ICTY and ICTR statutes did not add much to what had been previously established in the Charters and jurisprudence of the IMT and IMTFE. However, the ICTY and ICTR Statutes gave the judges the prerogative of developing rules of procedure and evidence applicable to their respective proceedings. These statutes did not however delegate to the judges the prerogative of adopting "general part" norms. But, since the two statutes did not "legislate" sufficient "general part" norms, the two tribunals' jurisprudence had to determine them. The process resembled that of the development of common law with all that system's advantages and shortcomings. The rules enacted by the judges and the jurisprudence of these two tribunals nevertheless filled the "legislative" gap, even though raising doubts about the fairness of this judge-made approach which often provided little advance notice to the parties of the applicable rules.

An assessment of the judge-made procedural rules of the ICTY and ICTR and the substantive jurisprudence of these bodies reveals that the rules of procedure and evidence and the contents of the "general part" are the product of an intuitive process whereby the judges on the basis of their individual knowledge, integrated international norms of due process contained in various international human rights law conventions and "general principles of law" deriving from the world's major criminal justice systems. This process was not the product of an established legal methodology or technique, particularly with respect to the identification of "general principles of law." Thus, while the exercise was necessary, the method by which it was achieved is open to question.

The elaboration of the ICC Statute, which began in 1994, resulted in the inclusion of a detailed "general part" and "procedural part" in the Rome Statute. Subsequent to the adoption of the Treaty in 1998, a United Nations Preparatory Commission was established with a mandate that included the development of "elements of crimes" and "rules of procedure and evidence" to supplement the provisions of the Statute. They were completed in June 2000, but they have still to be adopted by the Assembly of States-Parties which will occur after the ICC Statute enters into effect when sixty states have ratified the Treaty.

The process by which these two aspects of international criminal law were developed in the ICC Statute and the work of the Preparatory Commission was a treaty-negotiated exercise of identifying norms and rules deriving in part from international human rights law instruments, and in part from "general principles of law" arising out of the world's major criminal justice systems. Because that process occurred in the context of diplomatic negotiations, it was necessarily affected by political judgments. Scholars and experts in comparative criminal law and procedure have therefore questioned the validity or wisdom of some of the choices made, as well as the wording of some of the norms and rules which were elaborated. Nevertheless, there now exists a set of norms applicable to the "general part" and a set of rules applicable to the "procedural part" of international criminal law, even though the application of these two sets of norms and rules is limited to the ICC.

In time, as more states ratify and accede to the Rome Treaty, the ICC's norms and rules as developed by the court's jurisprudence will become customary international law. Until then however this new body of international criminal law will remain in the making, a work in progress.

The law and jurisprudence of the ICTY, ICTR, and ICC will require development, and this book is the first doctrinal analysis of defenses in the "general part" of international criminal law. It establishes the basis and rationale for defenses in international criminal litigation, tracing them to their historical origins in international criminal law, while drawing their evolution from comparative criminal law doctrine. Thus, the analysis seeks to merge the dual tracks of comparative criminal law and the law and jurisprudence of internationally established judicial bodies arising out of the IMT, IMTFE, ICTY, and ICTR. The author does so on a selective basis, in part not to overburden the book with lengthy historical references and doctrinal debate and in part because of his practitioner's orientation toward these complex questions.

The book also has another dimension which one would not expect to be associated with the treatment of "general part" questions. It pertains to certain procedural and evidentiary aspects applicable to international criminal proceedings. The author's reason for combining these two aspects of international criminal law is that they interface in the course of criminal proceedings before international bodies.

The author first explains in Chapter I his methodological approach which is in part carried forward in Chapter II with an examination of defenses as they originate in what the author identifies as being part of customary international law. To a large extent, this analysis is self-contained though it is logically pursued in Chapter III with an examination of defenses in what the author refers to as comparative criminal law sources. This division reveals the important methodological distinction between two different sources of law.

Throughout the first three chapters, the author examines the concepts of individual criminal responsibility and of command responsibility, as well as the defenses of obedience to superior orders, duress and immunity for such persons as heads of state, self-defense, insanity and intoxi-cation. In so doing, he relies on the charters, statutes and jurisprudence of the IMT, IMTFE, ICTY, and ICTR and on the ICC Statute, as well as selected comparative criminal law analysis.

The legal juncture between international law and national law sources in international criminal law doctrine is that discipline's greatest challenge. Understandably, it could not be resolved in these first three chapters.

In Chapter IV, the author returns to the issue of command responsi-bility in the international regulation of armed conflicts and applies that concept to different contexts of collective military action, such as the use of U.N. and NATO mandated troops in peace-keeping operations. This is followed in Chapter V with a discussion of the concepts of justification and excuse and the manner in which defenses to criminal responsibility are applied in connection with the use of collective military force. In Chapter VI, the author addresses the issue of self-defense in the U.N. Charter and customary international law, and, at the same time, he addresses the individual concept of self-defense in the law of armed con-flict. Both concepts are obviously quite distinct and should be addressed separately.

In Chapter VII, the author leaves the "general part" and addresses issues of procedural rights in the context of international criminal adjudi-cation. These issues include: fairness of the proceedings, the rights of the defense, admissibility of evidence, burden of proof and the use of scien-tific and expert testimony. In so doing, the author draws upon the jurisprudence of the ICTY and ICTR, as well as the jurisprudence of the European Court of Human Rights. He also draws on normative sources in the International Covenant of Civil and Political Rights and the European Convention on Human Rights. He concludes in Chapter VIII with a discussion of what he refers to as "A New Concept of International Due Process" in which he addresses the challenges facing the defense of international criminal cases, the role of defense lawyers and prosecutors and "equality of arms" as a necessary component of fairness in interna-tional criminal proceedings.

It is not an easy task to try merging comparative criminal law and procedure, which has its own methods and techniques, and that which has developed through statutes of *ad hoc* international criminal tribunals and their jurisprudence. One of the difficulties is that there is no estab-lished legal method and technique to bridge the gap between different legal disciplines which are based on different sources of law. But that is not the author's goal. Instead his goal is to address the concerns of prac-titioners as to the applications of certain aspects of the "general part," namely defenses, in the context of international criminal adjudication.

The author is breaking new ground and is to be congratulated for his contribution to the knowledge and understanding of international criminal law in its practical application to international criminal proceedings.

*M. Cherif Bassiouni*
*Professor of Law,*
*President, International Human*
    *Rights Law Institute,*
    *DePaul University;*
*President, International Association*
    *of Penal Law; President,*
    *International Institute of Higher*
    *Studies in Criminal Sciences;*
*Chairman, Drafting Committee, U.N.*
    *Diplomatic Conference on the*
    *Establishment of the ICC.*
*Chicago, February 10, 2001*

# FOREWORD

This book contains an overview of legal defenses in International Criminal Law that may be sustained before International Criminal Tribunals against war crimes charges. With the advent of the International Criminal Court, the subject matter of this book seems to be a topical one. My interest, especially in the role of the *Rule of Law* with regard to these defenses, derives from my 1998 Ph.D. thesis on the subject of *"duress and law-finding,"* in which, *inter alia*, the Rule of Law was propounded. This current study and its themes, I submit, coincide clearly with my previous thesis. The Rule of Law affects various areas of International Law, and it appears to me that it must be extended to the difficult, controversial and even antagonistic role of legal defenses to war crimes, in order to create more understanding and generate more legal interest. Only compliance to the Rule of Law can endorse this better understanding of the international community. Moreover, the increasing importance of the Rule of Law in safeguarding the law and customs of wars during multinational military operations of the United Nations and NATO can no longer be denied.

Amsterdam, 4 December 2000
Geert-Jan Knoops

# ACKNOWLEDGMENTS

In thanking those who have assisted in the preparation of this study it is necessary to recall those who have contributed to the development of my intellectual career. Many persons have influenced and encouraged me in the field of international law.

My deepest gratitude goes to my wife Carry Juliette Hamburger, who is also my legal partner, for both her enormous substantive commentary on this study as well as her moral contribution. It was she who taught me to live and moreover made me conscious that—as John Donne once stated—*"no man is an island. . . ."* Rightfully she is therefore my life since she stood at the basis of my spiritual abandoning of this island and helped my writing immeasurably. This book is a clear result of her contribution to my intellectual life. I remain indebted to Carry as it is to her that I owe my career in international law.

I am grateful to my family, especially my children Aaron, Nico and Joël, my mother Josephine Knoops, my sister Jolanda and her family, my parents-in-law Dr. David and Janny Moffie, all for their trust in me. I also owe considerable debt to Dick F. Swaab, professor of neurobiology, for educating me in his specialization, knowledge of which is used in this book.

Further, I owe much gratitude and admiration to the staff of the Royal Netherlands Marine Corps for their support during the times I spent with them. I am especially indebted to my true friend Willem A.J. Prins, Brigadier-General of the RNLMC, and Flag Officer of the Netherlands Forces in the Caribbean, and his wife Helène for their confidence in me, and, above all, their friendship. This friendship, on a spiritual level, contributed to this book as symbol of our mutual perseverance.

Like the international criminal justice system itself, so aptly equated by M. Cherif Bassiouni to "human solidarity," those mentioned here merit respect for their contribution to the humanization of our civilization. In this context I remember with gratitude also the late Rabbi Barend Drukarch in Amsterdam, who taught me many values of humanity which are denominators of the law and therefore a living example for me.

Finally, I am greatly indebted to Prof. M. Cherif Bassiouni, who guided me further into this fascinating topic, gave considerable inspiration as well as instruments for further study on the subject, and reviewed the manuscript with due diligence several times. To me, he embodies both a scientist and a person of greatness because of his respect for human dignity and the Rule of Law. Prof. Bassiouni's "in memoriam" to Kemoko Keita, in his book *The Protection of Human Rights in the Administration of Criminal Justice*, is a clear example. I am beholden to him—a person who has dedicated his life to the eradication of injustice and the promotion of legal science at the highest level—because he trusted me with the writing of this book.

A study cannot do without a review of its language. For this formidable task I owe thanks and appreciation to Matthew Furbush, an extraordinary person, teacher and writer; Jaap N. Hamburger, Professor of Intervention Cardiology, my dearest and most erudite brother in law; my youngest son Joël Knoops as well as his friends David van Dijk and Dani Oppenheim; and last but not least, my highly skilled secretary Frederique Wessel for her ever lasting patience with the ways of the author, gentle reminders and substantial assistance to this task. I was fortunate having them in my academic environment. I further thank my publisher, Mrs. Heike Fenton, and my editor, Mr. Terence Hegarty, for their patient encouragement, tolerance and confidence, since the days of my dissertation.

May there be many others like the aforementioned persons, whom I have had the honour to have met in life, to pursue the task of ensuring justice in the world.

Amsterdam 4 December 2000
Geert-Jan Knoops

# INTRODUCTION

In his General Course on Public International Law delivered at the Hague Academy of International Law to commemorate the fiftieth anniversary of the foundation of the United Nations, Ian Brownlie remarks: "In any formal description of the sources of international law, 'judicial legislation' would not figure, and yet important sectors of the law, and especially the law of the sea, have been affected by what was, in effect, judicial legislation."[1] Considering the increasing importance and power of judicial reasoning, resulting in judicial legislation as a competent source of international public law, this aspect is also significant with respect to the treatment of legal defenses to international crimes. It is this role of the process of creative judicial reasoning concerning the admissibility of defenses to international (war) crimes, which will be the main topic of this study. The "awareness of the significant role of international tribunals in making law"[2] is an important notion in the framework of and study of defenses in international criminal law (hereinafter: ICL).

In this study I intend to explore the elements and scope of defenses to international war crimes indictments. The need for refinement in this field is even more challenging as since the Statutes of the two main post-World War II War Crimes Tribunals, the ICTY and ICTR, "fail to specify adequately the nature and scope of defenses."[3]

The absence of clear standards or precedents emphasizes the importance of judicial legislation or law making through the jurisprudence of International Criminal Tribunals. There is a need to extend the current political and judicial interest in international criminal law and the prosecution of international crimes[4] to the defenses to international crimes indictments, as well as to produce in this field a more methodical and systematic judicial framework of ICL. As Blakesley observes, if the ad hoc Tribunals for the former Yugoslavia and Rwanda allow substantive

---

1.  *See* IAN BROWNLIE, THE RULE OF LAW IN INTERNATIONAL AFFAIRS 28 (1998).
2.  I. Brownlie, *supra* note 1, at 2.
3.  Christopher L. Blakesley, *Atrocity and its Prosecution: The ad hoc Tribunals for the former Yugoslavia and Rwanda*, in THE LAW OF WAR CRIMES 204 (Timothy L.H. McCormack & Gerry J. Simpson THE LAW OF WAR CRIMES eds., 1997).
4.  Gerry J. Simpson, *War Crimes: A Critical Introduction*, in 30 (Timothy L.H. McCormack & Gerry J. Simpson, eds., 1997).

defenses, it is important to delineate their elements and scope carefully.[5] National jurisdictions as such, with respect to international crimes, have proven insufficient in developing such a framework.[6] The tension between the judicial and moral or emotional implications of defenses to international war crimes, adjudicated at national levels, can be considered as a non-constructive element for building such a framework.[7] Describing the prosecutions brought under the Israeli Nazis and Nazi Collaborators (Punishment) Law enacted in 1950—just two years after the establishment of the State of Israel—which only (retroactively) conceives those war crimes committed during the period of the Nazi regime, and which law dealt also with the criminal responsibility of the Judenrat ('Jewish council'; the Jewish police force responsible for some of the dirty work of the SS) and Kapos (Jewish policemen and policewomen forced to collaborate with the Germans in the concentration camps), Jonathan Wenig remarks that these last two subjects "provide an example of war crimes issues best dealt with by domestic courts and not by an International Tribunal."[8] Wenig argues that "the relative subjectivity of the Israeli Court allowed for greater understanding of the circumstances and greater recognition of the complexity of the notion of the victim" [the member of the Judenrat or Kapo; GJK] "as a war criminal under duress."[9] This view neglects, however, the fact that the *rule of law* ensures equal application of ICL, including a uniform application of the law to all crimes against humanity, war and peace, regardless of the status of the actor.[10] International criminal court trials minimize, more than domestic criminal proceedings, the risk of selective application of international law as well as the issue of partiality, therefore ensuring a just application of international criminal laws to individual defendants, which in turn increases the legitimacy of the jurisdiction of International Tribunals. The solution of war crimes prosecution can therefore not be attributed only to domestic criminal Courts.

Moreover, the international community's response to violations of human rights or acts in breach of the international community's norms of *jus cogens* requires the authoritative presence of International War Crimes Tribunals to endorse a more vigorous and effective enforcement of humanitarian law. The notion that International Criminal Tribunals contribute more than domestic courts to the restoration and maintenance of peace, as well as the fact that indictments of alleged international crimes

---

5. *See* Blakesley, *supra* note 3, at 219.
6. G.J. Simpson, *supra* note 4, at 29.
7. *See also* G.J. Simpson, *supra* note 4, at 3.
8. Jonathan M. Wenig, *Enforcing the Lessons of History: Israel Judges the Holocaust*, in THE LAW OF WAR CRIMES 121 (Timothy L.H. McCormack & Gerry J. Simpson eds., 1997).
9. Wenig, *supra* note 8, at 121.
10. *See* G.J. Simpson, *supra* note 4, at 11.

before International Tribunals can have an educational and moral impact on the general public or world community not to accept human atrocities,[11] forms an additional argument hereto.

Finally, according to the monistic (ethical) approach advocated by Lauterpacht, the supremacy of international law to municipal law is founded upon the notion that the well-being of individuals and human rights is at best served by the capacity of international law "to imbue the international order with a sense of moral purpose and justice founded upon respect for human rights and the welfare of individuals."[12] It is clear that the principles of good faith and protection of moral values of humanity are, as universal notions of law, more deeply embedded and preserved in international law than in most domestic law systems.[13]

The rule of law, which ought to enhance international criminal proceedings,[14] the principle of fairness to apply in these proceedings,[15] and the introduction in ICL—made by the Nuremberg and Tokyo Tribunals, of the notion of individual culpability for international crime,[16] facilitate supportive arguments to expand the international legal interest in, and development of, defenses to international indictments.

The rule of law in international affairs, recently described by Brownlie,[17] implies, with respect to international criminal cases, the maintenance of the basic norms of due process, including the right of defendants to be assisted by legal counsel, to cross-examine witnesses, to present disculpatory evidence, and last but not least the right to invoke defenses to international crimes indictments.[18]

One cannot ignore the impact of the rule of law with respect to the assessment of defenses to war crimes indictments. This role is exemplified in the essay War Crimes: A Critical Introduction[19] wherein the author, Simpson, remarks that "it is clear that in an area of law so thoroughly politicized, culturally freighted and passionately punitive as war crimes there is a need for even greater protections for the accused." In both the jurisprudence and literature of international law, a coherent synthesis of the concept of the rule of law and the admissibility of defenses to war crimes remains an unresolved issue. One of the purposes of this study is

---

11. *See* Theodor Meron, *The Case for War Crimes Trials in Yugoslavia*, in WAR CRIMES LAW COMES OF AGE 187, 197 (Theodor Meron, ed., 1998).

12. *See* MALCOLM N. SHAW, INTERNATIONAL LAW 101 (1997).

13. *See* e.g. Article 26 of the Vienna Convention on the Law of Treaties.

14. *See* for the Rule of Law in International Affairs: I. Brownlie, *supra* note 1.

15. G.J. Simpson, *supra* note 4, at 4 and 30.

16. *See* Timothy L.H. McCormack & Gerry J. Simpson, *Preface*, in THE LAW OF WAR CRIMES 22 (Timothy L.H. McCormack & Gerry J. Simpson, eds., 1997).

17. *Supra*, note 1.

18. *See* for norms of due process: Th. Meron, *supra* note 11, at 189.

19. *Ibid..* at 15.

to provide or propound a theoretical perspective for such a synthesis. From this point of view, it is necessary to observe that both the Nuremberg jurisprudence and the post-Nuremberg International Tribunals show reluctance to accept a plea of duress and the defense of superior orders.[20]

The first major section (Chapters I–III) of this study explores the sources and content of international criminal law defenses. The most appropriate methodology to establish these defenses is presented in **Chapter I**. The various criminal law defenses to international crimes, evolved from customary international law, are examined in **Chapter II**. **Chapter III** examines international legal defenses which emerges from comparative criminal law. In the realm of international military operations, two additional legal defenses emerge: namely the defenses of necessity and prevention of crime. Chapter III includes a discussion of the relevance of these defenses as criminal law defenses in ICL. In addition, this chapter assesses current developments regarding international criminal law defenses, such as the (implicit) inclusion of neurobiological and neurotoxicological defenses within the ICC Statute, encompassing a relatively new area of ICL, on which few scholarly views are available.

The second major section (Chapters IV–VI) of this study deals with the application of criminal law defenses in armed conflicts, especially in the course of multinational military operations, a still-evolving aspect of ICL. Starting in **Chapter IV**, the specific concept of command responsibility in the course of these operations and conflicts is discussed, elaborating on the concept of the so-called Rules of Engagement applied during peacekeeping and peace-enforcement operations. From this topic, it is a small step to look into the subject of defenses in the sphere of multinational military operations, which are analyzed in **Chapter V**. This chapter is closely connected to **Chapter VI**, wherein the use of force by States, during the aforementioned operations, is observed and compared with the concept of individual self-defense as an international criminal law defense.

Until recently, exonerative norms relating to the use of force during law enforcement operations by Navy detachments on the high seas were not given much attention. It is against this background that **Chapter VI** tries to assess this topic, especially since it engages in a debate as to whether defenses such as individual self-defense emerge in this context. The relevance of this subject matter may seem clear in the light of the criminal law defense of prevention of crime, elaborated in Chapter V, considered as a judicial ground for the use of force conducted on the high seas in order to prevent international crimes.

The final major section (Chapters VII and VIII) of this study is more procedural than substantive. **Chapter VII** describes the procedural and

---

20.  Th. Meron, *supra* note 11, at 102–103, 190.

methodological aspects of international criminal law defenses; **Chapter VIII** considers the importance of the (international) Rule of Law and its implications for defenses to international criminal litigation. This analysis leads to the establishment of a concept or principle of international due process, to be maintained not only by International Criminal Courts but also by international criminal defense lawyers and prosecutors. From this perspective, this study views the substantive role of the international criminal defense lawyer as intermediary between the international criminal justice system and the defendant, emphasizing the application of international criminal law defenses, especially to war crimes. His or her role within the international criminal justice system is, from the perspective of the international community, unfortunately still not well understood. This book tries to look also into this antagonistic position of the international criminal defense counsel.

In conclusion, this study considers whether the assertion of Meron is justified: "In the matter of the defense of superior orders, for example, the Statute [of the International Tribunal for former Yugoslavia; GJK] reflects the black letter of the Nuremberg Charter without taking into account the more nuanced approach adopted by the Post-World War II war crimes Tribunals, literature and manuals of military law."[21] In this context the question will be examined whether such a "more nuanced approach" corroborates, or accords more, with principles of International Criminal Law, more especially the principle of procedural fairness, and Rule of Law, than the limited and reluctant application of the defenses of superior orders and duress practiced both by World War II Tribunals and ICTY and ICTR War Crimes Tribunals. The assumption that the increasing importance of the Rule of Law (principles) in International Affairs, recently extensively described by Brownlie,[22] can be of immediate relevance to criminal law defenses in International Criminal Court cases, forms the general basis of this study. I conclude this introduction by referring to Allen, saying with him that *"The notion of the rule of law is one that seeks to impose limits on and provide guidance for the exercise of official power."*[23] From this perspective, the role of defenses to international criminal litigation forms an essential device to the "limiting and guidance" of governmental powers.

---

21. Theodor Meron, *The Normative Impact on International Law of the International Tribunal for Former Yugoslavia* in WAR CRIMES LAW COMES OF AGE 224 (Theodor Meron, ed., 1998).

22. I. Brownlie, *supra* note 1, Preface.

23. *See* FRANCIS A. ALLEN, THE HABITS OF LEGALITY, CRIMINAL JUSTICE AND THE RULE OF LAW 14 (1996).

# CHAPTER I

## METHODOLOGY FOR DETERMINING A UNIFORM SYSTEM OF INTERNATIONAL CRIMINAL LAW DEFENSES

### 1  INTRODUCTION

The Post-World War II prosecutions, particularly the International Military Tribunal for the Far East at Tokyo (IMTFE), constitute a major historic development in the establishment of individual criminal responsibility under international law.[1] Heads of State were no longer given immunity (precedented only by Article 227 of the 1919 Treaty of Versailles, which defined the crime for which the Kaiser of Germany was to stand trial), and the traditional defense of "obedience to superior orders" was eliminated in the Far East. The establishment in 1999 of the International Criminal Court is, as Bassiouni observes,[2] a step in the direction of providing international criminal justice, incorporating a broad concept of legal defenses as an essential part of this fundamental justice. These historic facts reveal the development of the concept of the international criminal defense from an instrument of *realpolitik* to a general institution of international criminal justice. In order to achieve effective, independent, fair and impartial justice, resort to the rule of law, and not *realpolitik*, is required.

Under the ICC, the various modalities for achieving international justice in the area of defenses include those arising under customary (military and Humanitarian) international law, such as the concepts of command responsibility and superior orders, as well as those evolving from comparative criminal law, such as self-defense. Article 31 (3) of the ICC Statute seems to cover these two modalities, although the Statutes of the ICTY, ICTR and ICC show considerable constraints as to the admissibility of the former defenses—influenced by history and its connected *realpolitik*—whereas the latter defenses are built on a wider institutional legal basis, due to probably the absence of such a historical *realpolitik* in

---

1.    M. Cherif Bassiouni, *Combating Impunity in International Crimes*, 71 UNIVERSITY OF COLORADO LAW REVIEW 414 (2000).
2.    M. Cherif Bassiouni, *supra* note 1.

international criminal law (ICL). A perception of legal defenses which, due to political considerations, differs in Customary International Law and Comparative Criminal Law undermines the aforementioned goals of international justice and the principle of equal application of the law which should supersede *realpolitik*. Fortunately, in the Statute of the ICC, pursuant to Article 31(2) "the law of case" prevails with regard to defenses.

The enforcement of a uniform system of international justice, as well as the interrelationships between defenses stemming from customary international law sources and those emerging from comparative Criminal Law sources, should result in a uniform principle or rule as to the admissibility of defenses in ICL. This chapter focuses on the methodological arguments proposed to achieve and maintain such uniformity.

## 2    THE RATIONALE OF DEFENSES IN INTERNATIONAL LITIGATION

The first substantive argument for a uniform system of international criminal law defenses can be deduced from the *raison d'etre* of legal defenses. The rationale for the existence of defenses make it imperative not to exclude *ab initio* defenses in the era of ICL, more especially to war crimes indictments. There can be no question that the inclusion of defenses in the sphere of international criminal law constitutes an important stage in the recognition of the principle of fairness in international litigation and therefore the application of human rights standards in international criminal proceedings. This is reinforced by the judgment of the International Court of Justice in 1970, expressed in the so-called *Barcelona Traction* Case, in which the Court explicitly referred to obligations *erga omnes* in contemporary international law. These obligations were stated to include "the principles and rules concerning the basic rights of the human person, including protection from slavery and racial discrimination."[3] Accordingly, the International Court's fundamental principles of human rights form part of customary or general international law and subsequently of international criminal law, the latter being a sub-discipline of the former. This recognition can also be deduced from the final act of the Helsinki Conference of 1975,[4] enshrining a "Declaration of Principles Guiding Relations between Participating States," which enhances human rights. This section impresses on the participating States to fulfill "( . . . ) their obligations as set forth in the International declarations and agreements in (the) field (of human rights and fundamental free-

---

3.    ICJ Reports 1970, at 3, at 32.
4.    *See* IAN BROWNLIE, BASIC DOCUMENTS ON HUMAN RIGHTS 391 (1992).

doms), including *inter alia* the International Covenants on Human Rights, by which they may be bound." The significance of these notions with respect to defenses can be shown by referring to, *inter alia*, Article 6, Sections 1 and 3 of the European Convention on Human Rights and Fundamental Freedoms, ensuring that every defendant in a criminal case has the right to a fair trail and adequate facilities for his defense.[5] It is obvious that this includes the right to invoke defenses.

It can therefore be concluded that the idea of defenses to international (war) crimes indictments, as one of the fundamental general principles of international (humanitarian) law, is indirectly affirmed by the reference of the International Court of Justice to the existence of State obligations *erga omnes*, e.g. basic (defense) rights of the human person. The range of the concept of human rights encompasses, as Brownlie observes, the principle of fair trial,[6] which in turn includes the concept of defenses. It is the principle of fair trial which ensures also the high moral character of international criminal litigation.[7] From this principle, a uniform system of complete and absolute defenses to such litigation can subsequently be derived.[8]

## 3 NATURE OF INTERNATIONAL CRIMINAL LAW AND *MENS REA*

A second argument hereto relates to the interrelation between domestic criminal law systems and ICL, more especially the element of *mens rea*. As mentioned in the introduction, domestic judicial decisions and municipal acts of legislation provide *prima facie* evidence of the attitudes of states to international law and very often constitute the only available indications of the practice of states.[9] In the case of *Certain German Interests in Polish Upper Silesia*, the Permanent Court of International Justice expressed the proposition that "International Tribunals can take account of municipal laws as more facts," which implies *inter alia* that municipal law may be used to determine if conduct is in violation of a rule of treaty or customary law.[10] The supremacy of international law over municipal law in international tribunals does not mean, as Shaw points out, that the provisions of domestic legislation are irrelevant or unnecessary; on the contrary, the role of internal legal rules is vital to the workings of international

---

5.  *See* IAN BROWNLIE, PRINCIPLES OF PUBLIC INTERNATIONAL LAW 588–590 (1990).
6.  IAN BROWNLIE, THE RULE OF LAW IN INTERNATIONAL AFFAIRS 65 (1998).
7.  *See* for this high moral character also the appeals chamber decision of the ICTY in the *Tadić* case dated 2 October 1995, IT-94-1-AR72 para. 46.
8.  *Id.*
9.  Brownlie, *supra* note 5, at 55.
10.  Brownlie, *supra* note 5, at 40–41.

law.[11] The interaction between rules of municipal law and international law with respect to violations of international law endorses the fact that in the assessment of defenses in international criminal litigation, municipal rules are conclusive and decisive legal sources.[12] This assumption is based also on the knowledge that *"ICL is a complex legal discipline consisting of overlapping and concurrent sources of law and emanating from the international legal system and from national legal systems,"* thus endorsing *"an international legal regime"* from which *"certain norms and certain internationally established institutions 'emerge' that have some supra-national characteristics."*[13] General principles of law recognized by the world's major criminal law systems are an integrated collateral source of ICL, supplying ICL with the general part of criminal law, including, e.g., the prescriptions of requisite mental states and legal defenses to crimes.[14] National laws already possess a general part on defenses and perform a doctrinal basis for ICL.[15] Thus, in order to determine the admissibility of defenses in ICL, as well as their constituent elements or conditions, domestic doctrinal views can be supportive in achieving uniformity. Looking into the major domestic criminal law systems of the world, it is manifest that the overwhelming majority of them endorse the doctrinal view that, although no element of the crime *per se*, the absence of legal defenses when available is a prerequisite to the criminal liability of the accused. A doctrinal basis for one international system of defenses can be derived from this domestic principle. ICL did not move away from the concept of *mens rea*.

It is important to note that this study deals with legal defenses to international criminal litigation and therefore international crimes. At present there are twenty-five categories of international crimes. They are summarized by Bassiouni as follows: (1) aggression; (2) genocide; (3) crimes against humanity; (4) war crimes; (5) crimes against United Nations and associated personnel; (6) unlawful possession or use or emplacement of weapons; (7) theft of nuclear materials; (8) mercenary combat; (9) apartheid; (10) slavery and slave-related practices; (11) torture and other forms of cruel, inhuman, or degrading treatment; (12) unlawful human experimentation; (13) piracy; (14) aircraft hijacking and unlawful acts against international air safety; (15) unlawful acts against the safety of maritime navigation and the safety of platforms on the high seas; (16) threat and use of force against internationally protected persons; (17) taking of civilian hostages; (18) unlawful use of the mail; (19) unlawful traffic in drugs and related drug offenses; (20) destruction and/or theft of

---

11.  MALCOLM N. SHAW, INTERNATIONAL LAW 103 ( 1997).
12.  *See* also Theodor Meron, *Geneva Conventions as Customary Law*, in WAR CRIMES LAW COMES OF AGE 156 (Theodor Meron, ed., 1998).
13.  *See* M. CHERIF BASSIOUNI, I INTERNATIONAL CRIMINAL LAW 4 (1999).
14.  M. Cherif Bassiouni, *supra* note 13, at 16.
15.  *See* M. Cherif Bassiouni, *supra* note 13, at 4.

national treasures; (21) unlawful acts against certain internationally protected elements of the environment; (22) international traffic in obscene materials; (23) falsification and counterfeiting; (24) unlawful interference with submarine cables; and (25) bribery of foreign public officials. These crimes are reflected in 323 international interments elaborated in the period of 1815–1997.[16]

Besides the requisite basic *mens rea* in regard to all of these international crimes, some of them require a specific intent or *mens rea* in order to prove criminal liability. The existence of a specific intent has, as will be observed, implications for the admissibility of defenses.

*Mens rea* is a term which has no single meaning. Every international crime has its own *mens rea*, which can be ascertained only by reference to its definition in the relevant Convention or jurisprudence of international tribunals. In this context, one cannot neglect Article 30 of the ICC Statute. Although the *travaux préparatoires* of the ICC Statute indicate the intention that all the mental elements should be set out in the Statute, the latter fails by not containing these elements in one Article. Article 30 (1) states as prerequisite as to criminal responsibility, that *"the material elements are committed with intent and knowledge."* This implies that other relevant mental elements are to be found within the specific definition of crimes or other general principles of criminal law envisioned by the ICC Statute.[17] It is important to note that each of the terms *"intent"* and *"knowledge"* is specifically defined, in Article 30 (2) and (3) respectively. In the context of defenses, Article 30 (2)(a) asks for special attention: the words *"that person means to engage in the conduct"* signifies at a minimum that the conduct must be the result of a voluntary action on the part of an accused. To cite Piragoff: *"It includes the basic consciousness or volition that is necessary to attribute an action as being the product of the voluntary will of a person."*[18] Especially in relation to the special defenses of mental insanity, as well as the toxicological and genetic defenses to be discussed hereinafter, the relevance of this voluntary action will be clearly understood. In fact, this voluntary element is also contemplated by Article 30 (2)(b), which connects conduct and consequence and reflects the notion that specified consequences in the definition of a crime must causally follow from the person's conduct, and also defines the requisite element of the person's desire or means that such consequences occur, inclusive of the concept of *dolus eventualis*, i.e., the notion that specific consequences will occur in the

---

16. M. Cherif Bassiouni, *The Normative Framework of International Humanitarian Law: Overlaps, Gaps and Ambiguities*, in I INTERNATIONAL CRIMINAL LAW 629 (M. Cherif Bassiouni, ed., 1999).

17. *See* Donald K. Piragoff, *Article 30, Margin No. 3* in COMMENTARY ON THE ROME STATUTE (Otto Triffterer ed., 1999).

18. D.K. Piragoff, *supra* note 17, Margin No. 19.

ordinary course of events.[19] This detailed analysis is explicitly expressed in paragraph 3 of Article 30.

It is therefore possible only to define a general principle or presumption which governs the *mens rea* doctrine. Interestingly, the common law endorses, in crimes requiring *mens rea* (as distinct from negligence), the test that the accused should be liable only for that which he had *chosen* to bring about, or taken *the risk* of bringing about—i.e., that he intended or was reckless—of before all the elements of the offence, both results and circumstances, could occur. When the defendant had so chosen, he can fairly be held responsible for the occurrence of the *actus reus*, such act being the direct result of his intention or recklessness as to all the elements of the offence *mens rea* or the basic constituent of it.[20] Since the decision of the House of Lords in the *Caldwell* case,[21] however, this principle can no longer be based solely on the idea of choice in all cases. Here, an interrelation with, *inter alia*, the defense of duress appears, and, since the person's freedom of will is affected in case of duress,[22] it cannot be said that this person has *chosen* to take the risk. This view could be formalized also in regard to ICL in a general provision, pursuant to Article 24, section 1 of the English Draft Criminal Code Bill, which provides: "*Unless a contrary intention appears, a person does not commit a (n) ((international) crime unless he acts intentionally, knowingly or recklessly in respect of each of its elements ( . . . )*"

In sum, the concept of *mens rea*, being a requisite element of most international crimes, forms a decisive guiding principle to shape a uniform system of legal defenses in the international criminal law system.

Turning back to the major criminal law systems of the world, it is particularly important to observe that they differ, in one uniform juridical and, insofar as some crimes are excluded from the aforementioned impunity, one important effect of defenses. These different domestic perceptions regarding the scope of legal defenses can be seen in the defense of duress, a description of which is to be found in the Joint Separate Opinion of Judges MacDonald and Vohrah, submitted in the *Prosecutor v. Erdemović* decision of the Trial Chamber of the ICTY. Paragraphs 58–69 of this Opinion reveal the diversity of national criminal law systems with regard to defenses, i.e., the defense of duress.

In order to arrive at a general principle relating to duress, this opinion undertakes a limited survey of the treatment of duress as a complete defense in the world's legal systems. This survey is necessarily modest in its undertaking and is not a thorough comparative analysis. Its purpose, as we read in the aforesaid opinion, is to derive, to the extent possible, a

---

19.  D.K. Piragoff, *supra* note 17, Margin Nos. 21–23.
20.  JOHN SMITH & BRIAN HOGAN, CRIMINAL LAW 73 (1996).
21.  1982, AC 341, All ER 961; See also Smith & Hogan, *supra* note 20, at 701.
22.  *See* further: Chapter VII *infra*.

"general principle of law" as a source of international law. General principles are, however, by nature not specific, and thus often seem to be in contravention to the principle of legality. Therefore, general principles of law can in fact not act as primary sources of ICL, but serve as a source of interpretation for conventional and customary international law. As Professor Bassiouni points out, *"they constitute the guidelines or framework for the judiciary with respect to the interpretative and applicative functions of positive rules of law."*[23] The survey of judges MacDonald and Vohrah reads as follows:

## (a) Civil law systems

The penal codes of civil law systems, with some exceptions, consistently recognize duress as a complete defense to all crimes. The criminal codes of civil law nations provide that an accused acting under duress "commits no crime" or "is not criminally responsible" or "shall not be punished." It can be noted that some civil law systems distinguish between the notion of necessity and that of duress. Necessity is taken to refer to situations of emergency arising from natural forces. Duress, however, is taken to refer to compulsion by threats of another human being. Where a civil law system makes this distinction, only the provision relating to duress will be referred to.

### France

In the French Penal Code, promulgated on 22 July 1992, Article 122–2 provides: No person is criminally responsible who acted under the influence of a force or compulsion, which he could not resist. It is apparent from this article that French law recognizes duress as a general defense which leads to acquittal. The effect of the application of this provision is, speaking figuratively, the destruction of the will of the person under compulsion.

### Belgium

The Belgian Penal Code of 1867, Article 71, provides: There is no offence where the accused or suspect was insane at the time the act was committed, or where compelled by a force which he could not resist. This rule applies to every offence. The Court of Cassation has stipulated that for duress to be established the free will of the person concerned must not only be weakened but annihilated. As in French law, duress arising from one's own doing is not to be accepted as duress.

### The Netherlands

Article 40 of the Dutch Penal Code of 1881 reads: A person who commits an offence as a result of a force he could not be expected to resist

---

23. See M. Cherif Bassiouni, *A Functional Approach to General Principles of International Law*, 11 MICHIGAN JOURNAL OF INTERNATIONAL LAW 775 – 776 (1990).

*[overmacht]* is not criminally liable. The word *overmacht* means superior force and is sometimes translated as force *majeure*. The article applies to murder charges. In Dutch law, Article 40 appears to encapsulate both the notion of mental duress (threats overpowering the will of a person) and the notion of necessity.

## Spain

In the Spanish Penal Code of 1995, Article 20 provides that the criminal responsibility of an accused is removed where he is compelled to perform a certain act by an overwhelming fear.

## Germany

Section 35(1) of the German Penal Code of 1975 (amended as at 15 May 1987) provides: If someone commits a wrongful act in order to avoid an imminent, otherwise unavoidable danger to life, limb, or liberty, whether to himself or to a dependant or someone closely connected with him, the actor commits the act without culpability. This is not the case if under the circumstances it can be fairly expected of the actor that he suffer the risk; this might be fairly expected of him if he caused the danger, or if he stands in a special legal relationship to the danger. In the latter case, his punishment may be mitigated in conformity with section 49(l).

## Italy

Article 54 of the Italian Penal Code of 1930 (amended as at 1987) provides:

1. No one shall be punished for acts committed under the constraint of necessity to preserve himself or others from the actual danger of a serious personal harm, which is not caused voluntarily nor otherwise inevitable, and the acts committed under which are proportionate to the threatened harm.
2. This article does not apply to a person who has a legal duty to expose himself to the danger.
3. The provision of the first paragraph of this article also applies if the state of necessity arises from the threat of another person; however, in this case, the responsibility for the acts committed under committed, or the threat belongs to him who coerced the commission of the acts.

Article 54(2) is understood as referring to moral compulsion which arises from the external conditions to be ("contraint morale"). In addition, Article 46 of the Italian Penal Code provides: No one shall be punished for committing his acts under the coercion of another person by means of physical violence which cannot be resisted or avoided. In this case, the responsibility for the acts committed under duress goes to the person who coerces. Article 46 is in the category of factors that negate the subjective element of criminal responsibility (*mens rea*), as opposed to Article 54(2) which justifies the *actus reus* and therefore negates the objective element of criminal responsibility. No offence is excepted from the operation of these two provisions.

### Norway

Paragraph 47 of the Norwegian General Civil Penal Code (amended as at 1 July 1994) provides that: No person may be punished for any act that he has committed in order to save someone's person or property from an otherwise unavoidable danger when the circumstances justify him in regarding this danger as particularly significant in relation to the damage that might be caused by his act. It would appear that pleas of both duress and necessity may be brought under this paragraph.

### Sweden

Section 4 of Chapter 24 of the Swedish Penal Code provides for the defense of necessity [*nöd*]. *Nöd* includes both natural forces and threats by human forces. Section 4 provides: A person who in a case other than referred to previously in this Chapter acts out of necessity in order to avert danger to life or health, to save valuable property or for other reasons, shall also be free from punishment if the act must be considered justifiable in view of the nature of the danger, the harm caused to another and the circumstances in general.

### Finland

Section 10 of the Penal Code of Finland provides: If someone has committed a punishable act in order to save himself or another, or his or another's property, from an apparent danger, and if it would otherwise have been impossible to undertake the rescue, the court shall consider, in view of the act and the circumstances, whether he shall remain unpunished or whether he deserves full punishment or punishment reduced in accordance with s. 2(1).

### Venezuela

In the Venezuelan Penal Code of 1964, Article 65(4) absolves the criminal responsibility of an accused who acts under the compulsion (*constrenido*) of the need to save himself or others from a grave and imminent danger, which is not caused voluntarily and which cannot be avoided.

### Nicaragua

Article 28(5) of the Nicaraguan Penal Code of 1974 (amended as of July 1994) removes the criminal liability of a person "who acts under an irresistible physical force or is compelled by the threat of an imminent and grave danger." Article 28(6) exonerates the person "who acted under the necessity of preservation from an imminent danger which cannot otherwise be avoided, if the circumstance was such that he could not be fairly expected to sacrifice the threatened interests." Article 28(7) requires that, to be cleared of responsibility for committing a certain act to avoid an evil at the expense of other people's rights, the evil must be real and imminent and is greater than the harm caused by the act.

### Chile

In the Chilean Penal Code of 1874 (amended as at 1994), Article 10(9) provides that criminal liability shall be removed in respect of a person "who commits an offences due to an irresistible force or under the compulsion of an insuperable fear."

### Panama

In the Panamanian Penal Code of 1982, Article 37 reads: There is no guilt on the part of whoever acts under the compulsion or threat of an actual and grave danger, whether or not caused by the acts of a third person, if he may not reasonably be expected to act otherwise.

### Mexico

Under the Mexican Penal Code of 1931 (amended as at 1994) Article 15 sets out a number of grounds of exculpation. Article 15(9) states that there is no crime committed when: In view of the circumstances which are present in the completion of an illegal conduct, the author cannot reasonably be expected to have taken a different course of action, because it is not for him to decide to act legally.

### Former Yugoslavia

The Penal Code of the Socialist Federal Republic of Yugoslavia defined the general principles of criminal law, including the elements of criminal responsibility, and was applied by the constituent Republics and Autonomous Provinces of the former Yugoslavia which supplemented the federal code with their own specific penal legislation. In the 1990 amendment of the code, Article 3 provides for the defense of extreme necessity. Article 1 reads:

1. An act committed in extreme necessity is not a criminal offence.
2. An act is committed in extreme necessity if it is performed in order that the perpetrator avert from himself or from another an immediate danger which is not due to the perpetrator's fault and which could not have been averted in any other

way, provided that the evil created thereby does not exceed
the one which was threatening.
3.  If the perpetrator himself has negligently created the danger,
    or if he has exceeded the limits of extreme necessity, the court
    may impose a reduced punishment on him, and if he
    exceeded the limits under particularly mitigating circum-
    stances it may also remit the punishment.
4.  There is no extreme necessity where the perpetrator was
    under an obligation to expose himself to the danger.

## (b) Common law systems

### England

In England, duress is a complete defense to all crimes except murder,
attempted murder and, it would appear, treason. Although there is no
direct authority on whether duress is available in respect of attempted
murder, the prevailing view is that there is no reason in logic, morality or
law in granting the defense to a charge of attempted murder whilst withholding it in respect of a charge of murder.

### United States and Australia

The English position that duress operates as a complete defense in
respect of crimes generally is followed in the United States and Australia
with variations in the federal state jurisdictions as to the precise definition of the defense and the range of offences for which the defense is not
available.

### Canada

Section 17 of the Canadian Criminal Code deals with "compulsion by
threats" and provides: A person who commits an offence under compulsion by threats of immediate death or bodily harm from a person who is
present when the offence is committed is excused for committing the
offence if the person believes that the threats will be carried out and if the
person is not a party to a conspiracy or association whereby the person is
subject to compulsion, but this section does not apply where the offence
that is committed is high treason or treason, murder, piracy, attempted
murder, sexual assault, sexual assault with a weapon, threats to a third
party or causing bodily harm, aggravated sexual assault, forcible abduction, hostage taking, robbery, assault with a weapon or causing bodily
harm, aggravated assault, unlawfully causing bodily harm, arson or an
offence under section 280–330 (abduction and detention of young persons).

### South Africa

In an authoritative treatise on South African penal law, it is stated that
conduct otherwise criminal is not punishable if, during the whole period

of time it covered, the person concerned was compelled to it by threats which produced a reasonable and substantial fear that immediate death or serious bodily harm to himself or others to whom he stood in a protective relationship would follow his refusal. It is unsettled in South African law whether duress affords a complete defense to a principal to murder in the first degree.

### India

In the Indian Penal Code of 1960, amended as at March 1991, section 94 provides: Except murder, and offences against the State punishable with death, nothing is an offence which is done by a person who is compelled to do it by threats, which, at the time of doing it, reasonably cause the apprehension that instant death to that person will otherwise be the consequence: Provided the person doing the act did not of his own accord, or from a reasonable apprehension of harm to himself short of instant death, place himself in the situation by which he became subject to such constraint.

### Malaysia

Section 94 of the Penal Code of the Federated Malay States, which is based on the Indian Penal Code, reads: Except murder and offences against the State punishable with death, nothing is an offence which is done by a person who is compelled to do it by threats, which, at the time of doing it, reasonably cause the apprehension that instant death to that person will otherwise be the consequence: provided that the person doing the act did not of his own accord, or from a reasonable apprehension of harm to himself short of instant death, place himself in the situation by which he became subject to such constraint. Fear of instant death, as distinct from imprisonment, torture or other punishment, is a condition for the claim of duress in reliance on the section to be raised before the courts.

### Nigeria

In the Nigerian Criminal Code Act 1916 (amended as at 1990), section 32 provides: A person is not criminally responsible for an act or omission if he does or omits to do the act when he does or omits to do the act in order to save himself from immediate death or grievous harm threatened to be inflicted upon him by some person actually present and in a position to execute the threats, and believing himself to be unable otherwise to escape the carrying of the threats into execution: but this protection does not extend to an act or omission which would constitute an offence punishable with death, or an offence of which grievous harm is caused to the person of another, or an intention to cause such harm, is an element, nor to a person who by entering into an unlawful association or conspiracy rendered himself liable to have such threats made to him.

## (c)  Criminal Law of Other States

*Japan*

In the Japanese Penal Code of 9907 (amended as at 1968) Article 37(1) provides: An act unavoidably done to avert a present danger to the life, person, liberty, or property of oneself or any other person is not punishable only when the harm produced by such act does not exceed the harm which was sought to be averted. However, the punishment for an act causing excessive harm may be reduced or remitted in the light of the circumstances.

*China*

The 1979 Chinese Penal Code provides in Article 13: Although an act objectively creates harmful consequences, if it does not result from intent or negligence but rather stems from irresistible or unforeseeable causes, it is not to be deemed a crime. Article 18 of this Code reads that criminal responsibility is not to be borne for an act of urgent danger prevention that cannot but be undertaken to avert the occurrence of present danger to the public interest or the rights of the actor or of other people. Criminal responsibility shall be borne where urgent danger prevention exceeds the necessary limits and causes undue harm. However, consideration shall be given according to the circumstances to imposing a mitigated punishment or to granting exemption from punishment.

*Morocco*

Article 142 of the Moroccan Penal Code of 1962 provides that there is no crime, misdemeanor, or petty offence, *inter alia*, when the author was, by a circumstance originating from an external cause which he could not resist, physically coerced in committing, or was placed physically in an impossible position to avoid (the commission of) the offence.

*Somalia*

Article 27 of the Somali Penal Code of 1962 provides:

1.  No one shall be punished for committing his acts under the coercion of another person by means of physical violence which cannot be resisted or avoided.
2.  The responsibility for such acts belongs to the person who coerced (their commission).

*Ethiopia*

It would appear that the Ethiopian penal law remains embodied in the 1957 Penal Code promulgated by Emperor Haile Selassie. Article 67 of this code addresses "absolute coercion" and provides that whoever commits an offence under an absolute physical coercion which he could not possibly resist is not liable to punishment. The person who exercised the coercion shall answer for the offence. When the coercion was of a moral kind the Court may without restriction reduce the penalty or may impose no punishment. Article 68, addressing "resistible coercion," provides that if the coercion was not irresistible and the person concerned was in a position to resist it or avoid committing the act he shall, as a general rule, be punishable. The Court may, however, without restriction reduce the penalty, taking into account the circumstances of the case, in particular the degree and nature of the coercion, as well as personal circumstances and the relationship of strength, age or dependency existing between the person who was subjected to coercion and the person who coerced it.

In some legal systems duress figures only as a form of mitigation. The penal legislation of Poland and Norway concerning the punishment of war criminals explicitly rejects duress as a defense to war crimes in general and provides that circumstances of duress may at most be considered in mitigation of punishment. Article 5 of the Polish Law Concerning the Punishment of War Criminals of 11 December 1946 provides that the fact that an act or omission was caused by a threat, order or command does not exempt from criminal responsibility. In such a case, the court may mitigate the sentence taking into consideration the circumstances of the perpetrator and the deed. In this context article 5 of the Norwegian Law on the Punishment of Foreign War Criminals of 15 December 1946 provides that necessity and superior order cannot be pleaded in exculpation of any crime referred to in Article 1 of the present Law. The Court may, however, take the circumstances into account and may impose a sentence less than the minimum prescribed for the crime in question or may impose a milder form of punishment. In particularly extenuating circumstances the punishment may be entirely remitted.

In numerous national jurisdictions, certain offences are excepted from the application of the defense of duress. Traditional common law rejects the defense of duress in respect of murder and treason. Legislatures in many common law jurisdictions, however, often prescribe a longer list of excepted offences. Despite these offences being excluded from the operation of duress as a defense, the practice of courts in these jurisdictions is nevertheless to mitigate the punishment of persons committing excepted offences unless there is a mandatory penalty of death or life imprisonment prescribed for the offence. In the United Kingdom, section 3(31(a) of the Criminal Justice Act 1991 provides that a court "shall take into account all such information about the circumstances of the offence (including any aggravating or mitigating factors as is as available to it)."

Mitigating factors may relate to the seriousness of the offence, and in particular, may reflect the culpability of the offender. It is clearly established in principle and practice that where an offender is close to having a defense to criminal liability, this will tend to reduce the seriousness of the offence. In *R. v. Beaumont* the Court of Appeal reduced the offender's sentence because he had been entrapped into committing the offence even though entrapment is no defense in English law.

Similarly, in Australian sentencing jurisprudence and practice, the culpability of the offender is taken into account in sentencing. Section 9(2)(d) of the Penalties and Sentences Act 1992 (Qld) requires a court to take into account "the extent to which the offender is to blame for the offence." Section S(2)(d) of the Sentencing Act 1991 (Vic) refers to "the offender's culpability and degree of responsibility for the offence." In *R. v. Okutgen,* the Victorian Court of Criminal Appeal held that provocation is a factor mitigating crimes of violence. In *R. v. Evans,* credence was given to the principle that a sentence should reflect the degree of participation of an offender in an offence. The degree of participation is taken to reflect the degree of the offender's culpability.

In the United States, duress constitutes a specific category for mitigation of sentences under the Federal Sentencing Guidelines and Policy Statements issued pursuant to Section 994(a) of Title 28, United States Code, which took effect on 1 November 1987. Policy Statement 5K2.12, "Coercion and Duress" provides: If the defendant committed the offence because of serious coercion, blackmail or duress, under circumstances not amounting to a complete defense, the court may decrease the sentence below the applicable guideline range. The extent of the decrease ordinarily should depend on the reasonableness of the defendant's actions and on the extent to which the conduct would have been harmful under the circumstances as the defendant believed them to be. Ordinarily coercion will be sufficiently serious to warrant departure only when it involves a threat of physical injury, substantial damage to property or similar injury resulting from the unlawful action of a third party or from a natural emergency.

In Malaysia, section 176 of the Criminal Procedure Code refers to particulars to be recorded by the Subordinate Courts in a summary trial and by virtue of paragraph 176(ii)(r). One of the particulars that must be incorporated in the record is "[t]he Court's note on previous convictions, evidence of character, and plea in mitigation, if any." The practice of the High Court in Malaysia has been, without any statutory provision, to give an opportunity to the defense to submit a plea in mitigation although in cases where the death penalty is mandatory, such a plea is irrelevant.

Courts in civil law jurisdictions may also mitigate an offender's punishment on the ground of duress where the defense fails. In some systems, the power to mitigate punishment on the ground of duress is expressly stated in the provisions addressing duress. In other jurisdictions in which the criminal law is embodied in a penal code, the power to mitigate may be found in general provisions regarding mitigation of sentence.

The question arises if any general principal can be derived from this analysis? Having regard to the above survey relating to the treatment of duress in the various legal systems, it is in our view, a general principle of law recognized by civilized nations that an accused person is less blameworthy and less deserving of the full punishment when he performs a certain prohibited act under duress. We would use the term "duress" in this context to mean "imminent threats to the life of accused if he refuses to commit a crime" and do not refer to the legal terms of art which have the equivalent meaning of the English word "duress" in the languages of most civil law systems. This alleviation of blameworthiness is manifest in the different rules with differing content in the principal legal systems of the world as the above survey reveals. On the one hand, a large number of jurisdictions recognize duress as a complete defense absolving the accused from all criminal responsibility. On the other hand, in other jurisdictions, duress does not afford a complete defense to offences generally but serves merely as a factor which would mitigate the punishment to be imposed on a convicted person. Mitigation is also relevant in two other respects. Firstly, punishment may be mitigated in respect of legislatures of some jurisdictions. Secondly, courts have the power to mitigate sentences where the strict elements of a defense of duress are not made out on the facts.

It is only when national legislatures have prescribed a mandatory life sentence or death penalty for particular offences that no consideration is given in national legal systems to the general principle that a person who commits a crime under duress is less blameworthy and less deserving of the full punishment in respect of that particular offence.

The rules of the various legal systems of the world are, however, largely inconsistent regarding the specific question whether duress affords a complete defense to a combatant charged with a war crime or a crime against humanity involving the killing of innocent persons. As the general provisions of the numerous penal codes set out above show, the civil law systems in general would theoretically allow duress as a complete defense to all crimes including murder and unlawful killing. On the other hand, there are laws of other legal systems which categorically reject duress as a defense to murder. Firstly, specific laws relating to war crimes in Norway and Poland do not allow duress to operate as a complete defense but permit it to be taken into account only in mitigation of punishment. Secondly the Ethiopian Penal Code of 1957 provides in Article 67 that only "absolute physical coercion" may constitute a complete defense to crimes in general. Where the coercion is "moral" which we would interpret as referring to duress by threats, the accused is only entitled to a reduction of penalty. This reduction of penalty may extend, where appropriate, even to a complete discharge of the offender from ground of punishment. Thirdly, the common law systems throughout the world, with the exception of a small minority of jurisdictions of the United States which have adopted without reservation Section 2.09 of the United States Model Penal Code, reject duress as a defense to the killing of innocent persons.

Speaking about the case-law of certain civil law jurisdictions, the Joint Separate Opinion mentions that although the penal codes of most civil law jurisdictions do not expressly except the operation of the defense of duress in respect of offences involving the killing of innocent persons, the penal codes of Italy, Norway, Sweden, Nicaragua, Japan, and the former Yugoslavia require proportionality between the harm caused by the accused's act and the harm with which the accused was threatened. The effect of this requirement is that it leaves for determination in the case law of these civil law jurisdictions the question whether killing an innocent person is ever proportional to a threat to the life of an accused. The determination of that question is not essential to the disposal of this case, and it suffices to say that courts in certain civil law jurisdiction *may well* consistently reject duress as a defense to the killing of innocent persons on the ground that the proportionality requirement in the provisions governing duress is not met. For example, the case law of Norway does not allow duress as a defense to murder. During the last months of World War Two, three Norwegian policemen were forced to participate in the execution of a compatriot who was sentenced to death by a Nazi special court. After the war, they were prosecuted under the Norwegian General Civil Penal Code for treason (paragraph 86) and murder (paragraph 233) and pleaded duress (paragraph 47) as a defense. It was urged upon the court that if they had refused to follow the order, they would have been shot along with the person who had been sentenced. Whilst accepting the version of the facts given by the accused, the court nevertheless declined to call their act "lawful" and stated:

And when this is so, the Penal Code will not allow punishment to be dispensed with merely because the accused acted under duress, even where it was of such a serious nature as in the case at bar, since according to the decision of the court of assize it must be deemed clear that the force did not preclude intentional conduct on the part of the accused.

In other words, the Norwegian court found that the proportionality required between the harm caused by the accused's act and the harm with which the accused were threatened was not satisfied. Accordingly, despite the general applicability to all crimes of paragraph 47 as set out in the Code, it would appear that a Norwegian court when interpreting this general provision will deny the defense to an accused person charged with murder because paragraph 47 requires that the circumstances afford justification to the accused in "regarding (the) danger as particularly significant in relation to the damage that might be caused by his act."

In addition, the provisions governing duress in the penal codes of

Germany and the former Yugoslavia suggest the possibility that soldiers in an armed conflict may, in contrast to ordinary persons, be denied complete defense because of the special nature of their occupation. Section 35(1) of the German Penal Code provides that duress is no defense "if under the circumstances it can be fairly expected of the actor that he suffer the risk; this might be fairly expected of him . . . if he stands in a special legal relationship to the danger. In the latter case, his punishment may be mitigated in conformity with section 49(1)." Article 10(4) of the Penal Code of the Socialist Federal Republic of Yugoslavia provides that "[t]here is no extreme necessity where the perpetrator was under an obligation to expose himself to the danger."[24]

Thus, comparative criminal law teaches us that national criminal justice systems embody different essential characteristics governing the outcome of the application of defenses. This diversity is not so evident in the international criminal justice system. Since ICL purports to be—at least to a certain extent—hierarchically superior to national law, its legal regime must endorse uniformity and equity, reaffirming the need to ensure one regime regulating the admissibility of legal defenses. In addition, ICL has developed into a discipline that needs to be considered "as more than the sum total of several legal disciplines parts, but a new and complex discipline."[25] This new discipline must rely on a high degree of specificity as well as clarity—also due to the principle of legality—in order to supersede and combine national legal norms. International law has historically regulated the conduct of States and international organizations. It subsequently evolved to the notion that individuals are also its proper subjects, and it can thus impose proscriptions upon individual conduct. Since nowadays these individuals are the *rationae personae* par excellence of ICL, its binding power lies in a uniform system of legal norms as well as defenses.

## 4   INDIVIDUAL CRIMINAL RESPONSIBILITY IN ICL

A third argument emerges in support of one uniform system of legal defenses in ICL. It is particularly important that the international community implements the principle that under ICL guilt must be personal, including criminal responsibility for violations of the law of armed conflict.[26] Article 25 (1) and (2) of the ICC Statute reflects the universal accept-

---

24. *See* Joint Separate Opinion of Judges MacDonald and Vohrah to the Trial Chamber Decision of the ICTY dd. 29 november 1996, case no. IT-96-22-T, *Prosecutor v. Erdemović*, Paras. 59–69.

25. *See* M. CHERIF BASSIOUNI, I INTERNATIONAL CRIMINAL LAW 13 (1999).

26. *See* Jordan J. Paust, *Superior Orders and Command Responsibility*, in I INTERNATIONAL CRIMINAL LAW 223 (M. Cherif Bassiouni, ed., 1999).

ance nowadays of the principle of individual criminal responsibility as recognized by the Major War Crimes Tribunals and reaffirmed by the ICTY in the *Tadić* jurisdictional decision with regard to individual criminal responsibility for violations of common Article 3 of the Geneva Conventions.[27] The extensive scope of individual criminal liability, envisioned in Article 25 (3) of the ICC Statute, has its complement in the subsequent and specific rules on command and superior responsibility by virtue of Articles 28 and 33. The connection between Article 25 (3) and Article 28 is obvious. The latter provision expands individual responsibility for *omission*, i.e., liability of the superior for failure to prevent his or her subordinates from committing crimes or to punish them for these crimes. One can speak here of an extension of individual liability since the ICC Statute does not enhance the general rule on omission.[28] This reasoning indicates that exonerative circumstances depend on the particular defendant's capacity, which also confronts ICL with the individual as "subject" of international law, discounting the fact that normally and primarily the addressees of rules of international law are governments.[29] Thus the international community should examine not only criminal responsibility on its individual merits, but equally defenses to international crimes. Once this consistency is *in confesso*, achieving a uniform system of legal defenses is within reach.

## 5   SUSCEPTIBILITY OF DEFENSES IN ICL TO DOMESTIC CRIMINAL LAW ELEMENTS

This leads us to the question how to achieve such a uniform system of defenses. Faced with this question it seems axiomatic, in the light of the aforementioned, that "contrary to systems of national criminal laws, the system of international criminal law lacks the basic requirements for criminal responsibility of individuals," the reason for this being "( . . . ) that within a national criminal system there are several conditions for attribution and application of the concept of criminal responsibility, while this has not been regulated under international criminal law."[30] Existing ICL, being primarily general standards difficult to apply to individuals, does not provide for any legal test such as the common law's "ordinary reasonable person," a test decisive to both the subjective or mental element

---

27.   *See* Kai Ambos, *Article 25, Margin No. 1* in COMMENTARY ON THE ROME STATUTE (Otto Triffterer, ed., 1999).

28.   *See* K. Ambos, *supra* note 27, Article 25, Margin No. 42.

29.   *See* Brownlie, *supra* note 6, at 14.

30.   Farhad Malekian, *International Criminal Responsibility*, in I INTERNATIONAL CRIMINAL LAW 160 (M. Cherif Bassiouni, ed., 1999).

(hereinafter described) and the determination of criminal intent and exonerating factors.[31] Furthermore, the system of ICL is not familiar with essential and integral elements (varying from case by case) of national criminal systems, such as the element of consent to commit a crime or violation, implying that in the event of coercive causes to crime an *"( . . . ) accurate concept of criminal responsibility is not necessarily attributed to the relevant person."*[32] Neither it is familiar with the concept characteristic of national criminal systems that, in order to incur criminal responsibility, the defendant must have committed the act knowingly and not in ignorance.

Contrary to these concepts, within the ICL system, that evolved from World War II, individual criminal responsibility is governed by the principle that *"( . . . ) where the individual acts on behalf of, or under, the characterization of the State, he/she may be recognized as the perpetrator of any relevant international crimes because of the circumstances of State conduct."*[33] By its very nature, individual criminal responsibility under ICL—e.g. when the individual acts for the performance of State conduct—can exist even though the individual does not reflect all the necessary conditions essential to ensure criminal responsibility under national criminal systems.

The question is whether this approach should be modified in accordance with and pursuant to, more recent criminological and penological views of criminal behavior. Within ICL the human rights notion endorses a concept of individual criminal responsibility connected to principles of *mens rea* and free will derived from domestic laws.[34]

Bassiouni, upholding six denominators to determine this criminal responsibility, endorses a more sophisticated approach to individual criminal responsibility in ICL.[35] In his view ICL today encompasses an interaction between criminal liability and mental state; he proposes, as his third denominator, that *"ignorance of the existence of ICL is in principle no defense, but ignorance of a specific crime would be a legal excuse if it negates the mental element (my emphasis; GJK) of the crime."* Bassiouni considers as his fifth denominator the presumption that *"ICL should not recognize the principle of strict criminal responsibility, that is responsibility without intent, and intent presupposes actual knowledge of the law."*

Although current ICL does not comprise a particular form of legislation on the elements of the international criminal responsibility of individuals, it has developed elements and prerequisites essential to establish individual criminal responsibility under ICL for crimes committed in

---

31. F. Malekian, *supra* note 30, at 160–161.

32. F. Malekian, *supra* note 30, at 161.

33. F. Malekian, *supra* note 30 at 161.

34. *See* also Gerardus G.J. Knoops, *Het EVRM en de internationale overdracht van gevonniste personen*, 79 ADVOCATENBLAD 137–138 (1999).

35. M. CHERIF BASSIOUNI, CRIMES AGAINST HUMANITY IN INTERNATIONAL CRIMINAL LAW 363–364 (1992).

regard to the conduct of particular State. Malekian summarizes these elements clearly as follows:

1.  The principle that the individual has acted as a part of the machinery of the state for the completion of state conduct. Consequently, it is a general assumption that the state under the authority of which individuals act has knowledge of the international legal system including international criminal law. The state is therefore accordingly obliged to give all necessary information to its individuals before taking any step or measure in the international arena.[36]

2.  The individual was not at the time of the commission of the relevant international crime a mentally ill person.

3.  The individual was not at the time of the commission of an international crime under the age of majority acceptable to most national criminal systems.

4.  Medical drugs did not monopolize the will of the individual in the commission of certain international crimes.

5.  The fact that the individual at the moment of the commission of the relevant international crime was not threatened by any means by the acts of other individuals.

6.  The circumstantial fact that the individual at the time of the commission of the relevant crime was not a prisoner threatened by the death penalty.

7.  The commission of an international crime was not committed by the individual under threat of torture.

8.  The personal capacity of the individual at the time of the commission of an international crime was independent of any form of technical, computerized or other scientific modification.

9.  The fact that *duress per minas* was ineffective.[37]

10. That ignorance of the law was based on a decisive lack on knowledge of the law.

The topics mentioned under elements 2, 4, 5 7, and 9 run through the subject of defenses to international crimes like veins of ore in a mineral

---

36. For example, See article 49 of the First Geneva Convention for the Amelioration of the Condition of the Wounded and Sick Armed Forces in the Field, 1949. The article reads that: *"Each High Contracting Party shall take measures necessary for the suppression of all acts contrary to the provisions of the present Convention other than the grave breaches defined in the following Article,"* referring to Article 50 of the Convention.

37. It is a consolidated principle of criminal law that *duress per minas*—compelling a person to do some acts outside his/her capacity—invalidates the reason for criminality.

deposit and form, as we will observe hereafter, the constituent elements for these defenses. This approach can be considered a justified trend in the evolution of the contemporary system of ICL, especially now that the individual is recognized as a "subject" of this branch of public international law. Not only is ICL, in its final stage of implementation, indeed applicable to "physical persons," but also the theory of international criminal responsibility in ICL has developed from the concept of the criminal responsibility of *individuals*.[38] This approach can be derived from the view of the Nuremberg Tribunal, which noted that "*crimes against international law are committed by men, not by abstract entities ( . . . )*."[39]

In conclusion it can be stated that within the contemporary system of ICL, the criminal responsibility of individuals is nowadays—contrary to that of criminal responsibility of States—"juridically consolidated."[40] This consolidation includes also the notions of criminal intent and knowledge, *mens rea*, toxicological excuses and duress *per minas*, as basic principles that provide arguments for the inclusion of defenses in ICL. In recognition of the latter principles as an essential part of customary ICL, both these topics and the concept of international criminal liability of individuals are properly dealt with under ICL. On the one hand, they "consequently demand a general section with the codification of the ICL system."[41] On the other hand, such a general section is no ultimate solution, since "the concept of individual criminal responsibility for the commission of international crimes varies from case to case depending on the circumstances and the rules of the relevant tribunal enforcing the system of ICL."[42] Considering the fact, however, that the concept of criminal responsibility of individuals is currently recognized "( . . . ) *as an integral part of the* jus cogens *principles ( . . . )*,"[43] the system of ICL could be strengthened by such a general section.

## 6    APPLICABILITY OF DOMESTIC CLASSIFICATION OF DEFENSES TO ICL

In order to administer some kind of uniformity, reflections on the legal domestic classification of defenses are of interest. The common law on criminal law defenses distinguishes, in theory, between justifications and

---

38.   Malekian, *supra* note 30, at 158.
39.   22 International Military Tribunal, Trial of the Major War Criminals Before The International Military Tribunal, Nuremberg, Germany 466, 1947.
40.   *See* Malekian, *supra* note 30, at 153.
41.   *See* Malekian, *supra* note 30, at 153.
42.   *See* Malekian, *supra* note 30, at 162.
43.   Malekian, *supra* note 30, at 191.

excuses. Common law considers an act which is justified—i.e., when the legal community positively approves this act—to be a justification, while in the event of objective disapproval of the act but subjectively rightful acting of the accused (i.e., misappropriation to convict this person for his/her committed crime), the common law system qualifies this as an excuse.[44] In case of an excuse, the act is unlawful, but the actor is excused from criminal liability. Clearly such a distinction exists in fact. Such international crimes, as crimes against humanity, genocide, torture, rape, hijacking and terrorism, cannot be justified; only the possible exoneration of an excuse can be invoked, since nowadays nearly all these international crimes are ascribed to *jus cogens* norms. This means that though the causation of an *actus reus* with the appropriate *mens rea* remains unaffected, certain defenses may still be available. In the realm of the admissibility of legal defenses to crimes against humanity, one does not always distinguish between the dogmatic and different nature of justifications on the one hand and excuses on the other.[45] As to duress and superior orders, the opinion has been asserted that *"the correct approach is that no degree of duress or necessity may justify murder, let alone genocide."*[46] This general view may be legally correct when these two defenses, if successful, would lead to a *justification*. In these general terms, though, this cannot be upheld when these defenses are dealt with as excuses. As Kremnitzer states, criminal law is not the law regulating decoration of heroism.[47] Therefore, in the legal discussion whether the described defenses are admissible for international crimes against humanity, a differentiation between the justifiable and excusable effects of defenses must be taken into account.[48]

A more appropriate approach would be to formalize or even categorize the defenses related to justifications and those related to excuses. Despite the catalogue of defenses in Article 31 (1) of the ICC Statute, it fails to differentiate these two categories. In spite of this deficiency, however, the wording of this provision—framed by the words "( . . . ) *a person shall not be criminally responsible ( . . . )"*—allows for the application of the enumerated defenses only as "*excuses.*" In this respect, the ICC follows the common law approach, which accepts *de facto* a rather broad and undifferentiated concept of defenses, instead of the more accurate differentiation

---

44. *See* JOHN SMITH & BRIAN HOGAN, CRIMINAL LAW 193 (1996).

45. *See* e.g. Yoram Dinstein, *International Criminal Law*, 20 ISRAEL LAW REVIEW 236–238 (1985).

46. *See* Dinstein, *supra* note 45, at 235.

47. *See* Mordechai Kremnitzer, *The World Community as an International Legislator in Competition with National Legislators* in PRINCIPLES AND PROCEDURES FOR A NEW TRANSNATIONAL CRIMINAL LAW 345 ( Albin Eser & Otto Lagodny, eds., 1992).

48. *See* further Chapter III, section 4, *infra*.

between the two types of exclusionary grounds endorsed by most of the civil law systems.[49]

Moreover, the distinction between justifications and excuses is worthy of debate because of the legal consequences of third parties. It can be said that:

a.  it is lawful to resist an aggressor whose aggression is merely excused but not one whose aggression forms a justification;
b.  third party, accomplice or other participant in a crime remains criminally liable although the principal accused is excused, while in the event of a justification on behalf of the principal accused the accomplice may escape a conviction.

The development of the prohibition of certain international crimes towards a *jus cogens* character[50] and subsequent disconnection from the area of justifications implies that principals in the second degree (those who participated at the time when the crime was actually perpetrated) and accessories before the fact (those who participated at an earlier time) are criminally liable even when the principal offender[51] in the first degree is excused. This is of particular relevance with respect to the prosecution of, e.g., war criminals. In the course of this study, it is advocated, as a general principle of ICL that defenses to war crimes can only have an excusable result, with the exception of self-defense.

## 7   DEFENSES IN ICL DERIVED FROM NATIONAL LAWS OF THE WORLD'S LEGAL SYSTEMS

The absence of a general part of ICL is not remedied by the proviso of Article 31 of the ICC Statute, whose heading misleadingly suggests a complete compilation of all defenses. Apart from its clear supplementary function—stemming from its starting text *"in addition to other grounds for excluding criminal responsibility ( . . . )"*—several major defenses are not included in this proviso. Reference can be made, *inter alia*, to consent of the victim,[52] and to prevention of crime and necessity, which will be addressed in Chapter III. On the provisional basis of Article 31 (2) and (3), however, the ICC is empowered to adjudicate additional defenses, within the limits of its Article 21. Article 21 allows the Court to apply, besides its

---

49.  Albin Eser, *Article 31, Margin Nos. 2–3,* in COMMENTARY ON THE ROME STATUTE (O. Triffterer, ed., 1999).

50.  *See* Malekian, *supra* note 30, at 210–211.

51.  *See* for these parties to crime: Smith & Hogan, *supra* note 44, at 126–127.

52.  *See* for this topic Chapter III, section 3, *infra.*

Statute and Rules of procedure and evidence, not only treaties and principles or Rules of international law (of armed conflict) but also *"principles of law derived from national laws of legal systems of the world including, as appropriate, the national laws of states that would normally exercise jurisdiction over the crime ( . . . )."* The inclusion of paragraph 1(c) in Article 21 was essential to ensure that the ICC will consider not only principles derived from natural law or the conscience of humanity, but also those derived from national laws.[53] Close reading of the latter provision suggests that the ICC Judges are required to apply not the national laws of any particular State itself, but rather the principles underlying the laws of *the legal systems of the world*. In the realm of legal defenses such an exercise was conducted by the Trial Chambers of the ICC in the *Erdemović* case.[54] The admissibility of the defense of duress was partly based on an analysis of underlying principles on the law of duress in several national legal systems.

As observed already by McAuliffe de Guzman: *"In developing the international criminal law relating to defenses, it is essential that the Court be permitted to draw on principles of criminal law derived from national legal systems (Paragraph 1 (c)) . . . (which) therefore enhances the Court's ability to fill lacunae in the international criminal law."*[55]

In order to stimulate this development, the language of the ICC Statute is particularly supportive, since not only does Article 21 leave considerable discretion to the ICC Judges to assess which national laws have to be taken into account in deriving the mentioned general principles— presupposing that the application and interpretation pursuant to this Article are consistent with internationally recognized international human rights, analogous to Article 38 of the ICJ Statute—but also because of the fact that Article 31 (3) permits the Court to widen the admissibility scope of defenses.

## 8   LEGAL METHODOLOGY TO IDENTIFY INTERNATIONAL CRIMINAL LAW DEFENSES

The last section has shown that the process of the admissibility of defenses in ICL has not resulted in a uniform way, but rather in an *ad hoc* manner, mostly due to considerations of *realpolitik*, without an underlying philosophy that leads to a fair impartial way of applying defenses to

---

53. Margaret McAuliffe de Guzman, *Article 21, Margin No. 15*, in COMMENTARY ON THE ROME STATUTE (Otto Triffterer, ed., 1999).

54. *See* M. McAuliffe de Guzman, *supra* note 53, Margin No. 16; the *Erdemović* case will be analyzed in chapter II, section 4, and also in Chapter III.

55. *See* M. McAuliffe de Guzman, *supra* note 53, Margin No. 17.

international crimes. Until the Rome Statute of the ICC, ICL lacked a guiding principle with respect to the applicability of defenses. The underlying
rationale for defenses is the notion that, in particular circumstances, it is
not always reasonable to criminalize or punish an individual. *A fortiori*,
the international community must recognize this at the international level.
Once the international community has decided that this concept should
indeed be applied at the ICL level, the basis for uniformity is secured.

The key question is, however, how to arrive at this uniformity; that is
to say, how to establish a consistent international criminal law norm of
defenses. This question raises the issue of methodology of international
norms. At present, international comparative criminal law does not envision conceptual frameworks for identifying, developing and enforcing
internationally recognized legal defenses. Similar to international human
rights law, there are no formal rankings or classifications of legal defenses
for purposes of admissibility to war crimes indictments.[56] As opposed to,
*inter alia*, the human rights regime, criminal law defenses do not take the
evolutionary path to international recognition through enunciation in
nonbinding instruments, specialized international instruments and, lastly,
international instruments which criminalize violations of these rights and
provide for some enforcements.[57] It seems to me that this recognition is
more related to a convergence of international conventions (be it quite
modest, since these international conventions embody hardly any substantive provisions on criminal law defenses apart from an exclusion of
superior orders in, e.g., the Torture Convention), domestic laws and
jurisprudential evolutions of both international as well as domestic tribunals.[58] Therefore, a study of criminal law defenses, and the determination of whether a certain defense is sufficiently universal to rise to the
level of an internationally recognized general criminal law defense, is necessarily to be conducted by means of an *inductive method of inquiry*.[59] This
method, as presented by Bassiouni in analyzing international human
rights norms as binding general principles of criminal justice, implies the
technique by which *"general principles of international law are extracted from
domestic legal principles or norms discovered in the major legal systems of the
world."* To me, in the area of international criminal law defenses, this
method seems to be the most appropriate legal technique or methodol-

---

56.  *See* M. Cherif Bassiouni, *Human Rights in the Context of Criminal Justice:
Identifying International Procedural Protections and Equivalent Protections in National
Constitutions*, 3 DUKE JOURNAL OF COMPARATIVE & INTERNATIONAL LAW 236–237
(1993).

57.  *See* M. Cherif Bassiouni, *supra* note 56, at 237–238.

58.  Partly mentioned as sources of international law according Article 38 of
the Statute of the ICJ.

59.  *See* for this method with respect to human rights: M. Cherif Bassiouni,
*supra* note 56, at 239, 243.

ogy of comparative criminal law research, allowing jurists—who must overlook arguments of *realpolitik*—to effectively inquire whether certain legal defenses rise to the level of international legal defenses. With regard to the determination of these defenses, this method seems more decisive and conclusive as well, because of the rather distinct legal historical background of legal defenses. As will be observed in Chapters II and III, several originate from and owe their legally binding status to general or particular (international) custom, such as for instance the defense of obedience or superior orders; others (such as self-defense) stem from Constitutional laws from the various major legal systems of the world. It can be concluded, therefore, that these different origins are more appropriately transmitted and transpired by an *inductive method of inquiry*. Apart from the fact that *"this inductive research methodology is widely recognized and relied upon in connection with the identification of customary international law and general principles of international law as recognized by civilized nations,"*[60] this method also reflects the modern trend in comparative criminal law as evidenced by, *inter alia*, the issue of dual criminality in extradition cases.[61] Resort to this method with regard to the identification of criminal law defenses in ICL means that this analysis must be done by identifying and subsequently comparing criminal law defenses in international customary and military law as well as in the various national legal systems, in order to determine the existence of *"general criminal law defenses"* common to the major legal systems of the world. As noted, this comparative research requires a distinction to be made between the several legal defenses according to their exact origin. This survey reveals that these defenses and their inductive analyses may be grouped into major families, i.e. those derived from international customary law—focused on in Chapter II—and those ascertained through the discipline of comparative criminal law itself, examined in Chapter III. Now, no two legal systems are alike and certainly the legal provisions of different domestic systems with respect to legal defenses are not likely—as noted in section 3 above—to be identical. The question therefore arise (to quote Bassiouni again) *"( . . . ) whether sameness should be defined as: (i) identical normative formulation; (ii) identical legal elements; or (iii) a merely substantial similarity of norms or elements. In short, it must be decided whether it is necessary to seek sameness of normative provisions or only a comparative equivalence of normative provisions."*[62]

Following the approach of Bassiouni—saying here that the answer will depend on whether the inquiry in question involves a broad general principle of law or a specific one—the reaffirmation of legal defenses as

---

60. *See* M. Cherif Bassiouni, *supra* note 56, at 245.
61. *See* M. Cherif Bassiouni, *supra* note 56, at 246–247.
62. *See* M. Cherif Bassiouni, *supra* note 56, at 248.

internationally established criminal law defenses does not, according to my opinion, require sameness in terms of its specific normative proscription (*ad* (i) and (ii) *supra*), but rather a "*merely substantial similarity of*" its elements (*ad* (iii) *supra*). Not all domestic systems adhere to exactly the same legal elements; e.g., the various defenses as observed in section 3 above. The achievement of a system, or even a method of achieving such a system, of internationally recognized criminal law defenses as a general part of ICL, becomes illusory when greater similarity (*ad* (i) and (ii) *supra*) is the requisite standard of methodology. Moreover, future establishment of new norms of ICL and internationally accepted legal defenses would perhaps as a result be precluded. This would obstruct the process of unifying and endorsing a general part of ICL. We live in an age of rapid globalization, in which greater harmonization of the law is an absolute prerequisite for a proper legal balance within the international community. Developments in the various criminal justice systems of the world must correspond with this globalization and need for judicial harmonization, not only with respect to the procedural part of criminal law, but concerning substantive law as well. In order to achieve this important goal, the methodological and legal basis of evolving criminal justice must be found in the *inductive method of inquiry*. In this way the development of future ICL norms and defenses, and thus a general part of ICL, is secured and can more easily be used by international criminal tribunals.

The next step in establishing and identifying international criminal law defenses is the incorporation of defenses in the law-making process of the international criminal tribunals themselves. Once a defense is addressed on an international level, it remains to be seen whether it applies in a particular criminal case. These defenses must therefore be considered individually as to which adjudicatory level (following the *inductive method*) is the most appropriate. This adjudicatory technique *deduces* a rule or decision from the particular facts of the concrete case, the so-called *law of the case*, illuminated further hereinafter and particularly in Chapter VIII. What is of particular interest, showing the relevance of the inductive method, is the reality of ICL today: criminal law defenses most frequently arise at the lower military levels, not in the sphere of the higher military ranks, in international armed conflicts. As ICL and the complexity, number and nature of international armed conflicts expand, the relatively simple "*Nuremberg model*" (i.e., an international criminal trial of twenty major defendants in a certain conflict) is transformed into a more complex trial-model in which both the number of defendants and the involvement of lower military ranks increase. In such a model, how do we deal with available international criminal law defenses, such as drunkenness, insanity and duress? Elevating standard criminal law defenses to the level of international legal defenses, based upon just a few selected criminal cases, seems to me not a solid methodology. Further inductive analysis of domestic and customary laws, as well as case law of the major legal systems of the world, should be conducted to strengthen the international validity of each particular legal defense.

# CHAPTER II

# INTERNATIONAL CRIMINAL LAW DEFENSES ORIGINATING FROM CUSTOMARY INTERNATIONAL LAW

## 1   EVOLUTIONARY STAGES

In the identification process of defenses in ICL, a distinction has to be made—as already emphasized in Chapter I—between on the one hand the evolution of defenses from customary (military and humanitarian) international law—i.e. obedience of superior orders in connection with the concept of command responsibility, as well as duress and immunity of heads of state—and on the other hand legal defenses in ICL emerging from the discipline of comparative criminal law, such as self-defense, insanity and neurotoxicological as well as genetic defenses. In the past, war crimes defendants have resorted mainly to the former defenses, as evidenced by the Post World War II Tribunals and to a large extent by the ICTY and ICTR. With the advent and development of comparative criminal law, however, the international legal community is confronted with the difficulty of differentiating the aforementioned legal sources of these defenses. As Bassiouni states, some of these defenses, like obedience to superior orders, reprisals and *tu quoque*, arise under international criminal law, national military law, and national criminal law. Coercion and necessity arise essentially under national criminal law, but coercion also arises under international criminal law and national military law when it relates to obedience to superior orders. Lastly, immunity of heads of state arises under public international law and only since the Treaty of Versailles under international criminal law.[1] However, as concluded by Bassiouni in his analysis of defenses relevant to crimes against humanity, *"even though national legal systems differ as to the legal nature of these categories of defenses, their doctrinal basis, legal significance, and the scope of their application, the world's major criminal justice systems recognize the following defenses: insanity; self-defense; mistake of law or fact; compulsion (coercion and*

---

1.   M. CHERIF BASSIOUNI, CRIMES AGAINST HUMANITY IN INTERNATIONAL CRIMINAL LAW 449 (1999).

*duress); necessity; and in a limited way 'obedience to superior orders.'"*[2] The multiplicity of the legal sources defining defenses makes it difficult to ascertain with specificity their scope, content, and applicable legal standards. According to Bassiouni, the only way to ascertain such factors is by way of *"an inductive empirical approach from the world's major criminal justice systems in order to determine whether and to what extent they may be deemed a 'general principle of law.'"*[3] In order to seek and achieve the requisite uniformity as well as this inductive approach in ICL in this respect, the international community has to turn away from the policy-motivated basis of the former category of defenses and rely on legal principles. The purpose of this chapter is to catalogue all ICL defenses from this point of view, starting with sources in customary international law and proceeding (in the next Chapter) to comparative criminal law.

The phenomenon of war crimes defenses as such in ICL begins with the Post World War II prosecutions, which raised the impunity of defendants based upon obedience to superior orders. The need to render effective criminal accountability of persons accused of war crimes overshadowed a doctrinal or methodological analysis of the legal position of defenses within the system of ICL. This explains why one of the important aims of the Charter of the IMT, as it sought to establish international criminal responsibility of individuals for the commission of international crimes was to neutralize the plea of superior orders, which was often used to escape prosecution and punishment.[4] As noted by Malekian, the drafters of the IMT Charter intended to prosecute and punish all individuals without regard to rank. To this end, Article 8 of the Constitution of the IMT dealt with the noneffectiveness of a plea of superior orders in the proceedings of an International Criminal Tribunal. Interestingly, both the Control Council 10 and its proceedings, as well as the IMT, relied on the view that the provisions of Article 8 of its Constitution were in conformity with the provisions of all domestic criminal systems.[5] Later developments in ICL reaffirmed the view that obedience to superior orders does not relieve the accused from prosecution and penalty, but can only mitigate the given penalty.[6] An overview of the evolution of the defense of superior orders within ICL, stemming from customary international law, reveals, however, several inconsistencies and no uniform perception as to its exact legal status and standard.

---

2.    *See* Bassiouni, *supra* note 1, at 448.

3.    *See* Bassiouni, *supra* note 1, at 456.

4.    Farhad Malekian, *International Criminal Responsibility*, in I INTERNATIONAL CRIMINAL LAW 168 (M. Cherif Bassiouni ed., 1999).

5.    Malekian, *supra* note 4, at 169.

6.    *See* YORAM DINSTEIN, THE DEFENSE OF OBEDIENCE TO SUPERIOR ORDERS IN INTERNATIONAL LAW (1965); *see also* Malekian, *supra* note 4, at 170.

This evolution starts with a Commission established by the allies after World War I to assess the responsibility of German officers, which rightly assumed that concurrence of power to intervene, knowledge of crimes, and subsequent failure to act should render those concerned liable for the crimes of their subordinates.[7] Despite United States and Japanese dissent—the latter arguing that high-ranking officers should not be held personally responsible under international law, in accordance with the abstention theory of responsibility—trials instituted at the German Supreme Court in Leipzig recognized the existence of concrete duties pertaining to military commanders.[8] In addition to the famous *Peleus* case, an example is the criminal case against the commander of the German U-boat involved in the sinking of the Llandovery Castle, who was found liable of failure to punish, since the German Reichsgericht (Supreme Court) was not inclined to readily grant the accused a defense of obedience to superior orders.[9] Prior to the *Llandovery Castle* case, the same Leipzig Court acquitted the German commander Neumann, who had been charged with torpedoing the Dover Castle, a British hospital ship. The defendant claimed that he was acting pursuant to superior orders, issued by his naval superiors who asserted that they believed that allied hospital ships were being used for military purposes. The Leipzig decisions were in fact preceded by the Hague Conventions (IV regarding the Laws and Customs of War on Land (1907) and X regarding the Adaptation of the Principles of the Geneva Convention to Maritime War), which Conventions enacted already command duties in relation to the conduct of subordinate persons, providing a foundation for the concept of command responsibility.[10]

The defense of superior orders underwent significant elaboration in the proceedings of the World War II Tribunals. Although the IMT at Nuremberg addressed only the criminal liability of the highest Nazi officials, the Military Tribunal at Tokyo adjudicated upon the superior orders doctrine as to both military and non-military persons for failing to prevent or punish war crimes. Failure to control groups was a key element in this jurisprudence.[11] To Bassiouni, the most important decisions that

---

7. The Commission on the Responsibility of the Authors of the War and Enforcement of Penalties proposed that a tribunal be established to prosecute those who ordered or abstained from either preventing or repressing violations of the law or customs of war to be committed. Report Presented to the Preliminary Peace Conference, Versailles, March 29, 1919, reprinted in 14 AJIL 95 (1920).

8. *See* Ilias Bantekas, *The Contemporary Law of Superior Responsibility*, 93 AM. J. INT'L. L. 573 (1999).

9. *See* The British Cases, 16 AM. J. INT'L. L. 635, 639 (1922).

10. *See* Bantekas, *supra* note 8.

11. *See* e.g. The Hirota case, 3 JUDGMENTS OF THE INTERNATIONAL MILITARY TRIBUNAL FOR THE FAR EAST I (1948); *See* also Bantekas, *supra* note 8, at 574.

dealt with superior orders undoubtedly were rendered by the IMT at Nuremberg, where *"for the first time a rule was set down in positive international law that addressed the superior order defense,"* due to the fact that the Charter of the Nuremberg trial specifically excluded this defense, allowing it merely as a mitigating factor.[12]

The third phase in this development occurred in the proceedings of the European Tribunals after World War II, which serve also as important markers in the progression of the superior orders defense. Immediately following Nuremberg, each Allied power conducted separate trials of accused German war criminals. Known as the "Subsequent Proceedings," these trials were conducted under CCL 10, promulgated on December 20, 1945 by the Control Council of the four Occupying Powers in Germany.[13] The determination of the command responsibility issue by these tribunals was conducted by assessing the accused's capacity and opposition. Examples are the *Einsatzgruppen* trial, the *High Command* case, the *Hostage* cases, the *Ministries* cases, and the *Roechling Enterprises* case. All convictions in these cases were based on the rationale that persons in *de facto* control are responsible for persons under their power, irrespective of whether a military or civilian function was served, so that the doctrine of command responsibility was extended to all persons with power over others, whether it in a purely military context or not.[14]

This evolving jurisprudence on the concept of command responsibility notwithstanding, the Geneva Conventions of 1949 lacked a specific provision in this area, resulting in a decline of the application of this concept for over thirty years. During that period, many civil wars involving rebel armies without central organizations emphasized the need for consensus and a clear standard as to how a commander or superior in these kind of conflicts must be defined.

Although Articles 86 and 87 of the Geneva Protocol I of 1979 relating to the Protection of Victims of International Armed Conflict meant significant progress, it was not until the establishment of the ICTY and ICTR in response to civil conflicts in the former Yugoslavia and Rwanda that clear standards emerged to form a fourth phase in the evolution of the superior orders defense. As pointed out by Bantekas, the ongoing cases against Bosnian Croat General Blaškić and the judgment in the *Celebići* case influenced the development of Article 28 of the Statute of the International Criminal Court, making command responsibility a basis for criminal responsibility when international crimes are committed, which concept is—similar to the jurisprudence of ICTY and ICTR—available within the

---

12. M. CHERIF BASSIOUNI, CRIMES AGAINST HUMANITY IN INTERNATIONAL CRIMINAL LAW 469 (1999).

13. Bassiouni, *supra* note 1, at 473.

14. *See* Bantekas, *supra* note 8, at 574; *See also* Bassiouni, *supra* note 1, at 473–474.

ICC framework in both civilian and military settings.[15] On the one hand, considering the complexity of our world and its mixed conflicts, this is an encouraging development. On the other hand, an analysis of the afore-mentioned four evolutionary stages reveals indeed the absence of a clear legal standard of the defense of superior orders. Does it merit legal status as an absolute legal defense? Does it deserve a formal qualification as defense (Article 8, Nuremberg Charter) though not interpreted in that way by its jurisprudence? Or can this defense only be used in mitigation of punishment, as is the case in the Statutes of ICTY, ICTR and ICC? In other words, the question arises whether these past developments, embodying customary international law, should be stabilized in order to form a clear concept with permanent juridical validity within the system of ICL wherein this submitted first category of criminal law defenses in ICL are complete defenses. It is obvious that the principle of legality requires indeed a uniform concept.[16] In regard to the question of acceptance as a complete defense, several arguments for an affirmative answer emerge.

## 2  COMMAND RESPONSIBILITY AND THE DEFENSE OF SUPERIOR ORDERS

### 2.1 Expression of principle of individual criminal responsibility

There is nothing particularly novel in pointing out that international criminal law advocates the principle of individual criminal responsibility of superiors for acts and actions of subordinates if one had knowledge and power to prevent.[17] Moreover, it is a principle of current ICL that when an international crime is committed, it automatically gives rise to international criminal responsibility of the particular individual, within which the plea of superior orders as such is not exonerative, but merely mitigative in regard to the punishment. The *ratio decendi* of the above is the general rule that individuals carrying a superior order simply must be sure that the order is not criminal.[18] A textual analysis of some relevant treaty provisions in the categories of international crimes reveals that one of the main objectives of international criminal law conventions seems to be to exclude the defense of superior orders.[19] Article 33 of the Draft

---

15.  *See* Bantekas, *supra* note 8, at 575; this jurisprudence will be dealt with in Chapters IV and V *infra*.

16.  *See* Chapters I and IV *infra*.

17.  *See* Theodor Meron, *Crimes and Accountability in Shakespeare*, in WAR CRIMES LAW COMES OF AGE 82, 87 (Theodor Meron, ed., 1998).

18.  F. Malekian, *supra* note 4, at 168.

19.  *See* M. Cherif Bassiouni, *The Penal Characteristics of Conventional*

Statute of the International Criminal Court is a vivid recent example of this feature.[20] The *ratio decendi* of this approach seems to be to forestall the potential conflict between international criminal law and national law in the event the former establishes prohibition and the latter commands, permits or condones the very conduct prohibited. In response to such a potential conflict, international criminal law has developed specific norms on the defense of obedience to superior orders and command responsibility.[21] This especially applies to *jus cogens* crimes to which States cannot derogate, and in this respect ICL purports to be hierarchically superior to national law. The question whether there is a danger of individual subordinate responsibility under international law being used *de facto*, if not as a cloak behind which the responsibility of the State and its leaders or superiors can hide, and the question to which extent superior orders can function as a possible legal disculpation or excuse to international crimes, are thus strongly connected.

While it seems clearly justified that the international legal order should have effective means at its disposal for exercising criminal jurisdiction over both superiors and subordinates in instances where their individual responsibility exists, the international rule of law should provide an exception to this notion in extraordinary circumstances. However—the coexistence of both superior and subordinate responsibility as, in certain events, undermining the efficiency of international law as a body of law notwithstanding[22]—such a simple approach would neglect several main principles of international law.

## 2.2 Command responsibility and superior orders: correlative concepts?

The concept of criminal responsibility of superiors or commanders—the doctrinal basis being the idea that superiors are attributed with certain duties and obligations, with consequent responsibility to ensure all necessary and feasible measures to prevent the commission of international crimes by their subordinates[23]—and that of superior orders were both developed after World War II in order to prevent escape from pros-

*International Crimes Law* in 15 CASE WESTERN RESERVE JOURNAL OF INTERNATIONAL LAW 27 at 30.

20.   This article will be discussed in Chapters IV and V *infra*.

21.   M.Cherif Bassiouni, *The Sources and Content of International Criminal Law*, in I INTERNATIONAL CRIMINAL LAW 20–21 (M. Cherif Bassiouni, ed., 1999).

22.   *See* for co-existence of both individual and State responsibility: Malcolm D. Evans, *International Wrongs and National Jurisdiction*, in REMEDIES IN INTERNATIONAL LAW: THE INSTITUTIONAL DILEMMA 173 (Malcolm D. Evans, ed., 1998).

23.   *See* Malekian, *supra* note 4, at 171.

ecution and punishment and to maintain the principle of equal application of the law, regardless of the capacity or rank of the individual. The plea of superior orders and command responsibility developed in a similar way; provisions were enacted to ensure that these two concepts could not relieve the accused from prosecution. Examples hereof are Article 2, section 3 of the 1984 Torture Convention, excluding the plea of superior orders or the theory of obedience to the law as exoneration to prosecution,[24] and Article 11 of the 1995 Draft Code of Crimes Against the Peace and Security of Mankind. The latter ensures that subordinates' crimes violating the peace and security of mankind do not relieve their superiors of criminal responsibility, enabling only mitigation of punishment. The presupposition is that these superiors knew or could have known about the intended crime and abstained from preventing it. This Code reads: *"The fact that an individual charged with a crime against the peace and security of mankind acted pursuant to an order of a government or of a superior, does not relieve him of criminal responsibility if, in the circumstances at the time, it was possible for him not to comply with that order."*

Although it is clear that both subordinates and superiors are representatives of the particular State and their acts can legally be transposed to their Government, the consolidated principle of international criminal responsibility of superiors *"( . . . ) regardless of whether or not he/she was aware of the commission of (such) a crime"*[25] seems to be in conflict with the principle of ICL that individual criminal responsibility cannot be based on an abstract liability test but must be governed by the notion of concrete and individual guilt, which argument will be further assessed in Chapter III below. An analogous abstraction exists in customary ICL regarding the defense of superior orders, in that such a defense can only feature in mitigating the penalty, not as exclusion to the crime.[26] From this perspective we can conclude that both concepts—superior orders and command responsibility—have correlative characteristics. Although at present there seems to be a well-established consensus on the applicable law or legal standard determining these concepts, interpretation in practice remains a subject of debate. This debate does not center on the doctrinal conception of *mens rea*, nor does it focus on the principle of protection of individual soldiers within international law. A review of the aforesaid concepts in the light of both *mens rea* and the latter principle can be more revealing and instructive than a mere dogmatic approach to the concepts of command responsibility and superior orders.

The following subsections will explore the current scope of these two

---

24. *See* also Art. III of Apartheid Convention and Art. 8 of the Constitution of the IMT.

25. *See* Malekian, *supra* note 4, at 172.

26. *See* Malekian, *supra* note 4, at 170.

concepts with regard to the principles of protection of the individual soldier and that of *mens rea*. For now, it is important to recognize that the defenses of obedience to superior orders and command responsibility are closely linked. When the policy of international criminal responsibility places a greater burden on the commander, logically the subordinate can benefit from greater latitude with respect to the defense of superior orders. Whereas, in the event the responsibility of the commander is reduced, the consequence is that the burden of responsibility falls on the subordinate, unless it is obvious that the order was manifestly unlawful or their is a clear case of the element of duress. It can be observed that, not only in the Nuremberg jurisprudence but particularly in that of the Statutes of ICTY, ICTR and ICC, the international legal community has expanded the criminal responsibility of the commander while at the same time reducing the defense of superior orders related to the subordinate. Therefore the aforesaid logical interaction between command responsibility and defense of superior orders remarkably failed to materialize. It seems that the absence of this logical interaction establishes now a new policy of international criminal responsibility, which places a burden on both the commander and the subordinate in order to reduce the possibility of perpetration of war crimes.

### 2.3 The general scope of the defense of superior orders: the law of the case

The concept of superior orders has been a considerable source of legal controversy; its influence and importance in international legal practice have assumed great significance as a result of the increasing interventions of multilateral peacekeeping forces of both the United Nations and NATO in the last two decades of the twentieth century,[27] and as such will be examined closely in Chapters IV and V hereinafter in substantial detail.

These moral and practical controversies were in 1965 already outlined by Dinstein, concluding in his study that "( . . . ) *the fact of obedience to (superior) orders should be excluded as a defense per se, but permitted to be taken into account (as a factual element), among the other circumstances of the case, for the purpose of establishing a defense based on lack of* mens rea ( . . . )." As a scholar he has no doubt however that "the doctrine of *respondeat superior* authority has proved to be a chimera and the number of those who preach it is lessening."[28] There can be little question that the recognition of the

---

27. *See* also Gerardus G.J. Knoops, *Interstatelijk Noodweerrecht: disculpatiegrond voor internationaal-rechtelijke onrechtmatige daad*, 43 NEDERLANDS JURISTENBLAD 2013 et seq (1999).

28. YORAM DINSTEIN, THE DEFENSE OF OBEDIENCE TO SUPERIOR ORDERS IN INTERNATIONAL LAW 253 (1965).

doctrine of *respondeat superior*—the assumption that the fact of obedience to superior orders constitutes, automatically and *a priori*, a complete and absolute disculpatory defense against a criminal prosecution—should not be accepted.[29] This doctrine bears the danger of undermining not only *jus cogens* principles but also the interpretative character of international judicial reasoning. The closely linked concepts of command responsibility and superior orders have therefore to be elaborated on the basis of "*the law of the case.*" A justified legal approach dictates reference to the context, that it is to say the nature of the particular superior order and the purposive context that it presents. It is of considerable importance to distinguish obvious from non-obvious *contra jus cogens* superior orders. Although it may be that a military command is ordinarily a complete defense to the soldier who executes it, "because military discipline does not permit the subordinate to conduct a collateral inquiry as to the lawfulness of an order received ( . . . ),"[30] it is for subordinate clear that "an order to a sentry to kill anyone using 'opprobrious words' is 'obviously unlawful' and void (and) would not justify or excuse such a killing."[31] Likewise it is obvious that "an order to a soldier to assist his superior in the perpetration of rape is not a military command."[32] On the same criteria of "obviously illegal," the subordinate incurs criminal responsibility in case of murder of captured detainees under forced control, deliberate attack with machinegun fire on civilians torture or abuse of prisoners, and placing of civilians ahead of an army to clear a field of land mines.[33] One can address these diverse elements only through resort to "the law of the case." The defense of superior orders involves clearly a combination of law and facts. The consensus of the applicable law notwithstanding, establishing the facts is ultimately decisive as to the determinative and legal outcome of a criminal case. It is thus obvious that in this area of defenses, the factual basis seems to condition the law as opposed to the law conditioning the facts.

As a general outline, the presumption appears to be that "*servile compliance with orders clearly criminal for fear of some disadvantage or punishment not immediately threatened cannot be recognized as a defense*" (of duress and of superior orders; GJK).[34] The interplay between (international) military law and ICL in this era suggests that a more functional approach to the doctrine of command responsibility (and the closely linked concept of superior orders) should be through the notion or principle of protection of the individual soldier. In the event of conflicts between norms of ICL and the

---

29.  *See* also Dinstein, *supra* note 28, at 253.

30.  ROLLIN M. PERKINS AND RONALD N. BOYCE, CRIMINAL LAW 1062 (1982).

31.  Perkins and Boyce, supra note 30; *See* also Jordan J. Paust, *My Lai and Vietnam: Norms, Myths and Leader Responsibility*, 57 MILITARY LAW REVIEW 171 (1972).

32.  Perkins and Boyce, *supra* note 30, at 1062–1063.

33.  Paust, *supra* note 31, at 172.

34.  Paust, *supra* note 31, at 170.

law of the case, the appropriate answer depends not only on the nature of the particular order, but also on the notion—related to fairness and good faith—that individual soldiers, under certain circumstances, have to be protected against governmental military powers. This principle has to be relied upon because of the fact that, as expressed in Chapter I, the reality of ICL shows that criminal law defenses most frequently occur at the lower military levels, not in the area of the higher military ranks. Determination of the doctrine of command responsibility and superior orders has therefore to be conducted—apart from the applicable law or legal standard—in the light of the specific military operation and structure. This implies that, in the event of a conflict between the applicable legal standard and the law of the case, application of the former to the benefit of the individual soldier—presupposing that the superior order was not manifestly unlawful—reflects sometimes a more fair and functional interpretation.[35]

## 2.4 The specific scope of the defense of superior orders within the ICC: conception of *mens rea*

In the classical perception of superior orders, in doubtful cases command responsibility supervenes above subordinate responsibility, in recognition of the principle of *in dubio pro reo*, i.e., for the subordinate the order is to be presumed legal until an obviously illegal order arises.[36] In this context, subordinate criminal responsibility arises when the soldier personally *knows* the order to be unlawful or when faced with an obviously illegal order.[37]

Both State and individual responsibility are major concepts of international criminal law. Individual criminal responsibility is, in its operation, closely linked to the element of *mens rea*, i.e., the defense that a subordinate has not the requisite premeditation, criminal mind or criminal culpability.[38]

The determination of criminal liability in the field of superior orders can therefore be reduced to an analysis of its original *mens rea*, i.e., the accused "knew or should have known."[39] In the context of the defense of superior orders in international criminal cases, it is advocated that only lack of *mens rea*, of which obedience to orders constitutes circumstantial evidence, could serve as legal protection for criminal responsibility.

---

35. *See* for this view with regard to ROE: Chapter V *infra*.
36. *See* Paust, *supra* note 31, at 172.
37. Paust, *supra* note 31, at 171.
38. Paust, *supra* note 31, at 172.
39. Paust, *supra* note 31, at 172.

Therefore the admissibility of a defense of superior orders should be judged within the compass of a defense based on lack of *mens rea* (i.e., either mistake of law or fact or compulsion/duress), the fact of obedience to orders constituting only a factual element to be considered in conjunction with other factual circumstances of the particular case.[40] The application of this principle of *mens rea* is in accordance with the present view on the conditions of accountability of human beings for criminal behavior.[41]

Parallel to the endeavor of providing some kind of legal protection for the rather powerless individual soldier against the hierarchical machinery of the army—which protection is advocated in this chapter as well as in Chapters IV and V as regards actions pursuant to ROE—the *mens rea* principle appears to be a tenable solution of the antithesis between law and superior orders. This principle of protection of the individual soldier can, under some circumstances, be considered as a higher principle than that of legality. Even by holding that the mental element may be absent in the event the subordinate thinks by mistake that the order was lawful, the act remains illegal; only the defendant may be excused.[42] Moreover, to approach the concept of superior orders in ICL as an element in ascertaining the existence of *mens rea*—requisite to criminal liability—would merit a general principle of ICL, namely that of individual criminal responsibility.[43] It should be noted however that, in my opinion, the fact that one may view the defense of superior orders as part of the mental element does not detract from its use as a separate and independent defense.

The element of *mens rea* is now clearly envisioned by Article 33 (1)(b) and (c) of the ICC Statute, in conjunction with its paragraph 2. This conceptual framework appeared necessary *"or at least advisable after the Act of State doctrine had lost its validity and individual responsibility for crimes under international law became more and more accepted after the turn of the century and especially after the First World War."*[44] Since the goal of the ICC Statute in this matter was to ensure that subordinates could no longer hide behind the responsibility of their superiors or their States, the ICC Statute constitutes a framework within which State organs or officials, commanders and subordinates *"should be equally responsible"* through the Articles 25, 27, 28 and 33.[45] Article 33 expresses the view that the defense of superior orders,

---

40. Dinstein, *supra* note 28, at 88.

41. *See* further: Chapter VII, *infra*.

42. *See* Otto Triffterer, *Article 33, Margin No. 12*, in COMMENTARY ON THE ROME STATUTE (Otto Triffterer, ed., 1999).

43. *See* Hersch Lauerpacht, *The Law of Nations and the Punishment of War Crimes*, 21 BRIT. Y.B. INT'L. L. 58, 87 (1944).

44. Triffterer, *supra* note 42, Margin No. 10.

45. *Ibid.*

assuming it fulfills the requirements set out in paragraph 1, can never *justify* an act of the particular subordinate, based upon the corresponding order, but only and at the most can qualify as an *excuse*.[46] As observed, Article 33 (1) states three conditions under which superior orders may serve as an excuse for the subordinate:

— There must be a legal obligation to obey the order in question, which obligation must have existed at the time of committing the crime. In case the subordinate wrongfully believes himself to be under such a legal obligation, another defense emerges, namely the defense of mistake of fact or law by virtue of Article 32 of the ICC Statute. As a requisite element of this first condition, the particular superior must be legally empowered to impose a legally binding order on the subordinate in question.

— It is presumed that under the ICC Statute all orders are unlawful when "*a crime within the jurisdiction of the court has been committed.*"[47] According to Triffterer, in cases of doubt the ICC Statute, in favor of the subordinated accused, presupposes that the subordinate did not know about the unlawfulness of the order, so that his knowledge of this unlawfulness must be proven. In the absence of such knowledge, the condition of Article 33 (1)(b) does not apply. The Statute justifies this view by realizing the possibility of errors regarding the unlawfulness of the order.[48]

— The third condition involves, according to Triffterer, "*a sort of compensation for the strict acceptance of an error by the subordinate (even if avoidable) ( . . . ),*" as expressed by the above-mentioned second condition.[49] Similar to the first condition, this requirement forms an objective element by implying that, even if the first two conditions are fulfilled, the subordinate is not excused if the order was manifestly unlawful. Again here this "*manifestly*" element has to be proven by the prosecution, which also in this context results in the premise that "*as long as there remains doubt about this question, the order was, in favor of the subordinate, not manifestly unlawful.*"[50]

With regard to the scope of Article 33, it has to be noted that from its paragraph 2 (apart from the exclusion of the presumption mentioned in

---

46.  Triffterer, *supra* note 42, Margin Nos. 12 and 29.
47.  Triffterer, *supra* note 42, Margin No. 27.
48.  *Ibid.*
49.  Triffterer, *supra* note 42, Margin No. 28.
50.  *Ibid.*

paragraph 1(c)), it follows as consequential that this provision is only applicable in cases of war crimes and aggression.[51]

## 2.5 The applicability of the defense of superior orders to civilians in international armed conflicts

The establishment of command responsibility for civilian commanders notwithstanding, neither the ICTY, ICTR nor ICC Statutes contain a provision as regards the applicability of the defense of superior orders to civilians. The category of "superior" under Article 28 (b) of the ICC Statute includes civilian "commanders" such as political leaders, business leaders and senior civil servants,[52] since it refers to superior and subordinate relationships of non-military nature, as opposed to paragraph (a) which entails military or quasi–military structures resulting in exercise of command over forces. Likewise, the category of "subordinate" also embodies civilians; Article 28 (b) envisions any person who has a superior empowered with *de jure* or *de facto* (effective) authority to issue directives to one's activities as being a subordinate to that superior.[53] The inclusion within the ICC Statute of command responsibility of civilian commanders notwithstanding, the question still remains open as to the applicability of the defense of superior orders to civilians. It is my belief that, once the category of superiors is expanded to civilian leaders, it is a little step to the acceptance of this defense for civilians. Especially considering the broad concept of the category of subordinates, it would be illogical and legally inconsistent to prevent civilian subordinates from invoking this defense. Support for enlargement of this defense is provided by recent case law from French criminal cases as well as, to a certain extent, the Israeli trials of *Kapos* i.e., Jewish collaborators under the Nazis and Nazi Collaborators (Punishment) Law.

Illustrative in the first place is the French criminal case against the French collaborator Paul Touvier, the assistant of the former Gestapo Chief of Lyon Klaus Barbie. Touvier was sentenced to death *in absentia* twice, in 1945 and 1947, for various crimes against humanity but, unlike Barbie, he remained in France and was hidden and protected by Catholic fundamentalists. In 1969, Touvier's death sentences were rescinded and President Pompidou officially pardoned him. However, in 1973 private parties brought new charges of crimes against humanity, such as torture and the deportation of prisoners to concentration camps, against Touvier.

---

51.  Trifferer, *supra* note 42, Margin No. 30.
52.  William J. Fenrick, *Article 28, margin No. 16*, in COMMENTARY ON THE ROME STATUTE (Otto Trifferer, ed., 1999).
53.  Fenrick, *supra* note 52, Margin No. 18.

For eight years the French judiciary struggled to find an approach to the prosecution of crimes against humanity compatible with the French legal system. When at last the legal basis for prosecution was determined and the Cour de Cassation confirmed the imprescriptibility of crimes against humanity, investigation into the facts was resumed and an international arrest warrant was issued. In the meantime, however, Touvier had disappeared. For almost eight years he managed to evade the French authorities until he was finally arrested in May 1989 in a priory in Nice. Subsequently, the Indicting Chamber of the Paris Court of Appeals dismissed all five charges against Touvier; regarding four charges the Court considered the evidence inadequate and in regard to the fifth charge (the massacre of seven Jews at Rillieux-la-Pape, in which Touvier himself admitted his involvement) the Court concluded that Touvier lacked specific intent. The Cour de Cassation revised this decision in part and referred the case concerning the fifth charge to the Court of Appeals at Versailles.[54] In a decision of June 2, 1993 this Court finally raised charges against Touvier for the latter involvement.[55] In the subsequent proceedings before the Court at Versailles in Spring 1994 Touvier did not deny the charges, but argued that he had acted in a situation of distress and on superior orders of the German forces, asserting that he had tried his best to save other Jews from execution. However, during cross-examination he became entangled in contradictions and was ultimately found guilty on April 20, 1994 and sentenced to life imprisonment.[56] The trial of Touvier is exemplary for the defense of superior orders as raised by civilians.

Other examples are the Israeli criminal cases against the *Kapos* or Jewish policemen in the concentration camps. As pointed out by Wenig, although all of these Jewish collaborators were placed in incredibly difficult positions, some were guilty of terrible cruelty and of committing offences not excused by their situation.[57] Section 10 of the Nazis and Nazi Collaborators (Punishment) Law, enacted by Israel in 1950, provides for a defense where the act was done in order to save the perpetrator from the danger of immediate death threatening him, and the court is satisfied that he did his best to avert the consequences of the act or omission. Israel did not shy away from turning this law on its own war criminals. A remarkable example is the case of *The Attorney General of Israel v Hirsh Brinblatt*, which took place in 1964. Brinblatt, the head of the Jewish police

---

54. Judgment of Nov. 27, 1992; Cass. Crim., 1993 J.C.P. II G. No 21.977.

55. Judgment of June 2, 1993, Cour d'appel de Versailles (unpublished).

56. *See* Axel Marschik, *The Politics of Prosecution: European National Approaches to War Crimes*, in THE LAW OF WAR CRIMES 84–85 (Timothy L.H. McCormack & Gerry J. Simpson, eds., 1997).

57. *See* Jonathan M. Wenig, *Enforcing the Lessons of History: Israel Judges the Holocaust*, in THE LAW OF WAR CRIMES 118 –121 (Timothy L.H. McCormack & Gerry J. Simpson, eds., 1997).

force in the Polish city of Bendin, was charged with delivering up the Jews to the Nazis and organizing them into groups for transfer to concentration camps. As a civilian, he helped the Nazis organize the Jews and prevented them from fleeing or changing groups. Brinblatt was eventually acquitted on appeal, relying on the defense in section 10. Unfortunately the Court, as Wenig observes, shied away from dealing at length with the morality of the *Judenrat councils* as such and restricted its perspective only to the crimes of individuals, because (as the Court noted) the origin of the *Kapos* or *Judenrat* itself was not addressed by the legislation.[58] The main purpose in evaluating these Israeli criminal cases against *Kapos* is the fact that they obviously open the possibility for civilians to invoke the defense of superior orders.

Although these domestic trials leave much unanswered, the conclusion seems to be justified that the applicability of the defense of superior orders to civilians, under some circumstances, has to be left open, especially since it can provide for a more nuanced and comprehensive moral response to the (non-) sincerity of the intentions of defendants. To this end, amendment of Article 33 of the ICC Statute must be considered. Since the expression *"a legal obligation to obey orders"* refers to *"binding orders in general and not to the question of whether there was a legal obligation to obey this specific order to commit a crime,"*[59] and excludes civilians, revision of Article 33 (1)(a) in the light of this purpose could read: *"the person was, considering the factual situation or circumstances, under an obligation to obey orders ( . . . )."* Such a wording leaves adjudicatory leverage as to a differentiation between the three contexts of conflict: international, non-international and purely internal. With regard to the latter three contexts of conflict, one has to consider that, as pointed out by Bassiouni, a historical distinction separating international human rights law from IHL is now eroding.[60] While human rights law is known as the law of peace, international humanitarian law had developed as part of the international regulation of armed conflict, otherwise referred to as the law of war. Bassiouni notes that *"somehow these distinctions have not been totally eliminated, and thus international humanitarian law applies only in the context of armed conflicts, whether of an international or noninternational character."* It is my belief that, especially since international human rights protection nowadays strongly influences the content of IHL, the applicability of the defense of superior orders to civilians—assuming the civilian in question could reasonably rely on a not manifestly illegal order of a militarian—should in

---

58. *See* Wenig, *supra* note 57, at 119–120.
59. *See* Triffterer, *supra* note 42, Margin No. 26.
60. *See* M. Cherif Bassiouni, *Human Rights in the Context of Criminal Justice: Identifying International Procedural Protections and Equivalent Protections in National Constitutions*, 3 DUKE JOURNAL OF COMPARATIVE & INTERNATIONAL LAW, 242–243 (1993).

principle not differ according to the aforementioned three kinds of conflict. The principle of protection of civilians against military or government conduct, as well as the principle of equality envisioned by Article 14(1) of the ICCPR, is supportive of this view. The future of ICL will show whether this extensive modern approach to the concept of superior orders to civilians will be relied on.

## 2.6 Concurrence of duress and superior orders

Having examined the general outlines of the scope of superior orders as defense,[61] it is necessary to determine first the legal relationship between this form of defense and duress, since a judicially incorrect coherence is assumed between these two phenomena.[62]

In seeking the judicial boundaries of these defenses it becomes apparent that the position of a duress defense is rather different, although comparable in its performance, from the superior orders defense. The latter defense is based on "ignorance of the illegality,"[63] whereas duress arises when the actor's free will is impaired by an irresistible exterior force which imposes a mental compulsion. From this perspective, duress is not a form of superior orders "( ... ) although it may be involved in many situations in which superior's orders are raised as a defense."[64]

The military command structure imposes upon the subordinate an antagonistic and paradoxical necessity to respond. From the military legal jurisdiction emerges the duty of strict obedience and following superior orders, whereas the international judicial system enables him to act according to these military commands even when violating the international order, an example of concurrence of moral and legal choices *par excellence* which inevitably reveals an element of duress.[65] There can be no doubt that, in war situations, a legal connection exists between the defense of superior orders and that of duress (or necessity). It must be pointed out, however, that the special character of duress, as opposed to superior orders, appears in the constituent element "*to save from death or great bodily injury*," resulting in an "*inexcusable choice*."[66]

This applicable distinguishing characteristic of duress with respect to superior orders is described by Paust as follows: "*When a soldier does an*

---

61. *See* sections 3 and 4 below; *See* also Chapter III *infra*.

62. *See* Christopher L. Blakesley, *Atrocity and its Prosecution: The Ad Hoc Tribunals for the Former Yugoslavia and Rwanda*, in THE LAW OF WAR CRIMES 220 (Timothy L.H. McCormack and Gerry J Simpson, eds., 1997).

63. *See* Blakesley, *supra* note 62, at 219.

64. *See* Blakesley, *supra* note 62, at 220.

65. *See* for this concurrence also Blakesley, *supra* note 62, at 220.

66. Perkins and Boyce, *supra* note 30, at 1064.

*act known to be in violation of the law of war, he cannot plead duress as a defense unless there is a showing of circumstances such that a reasonable man would apprehend that he was in such imminent physical peril as to deprive him* (or close relations; GJK) *of his freedom to choose the right and refrain from the wrong."* This scholar affirms that "it would not be sufficient to argue that the sergeant or lieutenant would not want the soldier to disobey their order (but) there must be an honest belief of *an immediate threat of physical harm*" and "that the threatened harm must be more serious than the harm which will result to others from the act to be performed."[67] Bassiouni rightly describes both the distinctive and concurrent elements of duress and superior orders. In his study of 1999 one reads that: *"obedience to superior orders is not a defense under customary international law to an international crime when the order is manifestly illegal and when the subordinate has a moral choice with respect to obeying or refusing to obey the order. If the subordinate is coerced or compelled to carry out the order, the norms for the defense of coercion (compulsion) should apply. In such cases, the issue is not justification but excuse or mitigation of punishment."*[68] As indicated by the above scholar, even in certain rare circumstances obedience to superior order cannot be considered an essential reason for exclusion from prosecution. In other words: *"Individuals cannot escape from their own personal responsibility by resorting to superior orders as a reason for default."*

This description contains, as distinctive elements both the *"moral choice"* of the subordinate—absent in the event of superior orders—and the eventual concurrent element of coercion, in which event the superior orders defense will be transformed to a duress defense. Malekian argues that the validity of this approach follows from seven reasons:

i. The fact that the system of international criminal law today is a separate branch of international law having a consolidated position.

ii. The theory of acts of state does not any longer fit the contemporary needs of criminal proceedings.

iii. The practices of criminal courts in the prosecution and punishment of perpetrators of international crimes, in particular those of the IMT in Nuremberg, demonstrate that the plea of superior orders has no legal validity in the system of international criminal law.

iv. The fact that obedience to superior order is contrary to the provisions of international criminal conventions is applicable to all categories of defendants.

---

67. Paust, *supra* note 31 at 169–170, referring here to *United States versus Von Leeb* (1948) and *United States versus Ohlendorf* (1949).

68. M. CHERIF BASSIOUNI, CRIMES AGAINST HUMANITY IN INTERNATIONAL CRIMINAL LAW 483 (1999).

   v. The theory of obedience to superior order may disable the practical application of the system of international criminal law.

  vi. Defense of obedience to superior order is against the principle of *nullum crimen sine poena*; it may only slightly mitigate the punishment.

 vii. The practice of the International Tribunal for Violations of Humanitarian Law in the former Yugoslavia obviously denotes the invalidity of obedience to superior order within the framework of international criminal law in order to escape punishment.

A legal theory validated on the basis of a *petitio principii*—such as the reasons at (iii), (iv) and (vii) above—is not a particularly strong argument. Also, the assertion that the defense of superior orders is contrary to the principle "*nullum crimen sine poene*" seems to be artificial because this principle addresses no defenses.

The justification not to accept the defense of superior orders, in general terms, to international crimes can better be looked for in the legal distinction of defenses—derived from both common law and civil law systems—as either *justifications* or *excuses*, as will be elaborated in more detail in Chapter IV, section 4 below. In the event of the former, the contested crime is supposed to be justified *ab initio*, while in the latter case the contested act is and remains illegal although the accused can neither be blamed for having acted in this way or be excused. Recognition of the defense of superior orders (without duress) as exoneration would justify it unfairly. This seems to me a valid and major objection to the acceptance of this defense as being unconditionally part of customary ICL, since it suggests the legitimacy of the underlying act.

The general approach of the Yugoslavia Tribunal not to consider the two defenses of superior orders and duress as two self-containing dispositives, but allowing simultaneous consideration, is not commensurate with the specific nature of these defenses. This will be further elaborated in Chapter IV below.

## 2.7 Conclusion

A review of the evolution of the defense of superior orders in ICL leads, according to Bassiouni, to the conclusion that customary international law does not recognize this defense to an international crime when the order is manifestly illegal and the subordinate has no moral choice with respect to obeying or refusing the order. In case of coercion or compulsion to carry out the order, the latter defense can be invoked by the subordinate. Customary international law, at the time of World War I, contained no specific rule or norms disqualifying the defense of superior orders within ICL, nor provided for conclusive evidence. In contrast, the Leipzig trials following World War I provided substantial evidence whereby this defense was recognized in non-absolute terms. Once it is accepted that the entire question of obedience to superior orders should be viewed, pursuant to general principles of ICL, as part of the mental element of a crime (a prerequisite for individual criminal responsibility), it would be inconsistent to deny its status as an international criminal defense to international war crimes as well. This defense arises thus not from the authority of the order given, but from the absence of *mens rea*, due to moral-ethical considerations.[69]

## 3 THE DEFENSE OF DURESS: TRANSMITTING MORALITY AND *MENS REA*

### 3.1 Introduction

In the realm of international criminal litigation, there can be no question that duress is, together with superior orders, one of the most commonly arising defenses.[70] Although duress as a defense in ICL stems from customary and military international law, its partly comparative criminal law source cannot be denied.

In common law doctrine the defense of duress is only admissible under certain conditions. Both continental and common law systems, while justifying self-defense, do not recognize an excuse for intentional killing of an innocent person, even if necessary to save oneself from instant death. The only exception is the rule of duress, which excuses the commission of a prohibited act (with subsequent disculpation of the defendant of criminal liability) if reasonably believed to be necessary to save the actor from imminent death or great bodily injury.[71] In common law, this excuse is recognized in prosecutions for both minor offences (e.g. reckless driving) and grave felonies such as burglary, robbery and kidnapping. An essential element of the rule of duress is the fact that the defendant himself must raise the issue of duress and the prosecution, whenever this issue is raised, must prove the defendant guilty. Therefore the defendant does not need to prove duress, only to

---

69. Bassiouni, *supra* note 68, at 457.

70. *See* for the importance of a duress plea: *Prosecutor v. Erdemović*, Case no. IT-96-22-A, Appeals Chamber of the International Criminal Tribunal for the former Yugoslavia, dated October 7, 1997.

71. Perkins and Boyce, *supra* note 30, at 1059 and 1064.

attribute a preponderance of evidence;[72] i.e., if no facts from which duress might reasonably be inferred appear in the prosecution's case, the defendant has the "evidential burden" of laying a foundation for the defense by introducing evidence of such facts.[73]

The factual basis of duress originates in the impairment of the actor's ability to control his conduct or free will, and its judicial, doctrinal basis is the presumption that the alternative to committing the crime may have been so exceedingly unattractive that no reasonable person would have chosen it, even if there had been a choice.[74] Moreover, it should impose a mental compulsion on the defendant, caused by an irresistible exterior force.

As to Article 21 paragraph 1, sub c, of the Rome Statute of the International Criminal Court, it attributes "national laws of legal systems of the world" as the factual basis for the existence of general principles of law. Therefore domestic laws on defenses can undoubtedly serve as a factual contemplation for the contention in regard to defenses to international criminal litigation.

The common law doctrine in international criminal law is reflected in Article 25 (14) (B) of the U.S. draft rules of procedure and evidence for the International Tribunal for the Prosecution of Persons Responsible for Serious Violations of International Humanitarian Law committed in the former Yugoslavia,[75] defining the rule of duress as: *"( . . . ) a defense to any offense, except any crime involving killing, that the accused's participation in the offense was caused by a reasonable apprehension that the accused or another innocent person would be immediately killed or would immediately suffer serious bodily injury as a result of the accused's refusal to commit the act. The Trial Chamber may consider as a matter of mitigation in offenses involving killing the extent to which the accused was compelled by duress to commit the crime."*

The plea of duress, it may be noted, was recognized in such Nuremberg judgments under Control Council Law No. 10 as the *Von Leeb* and the *Ohlendorf* cases. The Secretary-General's Commentary recognizes that the tribunal "may consider the factor of superior orders in connection with other defenses such as coercion or lack of moral choice," but this, it is submitted, does not go far enough in reflecting the post-Nuremberg law.[76] The implementation of the defense of duress before international

---

72.  *U.S v. Calfon*, 607 F. 2d 29, 2d Circuit, 1979.

73.  *See* JOHN SMITH AND BRIAN HOGAN, CRIMINAL LAW 248 (1996).

74.  Smith and Hogan, *supra* note 73, at 238.

75.  Presented by letter dated November 18, 1993, from the United States Embassy at The Hague to the Secretary-General of the United Nations for transmission to the judges of the Tribunal.

76.  *See* C. O'Brien, *The International Tribunal for Violations of International Humanitarian Law in the Former Yugoslavia*, 87 AMERICAN JOURNAL OF INTERNATIONAL LAW 654, 693 (1993).

tribunals as being a legal, permanent and independent defense is an appropriate accommodation to the complex interrelation with the non-physical element of *mens rea*. As observed in Chapter I, the element of *mens rea* is currently accepted as being one of the constituent elements invoking individual criminal responsibility under ICL.

The element of *mens rea* is derived from the common law principle *"actus non facit reum, nisi mens sit rea,"* meaning that although essential to criminal responsibility, the *actus reus* alone is not sufficient without the necessary *mens rea* (i.e., a guilty state of mind), the latter being thus also essential to crime and subsequent criminal responsibility. *Mens rea* establishes therefore the mental element as a prerequisite for the fulfillment of the definition of the particular crime.[77] It is this mental element that causes the *actus reus*, a specific level of intention needed to activate the particular crime. The significance of the element of *mens rea* in international criminal affairs is clear with respect to the interpretive judgment of the scope of individual criminal responsibility, e.g., that provided in Article 7 (1) of the Statute of the former Yugoslavia Tribunal. To qualify the behavior of a defendant as "planned, instigated, ordered, committed, or otherwise aided and abetted in the planning," the condition of the necessary *mens rea* must be fulfilled.

The *ad hoc* Yugoslavia and Rwanda Statutes do not prescribe the specific mental state which is required to constitute the particular international offences, subject of the Statutes, although the International Criminal Tribunal for the former Yugoslavia refers to "the *mens rea* of the offence" as a condition for establishing the offence itself.[78]

This non-specifying of the particular required mental state is also a principal characteristic of domestic criminal judicial systems,[79] and is arguably due to the complementary role of defenses in international criminal affairs before both the Yugoslavia and Rwanda Tribunals as mitigation-mechanisms.[80] Under the Draft Statute of the International Criminal Court as it stands, and as Article 30 submits, the *mens rea* element is a condition to criminal responsibility under the Rome Statute with regard to "intent and knowledge." The innovating element in this Statute, compared with the *ad hoc* Tribunal Statutes, is its definition of this *"intent"* in paragraph 2 of Article 30. The Statute determines for its purpose this criminal intent as follows: that the defendant meant to engage in this conduct with a certain consequence, namely that the defendant meant to cause that

---

77. Perkins and Boyce, *supra* note 30, at 831; Smith and Hogan, *supra* note 73, at 56.

78. S14, *Prosecutor v. Erdemović*, at 29–11–1996, Case No. IT-96-22-TJ.

79. Blakesley, *supra* note 62, at 204.

80. *See* for this mitigation aspect: Theodor Meron, *International Criminalization of Internal Atrocities*, in WAR CRIMES LAW COMES OF AGE 224 (Theodor Meron, ed., 1998) and Article 7 (4) of the Yugoslavia Statute.

particular consequence or was aware that it would occur in "*the ordinary course of events.*" With regard to the element of "knowledge," the Statute, under article 30, sub 3, makes clear that this "*means awareness that a circumstance exists or a consequence will occur in the ordinary course of events.*" However, this attempt to define more especially the element of *mens rea* does not resolve the fact that it invokes judicial interpretation, development and decision by the Court.

The difficulty with the concept of *mens rea* is (and remains) that it invokes interpretative adjudicatory analysis. The skeptic would say that the development that it represents involves evidence of a state of uncertainty, or even immaturity, rather than a new internationally appropriate legal standard. However, this assumption would be inconsistent in respect of both the principle of international customary law of individual criminal responsibility and the existence of *opinio juris* implying that duress imposes a defendant to an "( . . . ) excruciatingly difficult moral choice,"[81] or "lack of moral choice and the risk of death."[82] In any event, psychiatric, psychological and neurobiological elements and predisposition also determine this "moral choice."[83] These phenomena enable international criminal tribunals to analyze this "moral choice" and the constitution of *mens rea*. While the weight must vary according to the circumstances, most criminal systems of law regard the impairment of the free will of the defendant as an admissible condition for the defense of duress,[84] which also relates to the "excruciatingly difficult moral choice." This finding is indirectly criticized by arguing that the international law regime is morally more pluralistic and normatively consensual than domestic legal systems, thus arguing against ready transposition of the notion of crime from municipal to international settings.[85] Essentially the question is one of the acceptance of the concept of *mens rea* as a preliminary condition for individual responsibility of international crimes, a concept that depends upon the relevant judicial and psychological standards of free will.

The relative judicial inability of the present international criminal system, especially the system of the *ad hoc* Tribunals, to insist on the strict concept of *mens rea* or "free will" has inevitably given prominence to the facilitation of the present very strict admissibility of duress pleas. While there is an inevitable controversy or antagonistic tension between prosecution of international crimes and defenses to these crimes, such a view does not seem to be justified considering the described nature of the rule

---

81. Blakesley, *supra* note 62, at 220.

82. Meron, *supra* note 17, at 89.

83. *See* for these elements: Chapter III.

84. *See* Gerardus G.J. Knoops, *Neurogenetica in het Strafrecht: nieuwe visie op opzet en toerekeningsvatbaarheid*, 22 ADVOCATENBLAD 1125–1127 (1999).

85. Gerry J. Simpson, *War Crimes: A Critical Introduction*, in THE LAW OF WAR CRIMES 16 (Timothy L.H McCormack and Gerry J. Simpson, eds., 1997).

of duress. Chapter IX will focus further on the indispensability of the rule of law on the underlying concept of *mens rea* concerning defenses.

## 3.2 Duress as defense to genocide and crimes against humanity

A study of the case law of the common law shows that a defense of duress *in principle* does not apply in case of a murder indictment, only, under circumstances, for minor offenses and grave felonies as burglary, robbery, kidnapping, arson or treason. This is particularly made clear in *State v. Taylor.*[86]

In the present context particular significance attaches to the controversy between the absolutist versus the utilitarian opinion. This significance derives from the fact that according the former opinion a duress defense to crimes against humanity and war crimes involving willing or innocent persons is *prima facie* inadmissible, whereas the latter opinion does not deprive in all events a defendant of considering the particular facts of the case.

This differences of opinion and controversy are made clear in the case law of the Yugoslavia Tribunal, especially in the *Erdemović* case, which led to the ruling of the Appeals Chamber of the International Criminal Tribunal for the former Yugoslavia of October 7th, 1997,[87] that duress does not provide a complete defense for a soldier charged with offences against humanity and/or war crimes involving the killing of innocent persons, nor does it eliminate criminal responsibility.[88]

There can be no question that the defense of duress is not confined to only certain offences. This defense can apply in principle in connection with all crimes, while it is clear that there is no preliminary "automatic" denial of a duress plea, any more than there is an "automatic" admissibility of such a defense. In this sense, the alleged antithesis between the absolutist and utilitarian concepts is artificial.

The absolutist-utilitarian controversy was elaborated on in the *Erdemović* case decided by the Appeals Chamber of the ICTY. Erdemović had been sentenced to ten years imprisonment, due to his guilty plea to one count of a crime against humanity, regarding involvement in the mass execution of a large number of civilian Muslim men after the fall of Srebrenica. In this case the accused raised the defense of duress, based upon the assertion that, when he initially refused to participate in this massacre by

---

86. *See* Perkins and Boyce, *supra* note 30, at 1060; 22 Wn. App. 308, 589, p2d, 1250 (1979); *ibidem* for international murder crimes: Blakesley, *supra* note 62, at 220.
87. *Prosecutor v. Erdemović*, Case No. IT-96-22-A, Appeals Judgment.
88. *See* for this case: Meron, *supra* note 17, at 89–103; this case is described in this chapter.

a firing squad, he was told he would be killed himself together with the Muslim victims and therefore coerced by imminent threats.

In the dissenting opinion of President-Judge Cassese, the utilitarian approach was advocated, arguing that since the massacre was inevitable at that very moment (or would have occurred irrespective of the will of the accused), the refusal of the defendant to participate in the execution, resulting in the eventual loss of his own life, would not have saved any life but only led to the loss of another life. According to the dissenting opinion of Judge Cassese, the duress defense is in such situations admissible because of the lack of any real moral choice. For this purpose, paragraph 50 of his opinion is quite important:

> "More particularly, in applying the conclusions of law which I have reached above, in my view the Trial Chamber to which the matter is remitted must first of all determine whether the situation leading to duress was voluntarily brought about by the Appellant. In particular, the Trial Chamber must satisfy itself whether the military unit to which he belonged and in which he had voluntarily enlisted (the 10th Sabotage Unit) was purposefully intent upon actions contrary to international humanitarian law and the Appellant either knew or should have known of this when he joined the unit or, if he only later became aware of it, that he then failed to leave the unit or otherwise disengage himself from such actions. If the answer to this were in the affirmative, the Appellant could not plead duress. Equally, he could not raise this defense if he in any other way voluntarily placed himself in a situation he knew would entail the unlawful execution of civilians.
>
> If, on the other hand, the above question be answered in the negative, and thus the Appellant would be entitled to urge duress, the Trial Chamber must then satisfy itself that the other strict conditions required by international criminal law to prove duress are met in the instant case, namely:
> 1. whether Appellant acted under a threat constituting imminent harm, both serious and irreparable, to his life or limb, or to the life or limb of his family, when he killed approximately 70 unarmed Muslim civilians at the Branjevo farm near Plica in Bosnia on 16 July 1995;
> 2. whether Appellant had no other adequate means of averting this harm other than executing the said civilians;
> 3. whether the execution of the said civilians was proportionate to the harm Appellant sought to avoid. As I have stated above, this requirement cannot normally be met with respect to offences involving the killing of innocents,

since it is impossible to balance one life against another. However, the Trial Chamber should determine, on its assessment of the evidence, whether the choice faced by Appellant was between refusing to participate in the killing of the Muslim civilians and being killed himself *or* participating in the killing of the Muslim civilians *who would be killed in any case by the other soldiers* and thus being allowed to live. If the Trial Chamber concludes that it is the latter, then Appellant's defense of duress will have succeeded.

In addition, bearing in mind that, as stated above, the lower the rank of a serviceman the greater his propensity to yield to compulsion, the Trial Chamber, in determining whether or not Appellant acted under duress, should also take into account his military rank. Furthermore, the Trial Chamber should consider whether Appellant confessed at the earliest possible opportunity to the act he had committed and denounced it to the relevant authorities. If he did so, this might contribute to lending credibility to his plea of duress."[89]

Contrary to this approach, the absolutist doctrine, represented herein by judges McDonald and Vohrah in their joint separate opinion, rejects any balancing of harms and is based on the categorical prohibition of killing of innocent people, even under duress. This view endorses a legal policy approach, the policy element being the consideration of withholding future crimes against humanity.[90] Their opinion includes the following rationale:

"The *Masetti* approach proceeds from the starting point of strict utilitarian logic based on the fact that if the victim will die anyway, the accused is not at all morally blameworthy for taking part in the execution; there is absolutely no reason why the accused should die, as it would be unjust for the law to expect the accused to die for nothing. It should be immediately apparent that the assertion that the accused is not morally blameworthy where the victim would have died in any case depends entirely again upon a view of morality based on utilitarian logic. This does not, in our opinion, address the true rationale for our rejection of duress as a defense to the killing of innocent human beings. The approach we take does not involve a balancing of harms for and against killing,

---

89. Diss. Op. Cassese *Prosecutor vs. Erdemović*, Case No. IT-96-22-A, Appeals Chamber Decision 7 October 1997, discussed by Th. Meron, *supra* note 17, at 91.
90. *See* also Meron, *supra* note 17, at 91.

but rests upon an application in the context of international humanitarian law of the rule that duress does not justify or excuse the killing of an innocent person. Our view is based upon recognition that international humanitarian law should guide the conduct of combatants and their commanders. There must be legal limits as to the conduct of combatants and their commanders in armed conflict. In accordance with the spirit of international humanitarian law, we deny the availability of duress as a complete defense to combatants who have killed innocent persons. In so doing, we give notice in no uncertain terms that those who kill innocent persons will not be able to take advantage of duress as a defense and thus get away with impunity for their criminal acts in the taking of innocent lives."[91]

In my view, the duress test with respect to crimes against humanity must be a moderation of the aforementioned two approaches, wherein the leading principle should be that of the rule of law, which contravenes a strict absolutist doctrine, but rather favors the utilitarian arguments.[92]

Three additional arguments can be established to question a strict absolutist doctrine on duress:

1.  Contrary to the absolutist doctrine, which is focused on a general impact of a court decision on duress for the international legal community, in the utilitarian approach the particular facts of the case prevail over legal policy, which is a judicially purer standard.
2.  According the absolutist doctrine, Jews in Nazi concentration camps (as described by Meron) coerced to assist in operating the crematoria would be denied the defense of duress. Meron asks if this would be just.[93]

The twofold general justification for the existence of criminal law involves a state mechanism required to both ensure public order and safety as well as provide the legal community with authorization to punish those whose conduct harms individual or public interests. The *moral* justification for imposing punishment and criminal liability is the presumption that the individual had the ability and appropriate possibility to choose otherwise, and therefore actors may be exonerated because of compulsion, law enforcement, self-defense or necessity. Also, involuntary

---

91.  *See* Joint Separate Opinion dd. 7 October 1997, of Judge McDonald and Judge Vohrah, regarding *Erdemović* Judgment of the Appeal Chamber of the ICTY, Case No. IT-96-22-A, para. 80.
92.  See Chapter VIII, *infra*.
93.  Meron, *supra* note 17, at 91.

intoxication resulting in the lack of the ability to perform a purposeful intentional act[94] and profound mental illness may, under some circumstances, lead to exoneration. Juridically, the mental and moral ability to refrain from acting wrongly is therefore a *conditio sine qua non* to impose criminal liability and thus, from both the legal-philosophical and neurobiological perspective, the role of free moral choice is essential in attributing criminal responsibility.[95]

Some choices may be hard ones, but if the accused can be presumed to have had the *reasonable* ability, although unexercised, to do otherwise, he may be considered not excusable.[96] The test hereto should not be just one of objective measurement, but also elaborate on the subjective interpretations of the facts by the accused at the very moment of the crime.[97]

It seems to me that in the above-mentioned dissenting opinion of judges McDonald and Vohrah a legally incorrect standpoint is invoked. These judges seem to accept the assumption, referring to the case law regarding duress as a defense to murder in the common law, that duress does not destroy the will or would not affect the voluntariness of the *actus reus* or the *mens rea*.[98] From both a legal and neurobiological point of view this is not correct. The rationale of the defense of duress is ultimately based in the disabling of the accused from achieving a culpable state of mind. To quote Bakker, in discussing the determinants of the defense of obedience to superior orders relative to the plea of duress, "( . . . ) *a moral choice is available where subordinates have the* freedom to choose between right and wrong *(emphasis added, GJK) courses of conduct without suffering detrimental consequences.*"[99] Exactly because of the intensity of the external power, the state of mind of the accused and subsequently his or her free will is often so seriously diminished that it cannot form a culpable state of mind. The latter is required for an act to be legally considered a crime. According to standard doctrine, *mens rea* and the consequent responsibility for actions are an emerging concept because of the general assumption that individuals have free will and a possibility *de facto* to choose.[100]

---

94.   *See* Chapter I, *supra*.

95.   *See* Simon H. Dinwiddle, *Genetics, Antisocial Personality and Criminal Responsibility*, 24 BULLETIN OF THE AMERICAN ACADEMY OF PSYCHIATRIC LAW 95–108 (1996), especially at 98.

96.   Dinwiddle, *supra* note 95, at 98.

97.   *See* GERARDUS G.J. KNOOPS, PSYCHISCHE OVERMACHT EN RECHTSVINDING (transl: Duress and Finding Law) (1998).

98.   Joint Sep. Opinion Judges MacDonald and Vohrah, *supra* note 91, at paras. 70–71.

99.   J.L. Bakker, *The Defense of Obedience to Superior Orders: The Mens Rea Requirement*, 17 AMERICAN JOURNAL OF CRIMINAL LAW 72–73; *see* further Chapter VII, *infra*.

100.   *See* Jonathan S. Alper, *Genes, Free Will and Criminal Responsibility*, 46 SOCIAL SCIENCES MEDICINE 1600 (1998).

Therefore an accused is considered not to be criminally responsible for his/her acts only if the conduct was the result of factors preventing him or her from exercising his or her free will, which factors are in most events external to the person, such as is the case with duress.

It is thus dogmatically just to perceive the area of the plea of duress as the *"moral choice test,"* as applied by the International Military Tribunal, more especially in the *Von Leeb* Case. The Court, with respect to the plea of duress, held in this case that, in order to establish this defense, "( . . . ) *there must be a showing of circumstances such that a reasonable man would apprehend that he was in such imminent physical peril as to deprive him of freedom to choose the right and refrain from the wrong"* (emphasis added).

Clearly the exercise of free will is regarded as the primary basis of this defense. The Court's view also indicates that the discussed absolutist doctrine contravenes the aforementioned premise of *"showing of circumstances."*

Equal to the defense of superior orders, the true base of the defense of duress is the absence of the requisite criminal mind or criminal culpability in the sense of *mens rea*.[101]

This leads us to a third argument in favor of *a rule of law test* regarding duress concerning crimes against humanity, i.e. the rule of law itself. Law, like all other human institutions, is no static phenomenon. The concept of the rule of law should be seen in this perspective.[102] Within the changing pattern of human relations, resulting from international legal and political developments, the role of defenses to international crimes is constantly challenged, in line with changing circumstances. Not only the case law of the ECHR,[103] but also the case law of the *ad hoc* International Criminal Tribunals elucidates the rule of law in this sense.

Thus the basis of judging a duress defense in the area of crimes against humanity should be the test of the rule of law, especially while it is clear that the rule of law "( . . . ) *embraces a broader conception of justice than the mere application of legal rules prevailing in any particular state at any given time."*[104]

Moreover, the rule of law and its subsequent principles serve the same goal: to counterbalance the power of the State.[105] This notion leads to the important caveat that defenses to international crimes should not be considered and applied in isolation from the facts of the case and should not

---

101. *See* Jordan Paust, *Superior Orders and Command Responsibility*, in I INTERNATIONAL CRIMINAL LAW 225 (M. Cherif Bassiouni, ed., 1999).

102. *See* E.A. ALKEMA, THE ROLE AND INDEPENDENCE OF THE JUDICIARY AND THE ADMINISTRATION OF JUSTICE IN THE PERSPECTIVE OF THE RULE OF LAW 1.1 (1997).

103. *See*, e.g., Judgment ECHR of 21 February 1975 in the *Golder* Case, Series A, Vol. 18, para. 28–32 regarding the rule of law.

104. Alkema, *supra* note 102, at 1.1.

105. Alkema, *supra* note 102, at 2.2.

be elucidated within a legal policy framework or, at the expense of the particular facts of the case, solely on the basis of either utilitarian or absolutist approach. Fundamental norms of human defense rights can hardly be subject to qualification or amendment by policy actions or thoughts.[106] As international law matures, it is more and more likely to be made directly applicable to individuals, which is an additional reason to accept the view that human and defense rights of individuals cannot be subject to restrictions as a result of absolutist legal policy arguments. The task of an international criminal tribunal is not to enter the territory—not even by virtue of interpretation of its statutes or rules of evidence and procedure—of legal policymaking, but merely to interpret and apply a provision of law and procedural right (i.e. the defense of duress) in the light of both today's intellectual concepts or ideologies and present-day conditions or situations.[107]

Whereas judges are charged with the *"ultimate decision over life, freedoms, rights, duties and property of citizens,"*[108] legal policy should not act as a primacy test on defenses (or defense rights) to the detriment of the factual and actual circumstances of each case within the overall system of international criminal law. In this view, no absolute exception is appropriate for a duress defense (or other defense) to crimes against humanity. As judge Louise Arbour, Chief Prosecutor of the ICTY and ICTR in 1997 stated: *"International rules must at all costs not become a reflection of the political compromises between seemingly competing national approaches ( . . . ). They must constitute a system that creatively incorporates a diversity of fundamental concerns: the rights of the accused ( . . . )."*[109]

This conclusion can unequivocally be invoked in acceptance of the rule of law as a supervening principle regarding the judgments of legal defenses to international criminal litigation, even when it concerns crimes against humanity. One cannot derogate from principal rights and defenses

---

106. *See* also Marian N. Leigh, *The Yugoslav Tribunal: Use of unnamed witnesses against accused, Editorial Comments*, 90 AM. J. INT'L. L. 238 (1996).

107. *See* for the ECHR also F. Matscher, *Methods of Interpretation of the Convention*, in THE EUROPEAN SYSTEM FOR THE PROTECTION OF HUMAN RIGHTS 70 (MacDonald et al, eds., 1993).

108. *See* the "Basic Principles on the Independency of the Judiciary," Declaration of the UN High Commissioner for Human Rights, adopted by the Seventh UN Congress on the Prevention of Crime and the Treatment of Offenders, held at Milan from 26 August to 6 September 1985 and endorsed by General Assembly Resolutions 40/32 of 29 November 1985 and 40/146 of 13 December 1985.

109. *"The development of a coherent system of Rules of International Criminal Procedure and Evidence before the ad hoc International Tribunals for the Former Yugoslavia and Rwanda"*; Speech by Judge Louise Arbour, Chief Prosecutor of the ICTY and ICTR to the ISISC meeting on Comparative Criminal Justice Systems: Diversity and Approachment, 18 December 1997 at 12.

of the accused for policy reasons and diversify the rights depending on which charge is made. In relation to the admissibility of evidence or burden of proof, the Trial Chamber of the ICTY in the *Celebići* case ruled that in the trial of criminal offences of the most serious kind "( . . . ) *nothing less than the most exacting standard of proof is required.*"[110] Analogous hereto, no less a standard of judgment on legal defenses can be accepted in regard to the most serious criminal charges. Otherwise, in my opinion, the "achievement of international criminal justice"[111] is infringed. No ultimate concept can therefore be offered. The various situations and facts encountered in international law practice can only be adequately empowered by judging, on the basis of inductive interpretation, a duress defense in each case on its own merits, without reference to pre-existing general conditions. International criminal cases are about law and facts. International tribunals are expected to know the law, but elucidating the facts raises particular problems.[112] This bears the consequence that an absolutist approach in providing the basis for judicial fact-finding and the process of creative judicial reasoning encountering the particular defense, would therefore contradict the principles of both reasonableness and fairness.[113]

Although Art. 7 paragraph 4 of the Statute does not explicitly refer to the defense of duress, the Trial Chamber of the International Tribunal for the former Yugoslavia in the judgment of *Prosecutor versus Erdemović*, analyzing the relevant case-law of the two post-World War II Tribunals, did not explicitly eliminate duress as a defense to violations of international humanitarian law, providing that three essential conditions are fulfilled.[114] In this respect the defense of duress embodies a general principle of international law. This creates a second reason to rule out the absolutist view, because general principles of law are not static but develop along with the changing society.[115]

The denial of the value of the concept that the binding force of international criminal law can only be found in the authoritative and casuistic decision-making power of international tribunals would lead to an unjust policy-oriented approach, overriding the judicial authority of these tribunals and the international legal order. In the future one should proceed

---

110. *Celebići* case, IT-96-21–T, Decision on Mucić's Motion for the Exclusion of Evidence, 2 September 1997, para. 41.

111. Arbour *supra* note 109, at 12.

112. Malcolm N. Shaw, *A Practical Look at the International Court of Justice*, in REMEDIES IN INTERNATIONAL LAW: THE INSTITUTIONAL DILEMMA 41 (M.D. Evans, ed., 1998).

113. Knoops, *supra* note 97.

114. *See* Paragraph 17 of the *Erdemović* decision dated 29–11–1996; these three conditions will be considered in Chapter III, *infra*.

115. HENRI. G. SCHERMERS AND NIELS M. BLOKKER, INTERNATIONAL INSTITUTIONAL LAW 1338 (1999).

in this field in a sensitive and careful way. Thus, the precise precedent weight to be accorded to propositions that do not constitute the *ratio decidendi* of a judgment is another matter entirely, and one to be judged on a case-by-case basis in the light of existing international law. The appropriate method of judicial reasoning within the area of defenses should at least be analogous to the manner of focusing upon essential issues as performed by the International Court of Justice. The latter Court emphasizes in the *Libya/Malta* Case[116] that "it must be open to the Court, and indeed it is its duty to give the fullest decision it may in the circumstances of each case." This does preclude the need for an absolutist judicial process.

### 3.3 Institutionalizing duress as a defense before international criminal tribunals

So far, the focus of this section has been on the acceptance and legal basis of duress as a defense to international criminal litigation. An internationally accepted legal concept of duress has not yet crystallized. A significant Post World War II attempt at such an internationally accepted typology of duress has been made by the International Criminal Tribunal for the former Yugoslavia. Since the Statute includes no provision on duress,[117] the Trial Chamber of the Yugoslavia Tribunal, faced with a duress defense of defendant Erdemović alleging that by refusing the order to kill Bosnian males he would have endangered his own life, was led to inquire the relevant Post World War II international military[118] case law of the United Nations War Crimes Commission, thus entering a law making process based on precedents.

In evaluating these authoritative decisions, the Tribunal deduced the following three exponents as prerequisites of an admissible duress defense to violations of international humanitarian law:

1. The act charged was done to avoid an immediate danger both serious and irreparable;
2. there was no adequate means of escape;
3. the remedy was not disproportionate to the evil.[119]

---

116. Continental Shelf Libyan Arab Jamahiriya/Malta—application for Permission to Intervene, Judgment, ICJ Reports 1984, 3 at 25.

117. *See Erdemović*, para.11.

118. *See* the *Krupp* Case, U.S. Military Tribunal, Nuremberg, 17.11.1947–30.06–1948, Case No. 48, The UN War Crimes Commission Law Reports of Trials of War Criminals, Vol. X, London, 1949, at 147.

119. Referring to the ILC report 1996, at 86, *see* para. 17.

The adjudicatory regime of duress, as the Tribunal stipulates,[120] is relatively strict, since it relies also upon two additional conditions as to the applicable positive law of duress. International case law is receptive to the *culpa in causa* concept and the rank of the accused as determinative factors regarding the validity of a duress defense. The Yugoslavia Tribunal gave expression to these two elements in the *Erdemović* sentencing judgment:

> The absence of moral choice was recognized on several occasions as one of the essential components for considering duress as a complete defense. A soldier may be considered as being deprived of his moral choice in the face of imminent physical danger. This physical threat, understood in case-law as a danger of death or serious bodily harm, must in some cases also meet the following conditions: it must be "clear and present" or else be "imminent, real, and inevitable."
>
> These tribunals also took into account the issue of voluntary participation in an enterprise that leaves no doubt as to its end results in order to determine the individual responsibility of the accused members of the armed forces or paramilitary groups. The rank held by the soldier giving the order and by the one receiving it has also been taken into account in assessing the duress a soldier may be subject to when forced to execute a manifestly illegal order.[121]

The elucidation of this concept of duress is now enclosed and formalized in Article 31 paragraph 1, sub d, of the Rome Statute of the International Criminal Court adopted on July the 17th, 1998. It is remarkable that, contrary to the strict legal regime on duress envisioned by the jurisprudence of the ICTY hereon, the ICC Drafters seem to denote a more flexible approach. Article 31 (1)(d) of the Rome Statute tries to combine two different concepts: "*(justifying) necessity and (merely excusing) duress,*" which concepts were "*mixed up in one provision.*"[122] Apart from the fact that the provision of Article 31 (1)(d)—by referring to the words "*alleged to constitute a crime within the jurisdiction of the Court*"—limits the scope of defense to crimes according to Articles 5–8 of the ICC Statute, the partic-

---

120.  *Ibid.*, Paras. 18 and 19.

121.  The ICTY refers for these two criteria to *inter alia* the *Einzatsgruppen case*, the trial of *Wilhelm von Leeb and thirteen others*, the trial of *Friedrich Flick and five others*, tried before the U.S. Military Tribunals, Nuremberg, 1947–1948, and also the trial of *Lieutenant General Shigeru Sawada* and three others, tried by the U.S. Military Commission Shanghai, 1946, Case No. 25.

122.  *See* Albin Eser, *Article 31, Margin No. 35*, in COMMENTARY ON THE ROME STATUTE (Otto Triffterer, ed., 1999).

ular accused *"must see himself or another person exposed to a threat which can either be made by other persons, as is the case if the person concerned is the victim of coercion, or constituted by other circumstances beyond that person's control, as in the case of danger which does not result from another person's action, but from other sorts of endangerment by natural forces or technical menaces."*[123] Three additional requirements are embedded in this Article 31 (1)(d):

- The threat has to be related to *"imminent death or of continuing or imminent serious bodily harm,"* which requires *"more than easily healed superficial wounds."*[124] This involves an external event.
- The threat must subsequently result in duress, i.e. an internal mental force that limits the free will of the accused in such a sense that he is unable to withstand the particular threat and is causally driven to the crime.
- Contrary to the prerequisites of reasonableness and proportionality for self-defense, Article 31 (1)(d) requires *"necessarily and reasonably acting"* of the accused. Eser observes that the latter requirement, compared to the prerequisites of self-defense, *"comes out to more or less the same: the act directed at avoiding the threat must be necessary in terms that no other means are available, reasonable in terms of being able to reach the desired effect, as well as adequate in terms of not being unreasonably disproportionate."*[125]

The more flexible approach on duress endorsed by the Drafters of the ICC clearly stems from the *travaux préparatoires*, which indicate a subjective conception of the *"lesser evil"* principle as to the assessment of this defense as well as to intertwining the classic defense of necessity (involving a balancing of conflicting interests) and classic duress (involving an excuse regardless of the greater or lesser harm). This balancing operation and solution is expressed by Eser as follows: *"( . . . ) this provision attempts to find a line in between: in objective terms, it is not required that the person concerned in fact avoids the greater harm by his criminal conduct, but in subjective terms he must intend to do so. Thus this defense requires less than justifying necessity would afford, and on the other hand requires more than excusing duress would be satisfied with. Therefore, it is up to the Court to find an adequate solution for the individual case according to paragraph 2."*[126] In order to find this adequate solution for each case, the legal basis of duress in ICL will be assessed in Chapter III below.

---

123. A. Eser, *supra* note 122, Margin No. 38.
124. A. Eser, *supra* note 122, Margin No. 38.
125. A. Eser, *supra* note 122, Margin No. 39.
126. A. Eser, *supra* note 122, Margin No. 40.

## 4    THE CONCEPT OF SOVEREIGN IMMUNITY AND HEADS OF STATE DEFENSES

### 4.1 Exclusion of any exonerative status

These limits lead to the so-called heads of state or sovereign immunity defenses. Equal to the defenses of duress and superior orders, the question of whether heads of state can be brought before an international criminal court for prosecution and punishment has been one of the most controversial and intricate questions of the system of ICL.[127] As clearly pointed out by Malekian, *"the theory that heads of state are not accountable and therefore have no international criminal responsibility under the system of ICL has no juridical validity within the system however."*[128] A special trait in scholarly views on war crimes is therefore the non-application of the defense of the *"act of state"* doctrine as well as the immunity of heads of state and diplomats.[129] This view is motivated by the fact that the State itself is involved in these crimes.[130] Contrary to the above described legal defense of self-defense, it is currently in fact one of the consolidated principles of ICL that heads of state bear international criminal responsibility for the commission of international crimes and consequently the subsequent defense is excluded from the international criminal law arena. This principle has especially developed since the start of World War I.[131] The concept of criminal responsibility of heads of state as well as the exclusion of the defense of sovereign immunity evolved more pronouncedly at the outbreak of World War II, when heads of state were attributed with liability for enormous atrocities, leading consequently to a codification of this concept in both the provisions of the IMT in Nuremberg and its judgments.[132] This development was also exemplified by Article II, 4 (A) of the Control Council Law No. 10, ensuring that *"The official position of any person, whether as head of state or as responsible official in a government department, does not free him from responsibility for a crime or entitle him to mitigation of punishment."*[133] As will be observed in more detail in Chapters III and V

---

127.  Malekian, *supra* note 4, at 174.

128.  Malekian, *supra* note 4, at 174.

129.  *See* Mordechai Kremnitzer, *The World Community as an International Legislator in Competition with National Legislators*, in PRINCIPLES AND PROCEDURES FOR A NEW TRANSNATIONAL CRIMINAL LAW 345 (Albin Eser and Otto Lagodny, eds., 1992), *See* also Yoram Dinstein, *International Criminal Law*, 20 ISRAEL LAW REVIEW 38–40 (1985).

130.  Kremnitzer, *supra* note 129, at 345.

131.  *Ibid.*

132.  *See inter alia* Articles 7 and 8 of the Nuremberg Charter.

133.  *See* also Chapter 2, sections 1 and 3; Chapter 3, section 1; and Chapter 7 of this Law.

hereinafter, neither *formal* command responsibility nor a direct chain of command is a requisite to leader responsibility, which concept includes both military and civilian leadership.[134] The concept of international criminal responsibility of heads of state—particularly embodied in the provisions of both the International Convention on the Prevention and Punishment of Crime and Genocide (Article IV), as well as the 1954, 1991 and 1995 Draft Articles on Crimes against Mankind (Article 13)—demonstrates the tendency of the international legal community towards prosecution and punishment of individuals regardless of their rank or position in government departments, as well as independently of the *domestic* law of leader responsibility.[135]

It can therefore be concluded that the concept of criminal liability of heads of state, considering the numerous international conventions on different international crimes, made a *progressive* development in ICL resulting in an *imperative* principle of exclusion of this legal defense in ICL as well as the exclusion of the sovereign immunity defense.[136] At present, the final result of this development is visualized in Article 27 of the ICC Statute, another provision to clarify the exact scope of individual criminal liability under ICL.[137] This exemplifies the Statute's goal of exposing official capacities to criminal prosecution by expressing that the Statute *"shall apply equally to all persons without any distinction based on official capacity."* Section 1 of Article 27 refers in particular to *"Head of State or government"* in which context it is decisive that the person in question holds such a position in a State government which is either established according to the law of the State, or at least acknowledged by the international community.[138] The element in section 1 referring to *"a member of a government of parliament"* includes *"all persons having a seat in one of these two institutions be they at the federal, state or local level and independent of whether such a person has been elected or nominated."*[139] Finally, the element of *"an elected representative or a government official"* denotes for also the lower ranks of the hierarchy and cover *"all possibilities not falling under the first two examples mentioned in paragraph 1."*[140]

In sum, the three categories envisioned by Article 27 (1) endorse indeed a broad concept of *"official capacity"* in order to protect the integrity of the ICL framework. As intended by the ICC Statute, and clearly

---

134. *See* e.g. Paust, *supra* note 31, at 182–183; INTERNATIONAL CRIMINAL LAW, CASES AND MATERIALS 1395–1396 (Jordan J. Paust et. al., eds., 1996).

135. *See* also Malekian, *supra* note 4, at 175.

136. *Ibid.*

137. Otto Triffterer, *Article 27, Margin No. 9* in COMMENTARY ON THE ROME STATUTE (Otto Triffterer ed. 1999).

138. Triffterer, *supra* note 137, Margin No. 14.

139. Triffterer, *supra* note 137, Margin No. 15.

140. *Ibid.*

envisioned by the fact that the enumeration in sentence 2 of paragraph 1 (by the wording *"in particular"*) embodies an exemplifying character, sentence 1 of this paragraph clearly intends to exclude *"any"* official capacity and sentence 2 explicitly prescribes that this official capacity *"shall in no case exempt a person from criminal responsibility."*[141] However this extensive context of the provision of Article 27 leaves open the possibility that the accused, unjustly claiming immunity based upon official capacity, can invoke other defenses under the Statute. Triffterer mentions the example of the lack of mental element required for a specific crime.

Finally the broad concept endorsed by Article 27 is, through paragraph 2, supported by expressing that the ICC can exercise jurisdiction over a person alleged to have official capacity and immunity irrespective of whether this immunity exists in national or in international law. It therefore *"makes no difference whether such immunity exclude criminal responsibility or only protect the respective person by a purely procedural rule against the exercise of domestic jurisdiction like arrest and prosecution before national courts."*[142]

## 4.2 Counterpart to the (non-) defense of superior orders

The consolidation of the submitted concept in positive ICL is to a certain extent understandable from the perspective of the reluctant or rigid application or acceptance in ICL of the defense of superior orders. A logical consequence of the strict and limited perception of the latter defense is a subsequent acceptance of judicial liability of the leaders or heads of state in question, for the particular order(s). It can thus not be denied that these two legal concepts, i.e. the concept of heads of state responsibility and the doctrine of superior orders, are, in fact, each other's judicial counterparts, and can therefore lead to simultaneous criminal responsibility in war crimes litigation.

---

141.  *See* also Triffterer, *supra* note 137, Margin Nos. 16–17.
142.  Triffterer, *supra* note 137, Article 28, Margin Nos. 20–21.

# CHAPTER III

# INTERNATIONAL CRIMINAL LAW DEFENSES
# ORIGINATING FROM COMPARATIVE CRIMINAL LAW

## 1  INDIVIDUAL SELF-DEFENSE IN ICL

### 1.1 New aspects and the special nature of self-defense in ICL

In substance, all domestic laws in both civil and common law systems governing the law of crimes provide for an exclusion of criminal responsibility of individuals in the event of self-defense. This is especially significant in the case of serious violations of obligations of the law such as involuntary manslaughter, leading to the question whether the right of self-defense can be exercised when carried out with the use of deadly force. Especially in the realm of indictments regarding grave breaches of obligations of ICL or even war crimes charges, this question confronts us with contravening moral and legal standards. It is axiomatic that, as will be assessed in this chapter and in Chapter IV below, the Rome Statute of the ICC realizes to a certain extent the concept of self-defense with regard to war crimes indictments, i.e., allowing, in particular circumstances, the defendant (alleged victim) to commit a war crime under the protective shield of the right of self-defense. This is remarkable since the ICTY and ICTR Statutes—neither their rules nor their jurisprudence—accept the defenses of superior orders and duress *per se* in order to avoid the exoneration of defendants from war crimes prosecutions.

Growth marks the development of ICL in every respect. It is observed by Mueller and Besharov that one is "( . . . ) *quite familiar with the inflation of penal regulation as society becomes more complicated ( . . . )*," leading these authors to the conclusion that "*ICL grows and grows and has not stopped growing ( . . . ).*"[1] Viewed from this perspective, the right of self-defense by individuals is nowadays considered to be a norm of substantive ICL

---

1.    *See* Gerhard O.W. Mueller and Douglas J. Besharov, *Evolution and Enforcement of ICL*, in I INTERNATIONAL CRIMINAL LAW 258 (M. Cherif Bassiouni, ed., 1999).

since international sovereigns, through Article 31(1)(c) of the ICC Statute, decided to cede this *"slice of their criminal jurisdiction to a truly international community."*[2] Just like ICL itself, the concept of self-defense in the international criminal law era can be understood only in terms of a dynamic development which is pre-conditioned by cultural and ideological denominators of the common and civil law systems regarding this defense. On the basis of the observations in this chapter it is justified to assume that self-defense is gradually developing towards a primary defense, as opposed to other legal defenses.

This development is exemplified by a novelty in the ICC Statute, namely Article 31 (1)(c) that explicitly recognizes the element of *"military necessity"* as justificatory to war crimes charges. This accommodation, obviously designed primarily to mediate in case of conflict of laws of war norms, seems a clear deviation of the principles of IHL, although it has certain roots in domestic laws. It occurs to me that the current trend in favor of using substantive ICL to codify standards of procedural and substantive criminal law in order to create a Supranational Criminal Law has its limits; it can never be conducted at the detriment of the quality of law.

## 1.2 Contemporary criminal law as a source of self-defense to war crimes indictments

### 1.2.1   Introduction

The doctrine of self-defense in international criminal law (hereinafter ICL) is of perennial concern, but is of greater moment these days for a number of reasons. Firstly, the 1998 Statute of a permanent International Criminal Court (hereinafter ICC) with jurisdiction over private individuals in order to adjudicate on crimes with an international character, explicitly provides—as opposed to the Statutes of both *ad hoc* tribunals, i.e., the Statutes of the ICTY and ICTR—for defense of self-defense.[3] Secondly, increased judicial and political importance and power attaches to the concept of individual self-defense as a result of the increasing intensity of military peacekeeping and peace enforcement operations conducted by international organizations such as the UN and NATO. The general level of compliance by States to the analogous concept of the inherent right of self-defense with regard to individual military personnel, envisioned *inter alia* in both the standing Rules of Engagement (peace enforcement) for the United Nations and the NATO Rules of Engagement, MC 362 (both discussed hereinafter), emphasizes that this theme involves an important

---

2.    *See* Mueller and Bersharov, *supra* note 1, at 258.
3.    *See* Article 31 (1)(c) of the Rome Statute of the ICC.

subject of international law and merits separate analysis in order to examine possible parallels between the two concepts of self-defense and peacekeeping. It is necessary to examine the constituent elements of the doctrine of self-defense in the ICC. Before doing so, however, it is useful to analyze and synthesize this doctrine with the relatively new rules of ICL which have emerged within the short time span of the last decade, evidenced by *inter alia* the Rome Statute of the ICC.

After discussing this latter preliminary topic in subsection 2, this section examines in subsection 3 the current scope of self-defense in ICL, especially from the perspective of the drafters of the Rome Statute of the ICC, as opposed to the scope of the defenses of duress and superior orders to war crimes. As a third principal subject, subsection 4 describes the mechanism of private self-defense from the view of the drafters of multinational rules of engagement, i.e., States or international organizations such as the United Nations and NATO, in order to seek for parallels and analogous principles. The overall context will be the question whether self-defense, as a juridical phenomenon, may be regarded as exoneration to war crimes indictments. In subsection 5, this section concludes with an account of the possible developments likely to be endorsed by ICL in the future.

### 1.2.2 The implementation of self-defense laws in international criminal law

It is today an acceptable and consolidated rule of international law and ICL that an internationally wrongful act, giving rise to the concept of individual criminal responsibility, can be justified or excused when it was committed in self-defense. In this connection, self-defense is understood as *"the application of the use of force against another person which may otherwise constitute a crime when and to the extent that the actor reasonably believes that such force is necessary to defend himself or anyone else against such other person's imminent use of unlawful force, and in a manner which is reasonably proportionate to the threat or use of force."*[4] The legal literature discloses, however, a disagreement as to what crimes can actually give rise to the defense of self-defense and how a committed crime rises to that level. The basic reasons for this disagreement are the significant differences in legal-philosophical and legal policy premises of both the jurisprudential and scholarly views in civil and common law systems, although both these systems allow this defense as such. These differences apply mainly to value-oriented goals, for example preservation of the legal order and safeguarding of the fundamental right of life.

---

4.   INTERNATIONAL CRIMINAL LAW, CASES AND MATERIALS 1389 (Jordan J. Paust & M. Cherif Bassiouni et al., eds., 1996).

In order to integrate fully the concept of self-defense in the ICL system in a comprehensive way, it is therefore necessary to turn first to the absence of scholarly consensus on this issue. Only after an integration of domestic doctrinal systems with regard to self-defense can one answer the question whether this defense applies also to war crimes indictments. An additional argument hereto now emerges. This study earlier addressed the role of national criminal law systems as well as general principles as sources of ICL. Since ICL, because of its origins in disparate sources, lacks a general part of criminal law (i.e., offence definitions, prescriptions of requisite mental states, penalties and defenses), and national criminal laws already have a developed general part on, *inter alia*, defenses, domestic laws in these areas serve as sources of the general part of ICL.[5] Because the general part of substantive criminal law varies from one law system to another, a synchronization of, i.e., the concept of self-defense is a preliminary task. if we are to comply with the requirements of the principles of legality.

### 1.2.3    The self-defense doctrine in American law versus common law and civil law

#### 1.2.3.1    *The controversy between the subjective and objective approaches*

As to the first principal difference between the civil law and common law views on self defense, it is particularly important to keep in mind that the common law systems on this field, contrary to civil law systems, endorse the distinction between deadly force (force intended or likely to cause death or great bodily harm) and non-deadly force (force neither intended nor likely to do so), as well as the distinction, also contrary to the civil law systems, between force which is reasonable and force which is not reasonable.[6] Deadly force and reasonable force are neither mutually exclusive nor collectively exhaustive. This implies that deadly force is unreasonable if non-deadly force is obviously sufficient to avert the threatened harm, but may be entirely reasonable under other circumstances. Conversely, non-deadly force is unreasonable if it is obviously and substantially in excess of what is needed for the particular defense.[7] In this realm, common law systems apply the test of the so-called *"reasonable man,"* which is mainly an objective test.[8] In common law the standard in

---

5.    *See* M. Cherif Bassiouni, *The Sources and Content of ICL, a Theoretical Framework*, in I INTERNATIONAL CRIMINAL LAW 16 (M. Cherif Bassiouni, ed., 1999).

6.    *See* ROLLIN M. PERKINS AND RONALD. N. BOYCE, CRIMINAL LAW 1113 (1982).

7.    Perkins and Boyce, *supra* note 6, at 1113.

8.    JOHN SMITH AND BRIAN HOGAN, CRIMINAL LAW 261–262 (1996).

reasonableness should take account not only of the nature of the crisis in which the necessity of the use of force arises, but also the fact that even the reasonable man cannot be expected to judge the minimum degree of force required to a nicety.[9]

American law envisions a mixed subjective-objective test. In the latter system, the essence of the right of self-defense is the *"reasonable belief of the defender under the circumstances as they appear at the moment," which belief is "sufficient for this aspect of the privilege of self-defense."*[10] As stated by Perkins and Boyce, summarizing the American law approach on this topic, *"the question is not whether the jury believes the force used was necessary in self-defense, but whether the defendant, acting as a reasonable person, had this belief."*[11] In most systems of the United States,, such as those of New York and California as well as the federal system, the subjective opinion of the accused is decisive if it passes an objective test by which the subjective view of the defendant is considered reasonable by the jury.[12] This approach is clearly exemplified by the famous New York criminal case of *People v. Goetz*, decided by the Court of Appeal in 1986.[13] Thus the reasonableness (as objective criterion) of the personal interpretation (a subjective test) of the defendant forms the standard in most criminal law systems of the United States as well as its federal law system. The emphasis on the subjective opinion of the accused, relying on self-defense, is also envisioned by the distinction in American law between perfect self-defense and imperfect self-defense. The former occurs in the event the subjective opinion of the accused who was unlawfully attacked is qualified by the jury as reasonable, in which event the accused is acquitted. The latter variation occurs when the subjective opinion of the accused is considered not reasonable.[14] Thus, the subjective element plays a more central role in American law than in common law or civil law.

In civil law systems, the doctrine regarding self-defense tends to place much more, and perhaps too much, emphasis on adjudication based on objective, strictly dogmatic criteria, such as the tests of proportionality and subsidiarity. As observed, the common law doctrine relies on, besides on the reasonable person standard, the subjective apprehension of the factual situation during the crime by the defendant, whose subjective interpretation of the facts is respected for the purpose of allowing self-defense as

---

9.   *Ibid.*

10.   Perkins and Boyce, *supra* note 6, at 1113–1114.

11.   Perkins and Boyce, *supra* note 6, at 1114.

12.   *See* JOHANNES A.W. LENSING, AMERIKAANS STRAFRECHT, EEN VERGELIJKENDE INLEIDING 236–239 (1996).

13.   Court of Appeal 506 N.Y.S. 2d 18 (1986), described by Lensing *supra* note 12, at 237–238.

14.   *See* Lensing, *supra* note 12, at 239.

justification of the alleged crime.[15] This controversy between subjective-objective (common law) and a purely objective (civil law) standard of the admissibility of the right of self-defense is also reflected by two sub-principles of American law, endorsed—again contrary to civil law approaches—in this manner:

1.  A bona-fide belief regarding the accused, which is correct, will not be held to be unreasonable merely because the defender is unable to paint a word-picture explaining exactly how he knew what the real facts were.[16]
2.  The danger must be, or appear to be, pressing and urgent according to the *"reasonable person standard."*

The most important feature in the American law systems regarding the application of self-defense by defendants is therefore the manifestation of subjective indicators as to the legitimacy of this legal defense. By way of conclusion and emphasis, the common law provides the following jurisprudential and doctrinal determinative criteria:[17]

1.  Regarding the use of non-deadly force: one who is himself free from fault[18] is permitted to use non-deadly force in self-defense whenever *three conditions* are satisfied. The first is that he *reasonably* believes the assailant intends to commit a battery upon him, or unlawfully to imprison him, and this belief has been induced by the other's conduct. The second is that the defensive force used is not *unreasonable* in view of the harm that it is intended to prevent. And the third is that the defender *reasonably* believes he cannot avoid the threatened harm without either using defensive force or giving up some right or privilege.

    It is to be noted that reasonableness in the American law is determined by the standard of *a reasonable person under like circumstances* and the determination is to be made by the jury. But there are, however, certain rules with regard to the use of deadly force. One such rule is that deadly force is not permitted in defense against non-deadly force. The Court does not ask the jury to determine whether such use of deadly

---

15.  *See* for analysis of these differences in both legal systems: Lensing, *supra* note 12, at 250.

16.  *See* Perkins and Boyce, *supra* note 6, at 1114.

17.  *See* for a more detailed analysis: Perkins and Boyce, *supra* note 6, at 1116–1127.

18.  In common law it is not assumed that fault in any degree will always rule out all possibility of self-defense.

force was reasonable under all the circumstances. The instruction will be that if the jury finds as a fact that the defendant used deadly force to defend against force which he realized was non-deadly, he is not excused.[19]

2. According the American law doctrine,[20] the counterpart of the rule that deadly force is not authorized in defense "*against non-deadly force is that deadly force is authorized to defend against deadly force if this* reasonably *seems necessary to avoid death or great bodily injury. Whether it* reasonably *seems necessary is determined by the reasonable person standard, but whether or not it means that he can thus defend himself where he is depends upon rules, and these rules are far from uniform. At one point all agree. A trespasser does not forfeit his life by trespassing upon the property of another, and hence does not forfeit his privilege of self-defense by doing so. But he is not privileged to use any force, particularly deadly force, to defend himself, if he can safely avoid the harm by terminating his trespass—by retreating from the other's premises. At the other extreme, also, almost all agree. If an intruder murderously attacks an innocent dweller in his dwelling, the dweller can use deadly force to defend himself where he is. Even if he could safely avoid his assailant by running out of the house, he is not required to do so. Between these extremes the rules differ widely* (emphasis added)."

The common law approaches this topic on a more casuistic basis; it leaves the Court open to develop a wider defense when it concerns the extent to which self-defense may be invoked as a defense to other crimes. In an English criminal case, named *A-G's Reference*,[21] the defendant made and retained in his shop petrol bombs at a time when extensive rioting was taking place in the area. The Court of Appeal held that there was evidence on which a jury might have decided that the use of the petrol bombs would have been reasonable force in self-defense against an apprehended attack. In this reasoning, the accused possessed the bombs for lawful purposes and was not guilty of the offence of possessing an explosive substance.[22]

---

19. *See*, e.g., *Sikes v. Commonwealth*, 304 KY 429, 200 S.W. 2d 956 (1949); Perkins and Boyce, *supra* note 6, at 1117.

20. *See* Perkins and Boyce, *supra* note 6, at 1127.

21. 1984, QB 456, (1984) I AII ER 988, (1984) Crim LR 289 and commentary, CA.

22. *See* for this case also Smith and Hogan, *supra* note 8, at 267.

### 1.2.3.2    The principle of "(no) retreat"

Another major distinction between the civil and common law standards on the one hand and American law on the other hand, regarding
the law of self-defense by individuals, American law endorses the view
that the defendant, acting in self-defense, bears in principle no preliminary obligation to retreat from the crime scene.[23] This obligation especially
does not apply in the event of an attack in the defendant's own house or
"castle." In American law, the defendant may stand his ground and use
deadly force, if this reasonably seems necessary to save himself there.[24]
The underlying rationale is that liberty itself is threatened if a law-abiding
citizen can be forced from a place where he has a right to be,[25] whereas
this extreme and exclusive privilege is not granted to an *"aggressor."*
Therefore, according this American law view, one who started the
encounter with an unlawful attacks or who culpably engaged in an
unlawful exchange of blows, enjoys no such position. The *"fault"* of the
defendant who joins in the crime with no thought of causing death or
great bodily harm is entirely overshadowed if the other person willfully
changes it to a deadly encounter. The element of retreat—in the civil law
systems a prerequisite to the admissibility of self defense, in the context of
the condition of subsidiarity[26]—is in the American law only relevant to
the extent that if the defendant-victim retreats as far as he can in reasonable safety, he may use deadly force if this reasonably seems necessary to
save himself from death or great bodily harm.[27] In addition, according to
American law, if by reason of suddenness and fierceness of the change in
the nature of the contest, there is no *reasonable* opportunity to retreat, the
defendant may resort to deadly force where he is.[28] Although *the principle
of reasonableness* remains decisive in American law as to the legitimacy of
the defense of self-defense, it primarily rests upon the subjective opinion
of the accused. Consequently, more abstraction is envisioned as to the requisite dogmatic and objective civil law criteria of proportionality and subsidiarity. These latter principles lead to strict application of the "retreat
rule." With regard to the defenses of superior orders and duress, the principle of reasonableness was endorsed as the most conclusive and decisive
adjudicatory standard hereto.

American law embraces a substantial minority of jurisdictions which
have adopted the so-called "retreat rule." This rule requires that even the

---

23.  *See* JOHANNES A. W. LENSING, AMERIKAANS STRAFRECHT 251 (1996).
24.  Perkins and Boyce, *supra* note 6, at 1127.
25.  *See*, e.g., *State v. Bartlett*, 170 Mo. 658, 668, 71 S.W. 148, 151 (1902).
26.  *See* Lensing, *supra* note 23, at 251.
27.  *See People v. Hecker*, 109 Cal. 451, 42 P. 307 (1895); *People v. Miceli*, 101 Cal.
App 2nd 643, 226 P. 2d 14 (1951); Perkins & Boyce, *supra* note 6, at 1129.
28.  *See People v. Hecker, supra* note 27; *Pond v. People*, 8 Mich. 150 (1860).

innocent victim of a murderous assault must elect an obviously safe retreat, if available, rather than resort to deadly force. But even in this view, three exceptions are available in the event:

1. the defendant was in his "castle" at the time of the assault;
2. the assailant is a person he is lawfully attempting to arrest; or
3. the assailant is a robber.[29]

Regarding the American system, Perkins and Boyce argue that the contention that the "retreat rule" tends to enhance the risk of the innocent is without foundation, because proper application of even this rule never requires the innocent victim to increase his own peril for the safety of a murderous assailant.[30] A further extension of the common law scope in this area regarding self-defense, as distinct from the civil law systems, is the fact that, without any doubt, the former system tends to enlarge the "castle" concept. This concept figuratively enhances all places from which the innocent victim of a murderous assault is not required to retreat before resorting to deadly force. This concept encompasses, besides one's own dwelling, a particular place of business, including the private driveway leading to the place of business of a garage owner or even to an open field if that is where one works.[31] Furthermore, jurisprudential examples in the American law exist, holding that the privilege of self-defense in conjunction with the "castle" concept is available whenever the innocent victim is on his own premises at the time.[32] This type of extensive reasoning is reinforced in the common law, through the application of the legal rule that a person is not to be deprived of his right of self-defense merely because he attends a place where he might lawfully go, but where he *knew* he was likely to be attacked.[33] In the analysis of the civil law systems, a significant difference appears, as the aspect of attending the crime place is used to regulate and to channel a restrictive use of the right of self-defense by raising the "the self-defense exterminating" criterion of *culpa in causa*. This leads to a rather conservative application of this defense. It should be noted, however, that the use of deadly force merely for the protection of property, is *eo ipso* not to be considered reasonable.[34]

In conclusion, contrary to (generally speaking) most of the civil law systems, the tendency in American law on this topic has been towards

---

29. Perkins & Boyce, *supra* note 6, at 1133.
30. Perkins & Boyce, *supra* note 6, at 1134.
31. *See*, e.g., *State v. Sipes*, 202 Iowa 173, 209, N.W. 458 (1926) and *State v. Gordon*, 128 S.C. 422, 122, S.E 501(1924).
32. *See* e.g. State v. Hewitt, 205 S.C. 207, 31 S.E. 2d 257 (1944).
33. *See* Smith & Hogan, *supra* note 8, at 265.
34. *See* Smith & Hogan, *supra* note 8, at 266.

enlarging, rather than narrowing, the defensive privilege against murderous attack.[35]

### 1.2.4   Conclusion

Whilst there are substantive differences between the law on self-defense between civil law and common law systems on the one hand and American law on the other hand, there can be no doubt that in all these legal systems the right of self-defense by individuals represents a major defense, essential to the elementary rights of the individual in both civil and criminal law. The requirement that the defendant reasonably believes that forceful response is necessary is a common law requirement which is superfluous in civil law systems. On the other hand, the introduction of the requirement that the response be to an *"imminent"* use of unlawful force may by viewed under the common law as surplusage.[36] Whilst the weight of the subjective-objective (common law) and objective (civil law) adjudicatory criteria varies considerable according to these systems, an important common feature exists; in both systems the right of self-defense is in principle admissible, even when advanced with the use of deadly force.[37] It can be observed that regarding the admissibility of self-defense which leads to the use of deadly force or killing of others, a substantive difference from the legal defenses of superior orders and duress can be recognized. This distinction between the scope of self-defense on the one hand and that of superior orders and duress on the other hand affects the admissibility of these defenses to war crimes indictments, to be examined in section 3 below. Article 31(1) (d) of the ICC Statute, allowing self-defense by individuals in the context of ICL, finds support in civil law as well as common law and American law systems.

## 1.3 The ICL status of self-defense

### 1.3.1   The argument of independent assessment

The development of the system of ICL largely depends on the concept of criminal responsibility of individuals, which concept is nowa-

---

35.   *See* also Lensing, *supra* note 23, at 252; Perkins & Boyce, *supra* note 6, at 1137.

36.   INTERNATIONAL CRIMINAL LAW, CASES AND MATERIALS 1390 (Jordan J. Paust et al., eds., 1996).

37.   *See* for the common law also Smith & Hogan, *supra* note 8, at 263–270.

days without doubt an integral part of the legal framework of ICL.[38] Two sub-concepts of international criminal responsibility of individuals emerge:

1. The commission of certain international crimes which can solely be conducted under State authority or a State's international legal personality. These crimes need the use of the machinery of the State for their commission, and include, *inter alia*, genocide, apartheid, torture, crimes against humanity and war crimes; and
2. the commission of international crimes which have, in most instances, been committed under an individual's own personality without the State's authority, such as piracy, narcotic crimes, hijacking and terrorism.[39]

In this context it is of relevance to note that, in the realm of adjudicating upon war crimes indictments (i.e., concept 1 above), "*an individual criminal act is not (eo ipso; GJK) a state conduct, although the individual acts under the legal personality of the State.*"[40] Therefore, "*an individual who commits a war crime in the course of war is personally responsible for his criminal act,*" implying that the concept of international criminal responsibility of individuals does not automatically involve the concept of international criminal responsibility of the State. Equally, it can be held that the sole fact that war crimes have been committed and State responsibility emerges does not rule out the legal possibility that the defense of self-defense by an individual of the particular State may be invoked. The very fact that the concept of international criminal responsibility of individuals forms an independent phenomenon, to be abstracted from the concept of criminal liability of States,[41] ensures that the doctrine of self-defense in the realm of war crimes merits individual assessment, apart from State responsibility, as well as apart from the concept of (anticipatory) self-defense by States. From the foregoing emerges therefore the first reason to admit the defense of self-defense to war crimes charges.

---

38. *See* Farhad Malekian, *International Criminal Responsibility*, in I INTERNATIONAL CRIMINAL LAW 190 (M. Cherif Bassiouni, ed., 1999).
39. *See* Malekian, *supra* note 38, at 176.
40. Malekian, *supra* note 38, at 211.
41. This is a very controversial concept; *See* John Dugard, *The Criminal Responsibility of States*, in I INTERNATIONAL CRIMINAL LAW 239–253 (M. Cherif Bassiouni, ed., 1999).

1.3.2    The argument of customary international law status

Individuals can derive the second reason from the customary international law status of the right of self-defense. This is evidenced by, *inter alia*, Article 2(2)(a) of the European Convention on Human Rights and Fundamental Freedoms, providing that deprivation of life shall not be regarded as a contravention of Article 2(1) when it results from the use of force which is no more than absolutely necessary in defense of any person from unlawful violence. This provision is clearly enacted for the international community interests and the safeguarding of these interests under the framework of ICL. It is therefore tenable that the right of an individual to self-defense is now to be considered part of customary international law. To accept this right as part of *jus cogens*, more international pronouncements must be available. On this point the ICCPR does not entail a provision similar to Article 2(2)(a) of the European Convention. In the *North Sea* cases, the ICJ referred to *"emergent rules of customary international law,"*[42] a formulation which indicates a flexible approach to the criterion of *opinio juris* as one of the constituent sources of the formation of customary international law. In general the ICJ appears to be willing to assume the existence of an *opinio juris* on the basis of evidence of, *inter alia*, general practice or State practice.[43] The evidence of State practice consists of a variety of material sources, including diplomatic correspondence, policy statements, the published opinions of government legal advisors, manuals of military law,[44] recitals in treaties and treaties themselves.[45] It may be emphasized that customary international law is not a special department or area of public international law: it *is* international law.[46] Therefore it can be held that the right of self-defense by individuals is an established rule of international law and a *fortiori* of ICL, since there are four main collateral sources of ICL, the first of which is international and regional human rights law, consisting of conventions, customary international law and general principles of law.[47] It is obvious that the European Human Rights Convention is part of this source, containing both procedural and substantive norms. A more direct source forms now Article 31 (1)(c) of the ICC Statute, formalizing self-defense in ICL and requiring in essence two conditions of exclusion for the criminal responsibility: (a) a certain danger to a person or property by unlawful force, and (b) an appropriate

---

42.  ICJ Reports 1969, at 39, para. 63.
43.  *See* IAN BROWNLIE, THE RULE OF LAW IN INTERNATIONAL AFFAIRS 21 (1998).
44.  *See* Chapter IV, *infra*.
45.  *See* Brownlie, *supra* note 43, at 19.
46.  *See* Brownlie, *supra* note 43, at 18.
47.  *See* M. CHERIF BASSIOUNI, INTERNATIONAL CRIMINAL LAW 14–15 (1999).

defense against it whereby the latter requires more than mere involvement in a defensive operation.[48]

The development of the right of self-defense as a general rule of customary international law and subsequently a rule of ICL has considerable relevance to the role of this concept in the area of international criminal law war tribunals. The individual self-defense provision in the Rome Statute of the ICC is, as far as it concerns a defense against an unlawful attack, actually based on this general customary rule, envisioned by Article 2(2)(a) of the European Human Rights Convention as well as in the language used in the Model Penal Code.[49] The difference is that the European Convention does not mention the defense of property. Hereinafter, it will be observed that the defense of property has no basis in customary international law. Since the jurisdiction of the ICC encompasses adjudication upon war crimes indictments, there is no doubt that the defendant subject of war crimes litigation can invoke the right of self-defense. However, the self-defense proviso in the ICC Statute involves not an unlimited right, but is restricted by the principle of proportionality. Further, its limits emerge from the fact that *"the use of force as well as the danger to person or property must be objectively given and may not only exist in the subjective belief of the defender,"* thus excluding an expansion of self-defense to the case that the accused *"merely reasonably believes"* that there was a particular threat.[50] From this perspective, on the one hand the scope of self-defense under the ICC seems to be considerably limited compared to the self-defense doctrine under common law, the latter doctrine (as observed before) admitting self-defense in cases of such a *"reasonable belief;"* on the other hand, the ICC provision is much wider than common law and American law, because of the inclusion of the defense of property.

### 1.3.3  Codificatory problems of the scope of Article 31 (1)(c)

This leads to the third argument as to the applicability of the right of self-defense by individual defendants prosecuted on the basis of war crimes charges. Close reading of the text of Article 31 (1)(c) of the ICC Statute shows that it does not exclude this defense for a defendant standing trial regarding war crimes. The text of this provision explicitly refers to "( . . . ) *the case of war crimes"* in conjunction with *"property which is essential*

---

48.  *See* Albin Eser *Article 31, Margin No. 28*, in Commentary on the Rome Statute (Otto Triffterer, ed. 1999).

49.  *See* International Criminal Law, Cases and Materials, *supra* note 36, at 1390.

50.  *See* A. Eser, *supra* note 48, Margin No. 31.

*for the survival of the person or another person* ( . . . )," thus obviously ensuring the admissibility of this defense even when war crimes are committed in order to defend property essential for one's own or others survival. The precedent in favor of this view, i.e. the *US v. Krupp* case, demonstrated that the plea of self-defense may be successfully invoked in war crimes trials in much the same circumstances as in domestic trials.[51] The *Krupp* case, though, did not deal with the defense of property.

The contemporary system of ICL has evolved fundamentally from various concepts of international criminal responsibility. This important principle of self-defense serves as the basis of the ICL system, which deals with the international responsibility of both individuals and States. Whereas the former is juridically consolidated, the controversial notion of criminal liability of States is still undergoing codification.[52] These facts imply that the law of self-defense by individuals and that of States are not interchangeable, so that the former concept is an independent one. The criticism derived from international humanitarian law instruments and principles (to be discussed in paragraph 1.3.4 below) do not therefore apply equally to the doctrine of individual self-defense in ICL. The law of self-defense in ICL judicially limits the use of force, in principle abstracted from the nature of the attack. When, under exceptional circumstances, such as in case of defense against an unlawful attack, assault and even manslaughter can be excusable, certain presupposed criteria are fulfilled,[53] it would not be consistent to exclude this defense *a priori* in the event of war crimes charges. The legal responsibilities of an individual, as already noted, are not interchangeable with those of the State.[54]

Finally, the basis for the plea of self-defense of an individual is that it would be inhuman to require people to abstain from such action when necessary, let alone to require waiting until the death or bodily harm of people is irreversible. Self-defense in this view is a "natural right."[55] Article 31(1)(c) of the ICC Statute is an exponent of this view, since in principle it does not exclude this defense to war crimes charges.[56]

### 1.3.4   Self-defense to war crimes and military necessity

Self-defence in the new phenomenon of "military necessity" that emerges in Article 31 (1)(c), is, however, another matter. The regime of

---

51. *See* International Criminal Law, Cases and Materials, *supra* note 36, at 1389.
52. Malekian, *supra* note 38, at 153; *See* also J. Dugard, *supra* note 41.
53. *See* also Nico Keijzer, *Self-defence in the Statute of Rome*, at 4 (unpublished)
54. *Ibid.*
55. Keijzer, *supra* note 53, at 4–5.
56. Also Keijzer, *supra* note 53, at 5.

self-defense in ICL is, as observed, relatively flexible, contrary to, *inter alia,* the defenses of duress and superior orders to war crimes. A new note in the realm of private self-defense in ICL is sounded in Article 31 (1)(c) of the Rome Statute of the ICC, which reads as follows: *"In addition to other grounds for excluding criminal responsibility provided for in this Statute, a person shall not be criminally responsible if, at the time of that person's conduct:*
(a). . . . . . .
(b). . . . . . .
*(c) The person acts reasonably to defend himself or herself or another person or, in the case of war crimes, property which is essential for the survival of the person or another person or property which is essential for accomplishing a military mission, against an imminent and unlawful use of force in a manner proportionate to the degree of danger to the person or the other person or property protected. The fact that the person was involved in a defensive operation conducted by forces shall not in itself constitute a ground for excluding criminal responsibility under this subparagraph."*

This new provision in ICL, although the wide defense scope of property seems to have support in American law precedents,[57] is not uncontroversial and strongly criticized by four Belgian scholars, who argue that no political, military or national interest or necessity can justify a war crime.[58] The scholarly criticism is translated by Cassese as follows: *"While it seems admissible to extend self-defense to the protection of another person or to property essential to the survival of the person or of another person, it is highly questionable to extend the notion at issue to the need to protect 'property which is essential for accomplishing a military mission.' This extension is manifestly outside lex lata, and may generate quite a few misgivings. Firstly, via international criminal law a norm of international humanitarian law has been created whereby a serviceman may now lawfully commit an international crime for the purpose of defending any 'property which is essential for accomplishing a military mission' against an imminent and unlawful use of force. So far such unlawful use of force against the 'property' at issue has not entitled the military to commit war crimes. They could only react by using lawful means or methods of combat or, ex post facto, by resorting to lawful reprisals against enemy belligerents. Secondly, the notion of 'property essential for accomplishing a military mission' is very loose and may be difficult to interpret."[59]*

The fact that the defense of property is a most contested aspect of Article 31(1)(c) of the Rome Statute stems also from the *travaux préparatoires* of this Statute. Notwithstanding the inclusion of self-defense as justification in the Preparatory Committee's compilation of 1996, its concept

57. *See* section. 1.2.2 of this chapter.
58. *See* open letter to *La libre Belgique,* 15 April 1999 of A. Andries, E. David, J. Verhaegen and C. van den Wyngaert.
59. Antonio Cassese, *The Statute of the ICC: Some Preliminary Reflections,* European Journal of International Law 154–155 (1999); *See* also 144–171.

and phrasing remained *"highly controversial until the very last framing of this provision."*[60] As analyzed by Eser, the first sentence of present Article 31(1)(c) is derived from a proposal by the USA of June 1998, although the defense of property as such in case of war crimes was not mentioned, but merely "military necessity" as a separate ground for excluding criminal responsibility. Ultimately this separate ground was integrated into the first sentence of the present provision on proposal of the Working Group. The Drafting Committee added the last sentence of this provision, envisioning defensive operations, at the very last moment.[61] Therefore the defense of property is strongly related to the defense of "military necessity" under public international law.[62] The controversiality of the defense of property can be derived also directly from the provision itself; the drafters realized obviously that the words *"essential for the survival of the person concerned or another person"* are rather open, since the included clear limitation in the second sentence of this provision must be considered with due diligence.[63]

The controversiality of the defense of property follows also from the different approaches in domestic law systems. Contrary to American law, most domestic law systems do not embrace a defense of property in the form of Article 31(1)(c) of the Rome Statute. The Dutch Penal Code, for instance, in Article 41 (1), although in principle allowing a defense against property, only provides for a limited protection of property.[64] Under common law the defense of property is generally dealt with through the defense of *prevention of crime*; when the defendant is charged with an offence against another person and his defense is that he was defending his property, according to common law he can invoke the defense of *prevention of crime*.[65] The reservation as to the defense of property in common law is aptly summarized by Smith and Hogan, who state that *"it can rarely, if ever, be reasonable to use deadly force merely for the protection of property"* and ask if it would have been reasonable to kill even one of the Great Train Robbers to prevent them from getting away with their millions of pounds loot, or kill a man about to destroy a priceless old master.[66]

The question worthy of debate is indeed whether the doctrine of self-defense by an individual who commits a war crime can be legitimate, either from the judicial or moral points of view. Already now it can be said that the concept of "military necessity" seems to militate to the detriment of the principles of legality, being a "very loose" notion. An important

---

60.  *See* A. Eser, *supra* note 48, Margin No. 28.

61.  *Ibid.*

62.  *See* Preparatory Committee Report of 1996 to Article R, at 103.

63.  A. Eser, *supra* note 48, Margin No. 30.

64.  *See* TEKST EN COMMENTAAR STRAFRECHT 227 (C.P.M. Cleiren and J.F. Nijboer, eds.,1997).

65.  Smith and Hogan, *supra* note 8, at 286.

66.  *Ibid.*

domestic source is Article 5 of the Belgium War Crimes Act of 1993, excluding any political, military or national interest or necessity from justifying a war crime, even if committed by means of a reprisal. The reality is that unfortunately most war crimes are actually committed under the shield of accomplishing a military mission. This provision can therefore undermine the principles of international humanitarian law and abuse the law of war.[67] Contravention seems to be present in Article 4(2) of the ICCPR and Article 15(2) of the ECHR—both of which exclude the right of life and the prohibition against torture or inhumane treatment from suspension of conventional provisions in time of war or public emergency— as well as in the common Articles 62/63/142/158 of the Geneva Conventions and Article 60 (5) of the Vienna Convention on the Law of Treaties, according to which no substantive violation by a party to a multilateral Convention concerning international humanitarian law justifies another party to suspend its own compliance to that convention.[68] In contrast to the general determination of self-defense by individuals as to war crimes indictments, it can be held as main principle of ICL that no exonerative use of the concept of military necessity is legitimate as to violations of the laws and customs of war.[69] Several arguments emerge:

1.  The concept of military necessity in conjunction with protection of property essential to military mission is *eo ipso* not of an inherent interest to a human being namely not *per se* essential for his survival. Especially, recourse to the Articles 51(5)(b) and 57(2)(b) of Additional Protocol I to the Geneva Conventions—the intent of which is the balancing between exclusion of human suffering and inclusion of effective warfare—seem to prevent, based on the principle of proportionality, the notion of military necessity as justificatory to war crimes.
2.  The concept of the war exception to human rights obligations, pursuant to (as noticed) Articles 15 (2) of the ECHR and 4(2) of the ICCPR, excludes the aspect of military necessity.
3.  The concept of "military necessity" envisaged by the Drafters of Article 31(1)(c) of the ICC Statute can mask political and military abuse, based on hidden agendas, and points to vulnerable areas in the legal regime of self-defense. Keijzer provides an enlightening hypothetical example: "*Suppose a lightly armed unit is charged with the protection of a village, which harbors an important historic monument, e.g., a medieval church. The*

---

67.  *See* also Keijzer, *supra* note 53, at 2.
68.  *See* Keijzer, *supra* note 53.
69.  *See* Keijzer, *supra* note 53, at 6.

*enemy attacks this village by heavy mortar fire, especially aimed at*
*the monument. Air support, in order to put the mortars out of*
*action, is not available. Then, not seeing any other way to save the*
*church, the commander of the unit decides to send saboteurs, wear-*
*ing enemy military uniforms, in order to destroy the enemy ammu-*
*nition. The saboteurs do succeed in penetrating the enemy lines and*
*in blowing up an important ammunition depot, which results in the*
*mortar fire dying out. After the war, one commander has to stand*
*trial for attacking a historic monument in violation of Article 4–1*
*Cultural Property Convention, the other is charged with having vio-*
*lated Art. 23-(f) Rules of Land Warfare and Art. 39–2, Protocol I,*
*which prohibit the use of the uniforms of the adverse party while*
*engaging in attack. The latter commander can, in my view, fairly*
*plead that, taken into account the values at stake, he was justified in*
*what he did, or, if not justified, he should at least be excused, because*
*the choice he made was reasonable and the violation cannot reason-*
*ably be blamed on him. But it is clear that we do not reach this judg-*
*ment because the defense of the church was part of the commander's*
*military mission* (and constitutes military necessity; GJK) *but*
*because of the special value of that church for mankind."*[70]

This danger as to unjust abuse in this area especially is not unrealistic because, although it contains the principles of reasonableness and pro- portionality, Article 31(1)(c) makes no explicit reference to the principle of subsidiarity. In my view, this is no real obstacle considering the overall principle of *reasonableness and good faith.* In this context Keijzer, however, points to another textual danger of present Article 31(1)(c), i.e., *"the danger that individuals without legal training might read in Article 31(1)(c) that mili- tary necessity is a general justification cannot be completely ruled out."*[71] Therefore, the application of this provision in international legal and mil- itary practice has to be accompanied by serious adherence to the Articles 82 and 83 of Additional Protocol I. This need emerges especially since, as clarified by sentence 2 of Article 31 (1)(c) of the ICC Statute, justifying individual self-defense in question here cannot be invoked merely by ref- erence to a *"defensive operation"* in which the accused concerned was involved.[72]

In sum, it can be observed that Article 31(1)(c) of the ICC Statute, with regard to "military necessity" creates several problems of ICL and inter- national humanitarian law, since, in general, it tends to shift the responsi- bility for war crimes away from military authorities. However, the law

---

70. Keijzer, *supra* note 53, at 7–8.
71. Keijzer, *supra* note 53, at 9.
72. *See* A. Eser, *supra* note 48, Margin No. 34.

and especially ICL cannot foresee future judicial or factual developments. From this perspective, the enactment of the submitted provision is perhaps desirable on the basis of the exceptional value of property essential for military missions, which should not be banished from the purview of international criminal courts.[73] History has indeed taught that *exceptional* situations are conceivable in which certain violations of the rules of war, conducted to defend property essential for the success of military missions, cannot reasonably always be blamed on the perpetrator.[74] Pursuant to the aforementioned International Conventions on the Laws of War, resort to this "exceptional" form of self-defense by individual (military) persons must be adhered to with the utmost stringency on a strict individual basis. The articulation of this "ultimate exception," if acceptable at all, cannot ultimately be based on *"essential military interests"* as such, since such an adjudicatory ruling raises the unjust impression that military necessity as a concept should prevail over elementary rules of international humanitarian law and the law or customs of war. This would be a legal anomaly, especially as customary international law does not clearly recognize the defense of property, and moreover, domestic systems clearly show juridical reservations towards this phenomenon.

## 2 THE DEFENSES OF NECESSITY AND PREVENTION OF CRIME IN ICL

### 2.1 Introduction

As observed by Brownlie, since the latter half of the nineteenth century it has been generally recognized that there are acts or commissions for which international law imposes criminal responsibility on individuals and for which punishment may be imposed, either by properly empowered international tribunals or by national courts and military tribunals.[75] In the Charter of the International Military Tribunal (hereinafter IMT), annexed to the Agreement for the Prosecution and Punishment of the Major War Criminals of the European Axis, signed on 8 August 1945, Article 6 provides, *inter alia*, that *"the following acts, or any of them, are crimes coming within the jurisdiction of the Tribunal for which there shall be individual responsibility: (a) crimes against peace ( . . . ), (b) War Crimes, namely, violations of the laws or customs of war ( . . . ), (c) crimes against humanity ( . . . )."* In this context the individual is no longer seen in relation to the State, but as an entity endowed with independent *"legal responsibility."* This idea is

---

73. *See* also Keijzer, *supra* note 53, at 8.
74. Keijzer, *supra* note 53, at 7.
75. Ian Brownlie, Principles of Public International Law 561 (1990).

clearly reflected in the judgment of the IMT in the *Eichmann* case,[76] wherein the Tribunal on the status of individual criminal liability ruled: *"it was submitted that international law is concerned with the actions of sovereign States, and provides no punishment for individuals; and further, that where the act in question is an act of State, those who carry it out are not personally responsible but are protected by the doctrine of the sovereignty of the State. In the opinion of the Tribunal, both these submissions must be rejected. That international law imposes duties and liabilities upon individuals as upon States has long been recognized . . . the very essence of the Charter is that individuals have international duties, which transcend the national obligations of obedience imposed by the individual State* (emphasis added). *He who violates the laws of war cannot obtain immunity while acting in pursuance of the authority of the State, if the State in authorizing action moves outside its competence under international law."* It is apparent from subsequent international conventions[77] and the judgments of the ICTY and ICTR that this Article 6 has since amounted to a rule of customary international criminal law.[78]

The language employed in this ruling leaves no doubt that ICL considers the individual as being bound directly by the laws of war, but also it constitutes another major principle of both ICL as well as international humanitarian law (hereinafter IHL), namely *"( . . . ) that individuals have international duties which transcend the national obligations of obedience imposed by the individual State."* It was this very idea that led to the principle that excludes superior orders as legal defense to war crimes. To be justified, the concept of the individual as judicially a *"superseding"* entity in relation to the State in the realm of ICL must have its correlative in international rights. Exponents hereof are two legal defenses, in the era of ICL rather unexposed, namely those of *necessity and prevention of crime*, neither of which are explicitly provided for in the Rome Statute of the ICC nor the Statutes of ICTY and ICTR.

Admittedly, Article 31(1)(d) of the ICC Statute, according to its text, tries to combine two different concepts, namely justifying necessity and merely excusing duress. This is remarkable, because all pre-Rome Conference proposals and drafts made clear distinctions between the defense of necessity on the one hand and duress on the other hand.[79] Only at the end of the day, according to Eser, *"for whatever unclear reasons, they were mixed up in one provision."*[80] It seems to me that this mixture of these

---

76. *See* ILR 36,5.

77. E.g., Article VI of the Convention on the Prevention and Punishment of the Crime of Genocide.

78. *See* also Brownlie, *supra* note 75, at 562.

79. *See* A. Eser, *supra* note 48, Margin No. 35; *See* also Preparatory Committee of March/April 1996 at 16–18; and Draft Statute of April 1998, Article 31, para. 1(d) and (e).

80. *See* Eser, *supra* note 48, *Ibid*; *See* Working Paper of 22 June 1998 (UN Doc.

two defenses is not only unnecessary, juridical and inaccurate, but accounts also for an underestimation of the defense of necessity in ICL. This omission is, however, not insurmountable. This section will show why this defense deserves an independent place in ICL.

Article 31(3) of the ICC Statute demonstrates namely that its drafters envisioned no restrictive and closed system of legal defenses to international crimes, providing in this section that *"at trial, the Court may consider a ground for excluding criminal responsibility* other than those referred to in paragraph 1 (emphasis added) *where such a ground is derived from applicable law, as set forth in Article 21 ( . . . ),"* stipulating thus the possibility of invoking legal defenses to war crimes charges outside the codificatory range of international statutes, presupposing its judicial basis in *"general principles of law derived ( . . . ) from national laws of legal systems of the world including ( . . . ) the national laws of States ( . . . ),"* pursuant to Article 21 (1) of the ICC Statute. Nothing new is said by observing that general principles of national laws of States, and in particular their system of defenses, can produce defenses in international criminal litigation.[81]

It is the basic purpose of this section to examine two defenses which are in fact special exponents of the above-illustrated defenses of duress and self-defense, namely the defenses of *"necessity"* and *"prevention of crime."* For this reason this part of the chapter is devoted to the implementation of the latter two defenses within the system of ICL, advancing in subsections 2 and 3, to a comparison with the jurisprudence in common law, and augmenting the scope of the related Articles 31 (1)(c)(d). Subsection 4, deals with the relevancy of the two submitted defenses in the framework not only of ICL but also international humanitarian law (hereinafter IHL). As observed by Bassiouni, *"the individual criminal responsibility of soldiers and others in the lower echelons of State power is much more easily accepted by governments than that of political leaders and senior government officials and, as well, those in the governmental bureaucracy who carry out, execute and facilitate the policies and practices of crimes against humanity, genocide and even war crimes."*[82] In order to equalize this apparent inequality (which, according to Bassiouni, renders prosecution of the latter category of perpetrators virtually impossible) the defenses of necessity and prevention of crime may be invoked to avoid substantial criminal involvement of the lower echelons to war crimes. These defenses also apply to

---

A/CONF.183/C.1/WGGP/L.6) and Draft Report of the Drafting Committee to the Committee of the Whole, 14 July 1998, Article 30 para. 1(d), at 7.

81. Several other special defenses, not explicitly enunciated in the ICC Statute nor in ICTY or ICTR Statutes or Rules of Procedure and Evidence, such as genetic defenses, are not dealt with in this chapter.

82. M. Cherif Bassiouni, *The Normative Framework of IHL: Overlaps, Gaps and Ambiguities in International Criminal Law*, in I INTERNATIONAL CRIMINAL LAW 619 (M. Cherif Bassiouni, ed. 1999).

the activities of soldiers of all ranks during multinational military peace-keeping and peace enforcement operations, a subject discussed in subsection 4.

## 2.2 The common law approach to the defense of necessity: relevance for ICL

### 2.2.1   Necessity in international crimes: duress of circumstances

The first important inquiry is whether ICL allows a defense of necessity, derived from general principles of law recognized by national laws of the world's legal systems or national laws of States, amounting to an internationally accepted norm or standard, pursuant to Article 21 (1)(c) of the ICC Statute. Common law as well as continental law systems recognize such a defense. United States Courts have taken the position that *"Generally, necessity is available as a defense when the physical forces of nature or the pressure of circumstances cause the accused to take unlawful action to avoid a harm which social policy deems greater than the harm resulting from a violation of the law."*[83] Close reading of Article 31 (1)(d)(ii) of the ICC Statute teach that this defense is indeed narrowly connected to duress—not to say *"mixed up in one provision"*[84]—to be distinguished, however, by the very fact that in the event of the latter the crime emerges from an imminent threat, with death or deadly force conducted by another person against the defendant, whereas in the case of necessity the specific crime emerges actually on the basis of a *"choice of evils,"* which can occur also outside the realm of an imminent threat or other external force causing a mental pressure.[85] The distinction was clearly illuminated in the 1978 decision of the U.S. Supreme Court in *U.S. v. Bailey: "Thus, where A destroyed a dike because B threatened to kill him if he did not, A would argue that he acted under* duress (emphasis added) *whereas if A destroyed the dike in order to protect more valuable property from flooding, A could claim a defense of* necessity (emphasis added)."*[86] Common law practice has gradually blurred this distinction.[87]

The *"inexcusable choice"* requirement for necessity applies equally to the law of duress. While the common law never excuses one who makes a choice between oneself and an obviously innocent person by intentionally killing the latter in order to preserve one's life—this being the propo-

---

83.   *See* e.g., *State v. Diana*, 24 Wn. App. 908, 604 P. 2d 1312, 1316 (1979); *U.S. v. Cassidy*, 616, No. F. 2d 101, 102 (4th Circuit, 1979).

84.   *See* A. Eser, *supra* note 48, Margin No. 35.

85.   *See* also Lensing, *supra* note 23, at 253.

86.   *U.S v. Bailey*, 444 U.S. 394, 409/410 (1978).

87.   Lensing, *supra* note 23, at 253.

sition of the *"inexcusable choice"* as evidenced by the famous *U.S. v. Holmes* case of 1842 as well as the equally famous *U.K. v. Dudley* case of 1884,[88] exceptional situations occur which may incline to an exonerative character. After all, Article 31 (2) of the ICC Statute ensures a non-restrictive adjudicatory assessment of defenses, by virtue of the principle of individuality. Exoneration under the plea of duress or necessity for taking the life of an innocent person, even if necessary to save oneself from death, turns out to be a controversial morality issue in the jurisprudence of the ICTY as well as in common law.

*Holmes*, was a famous American case that arose out of a situation in which a ship struck an iceberg and sank in mid-ocean. Before the vessel went down boats were lowered, carrying the passengers and members of the crew. These boats were soon separated. One was so overloaded the people were barely able to move in their crowded positions, and the next day a squall developed, threatening to send the overcrowded craft (not a modern lifeboat) to the bottom. In this emergency the officer in charge gave the order to jettison a portion of the human freight. Holmes was one of the two sailors who carried out the mandate to eliminate every third man, by seizing fourteen men and throwing them overboard. The boat, thus lightened, managed to ride the waves until a rescue-ship arrived on the following day. The officer and most of the crew disappeared shortly after landing, but Holmes appeared in Philadelphia, where he was arrested for murder on the high seas, a crime under federal law. Although it was conceded that the boat would not have survived the storm if the boat had not been lightened, no excuse was recognized.

In *Dudley*, an equally famous English case, two men were indicted for willful murder, and on the trial the jury returned a special verdict stating, in effect, that the prisoners and another sailor, the deceased a boy of about seventeen, able-bodied English seamen and the crew of an English yacht, were cast away in a storm on the high seas 1600 miles from land and were compelled to put into an open boat. The accused stated that the food they took with them was all consumed in twelve days, and having been without food for eight days and without water for six days, the prisoners killed the boy; that the boy when killed was lying on the bottom of the boat, quite helpless and weak, unable to make any resistance, but did not assent to being killed; that the sailors fed upon the body and blood of the boy for four days, when a passing vessel picked them up; that at the time of the killing there appeared to the accused every possibility that unless they fed upon the boy, or one of themselves, they would die of starvation; that there was no appreciable chance of saving life except by killing someone for the others to eat; that there was no greater necessity for killing the boy

---

88. *See United States v. Holmes*, 26 Fed. Case 360, No. 15, 383 (1842) resp. The Queen v. Dudley & *Stephens*, 14 Q.B.D. 273, 286, (1884).

than any of the others. The court held that this special verdict showed no justification or excuse for the killing and rendered a verdict of guilty of willful murder.

As to the above-mentioned exceptional situations, scholarly opinions assert that the assumption that a killing in such extremity, as exemplified by the *Dudley* and *Holmes* cases, bears *eo ipso* the judicial qualification of murder, seems not a nuanced approach.[89] To cite Perkins and Boyce: *"While moral considerations require the rejection of any claim of excuse, they do not require that the mitigation of the circumstances be overlooked. A killing in such an extremity is far removed from cold-blooded murder, and should be held to be manslaughter."*[90] In effect, the common law courts, although rejecting the defense of necessity, resulted in *de facto* assertions of this defense; in *Holmes*, the Grand Jury refused to indict for murder and the subsequent conviction for manslaughter entailed only six months imprisonment. In the *Dudley* case, likewise, the sentence to death was converted to six months' imprisonment.

In sum, whilst common law has been unduly tardy and restrictive in granting the defense of duress in cases of any compulsion, other than personal violence or the threat thereof, a form envisioned by Article 31 (1)(d)(ii), the defense of necessity can in these situations constitute an excuse in certain extreme circumstances.[91] The question now to be answered is what these circumstances can be in relation to international crimes.

### 2.2.2   War crimes and choice of evils

Although criminal law was never intended to be a complete moral code,[92] ICL has and can continue to meaningfully contribute to regulating and thereby eliminating conduct falling far below proper moral behavior. The defense of necessity seeks to be a conflict-resolving mechanism between morality and criminal law adhered to by defendants where other defenses are deemed to fail or are not available.

ICL, evidenced by the Statutes and jurisprudence of the ICTY and ICTR as well as the Statute of the ICC, especially Article 31 (1)(d), dictates in fact that no one may choose between oneself and another, who may live and who must die, by intentionally killing an obviously innocent person; ICL also presupposes that no one may intentionally sacrifice human life for the protection of property, this being illustrated in Chapter IV below with regard to the element of military necessity as justification for self-

---

89. Perkins and Boyce, *supra* note 6, at 1058.
90. *Ibid*.
91. *See* also Perkins and Boyce, *supra* note 6, at 1066.
92. Perkins and Boyce, *supra* note 6, at 1073.

defense. ICL, however, is in itself not primarily concerned with the relativity of different harms but, like most domestic criminal laws, endorses the principle that no one should be punished *"for doing what any reasonable person would have done."*[93] This is exactly why common law doctrines accepts *"a defense if it can be established as a matter of law that the actor's conduct, in the only way that seemed reasonably possible under the circumstances, avoided greater harm than it caused,"* this being the so-called requisite *"choice of evils"* element of the defense of necessity.[94] It would appear therefore, in the context of a complete set of defenses, that whereas duress and necessity *in general* form a defense if one acts under such compulsion, from whatever source, that a person of reasonable firmness in such a situation would have been unable to resist doing so (relying upon the reasonable person standard for all situations except for intentional or reckless killing of innocent people), necessity involves a *specialis* of this *generalis;* namely the special requisite on the reasonable person standard that determines whether one harm was, or was not, greater than the other. This leads us to consider three thresholds or prerequisites as to the admissibility of the defense of necessity regarding war crimes charges:

- The act charged must have been done to prevent a significantly greater evil than inflicted;
- there must have been no adequate alternative; and
- the harm inflicted must not have been disproportionate to the harm avoided.[95]

The defense of necessity in ICL should be available if the accused *reasonably* believed at the time of acting that the first and second elements were present, even if that belief was mistaken. Contrary, the defendant's believe alone will not suffice as to the third element since ICL requires also an objective determination with regard to the weight of various forms of international crimes and their possible *jus cogens* character.[96] The *"reasonableness,"* in more objective context, emerges also from the duress provision, envisaged by Article 31(1)(d) of the ICC Statute, encompassing the requisite element in which *"( . . . ) the person acts necessarily and reasonably* (emphasis added) *to avoid this threat, provided that the person does not intend to cause a greater harm than the one sought to be avoided."* The wording of this provision, however, does not rule out a *subjective* interpretative possibility for the accused; the element of *"not intending"* counts. This suggests that the assessment of the scope of duress under the ICC Statute must be

---

93. *See* Perkins and Boyce *supra* note 6, at 1073.

94. *See* Perkins and Boyce, *supra* note 6, at 1072.

95. *See* for these three elements: *Cleveland v. Municipality of Anchorage*, decision of the Alaska Court, 631, P.2d 1073, 1078 (1981).

96. *Ibid.*

conducted with a mixture of both objective and subjective standards and address equally the strongly related defense of necessity.

Given the foregoing in the realm of war crimes charges, it seems that prosecution of these crimes needs to take into account the following possible exonerative guidelines, amounting to the possibility of necessity:

1.  In the event the *"choice of evils"* is the choice between destruction of life and the destruction of property, a decision in favor of life seems morally right, while a decision in favor of property is supposed to be so morally wrong as to call for a rejection of the defense of necessity since ICL, analogous to *U.S. v. Ashton*,[97] *"deems the lives of all persons far more valuable than any property."*[98] It would therefore be a contravention of both ICL and the principles of IHL to accept a defense of necessity in the case of committing an international crime, let alone a war crime, to prevent the loss or destruction of even very valuable property. I emphasize already here that soldiers or subordinates, acting in the course of military peacekeeping or peace enforcement operations, wherein war crimes may be committed, can abstain from these delicts by disobeying military orders and subsequent reliance on the defense of necessity.[99]

2.  The second possible exonerative situation in this context relates to events in which the jurisprudence of the present *ad hoc* War Crimes Tribunals has not included duress, namely in cases of compulsion in any form other than personal violence or the threat thereof.

    In the leading case on duress of the ICTY, *Prosecutor v. Erdemović*,[100] the Trial Chamber ruled that "while the complete defense based on moral duress and/or a state of necessity stemming from superior orders is not ruled out absolutely, its conditions of application are particularly strict."[101] Although therefore the Trial Chamber did not absolutely exclude the defense of duress, it left very little room for this defense, resulting in fact in only a mitigative option. As expressed by the Trial Chamber, "the defense of duress accompanying the superior order will ( . . . ) be taken into account at the same time as other factors in the consideration of mitigating circumstances," this on a case-by-case

---

97.  24 Fed. Cas. 873, No. 14.470 C.C. Mass., 1834.
98.  *See* also Perkins and Boyce, *supra* note 6, at 1069.
99.  *See* further section 2.3 below.
100. Decision Trial Chamber, Case No. IT-96-22-T dd. 29 November 1996.
101. *Ibid.*, Margin No. 19.

approach.[102] The Trial Chamber also distinguished clearly between duress and necessity, the former founded on a strong mental pressure stemming from external circumstances, whereas the latter relates to a choice of evils without being related to this mental pressure.

This means that war crimes, evolving from substantially impelling external, non-violent influences, so severe that a person of reasonable firmness in like circumstances would have been impelled to do what actually was done, fall outside the juridical scope of duress. However, these crimes can in extreme circumstances (e.g. extreme starvation) be met with the defense of necessity, except for the pre-mediated or intentional or reckless killing of the innocent. Like duress and superior orders, no qualification as a justification but merely a link to an excuse remains in this area.

3. The third guideline contains an ambiguous element. It is, for ICL, acceptable, following the legal view envisioned in common law as well in civil law systems that *"the greater the number of loss of life of innocent persons, the greater the harm,"* as well as the view that *"the harm avoided by saving several innocent people is greater than the harm resulting from the death actually caused if, but only if, more innocent were saved than were killed."*[103]

Examination of the question leads to an example connected to war crimes. Suppose a soldier is ordered by his commanding officer to perform a task that will necessarily involve an unlawful application of force, e.g. the torturing of an innocent civilian. Although the soldier is not threatened with death or serious bodily injury, he is told that, if he refuses, he will be court-martialed and fired from military service or degraded in rank. It goes without saying that the latter military interests are of lesser harm than battering or torturing an innocent civilian. Compared to the suffering of the innocent civilian, the illustrated interests of the subordinate are relatively unimportant or can be outweighed. Cases likely to get into Court will, however, mostly not be so clear but more nuanced and somewhere near the middle. In the light of the foregoing, it would appear that a court decision is more difficult in the event the same soldier is ordered to torture an innocent man in order to save the lives of three other innocent civilians—e.g., the three children of the man—who are otherwise being executed by his superior. On the one hand, it can be argued that the soldier, ultimately charged with the perpetration of war crimes before an international or national criminal court, can invoke the defense of necessity, since the three aforementioned conditions seem to be fulfilled. On the

---

102. *Ibid.*, Margin No. 20.
103. *See* for the Common Law: Perkins and Boyce, *supra* note 6, at 1070.

other hand, however, it is tenable that in this example the element of *"inexcusable choice"* excludes the admissibility of the defense of necessity. It has been observed that such a defense is available if what the defendant avoided would have caused a greater harm than was caused by his act, but this would be no defense to an accused who had made the *"inexcusable choice"* regarding the killing of an innocent person. As the above demonstrates, whether a person should actually have had such an *"inexcusable choice"* must be tested *circumstantially* on a *case by case basis*. Moreover, this threshold cannot, in any way, rule out the possibility of relying on the defense of duress, once it is established that this *"inexcusable choice"* was of a coercive or compulsive nature.

### 2.2.3   Conclusion

The controversy as to an objective or subjective approach regarding the legal test of *"reasonableness"*—an important facet of law in assessing this defense—can probably be best solved by the criterion that this defense is available if *"it was reasonable for the defendant to believe that the need to avoid the injury was greater than the need to avoid the injury the (law) seeks to prevent,"* equivalent to the standard that the defense is available if *"a reasonable person would have believed that the harm avoided was greater than the harm caused."*[104] These principles provide a standard that enables war crimes cases to be decided, on an acceptable basis, from an *inductive* law-finding perspective, whereby the determinative factor mainly focuses on the reasonable belief of the defendant at the time of committing the crime and not on an objective and extrinsic assessment *post factum*.

Today, world actuality and the complexity of multinational peace-keeping and peace enforcement operations teach that *"if it were necessary to bring in extrinsic evidence to determine the actual degree of the unrelated harms, the result might be in some case, although human life was in no way involved, that defendant would be convicted for doing what any ordinary person would have done under the circumstances—and that is not acceptable."*[105] To quote Paust, writing about the related topic of superior orders and command responsibility, *"the reasonable person, as in all areas of the law, represents the community or, as one might prefer, community expectations about how a similarly situated person should or should not have acted under the circumstances. In a sense, all criminal conduct is* second guessed (emphasis added) *by the community, or its representatives after the fact."*[106] The law relating to the defense of necessity is actually no different.

---

104.  *See* Perkins and Boyce, *supra* note 6, at 1071.
105.  Perkins and Boyce, *supra* note 6, at 1071.
106.  *See* Jordan J. Paust, *Superior Orders and Command Responsibility*, in I INTERNATIONAL CRIMINAL LAW 237 (M. Cherif Bassiouni, ed., 1999).

### 2.3 The common law approach on the defense of prevention of crime: relationship to self-defense in ICL

#### 2.3.1 Introduction

This section approaches a second legal defense upon the subject of international crimes and war crimes, i.e., the so-called defense of prevention of crime, the significance of whose role in ICL is not yet addressed in the literature. While the system of ICL is developing rapidly and will soon become one of the most consolidated branches of international law,[107] the issue of criminal defense is still controversial in litigation of human rights atrocities or war crimes. As pointed out in the foregoing subsection 2.2, this controversial question becomes much more complicated when it comes to the defense of necessity and to a certain extent also to the defense of "prevention of crime." On the one hand, in the sphere of maintenance of IHL and prevention of human rights atrocities the defense of prevention of crime may be desirable. On the other hand, it may be used to justify abuse of governmental powers, especially when applied by individual soldiers during multinational military operations.

Although juridically one cannot compare the concept of anticipatory self-defense by States with the defense of prevention of crime by individuals, several analogous aspects are visible.

#### 2.3.2 The use of force in the course of preventing crime: exonerative status as to war crimes charges?

Although the common law recognizes the individual privilege or defense of using force to prevent the commission or consummation, not only of a felony, but also of a misdemeanor amounting to a breach of the peace (i.e. public order), such as assault and battery,[108] the common law on this subject is both complex and rather uncertain.[109] As to all such offences, the question is not whether force may be used, but under what circumstances and to what extent. This implies that the use of deadly force for (international) crime prevention is not unlimited; it also demands, like necessity, *"reasonableness."* An appropriate definition of the defense of prevention of crime may be derived from the British Criminal Law Act of 1967, wherein one reads in Section 3 (1): *A person may use such force as is reasonable in the circumstances in the prevention of crime, or in effecting or*

---

107. Malekian, *supra* note 38, at 193.
108. Perkins and Boyce, *supra* note 6, at 1109.
109. Smith and Hogan, *supra* note 8, at 261.

*assisting in the lawful arrest of offenders or suspected offenders or of persons unlawfully at large,"* resulting in a justification that excludes both civil and criminal liability.[110] As to an enumeration of restrictions on the legal scope of this defense, and as to the question of when such use of force is reasonable, no overall and concrete criteria are available. However, ICL can rely in part on the *travaux préparatoires* of the 1967 Criminal Law Act. The Criminal Law Revision Committee, the drafters of this section, explained the test of *"reasonableness"* in this context as follows: *"No doubt if a question on clause (now section) 3 [arose], the court, in considering what was reasonable force, would take into account all the circumstances, including in particular the nature and degree of force used, the seriousness of the evil to be prevented and the possibility of preventing it by other means; but there is no need to specify in the clause the criteria for deciding the question. Since the clause is framed in general terms, it is not limited to arrestable or any other class of offences, though in the case of very trivial offences it would very likely be held that it would not be reasonable to use even the slightest force to prevent them."*[111] It is the position of this writer that like to all other defenses in ICL, reasonableness and good faith must govern the adjudicatory scope. Two indicative aspects emerge from common law doctrine, which are in fact similar to those proposed regarding the necessity defense. It cannot *eo ipso* be reasonable to cause harm, by means of the defense of prevention of crime, unless:

5. It is necessary to do so in order to prevent the crime or effect the arrest, and
2. the evil that would follow from failure to prevent the crime or effect the arrest is so great that a reasonable man might think himself justified in causing that harm to avert that evil.[112]

Scholarly opinions suggest that *"it is likely ( . . . ) that even killing [a person] will be justifiable to prevent unlawful killing or grievous bodily harm ( . . . ) where there is an imminent risk of his causing death or grievous bodily harm if left at liberty."*[113] The element of *"imminent risk of causing death or grievous bodily harm"* confines the criteria for self-defense. This connection is understandable when considering that the privilege of using force in crime prevention was, under the common law of England, one of the major privileges—particularly as to the use of deadly force—whereas self-defense was initially to be conceded as a secondary privilege to give some protection to a person who was too much at fault to be entitled to exer-

---

110. Smith and Hogan, *supra* note 8, at 261.
111. Smith and Hogan, *supra* note 8, at 261–262.
112. *See* Smith and Hogan, *supra* note 8, at 262.
113. Smith and Hogan, *supra* note 8, at 262.

cise the privilege of crime prevention. And the privilege of defending another through self-defense was, until several decades ago, very limited at common law.[114]

The confluence of the defenses of prevention of crime and self-defense raises the question of how to establish the standard of reasonableness concerning prevention of crime, compared to the advocated, more subjective standard related to self-defense. It has been held in a civil action leading to the 1989 Northern Irish case of *Kelly v. Ministry of Defense* that the objectives of the use of force are to be determined, not by the evidence of the subjective view of the user of force, but by the Court on the basis of an objective test.[115] This case involved a soldier, who asserted that his intention in shooting was to arrest the occupants of a car, whom he reasonably believed to be terrorists, and who could probably continue to commit terrorist offences, while getting away, thus invoking the defense of preventing crime. The Northern Irish Court, however, held that the use of force was not reasonable to make an arrest but was yet justified as being reasonable to prevent crime. Although the court applied a strictly objective test, one must bear in mind that this opinion was held in a civil action, which does not automatically embody (international) criminal law. In the latter case, the defendant is only obliged to present a *prima facie* case of prevention of crime or bear a *prima facie* evidential burden of proof. In the sphere of ICL, it is therefore arguable that soldiers of the Dutch battalion supervising on behalf of the UN the Srebrenica Moslem enclave in the former Yugoslavia in 1995 could probably have relied on the defense of prevention of crime had they used even deadly force directed at Serbian people or militias in order to prevent the separation of Moslem men and women people and subsequent killing or genocide.[116]

## 2.4 Conclusion

Although IC has, never clearly articulated the defense of prevention of crime—the Statutes of ICTY, ICTR and ICC are silent hereon—it is obvious that such a defense can be derived from the general principles of the world's national law systems or national laws, as sources of ICL envisioned by Article 21 (1)(c) of the ICC Statute. This is reinforced by the fact that, notwithstanding the absence of this defense in Article 2 of the European Convention on Human Rights (the justifications for taking life), the ECHR indirectly acknowledged its existence as a defense in certain cases.[117] It is

---

114. Perkins and Boyce, *supra* note 6, at 1112.
115. *See Kelly v. Ministry of Defense*, 1989, NI 341.
116. The aspect of UN Mandate is left out of this case example.
117. *See* Application No. 17579/90.

the opinion of this writer that this defense, as illustrated above, can play an important judicial and factual role in the endorsement and protection of human rights and *jus cogens* in ICL and IHL, especially in the practice of multinational peacekeeping and peace enforcement operations.

## 3    THE DEFENSE OF CONSENT TO SEXUAL ASSAULT AND MISTAKE OF FACT

Contrary to the rather general guidelines which are embodied in articles 89–98 of both the *ad hoc* Tribunals' "Rules of Evidence," Rule 96 includes particular sub-rules. Relevant for this section is Art. 96 Section ii, sub rule a of these Rules of Evidence, providing that in cases of sexual assault:

> *"Consent shall not be allowed as a defense if the victim:*
> a.  *Has been subjected to or threatened with or has had reason to fear violence, duress, detention or psychological oppression, or,*
> b.  *reasonably believed that if the victim did not submit, another might be so subjected, threatened or put in fear."*

This formulation seems to exclude an important defense for the accused against a sexual assault, i.e., the defense of consent. It does not, however, absolutely exclude this defense in the event both conditions a) and b) are not fulfilled.[118] Yet it imposes restrictions on the defense of consent by making it more difficult to invoke this defense with success, i.e., only when the accused satisfies the Trial Chamber *in camera* that the evidence of the victim's consent is, according to Art. 96(iii), relevant and credible. The burden of proof as to the presence of either condition (a) or (b) is on the prosecution, whereas the defense can by a preponderance of evidence establish the absence of both their criteria.[119] Although Rule 96 indicates neither who has the burden of showing that the conditions of subparagraphs (ii)(a) and (b) have been met nor the standard of proof required to fulfill these conditions, paragraph (iii) does suggest that, because the defendant has an opportunity to satisfy the Trial Chamber that evidence of consent is relevant and credible, the burden of proof is on the defendant.[120] The evidence must prove, *inter alia*, that the victim was not subjected to, threatened with, or had reason to fear, violence.

---

118.  *See* also Daniel D. Ntanda Nsereko, *Rules of Procedure and Evidence of the International Tribunal for the Former Yugoslavia*, 5 CRIMINAL LAW FORUM 548 (1994).
119.  *See* further Chapter III.
120.  *See* M. CHERIF BASSIOUNI AND PETER MANIKAS, THE LAW OF THE ICTY 953 (1996)

Bassiouni points to an alternative approach, wherein the burden of proof would be shifted to the Prosecutor to establish the conditions contained in subparagraph (ii)(a) and (b) after the defendant has fulfilled the requirement of paragraph (iii).[121]

The defense of consent to sexual assault is related to the defense of mistake of fact, which defense is likewise not excluded by Rule 96. Concerning the defense of mistake of fact, the U.S. Court established under Control Council Law No.10 dd. 20 December 1945 (also known as the "Subsequent Proceedings") ruled in *U.S. v. List* (The Hostages case) of 19 February 1948, *inter alia*: *"( . . . ) The destruction was as complete as an efficient army could do it. Three years after the completion of the operation, the extent of the devastation was discernible to the eye. While the Russians did not follow up the retreat to the extent anticipated, there are physical evidences that they were expected to do so. Gun emplacements, foxholes, and other defense installations are still perceptible in the territory. In other words there are mute evidences that an attack was anticipated. There is evidence in the record that there was no military necessity for this destruction and devastation. An examination of the facts in retrospect can well sustain this conclusion. But we are obliged to judge the situation as it appeared to the defendant at the time. If the facts were such as would justify the action by the exercise of judgment, after giving consideration to all the factors and existing possibilities, even though the conclusion reached may have been faulty, it cannot be said to be criminal. After giving careful consideration to all the evidence on the subject, we are convinced that the defendant cannot be held criminally responsible although when viewed in retrospect, the danger did not actually exist."*

Ignorance or mistake of fact can be a legal excuse for what would otherwise be a crime. This notion can emerge in the case of, *inter alia*, a soldier who shoots a prisoner of war, mistakenly believing him to be in possession of a weapon which turns out to be only a fork. Common law recognizes mistake of fact as an excuse in prosecutions for certain offences, including murder.[122] *Ignorantia facti exusat* as such, however, cannot be accepted unconditionally regarding crimes. Some modification is needed, such as that *"in some cases ignorantia facti doth excuse"* or *"an honest mistake of fact will generally exonerate criminal prosecution."*[123] In the common law, the following definition is proposed for the admissibility of this defense: *"It may be stated as a general rule (subject, however, to exceptions in certain events) that mistake of facts will disprove a criminal charge if the mistaken belief is:*

---

121. *Ibid.*, at 954.
122. *See* Perkins and Boyce, *supra* note 6, at 1044.
123. *See* Perkins and Boyce, *supra* note 6, at 1044–1095.

a.  *honesty entertained;*
b.  *based upon reasonable grounds and;*
c.  *of such a nature that the conduct would have been lawful and proper had the facts been as they were reasonably supposed to be."*[124]

The element *"honest and reasonable belief"* in the terms sub a and sub b of the aforementioned description, suggests two alternative conditions:

1.  that the belief must have been sincere; and
2.  that what was done would have been proper had the facts been as they were mistakenly supposed to be.

These conditions or elements express the same notion, i.e. that the possibility or excuse based upon mistake of fact can never be invoked where there is no honest belief, but merely a dishonest pretense resorted to in order to escape punishment.[125] The aspect of honest and reasonable belief can also be related to the question (to be answered by the Court) whether the circumstances of the case might reasonably have been expected to induce such a belief in an accused of ordinary firmness and intelligence, in which event the defense is admissible.[126] It must be considered, however, that if no specific intent or other special mental element is required for guilt of the offense charged, a mistake of fact will not be recognized as an excuse unless it was based upon reasonable grounds; but even an unreasonable mistake, if entertained in good faith, is inconsistent with guilt if it negates some special element required for guilt of the offence, such as intent or knowledge.[127]

The ultimate question in any international criminal litigation is indeed whether or not all the essential elements of guilt, including specific intent or other special mental elements, are established. Therefore if the defense of mistake of fact, even without the support of reasonable grounds, negates the existence of such a special element, guilt according the charge has not been substantiated. The English House of Lords has applied this concept of mistake of fact to the crime of rape, ruling that a mistaken belief that the woman was consenting would not be unreasonable if genuine, which mistake may exclude the element of *mens rea* required for the crime of rape.[128]

The *Foca* indictment[129] of the ICTY, confirmed on 26 June 1996, charges several persons with crimes against humanity, evolving from the system-

---

124.  *See* Perkins and Boyce, *supra* note 6, at 1045.
125.  *See* also U.S. Supreme Court, *State v. Carrell*, 160 Mo. 368, 371, 60 S.W. 1087, 1088 (1901).
126.  *See* Perkins and Boyce, *supra* note 6, at 1045.
127.  *See* Perkins and Boyce, *supra* note 6, at 1046.
128.  *See* House of Lords, *Regina v. Morgan*, 1976, AC 182.
129.  IT-96-23-I.

atic rape and enslavement of women in the city of Foca after its takeover by Bosnian Serb forces in April 1992, and ruled that acts of forcible sexual penetration of a person or forcing a person to sexually penetrate another, can constitute an element of a crime against humanity.[130]

When rapes are charged as crimes against humanity, the requisite specific intent must be proven, i.e., that the charged rape(s) is (are) not isolated acts, but, instead, represent a course of systematic conduct.[131] The defense of mistake of fact can thus affect this specific element of crimes against humanity. This especially accounts for the judgment of ICTY in the *Nikolić* case, upholding that *"( . . . ) rape and other forms of sexual assault inflicted on women in circumstances such as those described by the witnesses, may fall within the definition of* torture *submitted by the Prosecutor."*[132] Here, the requisite specific intent for torture can be affected by the defense of mistake of fact. Within the scope of the discussed Rule 96 of the Rules of Procedure and Evidence of the ICTY, it can be asserted that the defense of mistake of fact can be of relevance, although in the context of a *"course of conduct"* as to an underlying criterion of crimes against humanity, this defense is difficult to imagine. Nevertheless, the defense of mistake of fact is now incorporated in the present Article 32 (1) of the ICC Statute, formalizing the aforementioned general principle of ICL.[133] This proviso is strongly related to Article 30 (1) of the ICC Statute, requiring the mental element in order to establish individual criminal responsibility. A person who is not aware of a certain situation or a particular material element cannot be attributed with the requisite mental element.[134] The legal consequence of this view can result in the application of Article 32 (1): the accused is excused, but only when the particular mistake of fact *"negates the mental element required by the crime."*

Two consequences of Article 32 should be illuminated:

- When the defense of Article 32 (1) would not lead to exclusion of criminal liability, the Court can nevertheless qualify the alleged mistake of fact as a mitigative circumstance

---

130. *See* Art. 5 (g) of the ICTY Statute.

131. *See* the ICTY Trial Chamber II Decision on defense Motion on the Form of the Indictment, rendered on 14 November 1995 in the *Tadić* case, IT-94-1-T, at para. 11; *See* also Trial Chamber I Decision on the Review of Indictment Pursuant to Rule 62, rendered on 20 October 1994 in the *Nikolić* case, IT-95-2-R 61, para. 33: *"These allegations (rape and sexual assault during the detention of women and girls at Susica Camp) do not seem to relate solely to isolated instances."*

132. *See* JOHN R.W.D. JONES, THE PRACTICE OF THE INTERNATIONAL CRIMINAL TRIBUNALS FOR THE FORMER YUGOSLAVIA AND RWANDA 50 (1998).

133. *See* Otto Triffterer, *Article 32, Margin No. 11*, in COMMENTARY ON THE ROME STATUTE (Otto Triffterer ed., 1999).

134. Triffterer, *supra* note 133, Margin No. 25.

according to Article 78 (1) of the ICC Statute. Even though this possibility is not explicitly mentioned in Article 32, this option is open in all cases dealt with here.[135]

- A second consequence of this proviso involves mistake about facts *underlying a defense*, such as self-defense. In this context, the mental element of crime is not exempted; however, such an error may exclude punishment since the *practical consequence* of such a mistake is *"as if it were a mistake of fact,"* which view equally applies to justifications as well as excuses.[136] Triffterer aptly describes this approach when referring to the justification of self-defense;. in the event the accused believed his act to be justified as self-defense, but was in reality mistaken about one or more facts, the material elements of the particular crime remain intact but the material conditions for a justification of the crime are affected. As Triffterer remarks, *"they thus have been inspired to commit a crime by being mistaken in a comparable way to a person who is in error over the existence of a material element: in both cases suspects perceive the reality incorrectly,"* which leads this author to support Triffterer's conclusion that *"by reasoning based not on legal theory, but on the similarity of the result, they should be treated equally: neither should be punished for intentionally committing the crime."*[137]

This reasoning applies equally to other defenses, such as necessity or duress, when the accused wrongfully assumes the presence of the requisite elements for these defenses. Especially in the context of duress, analogous mistake of fact is realistic; several situations are imaginable in which the accused reasonably presumes the presence of certain facts and therefore the mental pressure on him/her is equally strong as to the situation in which all the requisite elements for duress are fulfilled.

## 4  INTERDISCIPLINARY DEFENSES IN ICL: MENTAL INSANITY AND TOXICOLOGICAL DEFENSES

### 4.1 Comparative criminal law and interdisciplinary relationships

Another category of defenses in ICL based upon comparative criminal law is strongly related to the interdisciplinary nature of criminal law. As already noted by Bassiouni, ICL is *"a blend of several disciplines, parts of*

---

135. Triffterer, *supra* note 133, Margin No. 27.
136. Triffterer, *supra* note 133, Margin Nos. 28 and 14.
137. Triffterer, *supra* note 133, Margin 14.

*which are different in their nature, sources, methods, subjects and contents,"* explaining why *"ICL is a complex discipline which needs to reconcile the inconsistencies of its sources of law within a doctrinal framework reflecting its polyvalent nature."*[138] Substantive ICL nowadays has thus to be receptive to developments in other scientific disciplines. In the context of European Union law, Craig & De Búrca observe a *"gradual move away from a strictly analytical and doctrinal approach to the study of law, and the increasing emphasis on the interdisciplinary nature of its subject matter ( . . . )."*[139] In the realm of International Criminal law, the topic of the so-called "special" defenses in particular suggests this interdisciplinary nature. Although both the Rules of Procedure and Evidence of the International Tribunal for the former Yugoslavia (1994)[140] and the Statute of the International Tribunal for Rwanda (1994)[141] refer to the judicial possibility of invoking *"any special defense, including that of diminished or lack of mental responsibility,"* they fail to circumscribe this domain. A clear interest in sustaining "special" defenses seems to have been the Rome Statute of the International Criminal Court, adopted on July 17th, 1998. Apart from an explicit reference to the absence of criminal responsibility in case of mental diseases or other mental defects,[142] the Rome Statute formalizes also an "intoxication defense"[143] and suggests the option of "other" defenses than those explicitly mentioned in article 31 paragraph 1.[144] This necessarily implies a certain view of possible further developments in this field and broadens the category of defenses which may fall within the limits of the Statute. This provision of the Statute is clearly an attempt to increase the flexibility for the parties, especially the defense, to submit to the Court new aspects of defenses within (of course) the context of the Statute.[145] Indeed, this very characterization of the Statute is essential because it challenges our flexible society and calls upon new developments of not only legal science but also behavioral sciences, psychiatry, psychology, genetic science, and neurobiology, the latter two of which, it may be asserted, modern legal fact finding in criminal law cannot do without. It is this realistic approach that allows us to look into the world of special defenses, such as "mental and genetic defenses."

---

138. M. Cherif Bassiouni, International Criminal Law 11 (1999).

139. Paul Craig & Grainne De Burca, Eu Law, Oxford University Press 3 (1998).

140. *See* Rule 67(A)(ii)(b).

141. *See* Article 14 jo. Rule 67(A)(ii)(b) of the Rules of Procedure and Evidence of the International Tribunal for the former Yugoslavia.

142. *See* Article 31, paragraph 1 sub a, which Article will be considered in subsection 4.2 below.

143. Article 31, paragraph 1, sub b.

144. *See* Article 31 paragraph 3.

145. *See* Article 21 of the Statute.

The field of special defenses can be considered to be a vivid phenomenon, rapidly developing in concurrence with the subject matter of individual responsibility—a keystone principle in the Statutes of international criminal tribunals[146]—so it is therefore indeed not possible to define the exact scope of these defenses. The field of special defenses opens the judicial door for fascinating but elusive phenomenon such as mental diseases or disorders, neurobiological or genetic defenses, and toxicological exceptions.

The purpose of this section is to analyze these three special defenses and the judicial role they can play before international criminal tribunals. I will also examine whether these defenses are reconcilable with the nature of the principles of public international law.

The theme of special defenses has several significant points of relationship with the theme of the Rule of law in international law, and also ensures a certain moral dimension in international law. According to Bonnie, *"the insanity defense, in short, is essential to the moral integrity of the criminal law."*[147] Endorsing a standard of morality in international criminal law is certainly one of the purposes of the fair trial and guarantees the statute and rule of procedure and evidence of the ICTY. In the *Tadić* case, the ICTY was clear about this.[148] There are many examples of new rules of public international law emerging from customary rules. According to this view, scientific (new) developments and opinions can count as evidence of State practice for the purpose of assessing the generality of State practice.[149] The Statute of the International Court of Justice refers to "International custom, as evidence of a general practice accepted as *law."*[150] Does this exclude non-legal norms or opinions? In general the International Court appears to be willing to assume the existence of an *opinio juris* not only on the basis of evidence of a general practice or previous decisions of the Court itself or other international tribunals, but also on a certain consensus in the literature. The latter source ensures the possibility of determining special "customary law" defenses, reflecting consensus in a particular field of science, such as neurobiology or psychiatry. Another argument for this analogy can be derived from the jurisprudence of the International Court of Justice on the formation of public interna-

---

146. *See* Article 7 sub 1 of the Statute of the International Tribunal for the former Yugoslavia and Article 6 sub 1 of the Statute of the International Tribunal for Rwanda.

147. Richard J. Bonnie, *The Moral Basis of the Insanity Defense*, in LAW AND PSYCHOLOGY 283 (Martin Lyon Levine, ed., 1995).

148. *See* Appeals Chamber Decision of the ICTY dated 2 October 1995, para. 46, referring to Art. 1.3 section 1 of this Statute.

149. *See* for the formation of General International Law: I. Brownlie, *supra* note 43, at 18–23.

150. Art. 38 sub 1. b.

tional law based upon general principles of law. Such principles often play a significant role as part of the legal reasoning in decisions of international tribunals.[151] International tribunals have accepted and applied their legal reasoning judicial concepts based upon principles of good faith and equity.[152] This principle of good faith and equity implies the recognition of legal provisions as special defenses, amounting to the "moral integrity" of public international law. Although the literature of public international law has not provided much elaboration of this theme, it complies in my opinion nevertheless with the judicial reasoning of the International Court of Justice which has appeared thus far.

As further introduction, it is appropriate to look first at the present influential neurobiological scientific opinions with respect to criminal behavior. This view is inevitable because of the principle that criminal law rests on the assumption that defendants had the capacity for moral choice and nevertheless chose to do wrong; the centrality of the choice between good and evil, bringing blessings or punishment, is not only the base of the insanity defense (i.e. the defendant was insane at the time of the crime and therefore bears no criminal liability), but also a vision dating back to *Deuteronomy* 11 and 27–28. In this reasoning, international criminal law rests upon the defendant's capacity for moral choice and is validated by acquitting those few individuals who, because of their mental illness, do not have that capacity. This justifies a cross-view that is legitimate since certain defendants appearing before international tribunals lack the moral and intellectual equipment of ordinary people, while others, whose capacity for moral choice among alternatives is severely limited for reasons quite different from mental illness, are therefore not generally accorded the insanity defense.[153] Moreover, the genetic and social-emotional (heritable) "baggage" we carry with us from our childhood, conditioning our perceptions of current realities and human relationships, often impinges on our legally relevant behavior. Legal scholars have much to learn from current neurobiological research on the functioning of the human mind in relation to criminal behavior, and its possible contribution to judicial reasoning in international criminal law. By calling attention to this perception, the possible contribution to public international law is not in suggesting how international tribunals should deal with medically abnormal defendants, but in protecting and developing the above-mentioned principle of good faith and equity in international proceedings, judging each defendant and each case on its own merits.

---

151. *See* I. Brownlie, *supra* note 43, at 23 referring to the decision of the ICJ in the *Barcelona Traction, light and Power Company, Limited* case.

152. Brownlie, *supra* note 43, at 25.

153. Martin Lyon Levine, *Introduction*, in LAW AND PSYCHOLOGY XVIII (Martin Lyon Levine, ed., 1995).

A long-standing view held by many criminologists is that, while biological processes may play a minor role in predisposing to crime in a small, disturbed subgroup of offenders, social and political factors are the primary determinants of crime; a perspective which in the last decade has been challenged by neurobiological experts, especially in the genetic field, regarding developments with respect to predisposition to crime.[154] This section introduces the question, both critical and undeveloped, of whether human rights standards and principles of procedural fairness in international criminal law[155] should take the present neuroscientific view of genetic and neurobiological predisposition on crimes into account, a view which can perhaps also enhance the domain of international (war) crimes adjudicated by international tribunals.

Due to the complexity of the issues discussed here, it is worth analyzing the common ground between the litigation of violations of international humanitarian law and the role of genetic predisposition to these crimes as exculpatory elements. This not only facilitates analysis of the international legal practice of the scope of defenses, but also opens the issue of the neurobiological factor in crimes. Following a general discussion of the insanity defense, I will assess the possibility of raising toxicological defenses to international litigation, since explicit reference is made hereto in the Statute of the ICC and indirect basis for this particular defense can be found in rule 67 section a (IV) of the Rules of Procedure of Evidence and the ICTY.

## 4.2 Mental insanity and international crimes

An accused person's sanity may become relevant at two stages before criminal trial on indictment before the ICTY as well as the ICC. First, in the phase of the preliminary proceedings, it is inaccurate to speak of a "defense," since the effect of a finding of insanity of the appropriate kind is to prevent the accused from being tried before an international criminal Tribunal at all. Secondly, a person's sanity may be invoked during the stage of the trial itself before the ICTY, ICTR and ICC. This paragraph will focus only on the trial stage of international criminal litigation.

In this stage, it has to be presupposed that the accused is found fit to plead or, if that issue is not raised, the defendant may raise the defense of

---

154. *See* also Adrian Raine, Peter Brennan, B. Mednick & S.A. Mednick, *High rates of violence, crime, academic problems and behavioral problems in males with both early neuromotor deficits and unstable family environment*, 53 ARCHIVES OF GENERAL PSYCHIATRY 544–549 (1996).

155. *See* Gerry J. Simpson, *War Crimes: A Critical Introduction*, in THE LAW OF WAR CRIMES 13 (T.C.H. McCormack & G.J. Simpson, eds., 1997).

insanity at the trial stage itself. It is important to notice that, whereas at the preliminary stage of criminal proceedings ICL is concerned with the accused's' sanity *at the time of the inquiry*, during the trial stage ICL focuses on the accused's sanity *at the time when he did the act*.[156] The fact that the defendant was insane in the medical sense of the word is *eo ipso* not sufficient to grant the defense of insanity to international crimes.

Article 31 (1)(a) of the ICC Statute, contrary to the ICTY and ICTR Statutes, mentions explicitly, as observed, the special defense of mental diseases or other mental defects, but fails to define these notions. It is therefore worth linking to the domestic interpretation of this defense in common law. Common law exhibits a legal criterion of responsibility, set out in the authoritative so-called *M'Naghten Rules* formulated by common law judges in 1843. These Rules are derived from the criminal case against defendant Daniel M'Naghten, who intended to murder Sir Robert Peel, and killed the statesman's secretary by mistake. His acquittal of murder on the basis of insanity provoked controversy and was heavily debated in the House of Lords, which sought the advice of the judges and submitted to them a number of questions. The answers to those questions emerged with these famous Rules. In fact, these Rules envision *hypothetical questions*. The issue was whether such Rules did contravene the nature of criminal law. In the *Sullivan* case of 1984 it was however accepted by the House of Lords that these Rules contained a *comprehensive definition* of insanity.[157]

For ICL and for war crimes trials, these Rules form the provenance of the legal test of responsibility of the mentally abnormal, and also ensure a limit to the defenses of automatism. The main achievement of these Rules remains, however, the endorsement of a basic proposition of the law on insanity, to be found in the answers to questions 2 and 3: "( . . . ) *the jurors ought to be told in all cases that every man is presumed to be sane, and to possess a sufficient degree of reason to be responsible for his crimes, until the contrary be proved to their satisfaction; and that to establish a defense on the ground of insanity, it must be clearly proved that, at the time of the committing of the act, the party accused was laboring under such a defect of reason, from disease of the mind, as not to know the nature and quality of the act he was doing, or if he did know it, that he did not know he was doing what was wrong*."[158]

Because of the absence of a clear definition in ICL, this description of insanity has also significant value with regard to the interpretation of the defense to war crimes, pursuant to Article 31 (1)(a) of the ICC. In fact, in this area two lines of defense are available to an accused person faced with a war crimes indictment:

---

156. *See* Smith and Hogan *supra* note 8, at 201.

157. 1984, AC 156, (1983) 2 ALL ER 673; *See* also Smith and Hogan *supra* note 8, at 201.

158. Smith and Hogan *supra* note 8, at 202.

1. The possibility of acquittal in the event the defendant, due to a disease of the mind, did not know the nature and quality of his criminal act; or

2. the possibility of an acquittal in the event the defendant was aware of this nature and quality, but, because of a disease of the mind, he did not know it was a crime.

It must be emphasized that the question whether the defendant has raised a valid defense of insanity is *one of law for the judge*, equally with regard to international crimes. As to introducing medical witnesses in this field, the medical interpretation of "insanity" is therefore not conclusive for the judgment of this subsequent defense. The expert witnesses may thus testify as to the factual nature of the mental condition of the defendant, but it is, however, ultimately an assessment of the International Criminal Court as to whether this can judicially lead to the admissibility of the insanity defense. Adjudication upon the defense pursuant to Article 31 (1)(a) remains a strictly legal, not medical, concept.[159]

As to its merits, the exclusionary norm of Article 31 (1)(a) contains two basic conditions: (a) a defective mental state (b) in which the capacity to either appreciate the unlawfulness or to control the conduct is destroyed.[160]

Ad a: As observed by Eser, this requirement is narrow in one respect, and rather broad in another. In the restrictive perspective, this provision limits its scope to *mental defects*, thus excluding "psychic disturbances" as long as they do not affect the cognitive or intellectual capacity of the person concerned; in this respect the Statute certainly trails national laws which would also take psychic affections or deep emotional disturbances in consideration.[161] This limitation does not evade the possibility of relying on Article 31(3). In the extended perspective, the provision does not limit its scope *"to a specific mental 'disease,' but rather recognizing any 'defect' that destroys the person's relevant capacity."*[162] It is important to note that Article 31(1) (a) uses the term *"suffers,"* which implies more than a temporary or momentary mental defect, but on the contrary amounts to a disturbance of some duration.

Ad b: the second condition seems to relate to the strict wording of this provision, referring to wording *"that destroys that person's capacity ( . . . )."* This seems to imply that the doctrine of diminished mental insanity or diminished responsibility does not apply under the Statute of the ICC.[163] This doctrine forms an established concept of defense under common law,

---

159. Smith and Hogan, *supra* note 8, at 203.
160. *See* A. Eser, *supra* note 48, Margin No. 20.
161. A. Eser, *supra* note 48, Margin No. 21.
162. *Ibid.*
163. A. Eser, *supra* note 48, Margin No 22.

which entitles the accused—in case of, for example, murder—not to be acquitted altogether, but to be found guilty only of manslaughter.[164] Although in theory this concerns not a general defense, but forms a defense which only applies to murder, in practice defendants can rely on the defense also outside murder cases.[165] Either by way of reference to Article 31 (3) or through application of Article 78 (1) of this Statute, the ICC can however allow this special defense of diminished mental insanity, or take this aspect into account in determining the sentence.

The requisite instruction of this provision can relate to either the cognitive appreciation of the unlawfulness or nature of the conduct or the volitional control if the conduct is destroyed. A clear distinction has to be made hereto with the situation of a person's ability or awareness of acting. In the latter situation it is questionable if the requisite mental element enshrined by Article 32 (1) of the Statute exists at all, whereas in the former situation, Article 31 (1)(a) can be applied.

As to the boundaries of this legal defense in ICL, the future has to survey carefully in order to demarcate its exact scope with regard to war crimes indictments. It is interesting to note that, according to the M'Naghten Rules, an extension of the defense of insanity (in principle only applicable in case of internal factors) can also, under certain circumstances and due to external causes, be accepted. However, the distinction between external and internal factors seems artificial, since an internal factor can be a consequence of an external factor, such as a blow on the head, an injection, or the inhalation of toxic fumes. A blow on the head can, *inter alia*, inflict brain damage and cause a subsequent internal factor, which may give rise to the defense of insanity.[166] This concept of insanity cannot be excluded from the arena of international criminal tribunals. Suppose that, for example, a subordinate of a belligerent party or army is hit by a military vehicle or shot in the head and severely wounded, eventually causing brain damage. After re-entering his unit of force, this subordinate commits a war crime and, standing trial before the ICTY on the basis of a war crimes indictment, invokes the defense of insanity, which defense is covered by Rule 67 (a)(ii)(b) of the Rules of Procedure and Evidence of the ICTY and ICTR. Under special circumstances this defense cannot *eo ipso* be denied, its existence within ICL being not incompatible, in the absolutist sense, with principles of legality.[167]

---

164. *See* Smith and Hogan, *supra* note 8, at 216.
165. *Ibid.*
166. *See, e.g., Bratty v. A-G for Northern Ireland* (1963), AC 386, (1961) 3 ALL ER, 523; *see also* Smith and Hogan, *supra* note 8, at 206.
167. *See* Chapter III.

## 4.3 Neurotoxicology and toxicological defenses as new collateral sources and content of ICL

### 4.3.1 Introduction: a neurotoxicological framework

As already noted in Chapter I, international criminal law (ICL) is a relatively new discipline that consists of the penal and procedural aspects of international law and the international procedural aspects of national criminal law.[168] Aside from ICL's principal sources of law as enunciated in Article 38 of the International Court of Justice's Statute,[169] additional collateral sources of ICL exist, namely, *inter alia*, "( . . . ) *emerging international criminological perspectives.*"[170] As Bassiouni clearly observes: "ICL is ( . . . ) a *blend of several disciplines, parts of which are different in their nature, sources, methods, subjects and contents,*" assessing that this is "*why ICL is a complex discipline which needs to reconcile the inconsistencies of its sources of law within the doctrinal framework reflecting its polyvalent nature.*"[171] Moreover, since the post-World War II War Tribunal cases, ICL has continually expanded its scope and content. In the course of these two developments new scientific disciplines, supportive to developing ICL's sources, are postulated. In the interaction between actual sources of ICL and national criminal law, from the latter system newly emerging scientific visions on individual criminal responsibility need to be considered. ICL is indeed "( . . . ) *more than the sum total of several legal disciplines' parts, but a new and complex discipline.*"[172] Since the collateral sources of ICL also enhance the emerging international criminological and penological considerations, a discourse on not only genetic but also toxicological assessments of requisite mental states forms a prerequisite condition to the authority of ICL, i.e., its imposition of individual criminal responsibility.

Moreover, ICL has clearly accepted the general principles of law recognized by the world's major criminal law systems as a second additional collateral source of ICL.[173] This view is now enshrined also in Article 31 (3) in conjunction with Article 21 of the ICC Statute. From these general principles, norms have evolved also for constituting individual criminal

---

168. *See* M. CHERIF BASSIOUNI, I INTERNATIONAL CRIMINAL LAW 8 (1999).

169. Only the first three of those sources, conventions, customs and general principles apply to ICL; the fourth source *"the writing of the most distinguished publicists,"* cannot be deemed a source of ICL because it would violate the principle of legality, recognized by most domestic legal systems; *See* M. Cherif Bassiouni, *supra* note 168, at 4.

170. M. Cherif Bassiouni, *supra* note 168, at 10.

171. M. Cherif Bassiouni, *supra* note 168, at 11.

172. M. Cherif Bassiouni, *supra* note 168, at 13.

173. M. Cherif Bassiouni, *supra* note 168, at 14 and 16.

responsibility. Especially in the field of the general part of the law, enhancing *inter alia* the prescriptions of requisite mental states and defenses to crimes, national criminal laws (possessing already a developed general part of the law on e.g. defenses) can mediate as an important source of the general part of ICL.[174] With respect to the judicial assessments of requisite mental state and legal defenses, national criminal systems evaluate toxicological influences on the basis of developing and sometimes evolutionary scientific views.

### 4.3.2   Neurotoxicological interrelationships with ICL

Although the current system of ICL does not envision any general provision or section on the constituent elements of international criminal responsibility of individuals, as part of customary ICL—and on this plane today—the concept is accepted that *"the will of the individual in the commission of certain State conduct related, GJK) international crimes was not monopolized by medical drugs."*[175] The Rome Statute of the International Criminal Court[176] expresses this view clearly in Article 31 section 1(b), although Eser observes that this provision involves *"a world-wide highly controversial ground for excluding criminal responsibility."*[177] This provision asserts that the accused shall not be criminally responsible if, at the time of that person's conduct, this person *"( . . . ) is in a state of intoxication that destroys that person's capacity to appreciate the unlawfulness or nature of his or her conduct or capacity to control his or her conduct to conform to the requirements of law ( . . . )."* Like Article 31 section 1 (c), this provision is derived from the *mens rea* doctrine of the Common Law; i.e. the concept that there is no crime without a mind at fault. This concept is one of the great contributions of the common law to criminal law.[178]

In the analysis of Eser, this provision can be separated into two positive elements by requiring (a) a certain state of intoxication (b) by which the person's capacity of appreciation and control is destroyed. Furthermore, this provision entails also a negative element by (c) excluding exculpation if the person was mentally intoxicated.

Ad a: the drafters of this provision obviously chose explicitly not to limit the requisite *"state of intoxication"* to certain substances or causes, like alcohol or drugs, as sources of intoxication. The nature of intoxication, however, involves *"a state of toxic impact,"* so that *"it would not suffice that*

---

174. *See* M. Cherif Bassiouni, *supra* note 168, at 16.
175. F. Malekian, *supra* note 38, at 162.
176. Rome Statute of the International Criminal Court dd. 17 July 1998.
177. A. Eser, *supra* note 48, Margin No. 24, especially note 35.
178. *See* R.M. Perkins and R.N. Boyce, *supra* note 6, at 828.

*the person acted in a state of excitement or acceleration as may follow from endo-
genic causes of external circumstances, though in its effect comparable to drunkenness or drug consumption.*"[179] Therefore the intoxication envisioned by
this provision must be related to *"consumption of an exogenic substance with
the effect of intoxication."*

Ad b: Similar to the defense of Article 31 (1)(a), the defense of intoxication is not admissible in case the person's capacity based upon intoxication is merely diminished. Article 31 (1)(b) explicitly mentions the
element of *destruction* of a person's capacity to appreciate the unlawfulness or nature of his or her conduct.[180]

Ad c: Intoxication is not, and never has been, a defense in itself. If the
defendant had the *mens rea* for the crime charged, he can be convicted,
even though drink impaired or negated his ability to judge between right
and wrong or to resist temptation or provocation, and even though, in
his drunken state, he found the impulse to act as he did irresistible. In
this connection it is not decisive whether the accused was intoxicated voluntarily or involuntarily.[181] Under the Rome Statute the defense of intoxication can apply, however, in the event of involuntarily intoxication,
where Article 31 section 1 (b) refers explicitly to this defense *"unless the
person has become voluntarily intoxicated under such circumstances that the
person knew, or disregarded the risk, that as a result of the intoxication, he or
she was likely to engage in conduct constituting a crime within the jurisdiction
of the Court."*

The intent of the drafters of the ICC, by excluding exculpation of the
defendant in case of voluntarily intoxication, is to prevent *a mala fide* fab-
ricated state of incapacity. As observed by Eser, *"instead of denying any voluntary intoxication and exculpation, however, the Statute follows the principle
of actio libera in causa by presupposing that the person was aware of the risk
and likelihood of getting involved in criminal conduct at the point of becoming
intoxicated."*[182] The consequences of this negative element are, according
to Eser, that the defense of intoxication is only excluded in case (a) the
accused intentionally became drunk or otherwise intoxicated and (b)
knowingly or recklessly took the risk that, due to the intoxication, he
would commit or otherwise would be involved in a crime.

As a result of involuntary intoxication, the accused lacks the *mens rea*
of the particular crime, and a conviction is not justified. The ultimate test
of this is thus whether *mens rea* can be proven in regard to the defendant.
Two situations emerge:

---

179. A. Eser, *supra* note 48, Margin No. 25.
180. A. Eser, *supra* note 48, Margin No. 26.
181. *See* J. Smith and B. Hogan, *supra* note 8, at 225.
182. A. Eser, *supra* note 48, Margin No. 27.

1. In the event of *voluntary* intoxication—as intoxication almost always is—the defense of intoxication can only apply when both:
   a. the element of *mens rea* is affected (e.g., because of a drunken mistake of fact); and
   b. the accused raises the defense that the intoxication was involuntary or not self-induced by means of preponderance of evidence (an evidential burden), in which event the onus of proof for the contrary will be on the prosecution.[183]

   Under the ICC Statute, voluntary intoxication as a defense is admissible in the event the accused *"was not aware of the risk that he could engage in criminal conduct as a ramification of the intoxication."*[184] According to Eser, even if the person was aware of such likelihood, the defense of intoxication is only excluded if the alleged crime falls within the jurisdiction of the court. Article 31 (1)(b) entails namely at the end the words *"( . . . ) in conduct constituting a crime within the jurisdiction of the court."* These last words are not without meaning, but aptly emphasized by Eser as follows: *"this means that even in a case in which a soldier is aware that, due to his drunkenness, he might commit a murder, he could hardly be barred from invoking intoxication as a defense as long as he was not aware of the genocidal or anti-humanitarian character of the murder in terms of Article 6 or 7 of this Statute."*[185]

2. Where as a result of involuntary intoxication the necessary *mens rea* cannot be proven, a conviction is excluded. This can occur when it is established that the accused was unaware that he was taking an intoxicant, and in the special situation where a person becomes intoxicated through taking drugs in accordance with a medical prescription.[186] Involuntary intoxication does not occur merely because of underestimating the consumed amount of alcohol or the affect.

In the leading common law case of *Beard*, it was held that intoxication was a defense only if it rendered the accused incapable of forming the *mens rea*.[187] Proof of incapacity is of course conclusive that *mens rea* was not present; but it is now established in common law that it is not necessary to go so far. Smith & Hogan illustrate this notion by referring to the

---

183. *See* e.g.: Bailey, 1983, All ER 503, at 507.
184. *Ibid.*
185. Eser, *supra* note 48, Margin No. 27.
186. Smith and Hogan, *supra* note 8, at 225.
187. (1920) AC 479, at 501–502.

possibility of raising the defense of intoxication of a sober man, though he was perfectly capable of forming the intent required; but not, however, on the occasion in question.[188] Equally, as these authors argue, a drunken man may be capable, notwithstanding his drunkenness, of forming the intent to kill and yet not do so. With regard to litigation of international crimes the main question hereto is therefore, if, taking the intoxicated state of the defendant into account, he or she did in fact form the necessary intent. The onus of proof is clearly on the prosecution to establish that, notwithstanding the alleged intoxication, the accused formed the requisite intent. In the common law system, evidence of intoxication negating *mens rea* forms a defense in the following situations:

1. In crimes requiring a "specific intent," whether the drink or drug was taken voluntarily or involuntarily. In this respect the system deviates from the draft article 31 section 1(b) of the Rome Statute of the ICC, which envisions the exclusion of this defense in principle in cases of voluntarily intoxication. "Specific intent" is *inter alia* required in regard to the Article 6 (genocide), Article 7 (crimes against humanity) and Article 8 (war crimes) section 2 (a, b and e).
2. In all crimes, where the drink or drug was taken involuntarily. If the accused is presented lemonade which is laced with vodka, and he is *unaware* that he has consumed any alcohol, he can rely on evidence of his drunken condition. Similarly, perhaps, where he has taken drink *under duress* for example when someone is forced to drink alcohol.
3. In all crimes, where the drink or drug is taken voluntarily but in *bona fide* pursuance of medical treatment or prescription. For example, a defendant could rely on evidence that he had taken insulin, though voluntarily, and it was recognized that an anesthetic would have a similar effect. This is likely to be rarely applicable to alcohol but it might apply where, for example, brandy is administered to the defendant after an accident or injury.

It should be noted that the above-mentioned three principles do not apply when a crime (not requiring a specific intent) was involved, whereby the drink or drug was taken voluntarily. This rule is explicitly endorsed by the House of Lords in the case of *Director of Public Prosecutions v. Majewski*.[189] Thus, in case of a crime, not requiring specific intent, the accused may in principle be convicted if he was voluntarily

---

188. Smith and Hogan, *supra* note 8, at 227.
189. (1977) AC443, 2 ALL ER 142, 1976.

intoxicated at the time of committing the offence, though he did not have the *mens rea* required in all other circumstances for that offence and even though he was in a state of automatism at the time of doing the act.[190] It is therefore in that event immaterial that the accused lacked *mens rea* of the particular crime and even that he was unconscious. A further implication of these principles contains the rule that, where the accused relies on voluntary intoxication as a defense to a charge of an international crime, not requiring specific intent, the prosecution is not obliged to prove any intent or foresight, whatever the definition of the international crime may say, nor indeed any voluntary act.[191]

Although in principle *mens rea* must be proven, there seems to be an exception wherein the accused was intoxicated through voluntary taking of drink or drugs and no specific intent underlies the particular international crime. The nature of *specific intent* is thus a matter of great importance. A careful analysis of the common law decisions in this area suggest, however, that no consistent principle can be revealed. The only clear conclusion seems to be that *crime requiring specific intent* means a crime where evidence of voluntary intoxication negating *mens rea* is a defense.[192] In order to establish the classification of an international crime for this purpose, the conventions or statutes of international courts must tell us if the crimes, envisioned in these instruments require a specific intent. International criminal law nowadays enhances the following crimes requiring specific intent: genocide, crimes against humanity (e.g., enslavement, torture, forced pregnancy, persecution, the crime of apartheid), and certain war crimes such as intentionally directing attacks against a civilian population or civilian objects.[193] The conclusion emerges that almost all of the main international crimes require a form of specific intent. The Genocide Convention, *inter alia*, protects three groups, i.e. national, ethnic and religious. It also specifies that there must be a specific *"intent to destroy (the protected group) in whole or in part."*[194]

For this purpose it is clear that emphasizing the distinction between offences of either specific or basic intent has repercussions on not only the admissibility of both neurobiological and neurotoxicological defenses, but also on the topic of the burden of proof. When the accused is charged with an international crime not requiring specific intent, and claims that he did not have *mens rea* to support his defense with evidence that he had taken drink and drugs, the prosecution is in fact relieved from the burden of

---

190. Smith and Hogan *supra* note 8, at 228.
191. *See* also Decision House of Lords in *Lipman*, 3 ALL ER 410, 1969.
192. Smith and Hogan, *supra* note 8, at 229.
193. *See* for these international crimes, requiring a specific intent: the definitions of these crimes set out in article 6, 7 and 8 of the Rome Statute of the ICC.
194. For the topic of specific intent and *mens rea, see* further Chapter I, *supra*.

proof, which until that moment lay upon it, of proving beyond reasonable doubt that the accused had *mens rea*.

### 4.3.3   Intoxication otherwise than by alcohol or dangerous drugs

From common law jurisprudence some case law emerges regarding intoxication other than by alcohol or dangerous drugs. In the decision of the House of Appeals in the *Bailey* case, a diabetic failed to take sufficient food after having taken insulin,[195] whereby the accused caused grievous bodily harm and the defense contained the assertion that because of this intoxication, the accused was in a state of automatism. It is notable that the Court of Appeals held *"self-induced automatism, other than that due to intoxication from alcohol or drugs, may provide a defense to crimes of basic intent."* Although the alleged automatism seems to have been interpreted by the Court as arising from the failure to take food, rather than from the taking of the insulin, the Court drew a distinction between two types of drug, ruling that *"it is common knowledge that those who take alcohol to excess or certain sorts of drugs may become aggressive or do dangerous or unpredictable things ( . . . ) but the same cannot be said, without more, of a man who fails to take food after an insulin injection."* This distinction is also endorsed in the *Hardy* decision of the Court of Appeals of the United Kingdom, where the judge was confronted with the accused who had taken valium, a sedative drug to calm his nerves, the defense of intoxication was raised, precluding—as it was asserted—the *mens rea*. The Court of Appeals decided that concerning this kind of intoxication the *Majewski*-rule was not applicable, because valium *"is wholly different in kind from drugs which are liable to cause unpredictability or aggressiveness, ( . . . ) if the effect of a drug is merely soporific or sedative, the taking of it, even in excessive quantity, cannot in the ordinary way raise a conclusive presumption against the admission of proof of intoxication for the purpose of disproving* mens rea *in ordinary crimes, such as would be the case with alcohol intoxication or incapacity or automatism resulting from the self-administration of dangerous drugs."*[196]

The conclusion may be drawn that in cases where intoxication is self-induced other than by alcohol or dangerous drugs, the test of liability to apply, analogous to the common law doctrine, is to be one of recklessness, i.e. when the accused *"appreciate the risk that failure to take food (or other than* eo ipso *dangerous drugs) may lead to aggressive, unpredictable and uncontrollable conduct and he nevertheless deliberately runs the risk or otherwise disregards it, this will amount to recklessness,"*[197] and therefore an inadmissibility

---

195. *Bailey* case, 1983, 2 ALL ER 503.

196. *See* Court of Appeal, 1984, 3 ALL ER 848 (1985), at 853.

197. This criterion is deduced from the Court of Appeal decision in the *Bailey* case, *supra* note 57.

of the defense of intoxication. It is obvious that the prosecution bears the onus of proving this kind of recklessness.[198]

### 4.3.4   Intoxication causing mental insanity

The previous section provokes the question whether a defense exists to international crimes in the event that excessive drinking would cause actual insanity, such as delirium tremens, and in so far as Article 31 (1) (A) of the ICC Statute can be applicable, i.e. regarding the defense of mental defects or diseases or abnormality of mind. This view does seem to corroborate the doctrine hereto in common law, where it is advocated that the M'Naghten Rules can be applied in exactly the same way as where insanity rises from any other causes.[199] In the aforementioned ruling of the House of Lords in the *Beard* case of 1920, it was held that "( . . . ) *drunkenness is one thing and the diseases to which drunkenness leads are different things; and if a man by drunkenness brings on a state of disease which causes such a degree of madness, even for a time, which would have relieved him from responsibility if it had been caused in any other way, then he would not be criminally responsible.*"[200] It has to be kept in mind however, that a distinction exists between temporary insanity induced by drinking and simple drunkenness. Only in the former event is an insanity defense tenable, contrary to the latter case. Excessive drinking itself cannot legitimate any crime, let alone a war crime. In the realm of the prosecution of war crimes, resort to the defense of self-induced intoxication must be considered unacceptable, unless the defendant by means of *prima facie* evidence establishes[201] that the craving for drink or drugs is in itself an abnormality of mind.[202] In this sphere, the notion that drinking can inflict a toxic effect on the brain deserves due diligence. It is thus tenable that such effect constitutes a mental defect or disease, envisaged by Article 31 (1)(A) of the ICC Statute, especially when this results in a more or less permanent situation.

In sum, the issue of intoxication by alcohol or drugs in conjunction with the doctrine of (temporary) mental insanity provokes a serious question of legal defenses to international crimes. The tentatively drawn conclusion is that such a situation can *eo ipso* not be excluded from the legal defenses scope of the field of ICL, as qualified under Article 31 (1)(A) of the ICC Statute.

---

198.  Smith and Hogan, *supra* note 8, at 234.
199.  Smith and Hogan, *supra* note 8, at 234.
200.  *See Director of Public Prosecutions v. Beard*, 1920, AC 479, at 501.
201.  *See* for this aspect Chapter VII, *infra*.
202.  *See* also for common law: Smith and Hogan, *supra* note 8, at 235.

### 4.3.5    Intoxication induced with the intention of committing crime

The latter question raises another important legal defense issue regarding war crimes. Suppose the defendant, an officer or subordinate in the course of a military operation or a defendant otherwise, intends to commit a crime—to be qualified as an international crime or even war crime—and takes drink or drugs in order to give himself *"Dutch courage"* to carry out such a crime. Can this defendant, according to ICL, resort to a legal defense to subsequent war crimes indictments such as the exoneration of induced insanity according the M'Naghten Rules, or the assertion that the state of drunkenness in question negates a *"specific intent"* condition? In the common law, an interesting precedent hereof is available, leading to the decision of the Court of Criminal Appeal of Northern Ireland in the case of *Northern Ireland v. Gallagher* in 1963. Here a defendant, having decided to kill his wife, bought a knife and a bottle of whiskey, drank an excessive amount of this whiskey in order to kill his wife with the knife, which eventually he did. After being convicted in the first instance with rejection of his defense plea of insanity or absence of requisite *mens rea* at the time of the crime, the Northern Irish Court of Appeal reversed this conviction for murder, based on the ground that the lower Court had misdirected the jury by instructing them to apply the M'Naghten Rules to the defendant's state of mind only at the time before taking the alcohol and unjustly not to extend these rules to the time of committing the act itself.[203]

The factor referred to by the Court entails in fact a variation of the M'Naghten Rules, which definitely fix the crucial time as the time of committing the act. An opposite view arguing that the mere wickedness of the defendant's mind before he got drunk suffice as to a conviction for murder, implies an intention to act some time in the future, which view does not comply with the requisite *mens rea*. In principle, the *mens rea* must coincide namely with the conduct itself, which causes the *actus reus*.[204] Conversely, when the Court would follow the reasoning that the defendant is to be held liable for inducing in himself a state of irresponsibility with the intention to kill his wife while he was in that state, a conviction would not be incompatible with the wording of the M'Naghten Rules, nor with the criterion applied in civil law systems of the *culpa in causa*.[205]

In conclusion, the assessment of legal defenses based on the phenomenon of self-induced intoxication with premeditated intention of committing a crime requires cautious adjudicatory law-making, whereby the

---

203. Northern Ireland Court of Appeal, 1963, AC 349, 3 ALL ER 299.

204. Smith and Hogan, *supra* note 8, at 236.

205. *See* for this principle regarding duress and alcohol: GERARDUS G.J. KNOOPS, PSYCHISCHE OVERMACHT EN RECHTSVINDING 148–156 (1998).

decisive principle, according to my view, has to be that of *reasonableness and good faith on a case-by-case law-making basis,* equal to the assessment of the defense of duress and superior orders to war crimes, described in Chapter II above.

### 4.3.6 Summary: individual assessment of neurotoxicological defenses to international crimes

The appearance of Article 31 (1)(b) of the ICC Statute in the sphere of ICL has, in conjunction with present views on toxicological defenses, mainly support in common law precedents. It is clear that this special defense has to be stabilized and thoroughly implemented in the ICL system in order to develop this provision as a clear and sophisticated legal defense, equal to *inter alia* the defense of self-defense. It is clear to me that a highly selective and nuanced application of this relatively new defense is appropriate, encouraged by adherence to a strict casuistic and inductive law-finding approach. Although with regard to war crimes the result of penalty-free delinquents due to toxicological defenses forms a strong factor of interference, the applicability of these defenses in the era of international crimes, as such, is not incompatible with principles of ICL, especially not with those principles already analyzed in Chapter I above.

## 5   GENETIC DEFENSES AND NEUROBIOLOGICAL RELATIONSHIPS TO THE DEFENSE OF DURESS TO INTERNATIONAL CRIMES

In order to assess the scope of the "special" or "other" defenses envisaged by Article 31 (3) of the ICC Statute this section discusses the evolution of so-called neurobiological or genetic defenses in criminal law, currently a serious subject of defenses in American law. The question arises to what extent these defenses can be invoked to war crimes. Notwithstanding a scientific investigation in order to obtain a psychiatric explanation for the atrocities conducted by the Nazis during World War II by Dr Cohen in 1956,[206] no clear answers are available to explain how defendants are able to conduct these enormous atrocities, such as those committed during World War II and those currently presented before the ICTY and ICTR. Therefore it is worthwhile, especially from the perspective of ICL, to search further with the help of the present scientific knowledge based upon neurogenetical information about human behavior and aggression. Moreover, this search is useful because of the relation to the

---

206. E.A. COHEN, HET DUITSE CONCENTRATIEKAMP, EEN MEDISCHE EN PSYCHOLOGISCHE STUDIE (1956).

above-mentioned special and "other defenses," enabled by the ICC Statute as well as by the ICTY Statute. Finally, one has to consider that the various areas of forensic expertise have grown in the past based upon knowledge as well as upon personal interests of scientists. Jakobs and Sprangers observe that, as different areas of forensic science expertise may belong to a single basic natural science, overlap can occur between forensic experts of different areas of expertise, and in addition new developments in the various natural sciences, leading to new sub-areas of forensic expertise, will always be occurring.[207]

Whereas the goal of neural science is to understand the human mind,[208] one of the goals of criminal law is to cope with this human mind. The fact that there are two general components of every crime, a physical and a mental one, the latter also named *mens rea*,[209] emphasizes the existence of a causal relationship between neural science and criminal law.

Today neural science advocates the central principle that behavior is an expression of neural activity and that even (human) consciousness is the product of the nervous system.[210] This prominent role of neural science in the understanding of the human mind has not yet been established in criminal law and especially not with respect to the rule of duress, in which the human mind is strongly involved.

While both continental and common law do not recognize, except with respect to the law of self-defense, an excuse for the intentional killing of an innocent person, even if necessary to save oneself from instant death, this is an exception to the rule of duress, which is that the doing of a prohibited act is excused (and therefore the defendant is not criminally liable) if reasonably believed to be necessary to save the actor from imminent death or great bodily injury.[211] This excuse is recognized in prosecutions for both minor offenses (e.g., reckless driving, malicious mischief) and also grave felonies such as burglary, robbery and kidnapping. The essential element of the rule of duress is the fact that the defendant himself must raise the issue of duress and the government, whenever the issue is raised, must prove the defendant's guilt. The defendant does not have the burden of proving duress.[212] The fact that the judicial base of duress originates from the impairment of the actor's ability to control his conduct or to con-

---

207.   Livia E.M.P. Jacobs and Wim J.M. Sprangers, *A European View on Forensic Expertise and Counter-Expertise*, in HARMONISATION IN FORENSIC EXPERTISE 224 (J.F. Nijboer & W.J.J.M. Sprangers, eds., 2000).

208.   Eric R. Kandel, *Brain and Behaviour*, in PRINCIPLES OF NEURAL SCIENCE 5–17 (E.R. Kandel, J.H. Swartz & Th.M. Jessell, eds., 1993); *See* also Preface of this book.

209.   R.M. Perkins and R.N. Boyce, *supra* note 6, at 831.

210.   Kandel et al., *supra* note 208, Preface and at 1009; EUAN M. MACPHAIL, THE EVOLUTION OF CONSCIOUSNESS 212–213 (1998).

211.   Perkins and Boyce, *supra* note 6, at 1059.

212.   *U.S. Versus Calfon*, 607 F. 2d 29, 2d Circuit, 1979.

trol his free will implies a close relationship with neural science.[213] Therefore, matching the progress made in molecular neural science with the judicial view of duress can be an important aim of ICL. Perhaps it is time to stress more vigorously that future judicial development of duress is intimately tied to that of molecular neural science. Subsequently, in the era of ICL it is—similarly as to domestic criminal law cases—of importance to determine whether a genetic predisposition exists that contributes to possible vulnerability of a person to duress situations. Later, in Chapter VII, I will look into the methods for this introduction of neurobiology in criminal cases as far as it concerns duress.

---

213. P.H. ROBINSON, CRIMINAL LAW DEFENSES 350, 353–355, 366 (1986).

# CHAPTER IV

# INDIVIDUAL AND INSTITUTIONAL COMMAND RESPONSIBILITY AND THE INTERNATIONAL REGULATION OF ARMED CONFLICTS

## 1    INTRODUCTION

Despite the inevitably and increasingly important United Nations (hereinafter: UN) Peacekeeping and Peace enforcement operations during the last decade for the international community,[1] no clear analysis or determination has thus far been conducted as to the command responsibility for war crimes in multinational operations. In 1986 the *Nicaragua* case of the ICJ was called to assess this concept. The Court ruled that when an intervening state gives *"direct and critical combat support"* to an insurgent force and insurgent operations reflect *"strategy and tactics wholly devised"* by the intervening state, then an agency relationship is established.[2]

In section 2, this Chapter *first* explores whether this principle affects or has to affect the command responsibility in the context of multinational operations, since the judgment of the ICJ in the *Nicaragua* case encompasses only state responsibility. *Secondly*, this chapter will assess, in sections 3–6, the scope of both institutional (section 4) and individual (section 5) command responsibility to war crimes occurring in multinational operations endowed with various mandates (section 6). In the light of present international humanitarian law (hereinafter IHL) developments, the question will be examined whether the present standards hereto suffice. A complicating factor to be considered is the interplay between IHL and international criminal law (hereinafter ICL) regarding the doctrine of superior responsibility; this doctrine *"requires that crimes have occurred or are likely to occur, and that no action is taken to prevent or*

---

1.    *See* Gerardus G.J. Knoops, *Interstatelijk Noodweerrecht: disculpatiegrond voor Internationalrechtelijke Onrechtmatige Daad?* 43 NEDERLANDS JURISTENBLAD 2016 (1999).

2.    *See Nicaragua v. U.S.*, Merits, ICJ Reports 1986, 14 at 61–62; *See* also Ilias Bantekas, *The contemporary law of superior responsibility*, 93 THE AMERICAN JOURNAL OF INTERNATIONAL LAW 594–595 (1999).

*punish them.*"[3] This interplay is clearly envisaged by the premise that while IHL acts in advance to assure that commanders promote its objectives, ICL intervenes when breaches have occurred.[4] Command responsibility to war crimes in multinational operations can be positioned in both areas, as envisaged by the so-called *Rules of Engagement* (hereinafter ROE) enacted for these kind of operations. Because these ROE have to be examined more thoroughly, the third and final question as to the status of these ROE in the realm of both IHL and ICL is considered in section 7.

## 2  COMMAND RESPONSIBILITY: CONCURRENCE OF STATE RESPONSIBILITY AND INDIVIDUAL SUPERIOR RESPONSIBILITY

Under IHL a military commander is not *eo ipso* responsible because he is in a position of authority, nor does such function carry burdens of vicarious or strict liability. This evolves from the criminal (compulsory) elements envisaged by Articles 7 (3) and 6 (3) of the ICTY statute respective of the ICTR Statute.[5] The choice of law differs here with regard to the basis of State responsibility, which is qualified as a concept of *"relatively strict liability"*[6] in which context it is argued that *"governments act through agents"* while *"the effectiveness of international duties would be much reduced if the complainant State has to prove some level of knowledge or intention at a high level of government in respect to the acts or omissions of subordinate officials"* (emphasis added; GJK).[7] Therefore, the aforementioned concept of state responsibility as such seems not—for two reasons—to be legally applicable as to command responsibility.[8] In the first place, ICTY in the *Celebići* case rejected a presumption of knowledge of military leaders where crimes under one's command were widespread and notorious. The Tribunal referred hereto—seemingly in opposition to the High Command cases decision[9]—to the fact that the assessment of the element of knowledge must have taken place on an *individual* basis by adjudicating upon, on the one hand, the extent and severity of the atrocities, and on the other hand the absence of communications.[10]

---

3.   *See* Bantekas, *supra* note 2, at 593.
4.   *See* Bantekas, *supra* note 2, at 594.
5.   *See* commentary on the Additional Protocols of 8 June 1977 to the Geneva Conventions of 12 August 1949, para. 3543; *see also* Bantekas, *supra* note 2, at 577.
6.   IAN BROWNLIE, THE RULE OF LAW IN INTERNATIONAL AFFAIRS 84 (1998).
7.   Brownlie, *supra* note 6, at 85.
8.   In the context of the principle of criminal liability, state responsibility can, however, serve as a precedent for institutional liability. *See* section 4.
9.   *U.S. v. Von Leeb*, 1 Trials of War Criminals before the Nuremberg Military Tribunals under Control Council Law No. 10, at 1, 462 (1950).
10.   *See Prosecutor v. Delalić*, Judgment No. IT-96-21-T of 16 November 1998, at para. 385; Bantekas, *supra* note 2, at 589.

The second reason makes a comparison between the concept of state responsibility and that of command responsibility difficult, the difficulty emerging from the so-called *"delegation principle"* which is nowadays accepted as a general principle of ICL and which is derived from the *Yamashita* case.[11]

*Yamashita*'s conviction was upheld for acts of troops beyond his *de facto* control, for the reason that operational command responsibility couldn't be ceded for the purposes of the doctrine of command responsibility even though the specific aspects of such command are actually ceded to others. It was interesting that the accused, Supreme Military Commander of the Japanese Imperial Army of the Philippines, was charged with violating his duty to control his troops, this resulting in implicit permission to perpetrate grave atrocities; Yamashita ordered, just before the U.S. invasion, a partial evacuation, and divided the remainder of his forces into three separate fighting units, ceding full command of two and maintaining the command of the other. Contrary to his orders, the evacuation did not occur, leaving Yamashita isolated in the mountains as well as *incommunicado* with the other two commanders and his own headquarters. With regard to command responsibility to war crimes in multinational operations, the *Yamashita* ruling implies that in the event of multinational military operations under command of International Organizations such as the UN and NATO, the command responsibility to possible war crimes cannot be exclusively delegated to the respective military commanders of the participating powers in order to avoid criminal responsibility of international organizations, such as NATO and the UN itself. In section 4 below, the subject of institutional criminal liability will be examined further.

## 3 THE RELEVANT COMMAND STRUCTURE OF MULTINATIONAL MILITARY OPERATIONS

### 3.1 Introduction

The latter tentatively drawn conclusion has to be further assessed from the perspective of the command structure within multinational organizations such as NATO and the UN, which are involved in multinational peacekeeping and peace enforcement operations.

---

11. *See Yamashita v. Styer*, 327 U.S. 1, 16 (1946); *See* Bantekas, *supra* note 2, at 585.

## 3.2 Alignment of UN and NATO to IHL

Before analyzing this structure, one must observe whether, pursuant to customary IHL, the UN and NATO as such—i.e., as international organizations empowered with international legal personality[12]—are nowadays bound by the rules of IHL, especially the Geneva Conventions and Additional Protocols I and II, notwithstanding the fact that several member states of NATO and the UN did not ratify Additional Protocol I. The mere fact that NATO or the UN as such are not parties to the Geneva Conventions or Additional Protocols does not suffice to prevent alignment to instruments of IHL. *Firstly* both NATO and UN forces are composed of national contingents contributed by States who are invariably parties to the Geneva Conventions and most of whom are also parties to the Protocols.[13]

Those States are required by Article 1 of the Conventions and Article 1 of Additional Protocol I to ensure that the members of their armed forces respect the provisions of the Conventions and the Protocol *"in all circumstances."* This especially applies to peace enforcement or other enforcement operations, whereby the UN or NATO (States) are in fact a party to the armed conflict.[14]

*Secondly*, although these Conventions do not explicitly provide for the accession of International Organizations—referring only to *"powers,"* arguably meaning only States[15]—this fact does not preclude the applicability of international customary law. The UN and NATO are both subject to international law having international legal identity, and are therefore bound by and capable of having rights and duties like States.[16]

Substantial parts and provisions of both the Geneva Conventions and Additional Protocols are at present considered to have customary status.[17] Moreover, the main principles of Additional Protocol I, such as Articles 48, 51(2), 52(1), 51(5)(b), 57(2) (a) (iii), 54, 57 and 58, are nowadays accepted as being part of customary IHL.[18] Noteworthy, and for this study

---

12. *See* Reparations for Injuries suffered in the service of the UN, ICJ-Advisory Opinion of 11 April 1949, ICJ Reports, 1949, at 174.

13. *See* Christopher Greenwood, *IHL and UN Military Operations*, I YEARBOOK OF INTERNATIONAL HUMANITARIAN LAW 17 (1998).

14. *See*, e.g., the enforcement interventions of NATO in Kosovo; Greenwood, *supra* note 13, at 27.

15. *See* Article 96 (2), Additional Protocol I.

16. *See* Martin Zwanenburg, *The Secretary-General's Bulletin on Observance by United Nations Forces of IHL: Some Preliminary Observations*, at 3; *See* also Reparations for Injuries suffered in the Service of the UN, Advisory Opinion of 11 April 1949, ICJ Reports 1949, at 174.

17. *See* Zwanenburg, *supra* note 16, at 3.

18. *See* Christopher Greenwood, *Customary International Law and the First*

relevant, is the fact that most, if not all, of the coalition States which participated in the international force against Iraq in the Gulf War and party to Protocol I have incorporated the standards of the Protocol into their training and military manuals, so that the standards laid down in the Protocol have become part of the military doctrine of their armed forces.[19] This result reaffirms that the status and interpretation of many of the provisions, especially those relating to the protection of civilians from the effects of war, are ascribed with a *peremptory* character regarding unilateral or multinational military operations.

*Thirdly,* notwithstanding the fact that the UN on the one hand always asserted that it is not a party to any treaty of IHL, particularly not the 1949 Geneva Convention as well as their Additional Protocols, and IHL as such would not apply to UN Peacekeeping, the UN contrarily has explicitly held that *"the UN Peacekeeping operation shall observe and respect the principles and spirits of the general international conventions applicable to the conduct of military personnel."* They then added that these international conventions include the four Geneva Conventions of 12 August 1949, their Additional Protocols of 8 June 1977 and the UNESCO Convention of 14 May 1954 on the Protection of Cultural Property in the event of armed conflict.[20]

The UN hereto obligates the participating States to ensure *"that the members of its national contingent serving with the UN peace-keeping operation be fully acquainted with the principles and spirits of these Conventions."*[21] Admittedly, it goes without saying that being constrained by the *"principles and spirits"* of IHL is not fully equal to being party to the International Conventions as such. Violations of these principles and spirit entail, however, surely analogous criminal responsibility of the UN and NATO as international legal entities as well as towards the particular military commanders.[22] Although it is clear that customary IHL, including the four Geneva Conventions, binds all States contributing to a UN or NATO operation, the literature questions whether the same counts for Additional Protocol I.[23] Greenwood thus posits that the paradoxical dichotomy is possible *"that different contingents in the same force could be subject to different legal obligations, thus creating serious problems to interoperability."*[24] With

*Geneva Protocol of 1977 in the Gulf Conflict*, in THE GULF WAR 1990–1991 IN INTERNATIONAL AND ENGLISH LAW 64–65, 88 (P. Rone, ed., 1993).

19. *See* Greenwood, *supra* note 18, 1993, at 65.

20. *See* Article 28 of the Draft Model Agreement between the UN and Member States contributing personnel and equipment to the UN peacekeeping operations of 23 May 1991, UN Doc. A/46/185.

21. *See* article 28 of the Draft Model Agreement, *supra* note 20.

22. *See also* Zwanenburg, *supra* note 16, at 2.

23. *See* Greenwood *supra* note 13, 1998, at 19.

24. *See* Greenwood, *supra* note 13, 1998, at 19.

regard to multinational enforcement operations of UN or NATO "*which (were) designed to, and did, in fact engage in hostilities on a large scale, the whole of the relevant IHL would apply to that operation.*"[25] This approach is clearly envisioned by article 2 (2) of the 1994 Convention on the Safety of UN and Associated Personnel, providing that "*this convention shall not apply to a UN operation authorized by the Security Council as an enforcement action under Chapter VII of the Charter of the UN in which any of the personnel are engaged as combatants against organized armed forces and to which the law of* International armed conflict *applies*" (emphasis added; GJK).

Similarly, this view is espoused by Section 1 of the recent UN Secretary-General's Bulletin, "*Observance by UN forces of IHL*" of 6 August 1999, wherein it is noted that "*the* fundamental principles and rules *of IHL* (my emphasis; GJK) *set out in the present bulletin are applicable to UN forces when in situations or armed conflict they are actively engaged therein as combatants*[26] ( . . . )."

With regard to peacekeeping and peace enforcement operations, it is arguable that forces acting within these types of operations under UN command and control have both *legal* and moral obligations to ensure that at least "*the principles and spirits*" of IHL are respected.[27]

The conclusion of the aforementioned is that the theoretical mandate of a multinational force—of the UN, NATO or otherwise—and its classification as to enforcement, peace enforcement or peacekeeping, is not decisive to the applicability of IHL. Nor does it affect the subsequent command responsibility in multinational operations to violations of IHL and war crimes. Ultimately, as stated by Greenwood, multinational forces, faced with serious violations of IHL and participating in an operation not set up with the specific purpose of enforcing IHL or human rights, but rather to conduct traditional peacekeeping or humanitarian aid, have "*an (implicit) right to take such (military) action.*" This right also emerges from the Geneva Conventions as such, notwithstanding the absence of a "*legal basis for the existence of such a duty.*"[28] In addition it has to be highlighted that from a judgment of the Belgian Military Court at Brussels, rendered in 1997 regarding the UN peacekeeping operation in Somalia, it emerges that a UN Peacekeeping Force can become a party to the conflict and thus constrained by rules of IHL in the event of a "*protracted, generalized and structured engagement to the conflict.*" Without any doubt this involves the concept of superior responsibility.

The compliance of NATO and UN to the Geneva Conventions already implies their own legal (criminal) responsibility as to violations of these

---

25. *See* Greenwood *supra* note 13, 1998, at 20.
26. *See* also section 3 of the Bulletin.
27. *See* Greenwood, *supra* note 13, 1998, at 20–21, 33.
28. *See* Greenwood, *supra* note 13, 1998, at 32.

Conventions and subsequent war crimes. Therefore, an exclusive delegation of criminal responsibility from these organizations, or even the member states, to force to adherence battlefield commanders of the participating states of multinational operations cannot be imputed.

## 3.3 Multinational command structure

From the perspective of the command structure of the UN or NATO, independent criminal responsibility of these organizations can also be upheld. The traditional defense structure of a state consists of *four* general command stages: the *policy* and *strategic* military levels (both concerned with the power to commit or withdraw military forces, as well as producing a viable military plan to achieve policy military objectives), the *senior military* level (empowered to implement an earlier authorized battle plan at Corps or Division level by directing operational mid-level commanders), and finally the tactical level where tactical field commanders of any rank direct command of troops. Contrary to this structure, the command structure is divided differently in multinational forces. The UN endorses a command structure whereby the Security Council, and to a rather limited degree the Secretary-General,[29] exercise both policy and strategic command. Because peacekeeping and peace enforcement forces are composed of national contingents which retain a distinguishable national identity despite forming part of a UN institution, four hierarchical/organizational levels are to be distinguished with regard to the most common model, i.e., an operation under full UN command and control:

1. The principal organ, which creates the peace-keeping or enforcement forces;
2. The Secretary-General, according to Arts. 97–99 of the UN Charter, empowered with a wide range of administrative and political functions inclusive (Art. 99) of the right to political initiative to act in an international peace-threatening situation;
3. The Commander-in-Chief and his staff;
4. National contingents headed by a contingent Commander.[30]

---

29. *See* Bantekas, *supra* note 2, at 579; *See* Article 8 of the 11th report of a Working Group of the UN Special Committee on Peacekeeping Operations, UN Doc. A/32/394/Annex II, App. I, 2 December 1977.

30. *See* for this internal structure of peace-keeping operations: *The Charter of the United Nations, A Commentary* (B. Simma, ed.), Oxford University Press, 1994, at 593.

In this model, a UN operation thus encompasses a Force Commander who exercises operational command over the respective contingents provided by member States. Important to observe is that for the duration and purposes of the specific multinational operation, military personnel under the Force Commander are to be considered *"international personnel,"* although they remain in national service.[31] Aside from this common model, one cannot overlook two other models of multinational (UN) operations, i.e., operations conducted under national command and control, but authorized by the Security Council (the model adopted in the Gulf conflict) and another model at present likely to be applied to any peace enforcement operation and operations in which a force under UN command operates alongside other forces under national command and control, e.g., UNODOM I and UNOSOM II, but also UNPROFOR which, as a UN Force, operated with the support of NATO Air Forces, the latter acting under authorization of the Security Council and in response to UN requests for military assistance.[32]

Despite the mainly political-administrative differences between these three operative models, in essence these are not of significance as to the fact of the application of the doctrine of superior responsibility, in theory and practice, nor as to liability of the multinational organizations. In practice, observed by Bantekas, Force Commanders operative in multinational forces have been granted *"full authority"* over their forces and have as a result been held *"operationally responsible"* for their performance.[33] This concept is exemplified by, *inter alia*, the Allied Command Europe Mobile Force (AMF) of NATO, the NATO quick intervention force, which consists of military personnel of 12 NATO member states, and which recently accepted Poland and Czechoslovakia as members.[34]

According to the 1995 NATO Handbook, however, only operational command or control over forces is assigned to NATO by member States, whereas full command over all tactical aspects of the operation and administration of forces is retained by the national governments. Operational command or control over forces implies consequently an element of criminal responsibility for war crimes to the detriment of NATO. This approach is reinforced by the fact that since the end of the cold war military alliances have viewed their structures and operations more

---

31.  Bantekas, *supra* note 2, at 579.
32.  *See* for these three models; Greenwood, *supra* note 13, at 12–13.
33.  Bantekas, *supra* note 2, at 579.
34.  *See*, e.g., also Art. 11 of the UN Force in Cyprus Regulations (UNFICYP) of 1964; for other examples see note 61, Bantekas *supra* note 2.

broadly, in accordance with peacekeeping and regional defense requirements. This subsequently led to a military structure of the multinational or national contingent force operating within the context of a multinational operation whereby this contingent may have two command chains, according to the nature of its missions, as evidenced by the Quick Reaction Force (QRF) in Somalia. This force solely contained U.S. troops and was attributed with a U.S. command chain, although in the event of emergency situations it was planned to have as superior command the UN Operation commander in Somalia II (UNOSOM II).[35]

The conclusion therefore follows that criminal responsibility for war crimes committed during multinational (UN or NATO) peacekeeping and peace-enforcement operations cannot solely be attributed to field commanders of the participating contingents but is, depending on the circumstances, exclusively or simultaneously applicable to the UN Commander-in-Chief in question (third level; level c. *supra*) as well as the multinational military organization as such.

## 4   THE LEGAL BASIS OF INSTITUTIONAL LIABILITY TO WAR CRIMES IN MULTINATIONAL MILITARY OPERATIONS

This section will concentrate on the application and judicial basis of criminal responsibility to multinational military operations.

*Firstly*, it is legitimate to accept as premise that the relationship between multinational forces and criminal liability be influenced by the fact that IHL is *"not concerned with the interests of the parties to the conflict"* but involves the protection and *"general considerations of humanitarian and human dignity."*[36] This principle entails already a substantial obligation of multinational organizations to be adhered to during the submitted military operations.

*Secondly*, since neither the UN nor any other multinational organization has law enforcement and judicial organs of its own, recourse to national criminal and disciplinary law is necessary as it concerns criminal and disciplinary jurisdictional powers over the members of the multinational force. In this sense these domestic rules enforce obligations vis-à-vis the UN.[37] To the extent that these rules of national criminal and disciplinary law serve the purpose of enforcing international legal rules and IHL, they *"no longer deal with the international obligations of the* state,

---

35.   *See* Bantekas, *supra* note 2, at 579.

36.   *See* HANS P. GASSER, INTERNATIONAL HUMANITARIAN LAW, AN INTRODUCTION 90–99 (1993).

37.   *See* THE CHARTER OF THE UNITED NATIONS, A COMMENTARY 597 (Bruno Simma, ed., 1994).

*but rather with the decisive international obligations of the* UN (emphasis added; GJK)."[38] Therefore, from this principle of indirect enforcement— i.e., the application of national criminal law to implement the international obligations of the UN—on which substantive ICL so far has relied,[39] the international (criminal) responsibility of the UN (or other organizations empowered with legal power and identity) for the acts of the multinational force, emerges.[40] This approach seems to be challenged by the observation that it would be *"highly objectionable"* to require that violations of IHL committed by members of multinational forces be sanctioned, whereas *"no clear legal determination of the obligation of the participating states for the newer peace-keeping operations"* would be available.[41] This criticism does not affect, however, the principle of liability of the UN as such, especially because, as will be considered in section 7, recourse to such *"legal determination of obligations"* can be conducted through the Rules of Engagement.

*Thirdly,* the submitted criminal responsibility of multinational organizations is in accordance with the principles of ICL. The concept of state responsibility is nowadays accepted by international law.[42] This view is also supported by Article 3 of the 1907 Convention on the Laws and Customs of War on Land, providing that any member state violating those laws and customs *"shall be responsible for all acts committed by persons forming part of its armed forces,"* and *"shall, if the case demands, be liable to pay compensation."*[43]

State criminal responsibility is premised on the distinction between particularly serious wrongs committed by states (*crimes*) and less serious wrongs (*delicts*), a distinction which has its roots in obligations *erga omnes* and the doctrine of *jus cogens.*[44] Similar to a major objection to state criminal responsibility, one could argue that criminal responsibility for international (military) organizations differs so fundamentally from criminal liability in domestic law, as to *inter alia* the punishment, that it would fail

---

38. Simma, *supra* note 37, at 597.

39. *See* M. Cherif Bassiouni, I International Criminal Law 14, 110–115, 267 (1999).

40. *See also* Simma, *supra* note 37

41. *See* Simma, *supra* note 37, at 597.

42. *See* John Dugard, *Criminal Responsibility of States,* in I International Criminal Law 251 (M. Cherif Bassiouni, ed., 1999); *See* also Gerardus G.J. Knoops, *De Lockerbie Affaire: transponering van internationalrechtelijke staatsaansprakelijkheid naar nationale jurisdictie: No hiding place for the state?* 29 Delikt en Delinkwent 601–613 (1999).

43. Christopher Greenwood, International Humanitarian Law and the Laws of War, Preliminary Report for the Centennial Commemoration of the First Hague Peace Conference 1899, 76–77 (1998).

44. Dugard, *supra* note 42, at 242.

to pass the test of analogy. As already observed by Dugard, these objections are without substance since:

1. The argument that organizations endowed with international legal personality are incapable of committing a crime is unconvincing, for both common law countries and an increasing number of civil law countries recognize the criminal liability of corporations, and

2. the assertion that international organizations can, as stated, not be subject to criminal punishment (as imprisonment) contravenes the fact that it equally applies to the liability of corporations. Despite this assertion, many domestic legal systems ensure criminal liability of corporations. Moreover, equal to economic, penal sanctions imputed on corporations, public international law entails sanctions analogous to criminal punishments, such as military, economic and diplomatic sanctions imposed under Chapter VII of the UN Charter,[45] and

3. finally, the objection that no *mens rea* can be imputed to an entity such as a state or international organization can be answered by referring to the concept of *"vicarious"* liability for the acts of its officials respective of its personnel, similar to the acts of shareholders, directors or personnel of a company in the municipal criminal laws of civil and common law countries.[46]

In conclusion, the question to be addressed is in fact not whether an international (military) organization may be held criminally liable for war crimes committed during multinational military operations—a liability shown to exist—but whether the international legal community recognizes or should recognize such liability. State practice—as evidenced, *inter alia*, by the actions taken by the UN against South Africa to compel it to abandon its apartheid policy, the Resolutions of the Security Council following Iraq's invasion of Kuwait, and its Resolutions directed at Libya over its refusal to extradite the suspects of the destruction of Pan Am flight 103 over Lockerbie—leads to an affirmative answer.[47] This especially applies to violations of IHL committed by the multinational organizations in question.

---

45. *See* Dugard, *supra* note 42, at 246–247.
46. Dugard, *supra* note 42, at 248.
47. *See* Dugard, *supra* note 42, at 243–246.

## 5   SIMULTANEOUS INDIVIDUAL COMMAND RESPONSIBILITY TO WAR CRIMES IN MULTINATIONAL MILITARY OPERATIONS

The fact that battlefield or tactical commanders on the third and fourth organizational level in the context of multinational operations, as described in section 3.3, are to be considered as *"international personnel"* does not exonerate them as to their own criminal liability for war crimes as separate from the liability of the multinational organization in question. In other words, the presence of such an organization cannot act as a cloak behind which (multinational) force commanders, tactical or battlefield commanders can legally shelter. Several arguments support this view.

*Firstly*, without doubt it can be held that an opposite view would contravene Art. 86 (1)(2) and Article 87 (1), of Additional Protocol I to the Geneva Convention of 1949, providing penal or disciplinary responsibility for superior military personnel as well as State responsibility envisaged by Article 87 (1) of Additional Protocol I, without restricting this to only unilateral military operations. This provision leaves therefore the extension to unilateral (individual) command responsibility in conjunction with multinational operations open.[48]

*Secondly*, the UN has recognized the significance of the element of simultaneous superior responsibility. The Secretary-General's Bulletin of 6 August 1999, titled *"Observance by UN forces of International Humanitarian Law,"* provides explicitly that *"in case of violations of IHL members of the military personnel of a UN Force are subject to prosecution in their national court."* It may be assumed that this principle, applicable in both UN enforcement and peacekeeping actions regarding forces under UN command and control when the use of force is permitted in self-defense, can be invoked in the context of international criminal litigation.

*Thirdly*, the concept of (independent) individual command responsibility in multinational operations is clearly reflected in the *Rules of Engagement* (ROE) which are developed among the coalition parties or coalition combatant forces attending these operations. The ROE governing these operations of Military Alliances under supervision of the UN (and to be adhered to), are known as the *"Standing Rules of Engagement (peace enforcement) for the United Nations Forces."* The UN ROE entails in Section 4 the concept of individual Commanders' responsibility, providing that *"UN commanders* at all levels (emphasis added; GJK) *are required:*

a.   *To have the ROE disseminated to every subordinate under their command and have translated, if required; and*

---

48.   *See* also Art. 31 (1) of the Vienna Convention on the Law of Treaties regarding the application and interpretation of Treaties according good faith, as well as in the light of its object and purpose.

b. *To ensure that every subordinate under their command:*
   1. *is instructed and refreshed on the meaning and application of these rules as they relate to assigned missions,*
   2. *understands and complies with the contents of this document, and*
   3. *has the opportunity to seek additional clarification, guidance or direction if these ROE require further explanation.*

   *UN commanders shall issue orders on the readiness of personal weapons to be maintained, appropriate to the situation.*
   *The UN force Commander may not restrict the inherent right of self-defense."*

In conclusion, apart from and simultaneous to (criminal) responsibility of multinational organizations such as the UN or NATO regarding war crimes, both ICL and IHL endorse individual superior responsibility in multinational operations.

Although the importance of preventing violations of IHL has to be recognized by the UN and NATO themselves, as well as by the principal States and secondarily by force commanders,[49] these multinational organizations bear the legal and moral responsibility of not only setting up the particular multinational operation, but also determining the relevant body of law and transforming this body to the force levels. In order to achieve this purpose, the so-called Rules of Engagement (ROE), for which these organizations are equally responsible, are operative.

## 6   CRIMINAL RESPONSIBILITY AND VARIOUS FORMS OF MULTINATIONAL MILITARY MANDATES

The question now arises whether the extent of criminal responsibility of international organizations such as the UN or NATO, and subsequent individual superior responsibility, depends on the exact *nature or type* of Multinational operations, which can be classified into the following three primary categories:

1. Peace-keeping operations,
2. peace-enforcement operations, and
3. enforcement operations.

With regard to the first kind of operations, the use of force is only authorized in the case of self-defense, including the protection of UN

---

49.   Greenwood, *supra* note 13, at 33.

premises and personnel,[50] whereas peace-enforcement operations will generally authorize a wider scale of options, including the use of military force in the traditional, military way, i.e., in order to achieve submissions on the part of an opposing force and to carry out humanitarian operations.[51]

The authority to use force in traditional (UN) peacekeeping operations is limited, i.e., only allowed in the event of self-defense or in attempts by forceful means to prevent the peacekeeping forces from discharging their duties under the particular mandate. Therefore the use of force beyond this nature and mandate by peacekeeping commanders, including the national superiors operating on the third and fourth level, gives rise to command responsibility at an individual (national) level, which *a fortiori* applies to war crimes. Moreover, this individual command responsibility can be adhered to when considering that the nature of peacekeeping operations requires that peacekeeping forces should never become a party to the conflict in which they have been called upon to intervene.[52] Further, the opinion in the literature that the law of armed conflicts does not apply to the conduct of traditional peacekeeping operations[53] does not exclude command responsibility for war crimes committed in these operations. This especially would not be acceptable since both the principles of proportion and subsidiarity are fully applicable in these operations,[54] as are behavioral directives to the military personnel attending these operations, including the use of force. These directives are ensured by the so-called Rules of Engagement (ROE).[55]

On the contrary, violations of the latter principles and ROE can, aside from liability of the UN or NATO as such, impose command responsibility on national commanders participating in multinational operations.[56]

In the realm of command responsibility to war crimes in multinational peacekeeping operations it is, however, questionable whether the law of armed conflicts, as the UN advocates, is indeed not applicable during

---

50. *See* Articles 2 (4) and 51 of the UN Charter; *See* TIMOTHY L.H. MACCORMACK, SELF DEFENSE IN INTERNATIONAL LAW 111–149 (1996).

51. *See* Gert-Jan F. van Hegelsom, *The Law of Armed Conflict and UN Peacekeeping and Peace-enforcing Operations*, 6 HAGUE YEARBOOK OF INTERNATIONAL LAW 47 and 57 (1993), in which the author points out, however, that grey areas occur between these forms of operations.

52. Van Hegelsom, *supra* note 51, at 54.

53. Van Hegelsom, *supra* note 51, at 54.

54. *See* Aide-Memoire of the Secretary General concerning some questions relating to the function and operation of the UN Peace-keeping Force in Cyprus, UN Doc. S/5653 of 11 April 1964, at paras. 16–18.

55. *See* paragraphs 7.3 and 7.4 for the judicial character and legal consequences hereof.

56. *See* further paragraph 7.5.

these kind of operations. When we accept that the mandate hereto implies always the inherent right to the use of force by virtue of self-defense, the law of wars emerges and thus the adjustment of the Geneva Conventions and Additional Protocols.[57] This conclusion was already in other contexts drawn in section 3.3 above.

## 7 THE NATURE OF THE RULES OF ENGAGEMENT: BASIS FOR SUPERIOR RESPONSIBILITY AND/OR EXONERATION TO WAR CRIMES IN MULTINATIONAL OPERATIONS?

### 7.1 Introduction

It is inevitable that sophisticated modern-day armed forces have to be given significant assistance with regard to the application *in concreto* of the use of force during multinational operations. This aid is needed to ensure a uniform, controllable achievement of the purpose of the operation in question as well as to ensure compliance with both national and international law. To this extent the concept of the ROE can be adhered to; in fact, their aim is to improve the relationship between military or operational planning and the constraints of international humanitarian law. The Standing ROE (Peace Enforcement) for the United Nations Forces highlights on page one this functionality by mentioning that *"these ROE establish fundamental policies and procedures governing the actions undertaken by Force Commanders in United Nations Peace-Enforcement Operations under Chapter VII of the UN Charter,"* and this *"( . . . ) to be used (at all levels) as fundamental guidance for training and directing their forces."* Moreover, it is noted herein that *"these ROE provide general guidelines on self-defense and specific guidance governing the use of force consistent with mission accomplishment."* The ROE contains both prohibitions and permissions to be undertaken by both the (UN) Force Commanders at all levels and the Multinational Forces as such.

Thus, the ROE are potentially of great importance not only for the application of IHL in multinational operations, but also regarding the interpretation of the doctrine of individual superior and State criminal responsibility as well as possible exoneration to international criminal litigation. The purpose of this section is therefore to examine the practice of the ROE in multinational operations and to observe what light it sheds upon the aforementioned superior responsibility or exonerative standards. The principal focus of attention will be upon the *individual* superior responsibility or exculpation.

---

57. For another opinion: Van Hegelsom, *supra* note 51, at 51.

## 7.2 Multinational rules of engagement: direct sources of customary international law or law of the soldier?

Before assessing this principal focus, this subject requires analysis as to the international legal character or qualification of these ROE enacted by an international organization such as the UN or NATO. What is their international legal status in general or for the individual soldier in particular? This question leads to a collision, or at least an interaction, between (international) military penal law as part of international customary law on the one hand and contemporary international criminal law—especially the doctrines of command responsibility and superior orders—on the other. Sophisticated modern-day military law and IHL ask for a remedy in order to synchronize these two areas of international law.

As far as law making in ICL is concerned, the starting point is, logically, the practice of States and international organizations. In the context of human rights and international humanitarian law, it is observed that *"the gap between the norms stated and actual practice tends to be especially wide."*[58] This accounts equally for the legal norms ensured by international criminal law and military law on the one hand and the practice or practical necessities of using military forces both in armed conflict and peacekeeping operations on the other hand. Of course, the law-making process cannot foresee all future events, and the behavior of States and military forces in armed conflicts and *"crisis-response"* operations.[59] Under exceptional, not foreseeable conditions, military practice or rules can easily collide with political interests and norms of ICL.

In addition to codifying the actual behavior of States, international crimes, and the enactment of procedures for international criminal tribunals, the time has also arrived to promulgate more preventive and protective rules of conduct—as a mixture of actual and desired practice with ICL—for military forces operating on behalf of the international community in armed conflicts and crisis-response operations. This should be done in order to prevent breaches of ICL, and also to encourage broader compliance with both norms of ICL and international customary law. This approach could also result in a promotion of the acceptance of norms of ICL.

In the Joint Separate Opinion to the Appeals Chamber decision of the ICTY in the *Erdemović* case, judges McDonald and Vohrah pointed out that

---

58.  Theodor Meron, *Geneva Conventions as Customary Law*, in WAR CRIMES LAW COMES OF AGE 158 (Theodor Meron, ed., 1998).

59.  *See* also Jordan Paust, *Superior Orders and Command Responsibility*, in I INTERNATIONAL CRIMINAL LAW 237 (M. Cherif Bassiouni, ed., 1999), observing that the law relating to superior orders and command responsibility is "second-guessed" by the community after the fact.

their view (i.e. the rejection of duress as a defense to the killing of innocent human beings) "( . . . ) *is based upon a recognition that international humanitarian law should guide the conduct of combatants and their commanders*" and that "*there must be legal limits as to the conduct of combatants and their commanders in armed conflict.*"[60] Due consideration has to be given to this philosophy when it concerns the task of ICL; this counts especially for its rules in regard to self-defense and superior orders, which call for clear standards to be maintained by field-commanders and subordinates.

To endorse these purposes, as well as to diminish the aforementioned gap and to compose clear protective, preventive rules for international military forces, e.g. KFOR and other NATO or UN forces or others acting as such, semi-legislative instruments are created, i.e. the *Rules of Engagement*. From this perspective therefore, independent of the possible parallel to military manuals, ROE enacted by international organizations could be considered part of international humanitarian law. Supportive hereto is the fact that, although the various allied contingents in the Gulf War of 1990–1991 were not (at least in the formal sense) subject to a single unified command, there seems, according to Greenwood, to have been general agreement amongst the coalition states regarding targeting policy which agreement actually was based on the *Rules of Engagement*.[61] In discussing these ROE which were applied during the Gulf Conflict, the Pentagon Interim Report notes that "*as military command relationships developed among the coalition, US ROE became effective for, or were consistent with, all coalition combatant forces.*"[62] This leads Greenwood to the conclusion that a wide measure of agreement on military policy targets and proceedings was itself reflected (in the ROE) as the applicable law. In other words, the codification of a hitherto unwritten policy by means of ROE, enacted by an international organization, can *de facto* become binding as part of customary international law, since the three conditions to be met hereto seem to be fulfilled.[63] Both the norm-creating character of the provision in question and the elements of *state practice* and *opinio juris* are present with regard to internationally drawn ROE. In the *North Sea* cases, the ICJ referred to "*emergent rules of customary international law,*"[64] a formulation which indicates a flexible approach to the criterion of *opinio juris*. In general, the ICJ appears to be willing to assume the existence of *opinio juris* on the basis of evidence of, *inter alia*, a general practice.[65] It can be held that, certainly when it concerns enactment of ROE for multinational

---

60. Decision 7 October 1997, Case no. IT-96-22-A, para. 80.

61. *See* Greenwood, *supra* note 18, 1993, at 66.

62. *See* Greenwood, *supra* note 18, 1993, at 66.

63. *See* for these conditions: Judgment ICJ in the *North Sea Continental Shelf Case*, ICJ Reports, 1969, 3.

64. ICJ Reports 1969, para. 63.

65. *See* IAN BROWNLIE, THE RULE OF LAW IN INTERNATIONAL AFFAIRS 21 (1998).

operations, their content represents customary law, based on both *State practice* and a *general practice*. Striking hereto is the clearness or readiness with which the UN ROE (Peace Enforcement) for the United Nations are enacted when it concerns their reflection of customary international law. In the "background notes" accompanying these ROE, the UN mentions that these Rules: "( . . . ) *reflect the principles of international, national and customary law and help ensure that the military force is aware of these principles in the conduct of its operations."*[66] Especially the ICJ's requirement of *"evidence of express consent"* to the relevant norms, as proof of *opinio juris*, seems to be fulfilled regarding these ROE.[67] In addition, in the realm of the state and general practice as required by the *North Sea Test*, it should be remembered that the adoption of the particular multinational ROE text itself forms an important piece of State practice, which suffices to become part of customary law or bring about a part of customary law. Especially because international judicial decisions are rare in respect to any of the multinational ROE, the requirements hereto have to be not unreasonably rigorous.[68] Notwithstanding the tenability of the assertion that multinational ROE—enacted by international organizations and conducted during multinational operations—under some circumstances can create a customary international legal basis for both superior responsibility and possible exculpation, an elaboration on its judicial values for the individual soldier is more constructive.

In the latter context, the way in which military manuals, being not codificatory, may come to affect customary law, or even become part of it, calls for a parallel approach with regard to these ROE. The assessment of the legal status of military manuals is thus a primary task. *"The few international judicial decisions on international humanitarian law reveal little, if any, inquiry into the process by which particular instruments have been transformed into customary law,"* and this assertion of Meron[69] equally applies to the judicial interaction between military (penal) rules and customary international (criminal) law.

A startling and interesting case on the relationship between international customary law and military rules is that of *United States v. List*, one of the judgments of the *International Military Tribunal* (IMT) for *the Trial of Major German War Criminals*.[70] Despite the fact that the 1929 Geneva Convention is silent regarding the defense of superior orders, the IMT observed that the recognition by States of such a defense in their manuals of military law was not a competent source of international law but might

---

66.  *See* page 1 of these "background notes."
67.  ICJ Reports 1986, at 98–101.
68.  *See* also Greenwood, *supra* note 18, at 69, regarding IHL treaties.
69.  Th. Meron, *supra* note 58, at 154.
70.  II Trials of War Criminals before the Nuremberg Military Tribunals under Control Council Law No. 10, at 1230, 1237.

have evidentiary value. The Tribunal ruled: *"We point out that army regulations are not a competent source of international law. They are neither legislative nor judicial pronouncements ( . . . ). But it is possible ( . . . ) that such regulations, as they bear upon a question of custom and practice in the conduct of war, might have evidentiary value, particularly if the applicable portions had been put into general practice. It will be observed that the determination, whether a custom or practice exists, is a question of fact."*[71]

This approach is, however, questionable. As Meron observes, this view appears to have been supported by an understandable reluctance to accept the defense of superior orders from German officers.[72] Manuals of military law frequently not only reflect domestic government policy but also policy of the international community, e.g. in regard to the rules of engagement enacted by the UN concerning peacekeeping operations (which rules will be discussed hereafter). Therefore, towards States, these military manuals create mutual expectations of compliance, resulting thus in the acceptance of these rules as norms of international customary law.[73] Confirmation of this view can also be deduced from the ruling of the ICJ in the *Nicaragua* case. Although the Court in this case did not discuss the formation of customary law in the direct context of military penal codes or military peace-keeping rules as such, the Court's law-making method also affects future adoption of customary law in various fields of international law, including not only, e.g., the Geneva Conventions,[74] but also (inter) national military regulations for both peace and warfare operations. In the *Nicaragua* case, the Court made only perfunctory references to the practice of States. Notwithstanding the variety of reasons which impel states to adopt their respective positions in international fora, the ICJ found *opinio juris* in verbal statements of governmental representatives to international organizations, in the content of resolutions, as well as in declarations and other normative instruments adopted by such organizations, including the consent of States to such instruments.[75]

Therefore, from the perspective of the military forces, military manuals establish (legal) obligations binding on members of the armed forces. Since the factual nature of ROE is similar to these, this equally counts for these ROE enacted by international organizations. *In concreto*, this means that the qualification of the factual nature of ROE is equivalent to a given

---

71. *United States v. List* (also known as the *Hostages* Trial), *supra* note 60, at 1230; *See* also Paust, *infra*, note 89; L.C. Green, *Superior Orders and Command Responsibility*, The Canadian Yearbook of International Law, 1989, at 180–184.

72. Meron, *supra* note 58, at 156.

73. *See* also Meron, *supra* note 58, at 156.

74. Meron, *supra* note 58, at 157.

75. *See* ICJ Reports, 1986, 14; *See* also Meron, *supra* note 58, at 157, referring to earlier antecedents of the ICJ, e.g., its Advisory Opinion in the *Western Sahara* Case, 1975, ICJ Reports 12, 30–7.

superior order. Especially in the event of not manifestly illegal ROE, the individual soldier reasonably has to or can rely on the legitimacy of the ROE in question. The consequence hereof is that, in case of a defense based upon such ROE which would eventually be rejected as being not according to ICL, it is not the individual soldier who should bear criminal liability, but the enactors. Leaving aside the international legally binding status of multinational ROE, the latter phenomenon forms a specific law for the individual soldier, equivalent to the concept of obedience of superior orders and ultimately—in case all requirements for the latter defense are fulfilled—resulting in criminal responsibility of the makers of these ROE.

### 7.3 Multinational ROE and superior responsibility

Assessment of the concrete relationship between multinational ROE and superior responsibility in multinational operations cannot be conducted without pointing to the decision of the Trial Chamber of the ICTY in the *Aleksovski* case. The Tribunal therein expressed that Article 7 (3) of the ICTY Statute makes clear that superior responsibility may be invoked if three concurrent elements are proven:

1.  a superior-subordinate relationship between the person against whom the claim is directed and the perpetrators of the offence;
2.  the superior knew or had reason to know that a crime was about to be committed or had been committed;
3.  the superior did not take all the necessary and reasonable measures to prevent the crime or to punish the perpetrator(s) thereof.[76]

Closely related to the topic of multinational operations under national, UN or combined command and control is the decisive criterion of the element of superior responsibility, which according to both customary international law and the case law of the ICTY, is the ability, as demonstrated by the duties and competence of the "superior," to *exercise control* instead of the formal legal status of the person in question as such.[77] In the recent *Blaškić* judgment, dd. 3 March 2000, Trial Chamber I further elaborated on this decisive criterion.[78] The Tribunal ruled that

---

76.   Judgment of 25 June 1999, *Prosecutor v. Aleksovksi*, case no. IT-95-14/1, para. 69.

77.   *See Aleksovski* Judgment, o.c. para. 76; *see* also Judgment of the ICTY *Prosecutor v. Celebići* dd. 16 November 1998, Case no. IT-96-21.

78.   *Blaškić* Case No. IT-95-14.

General T. Bla\u0161ki\u0107, as superior, was criminally responsible for the killing of Moslems in Central Bosnia in 1993 since, although not physically present during these massacres, he exercised *de facto* power and control, and did not prevent these war crimes. The ICTY case law expresses thus the view that the best approach to the doctrine of command responsibility should be through the *concept of control*.

Since these multinational ROE, as observed in paragraphs 7.2 and 7.3, entail customary international law, both the enacting organization and the force commanders *"at all levels"* have a legal duty to comply with these rules. The submitted UN Peace Enforcement ROE clearly enable the individual UN Force Commanders to *"exercise power and control,"* which is derived from Section 3 of these UN ROE. This section ensures that *"a (force) Commander (at all levels) has the authority to use all necessary means available and to take all appropriate action to defend his unit and other UN personnel under his protection from hostile acts or demonstrated hostile intent."* Section 3 notes that *"these rules do not limit the Force Commander's inherent* authority and obligation (emphasis added: GJK) *to use all necessary means available and to take all appropriate action in self-defense of the commander's unit and other nearby United Nations Forces, or civilians and property placed under his protection."* Together with the Commander's responsibility adhered to in Section 4 (as discussed), this formulation of ROE entails superior responsibility in case of failure to act or abuse these powers. The exact mandate of the UN Force is, in that event, actually not decisive as to whether the concept of individual superior responsibility is applicable.

### 7.4 Multinational ROE and criminal (superior) exoneration

A closely related question is whether multinational ROE can be adjusted with an exculpatory character. This question revolves around two issues:

I.   *Firstly,* how far these ROE as such imply a defense to international criminal litigation or war crimes regarding UN Force commanders relying on these ROE; and

II.  *Secondly,* how far these ROE legitimate or exonerate the use of force by multinational forces in the context of peacekeeping or peace-enforcement operations against other parties to the conflict.

Ad (I):
This modality is clearly exemplified by the massacre of members of the UN-Belgium peacekeeping contingent, part of UNAMIR in April 1994, during the Rwandan civil war. This massacre was a clear violation of

common Article 3 of the Geneva Conventions, since members of a (UN) multinational Force are, in principle, *"persons taking no active part in hostilities"* for the purpose of this Common Article 3. Acts of violence against them and hostage taking are therefore unlawful. The Security Council's condemnation of that attack as a violation of IHL is to be interpreted as a reference to that provision.[79] As already noted, the force commander of the Belgian contingent in question, Colonel Marchal, was prosecuted for failure to act, being superior responsible for the safety and action in self-defense on behalf of his (UN-) personnel, i.e., the ten killed Belgian para-commandos or *"blue helmets."*

Pursuant to the principle that members of UN Peacekeeping operations remain subject to the exclusive jurisdiction of their respective national states with regard to any criminal offences that may be committed by them,[80] Colonel Marchal was charged before his national Military Court at Brussels for involuntary manslaughter regarding the killed members of his unit. The Military Penal Court, in a judgment rendered on the 4th July 1996, acquitted him because it was accepted that the accused complied with the UN Mandate in question as well as the ROE drawn for this operation.[81]

The conclusion emerges therefore that multinational ROE merits, under some circumstances, legal protection for the members of such multinational forces and associated personnel, especially force commanders. Since it is arguable that these ROE reflect customary international law or form part of it, their protective character towards force commanders, such as Colonel Marchal, can be ascertained *on the basis of case-by-case law*. The degree of this protective recognition must depend largely on the question whether multinational peacekeeping or peace-enforcement forces are or are not a *party* to the international armed conflict in question. It is arguable that, in the event, e.g., a UN Force is not a party to an armed conflict, but is nevertheless subjected to attacks by one or more of the belligerent forces—as in Rwanda, where UNAMIR took no active part in hostilities and thus performed only peacekeeping—the protective value of ROE (and the reliance thereon) on behalf of force commanders or personnel participating in peacekeeping operations has to be given more weight. This especially counts for the rules and directives of the use of force in self-defense. From this perspective, the judgment of the Belgian Military Court, in the *Marchal* case, is controversial, since the Court did not in general uphold that the force commander *stricto sensu*

79.  *See* Greenwood, *supra* note 13, 1998, at 31.
80.  *See* Zwanenburg, *supra* note 16, at 2; *see* also Secretary-General Bulletin dd. 6 August 1999, o.c. Section 4; *see* also the NATO Status of Force Agreements with regard to transfer of jurisdiction to national courts.
81.  Case no. 13, R.G. 1996, *Le Ministre Public v. L.M.G.M. Marchal*, para. 3(a–i) and 4.

had an obligation to apply the ROE code of conduct for self-defense on behalf of his unit.

Ad (II):

As to the second question, the principle focus of attention is drawn to the assumption that the authority to use force in traditional UN (peace-keeping) operations *"( . . . ) shows how limited ( . . . ) the options (are) at the disposal of UN commanders."*[82] When considering the previously discussed *UN Standing Rules of engagement concerning Peace Enforcement*, this assumption seems inconclusive. With regard to the *"inherent right of self-defense"* of UN Force commanders, the definition of UN ROE held that *"at all times ( . . . ) the requirements of necessity and proportionality ( . . . ) will be the basis for the* judgment of the commander (emphasis added; GJK) *as to what constitutes an appropriate response to a particular hostile act or demonstration of hostile intent."* This implies a considerable discretionary power and assessment for UN Force commanders regarding the use of force. Interestingly, these UN ROE entail a very detailed determination of the above-mentioned four main constituent elements of self-defense, to be interpreted by the UN force commanders themselves.[83] The rather wide range of interpretive powers hereto of UN Force commanders, contrary to the introductory assumption, are also envisioned by, *inter alia*, the following provisions in the UN ROE regarding the definition of several self-defense elements:

- *"Hostile Force,"* which includes any force that *"has been* declared hostile by the force commander *or the appropriate UN authority"* (emphasis added; GJK).
- *"Reasonable belief,"* in the context of the element of proportionality, which is present *"when the* commander *or individual logically concludes that, based on the conditions and circumstances in which he finds himself, a threat exists that he is authorized to suppress."*[84]

Supportive to these substantive interpretative powers of UN Force commanders is the possibility of declaring a certain force hostile: *"only the appropriate UN authority or the force commander may declare a force hostile."*[85]

In conclusion, the nature of the UN ROE regarding peace enforcement does not restrain force commanders in their options as to the application of self-defense, but rather endows them with interpretive authority.

---

82. Van Hegelsom, *supra* note 51, at 54.
83. *See* section 5 of the UN ROE.
84. *See* section 4 and 6 of the UN ROE.
85. UN ROE, at 7.

Although this view respects their professional experience and case-by-case judgment, conversely the consequence hereof may be that failure to apply this authority in compliance with norms of ICL and IHL imputes a lower threshold of individual superior responsibility.

## 7.5 Multinational ROE in maritime (law enforcement) operations

Leaving aside jurisdictional issues with respect to suppressing illicit drug trafficking on the high seas, and presupposing the existence of such jurisdiction, the phenomenon of multinational ROE and command responsibility also emerge in the sphere of the use of force as such by maritime forces. International law distinguishes between the *jus ad bellum*—the right to go to war—and the *jus in bello*—the law governing the waging of war and the treatment of combatants and civilians in time of war.[86] Maritime law enforcement operations are mostly related to *jus ad bellum*. Apart from Article 51 of the UN Charter, no clear international legal guidelines are available and the only resort is to domestic law enforcement norms of a particular State.

In the realm of both *jus in bello* and *jus ad bellum*, the international community ensures uniform standards or norms regarding the application of force. These standards, also known as Rules of Engagement (ROE) were recently again applied by NATO in the Kosovo war, and meant to be *"the authorization for or limits on the use of force* during *military operations,"*[87] which are based on the unique requirements and objectives of each mission and the right of self-defense. It is my opinion that, with respect to the norms to be applied in a *jus ad bellum* situation, States should also agree to act in accordance with the principles and spirit of these ROE enacted by international organizations. In this context a parallel development can be observed concerning UN military operations and the application of norms of IHL. Even when not acting as a party to the armed conflict (*jus in bello*), a UN peacekeeping or peace enforcement contingent has a duty to comply with the principles and spirit of IHL norms.[88] The latter norms are mainly derived from the provisions of the Geneva Conventions, several of which nowadays can be regarded as stating rules of customary international law. The following provisions of Protocol I can, *inter alia*, be regarded as binding in customary law:

- The principle of distinction and the prohibition of attacks against the civilian population, individual civilians and civilian objects, laid down in Articles 48, 51 (2) and 52 (1);

---

86. *See* JOHN DUGARD, INTERNATIONAL LAW 431 (2000).
87. *See* Part I, Margin No. 1 of these ROE MC 362.
88. *See* C. Greenwood, *supra* note 13, at 33–34.

- the definition of a military objective in Article 52 (2);
- the principle of proportionality laid down in Articles 51 (5)(b) and 57 (2)(a)(iii); and
- the principle of the protection of cultural objects, envisioned by Article 53.[89]

Since, as is observed in the first chapter, ROE enacted by UN or NATO reflect these provisions, especially the principle of proportionality, it can be held that these ROE embrace also rules of customary international law.

In the present context, particular significance attaches to the fact that on the 1st December 1999 the Military Committee of NATO approved its Rules of Engagement named "MC 362," which were actually *de facto* applied during the Kosovo war. These Rules of Engagement (hereinafter ROE) enhance in annex D the requirements for the use of force in maritime operations (according to Article 3 applicable in both *jus in bello* as well as in peace time) and refer in Article 7 of this annex to, *inter alia,* enforcing "( . . . ) *prohibitions on the transport of specified persons or material ( . . . )*" derived from "( . . . ) *international law, treaty or convention or the resolutions or enactments of the UN ( . . . ).*" Thus these ROE seem to embrace also illicit drug trafficking envisaged by the 1988 Drug Convention. The system of annex D of the ROE MC 362 represents the elements of a use of force system in compliance with the legal regime relating to the analogous institution of the use of force by States. That is to say, it provides the practical basis for the effective application of the principles of proportionality and subsidiarity,[90] being these principles' essential boundaries in the system of international public order.[91] It was these principles which are affirmed and applied by the International Law Commission in its report to the General Assembly on the Work of the thirty-second session related to the use of force by States,[92] as well as adhered to by the International Court of Justice in the *Nicaragua* case[93] and *Corfu Channel* case.[94] In this realm, the question worthy of debate is whether a right to use force to detain vessels, in the context of *jus ad bellum,* exists on the basis of security or (anticipatory) self-defense. Apart from scholarly support by mainly English authorities, this view seems to contravene current public international law. In the absence of an attack on other shipping by the vessel sought to be detained, the requirements for the use of force by means of

---

89. *See* C. Greenwood, *supra* note 18, at 63–88.
90. *See* Articles 11–15 of Annex D of the ROE, constituting a framework of gradually increasing enforcement measures including, as last resort, disabling fire.
91. *See* I. Brownlie, *supra* note 65, at 194–210.
92. ICL Yearbook, 1980, II, Pt. ii, at 52.
93. ICJ Reports, 1984, at 392.
94. ICJ Reports 1949 Merits, at 4.

self-defense are lacking.[95] In the present context it is significant that the International Law Commission (ILC), and the majority of State opinions, do not accept the legality of security zones (as to support a claim to visit and seize vessels on the high seas) *"and therefore are unlikely to regard an ambulatory exercise of a right of (anticipatory) self-defense with any favor."*[96] In its comment on the draft Article which later appeared as Article 22 of the Convention on the High Seas, the ILC stated: *"The question arose whether the right to board a vessel should be recognized also in the event of a ship being suspected of committing acts hostile to the State to which the warship belongs, at a time of imminent danger to the security of that State. The Commission did not deem it advisable to include such a provision, mainly because of the vagueness of terms like 'imminent danger' and 'hostile acts,' which leaves them open to abuse."*[97] The absence of an internationally juridical basis for visiting and seizure of suspected vessels on the high seas based upon the concept of (anticipatory) self-defense can serve as an additional argument for implementation and application of the contents of Annex D of the ROE MC 362 to render the denominators for the use of force in the area of law enforcement operations by maritime forces on the high seas, especially in the context of counter drug (CD) operations.

In the sphere of international law enforcement, another precedent and legal framework emerges, i.e., the enforcement rules of the US Coast Guard *"use of force policy."* These rules involve the implementation of a use of force continuum against individuals to be conducted in law enforcement situations. This continuum recognizes four basic types of force starting at a passive level towards active levels. Interestingly, this framework entails in rule 4.10.9 the doctrine of *"disabling fire,"* defined as *"a special method of stopping a vessel."* It is important to note that US federal statutory law specifically allows the use of disabling fire, (14 USC 637). This law enables a US Navy surface vessel with a Coast Guard LEDET aboard and operating under Coast Guard TACON, after firing a warning shot, to fire—as a last resort and under certain restrictive conditions—into a vessel which is subject to seizure or examination if it does not stop upon being ordered to do so, for the sole purpose of stopping a vessel after obtaining permission through the Statement of No Objection (SNO) process pursuant to Article 17(4) of the 1988 Drug Convention. This concept presupposes also a statutory basis in the Dutch Penal Code as well as the Antillean equivalent. To that end, the present Dutch domestic statutory powers concerning the arrest of individuals can be extended or refined.

Universal jurisdiction is one thing, and the use of force and law enforcement (on the high seas) is another. The Israeli government and

---

95. *See* IAN BROWNLIE, PRINCIPLES OF PUBLIC INTERNATIONAL LAW 245 (1990).
96. *Ibid.*
97. Yearbook ILC, 1956 (ii) 284.

Courts justified the criminal trial against A. Eichmann in part on the principle of universality, but not the abduction of A. Eichmann by Israeli agents to Israel.[98] The latter aspect is comparable to the apprehension of defendants on the high seas by certain States. This example shows that the principle of universality does not empower States with an unlimited right to enforce the laws. As observed, law enforcement on the high seas forms an exception in so far as the five events of Article 110 of the 1982 Convention on the Law of the Sea are applicable.

A legal approach dictates reference to the context, that is to say, the necessity of self-defense and the purposive context which it presents. It is therefore important to emphasize that the analyzed ROE MC 362—as stressed in Part II of its "main body" named "self-defense"—*"does not limit this right"* and especially does not exclude the right *"to defend NATO forces and personnel against attack or an imminent attack."* Thus, once the use of force by apprehended vessels or its crew is launched in the course of maritime law enforcement operations against the executing forces, the concept of (anticipatory) self-defense applies, analogous to the provisions in the submitted NATO ROE.

In face of the present view in international law regarding the use of force by States, the increasing receptiveness of the international legal community,[99] and the perpetration of extreme forms of violence on the high seas committed by suspects in relation the security of maritime forces,[100] the time has arrived to give more recognition to the establishment of a clear international legal regime equal to the herein analyzed Annex D of the NATO ROE MC 362. Since these rules were clearly intended to restrict or minimize resort to the use of force in maritime operations and also resort to different forms of (armed) intervention by maritime forces, there can be no question that these denominators imply an effective instrument and include the prerequisites for use of force by States, especially because these rules reflect norms of customary international law, as observed before. No doubt a legal regime on this topic *"( . . . ) will always entail problems of application, and rules alone, however carefully formulated, will not induce States to behave in a civilized way."*[101]

However, the risks of governmental abuse of powers and use of force seem to decrease when enacted according the forcible intervention framework of the Articles 7–15 of the NATO ROE, MC 362, Annex D. By way of conclusion it is therefore appropriate to point to the entry of similar ROE (in this context regional or national) relating to the use of force by maritime forces in the high seas, especially with respect to the legitimacy for

---

98. *See also* TH. BUERGENTHAL & H.G. MAIER, PUBLIC INTERNATIONAL LAW 170 (1989).
99. *See* the described conventions.
100. *See* statistics of the Flag Officer Netherlands Forces in the Caribbean.
101. Brownlie, *supra* note 65, at 210.

resort to force by Dutch Navy forces participating in the LEDET on the Caribbean High Seas.

The creation of multinational ROE indicates how, in the course of time, confronted with the controversy between proponents of national law advocating the concept of *jus cogens* and proponents of legal positivism arguing that the principle of legality supersedes, *"a value-neutral approach is impossible, thus the only practical solution is* the codification of ICL (emphasis added; GJK)."[102] It must be emphasized that law enforcement powers on the high seas is an area that needs additional norms and improved mechanisms of control. Governments have to endeavor, more than ever, to obtain the codification of ICL, inclusive of the jurisdiction of powers to attain appropriate functioning of the present indirect enforcement system.

### 7.6 Multinational ROE and principles of legality: conclusion

It has frequently been suggested that both national and international law would be quite insufficient *"in relation to the command of the UN over national military contingents,"* which consequently would lead to *"an insufficient enforcement of the international obligation of the UN but also to an intolerable uncertainty as to the legal status of individual soldiers."*[103] It should be clear, however, that on the one hand, this *"insufficiency"* and *"uncertainty"* is only relative in the event both ICL and IHL would elaborate more on the nature, status and context of the multinational ROE. To erase this alleged "uncertainty," more clarification should be endorsed to the extent of both the inculpatory and exculpatory character of ROE with regard to force commanders as well as subordinate, individual soldiers. In practice, more advice and appropriate instruction to be given to the military commanders and soldiers of multinational forces about the factual and legal meaning of these Rules has to be ensured pursuant to Articles 82 and 83 of the 1977 Additional Protocol I.

On the other hand, though, all sources of ICL must satisfy certain *"principles of legality"* reflected in the Latin adagium *"nullum crimen sine lege, nulla poena sine lege (jus)."* The question and criticism of the aforementioned view regarding the international legal status of multinational ROE is: whether it can be left to the group of States or international organizations in question to enact ROE with the legal status of direct sources of International Customary Law, since it could contravene the principle of legality. It should first be noted, however, that the proposed substitution of the word *"jus"* for *"lege,"* with regard to the aforementioned adagium,

---

102. M. Cherif Bassiouni, *supra* note 39, at 44.
103. Simma, *supra* note 38, at 597.

is advocated in order to emphasize sources and normative bases other than written law.[104] Secondly, the principles of legality in ICL differ from those of many legal systems in that they are less rigorous than, *inter alia*, positivist legal systems.[105] Therefore the existence of a customary international law can depend upon various sources. Thirdly, no contravention as to the principles of legality appears, because the content of ROE as such does not constitute the alleged international crime; their content can only serve as *one of the components* to establish a possible in—or exculpation to a war crimes indictment in the sense that ROE dictate a high evidentiary level of command responsibility to war crimes or exculpation thereof.


## 8   SUMMARY AND CONCLUSIONS

This chapter has demonstrated that although guilt in ICL must in principle be assessed on a personal basis, there are circumstances where an individual not directly involved or even an (international) organization can be held criminally responsible for what one knew or should have known and failed to stop, prevent or correct.[106] Such a circumstance clearly encompasses the aforementioned analyzed situation of perpetration of war crimes or grave violations of IHL during multinational operations, such as those of UN and NATO, irrespective of the exact mandate as to peacekeeping or peace-enforcement, which imputes both individual superior as well as (institutional) criminal liability of the UN or NATO as such. Although an institutional framework for regulating the latter kind of liability until now is absent, the featured ROE—irrespective of status as part of customary international law—are sufficiently justified as to devising and assessing the scope of both institutional and individual criminal liability. This conclusion is justified since these multinational ROE, enacted on behalf of the submitted operations, envision a wide range of legal obligations, prohibitions, permissions and consequences for the particular military commanders, particularly regarding the use of force. On the one hand, they facilitate the determination as to when multinational Force commanders or the multinational organization itself has committed an international crime. On the other hand, they govern the law for the individual soldier in armed conflicts, for these individual military rules are equally binding to a superior order. A new approach is needed in the event these "ROE orders" are not manifestly illegal; the (consequential) better answer is that—in case of a rejection of a subsequent defense of

---

104.   INTERNATIONAL CRIMINAL LAW, CASES AND MATERIALS 7 (Jordan J. Paust & M. Cherif Bassiouni, et al., eds., 1996).

105.   *Ibid.*

106.   *See* also J.J. Paust, *supra* note 59, at 223–237.

superior orders—the enactors of these ROE incur criminal liability so that they will abstain from proclaiming frivolous ROE. Notwithstanding this fact, however, that state and institutional criminal liability is an accepted principle of ICL, there is a need to institutionalize acts of war crimes, accountable to multinational (military) organizations,[107] analogous to, e.g., the aforementioned Article 3 of the 1907 Convention on the Laws of War on Land.

---

107. Similar to state crimes: Dugard, *supra* note 42, at 253.

# CHAPTER V

# INTERNATIONAL CRIMINAL LAW DEFENSES AND THE INTERNATIONAL REGULATION OF ARMED CONFLICTS

## 1  INTRODUCTION

The seemingly inevitable antagonistic relationship between the defenses of superior orders and duress on the one hand and the doctrine of command responsibility on the other is well expressed by Green as he states: *"To some extent it may be considered that the defense of superior orders and the question of command responsibility are two counterparts of a single issue, for one raises the possibility of a person contending that he is not liable for his wrongdoing because he was merely following orders, while the other turns on the liability of a superior for the order he may have given that results in the commission of a criminal act."*[1]

Although both common law and civil law systems endorse the principle of individual criminal responsibility, it seems contradictory to observe that both conventional and customary international law do not accept the defenses of superior orders and duress as exculpatory to international crimes and to crimes against humanity as such, apart from an eventually mitigative effect.[2]

The reluctance to implement provisions as to the admissibility of these defenses—pursuant to the Statutes of both *ad hoc* Tribunals, the Statute of the ICC, Art. 8 of the Nuremberg International Military Tribunal (IMT) Charter and Art. 4 (2) of the Control Council Law No. 10—seems firstly to emerge from the fact that the establishment of these tribunals is founded upon three distinct but related areas of law: international criminal law (hereinafter ICL), international humanitarian law, and international human rights law,[3] this tripartite basis distinguishes these tribunals

---

1. Leslie C. Green, *Superior Orders and Command Responsibility*, 27 THE CANADIAN YEARBOOK OF INTERNATIONAL LAW 167 (1989).
2. *See*, e.g., HANS P. GASSER, INTERNATIONAL HUMANITARIAN LAW 86 (1992); M. CHERIF BASSIOUNI AND PETER MANIKAS, THE LAW OF THE ICTY 408 (1996). The Statutes of ICTY, ICTR and ICC exclude these defenses.
3. *See also* Anonymous, *Human Rights in Peace Negotiations*, 18 HUMAN RIGHTS QUARTERLY 258 (1996).

from their predecessors, resulting in a judicial compromise as to the adjudicatory framework of these Courts. Secondly, causation on this topic can be found in the fact that ICL lacks a general part on the doctrinal subject matters, such as the concept of legal defenses, which have in fact to be remedied in accordance with national laws.[4] Furthermore, this "lack of legislative inclusion" stems from the fact that ICL is based on an indirect enforcement system, under which States incorporate internationally established proscriptions into their national legal systems which are subsequently enforced through the respective domestic criminal justice systems.[5]

The purpose of this chapter is, first, to examine the present doctrine and jurisprudence of the *ad hoc* Tribunals and Draft ICC Statute as to legitimacy of the defenses of superior orders and duress in the area of armed conflicts and connected war crimes. Second, it intends to determine whether this doctrine and jurisprudence do comply with the principle of legality, as well as other principles of law. Finally, it investigates if customary international law standards such as the rules of engagement, *in casu* legal standards to be pursued by military commanders during (multi) national (peacekeeping-) enforcement operations,[6] may be accorded to the accused in the context of duress, superior orders or perhaps self defense.

## 2    DEFENSES OF DURESS AND SUPERIOR ORDERS UNDER ICTY AND ICTR JURISPRUDENCE

### 2.1  The restrictive approach on duress of the *ad hoc* Tribunals

When it comes to discussing whether war crimes indictments can be dismissed due to the defense of superior orders and duress, the ICTY and ICTR have not allowed superior orders and duress as a defense, but are only prepared to take this possible defense into consideration as a mitigating factor.[7] In the hereinafter to be analyzed *Erdemović* Case, the Trial Chamber of the ICTY ruled *inter alia* that *"with regard to a crime against humanity, ( . . . ) the life of the accused and that of the victim are not fully equivalent,"* continuing that, *"as opposed to ordinary law, the violation*

---

4.    *See*, e.g., the Trial Chamber's decision on duress in the *Erdemović* case, *infra* note 8, para. 17.

5.    *See* M. Cherif Bassiouni and P. Manikas, *supra* note 2, at 269.

6.    *See* for these three various forms of operations: Christopher Greenwood, *International Humanitarian Law and United Nations Military Operations*, I YEARBOOK OF INTERNATIONAL HUMANITARIAN LAW 12 (1998).

7.    *See* also Christopher L. Blakesley, *Atrocity and its Prosecution: The Ad Hoc Tribunals of the Former Yugoslavia and Rwanda*, in THE LAW OF WAR CRIMES 219 (T.L.H. McCormack & G.J. Simpson, eds., 1997).

*here is no longer directed at the physical welfare of the victim alone but at humanity as a whole.*"[8]

The ICTY's approach to the defense of duress is colored by the nature of war crimes and is inclined to demand from the accused virtually a *probatio diabolica*: "*the duty to disobey (a manifestly illegal order) can (according to the ICTY) only recede in the face of the* most extreme duress" (emphasis added; GJK).[9] The implicit burden of proof, which in fact bears on the accused (at least by a preponderance of evidence)[10] is for the latter problematic. How can he make this "most extreme duress" probable? The question arises whether this jurisprudence complies with the principle that, according to both Art. 21 (3) of the ICTY Statute and Rule 87 (A) of the Rules of Procedure and Evidence of the ICTY, the Prosecutor bears the onus of establishing the guilt of the accused beyond a reasonable doubt. This subsequently leads to the notion that the defendant is not obliged to prove beyond a reasonable doubt the existence of a legal defense; the accused may merely depend on the criterion of preponderance of evidence by presenting a *prima facie* case, analogous to Rule 66 (B) of the Rules of Procedure and Evidence of the ICTY and ICTR.[11] Since it is extremely difficult for an accused to fulfill the requirement of "the most extreme duress," it may be said that the present jurisprudence of the ICTY regarding duress constrains the procedural and material defense scope of the accused unjustly. The *de facto* acknowledgment thereof is entailed in paragraph 19 of the *Erdemović* judgment, wherein the Tribunal rules that "*( . . . ) while the complete defense based on moral duress and/or a state of necessity stemming from superior orders is not ruled out absolutely, its conditions of application are particularly* strict (emphasis added; GJK)," characterizing its test as the use of a "*rigorous and restrictive approach,*" the legitimacy of which test is conceded by "*the scope of its jurisdiction (which) requires it to judge the most serious violations of international humanitarian law.*" Is this legal policy argument justificatory as to narrowing the scope of defenses of duress and superior orders? The answer hereof will be further assessed in sections 3–9 below.

---

8.    *See Prosecutor v. Drazen Erdemović*, Sentencing Judgment, Case No. IT-96-22-T, 29 November 1996, paras. 18–20.

9.    *Erdemović* judgment, *supra* note 8, at para. 18.

10.    *See* Renee C. Pruitt, *Guilt by Majority in the ICTY: Does this meet the standard of Beyond Reasonable Doubt?*, 10 LJIL 557–578 (1997).

11.    *See* also decision Trial Chamber II in *Delalić et al.*, dd. 26 September 1996, IT-96-21-T, decision on motion by the accused Z. Delalić for the disclosure of evidence, para. 49.

## 2.2 Superior orders and moral choice

### 2.2.1 Superior responsibility as prerequisite to the defense of superior orders

The defense of superior orders is the legal and logical concomitant to the doctrine of superior responsibility, which doctrine originated in national military law and gradually became a basis of international criminal responsibility.[12] Thus, a nexus exists between these two legal concepts. It can therefore be asserted that the presence of superior responsibility forms a *conditio sine qua non* as to the application of the defense of superior orders. Should therefore the requisite elements for superior responsibility not be proved, no defense of superior orders would be available at all. In the words of Bassiouni: *"( . . . ) if a subordinate is to be exonerated from criminal responsibility for carrying out a superior's order, that superior should be accountable for issuing an order which violates ICL."*[13] Conversely, it can be held that absence of superior responsibility rules out the defense of superior orders. Let us therefore first turn to the former prerequisite, the concept of superior orders. Article 7 (3) of the ICTY Statute, as noted by the Trial Chamber of the ICTY, makes clear that superior responsibility may be invoked if three concurrent elements are proved, which constituent elements are clearly drawn from Article 86 (2) of Additional Protocol I and Article 6 of the Draft Code of the International Law Commission of 1996, enshrined also by Article 28 of the Rome Statute of the ICC:

1. A superior-subordinate relationship exists between the person against whom the claim is directed and the perpetrators of the offence;
2. the superior knew or had reason to know that a crime was about to be committed or had been committed; and
3. the superior did not take all the necessary and reasonable measures to prevent the crime or to punish the perpetrator or perpetrators thereof.[14]

If any one of these three constituent elements is absent, the defense of superior orders is deemed to fail.

Civil law tribunals have tried to solve the issue of command responsibility regarding unlawful orders by assessing the accused's capacity and (eventual) opposition. Military officers (exemplified in both the *High Command* case, where senior German officers were held criminally liable

---

12.  *See* M. Cherif Bassiouni & P. Manikas, *supra* note 2, at 346.
13.  Bassiouni & Manikas, *supra* note 2, at 346.
14.  *See Prosecutor v. Z. Aleksovski*, Judgment 25 June 1999, paras. 69–70.

for participating in Hitler's extermination plan,[15] and in the *Hostage* case),[16] as well as non-military persons with power over others (exemplified in both the *Ministries* case, related to the power of German government officials to oppose the extermination of the Jewish people,[17] and the *Roechling Enterprises* case, where the Tribunal held German industrialists criminally liable for acts of slave labor and ill-treatment of civilians and POWs who worked within their power)[18] were found subject to the doctrine of command responsibility based on the rationale "*that persons in de facto control are responsible for persons under their power, irrespective of whether a military or civilian function was served.*"[19] This rich jurisprudence did not result in an express provision on superior responsibility in the Geneva Conventions of 1949. Actually, the increase in civil wars since 1950, involving rebel armies and rebel "command" structures, has led to the implementation of Articles 86 and 87 of Geneva Protocol I (1977), accumulating this development in the establishment of the ICTY and ICTR, where the doctrine of command responsibility in civil conflicts was applied to modern warfare.[20] Recent developments in the jurisprudence of ICTY and ICTR indicate a further extension of the scope of military and civilian superior responsibility under international law, whereas, until the *Celebići* case of the ICTY,[21] the Tribunals dealt only with charges of direct participation, not based on omissions by superiors. Although Article 7 (3) of the ICTY Statute and Article 6 (3) of the ICTR Statute, similar like Art. 28 (2) of the ICC Statute, pertain only to express formulations of (active) duties of commanders, in order to prevent their subordinates from violating the laws of war, the ICTY rendered convictions, in the *Celebići* and *Blaškić* cases,[22] on the basis of command responsibility due to criminal omissions or activities of the superiors in both civilian and military context, which subsequently inspired the enactment of Article 28 of the ICC Statute.

A further extension as to the doctrine of superior responsibility was formulated in the recent *Aleksovski* judgment of the ICTY Trial Chamber.[23]

---

15. See *U.S. v. Von Leeb*, 11 Trials of War Criminals before the Nuremberg Military Tribunals under Control Council Law No. 10, at 1, 462 (1950).

16. See *U.S. v. List et al.*, 11 Trials, *infra* note 15 at 759, 1230 (1951).

17. See *U.S.-Von Weiszsaecker*, 14 Trials, *infra* note 15, at 308 (1952).

18. See Judgment on Appeal to the Superior Military Government Court of the French Occupation Zone in Germany, 14 Trials *infra* note 15, at 1097; See also *U.S. v. Flick*, 6 Trials, *infra* note 15, at 1187 (1952).

19. See Ilias Bantekas, *The contemporary law of superior responsibility*, 93 THE AMERICAN JOURNAL OF INTERNATIONAL LAW 574 (1999).

20. See Bantekas, *supra* note 19, at 575.

21. See *Prosecutor v. Delalić*, Judgment No. IT-96-21-T, 16 November 1998.

22. *Prosecutor v. Blaškić*, No. IT-95-14 concerning the Bosnian-Croat General Blaškić who was convicted on 3 March 2000 because of tolerating various widespread crimes committed by combat units acting within his geographical area of command.

23. Judgment dd. 25 June 1999, *Prosecutor v. Z. Aleksovski*, paras 66–78.

The Tribunal put forth an interpretation of the generic term *"superior"* in Article 7 (3) of the Statute, which term, according the Tribunal, *"( . . . ) can be interpreted only to mean that superior responsibility is not limited to military commanders but may apply to the civilian authorities"* (who are in a similar position of command and exercise a similar degree of control with respect to their subordinates; GJK). The Court adds that this interpretation is *"( . . . ) in line with customary international law as the Trial Chamber in the* Celebići *case already noted."*[24] Superior responsibility is thus not reserved for official authorities. Any person acting *de facto* as a superior may, pursuant to the *Aleksovski* judgment, be held responsible under Article 7 (3), whereby the decisive criterion in determining who is a superior according to customary international law, as emphasized by the Tribunal, is not only the accused's *formal legal status* but also his *ability*, as demonstrated by his duties and competence, to exercise *control*.[25] The Tribunal further assesses the scope of this concept by defining that *"formal designation as a commander should not be considered to be a necessary prerequisite for superior responsibility to attach, as such responsibility may be imposed by virtue of a person's* de facto, *as well as* de jure, *position as a commander."*[26]

The international law doctrine of command responsibility is now, to a considerable extent, expanded and formalized in Article 28 of the ICC Statute. This provision entails the following requisite elements: (a) a military commander or person effectively acting as a military commander, (b) crimes committed by forces (c) under his effective command and control or effective authority and control, and (d) a failure to exercise a proper control over such forces.

Ad a: Forces include the armed forces of a party to a conflict, which encompass, pursuant to Article 43 of Additional Protocol I, all organized armed forces, groups and units subjected to an internal disciplinary system, including armed police units and paramilitary units.[27]

Ad b: The second element parallels the jurisprudence of the ICTY, namely the principle that forces under the effective command and control of a commander, pursuant to Article 28, entails forces which are subordinate to the commander in either *"a de jure or de facto chain of command and to which the commander may give orders,"* which orders may be transmitted directly or through intermediate subordinate commanders of lower ranks.[28] Like the jurisprudence of the ICTY, hereinafter to be discussed, the word "effective" in this provision means to cover both *de jure* and *de facto* command, as well as ensuring that multiple chains of command can-

---

  24. *See Aleksovski* Judgment, o.c., para. 75.

  25. *See Aleksovski* Judgment, o.c., para. 76.

  26. *Supra* note 25.

  27. *See* William J. Fenrick, *Article 28, Margin No. 6*, in COMMENTARY ON THE ROME STATUTE (Otto Triffterer, ed., 1999).

  28. W.J. Fenrick, *supra* note 27, Margin No. 7.

not serve as a shelter for operative commanders of higher ranks who are empowered to give the particular orders, this implying that subjective incapacity of such a commander forms no defense on his behalf.

Ad c: Subsequently, as a third element under the Statute, responsibility of commanding officers can also exist in case of *"effective authority and control,"* which relates to the situation of control over forces which are not placed under these commanders in a direct chain of command.[29]

Ad d: The fourth element of *"failure to exercise control properly"* seems to be derived from, *inter alia*, Articles 86 (a provision related to failure to act) and 87 of Additional Protocol I, enshrining the obligation of commanders, not only to control, prevent, suppress, and report breaches of the Geneva Conventions or its Protocols, but also the preventive duty to make their subordinates aware of these obligations under the Conventions and Additional Protocol I.

Article 28 of the ICC Statute subsequently provides for two concrete denominators to establish criminal responsibility of commanders. Article 28 (a)(i) aims at the situation in which the commander *"either knew or should have known."* Apart from proving actual knowledge on a circumstantial basis, in which event the responsibility seems obvious, the requisite *"should have known"* can be deduced from a scale of special circumstances, several of them analyzed by Fenrick: the number of legal acts, their type and scope, the time during which these acts occurred, the number and type of troops involved, the widespread scale of the acts, the *modus operandi*, the tactical actions, the officers and staff involved, and finally the location of the commander himself at the time of the atrocities.[30] Furthermore, Article 28 (a)(i) (with the element *"should have known"*) relates also to the jurisprudence of the World War II War Crimes Tribunals discussed above. It clearly covers the situation in which a commander, having duties under Articles 83, 86 and 87 of Additional Protocol I, fails to obtain or disregards clear indications as to the occurrence of the atrocities. It is logical that the drafters of the ICC Statute envisioned, in Article 28 (a)(ii), the situation of failure to take corrective measures available to commanders which are within their powers.

It must be emphasized, however, that under the ICC Statute a commander cannot automatically be held criminally responsible for acts of subordinates. According to Fenrick, in case offences are already committed, it is questionable if a commander has direct and complete control over military or civil justice systems. This leads Fenrick to the conclusion that, since a commander cannot direct that an accused be found guilty, the commander would have fulfilled his responsibility when alleged offences are

---

29. *See* Fenrick, *supra* note 27, Margin No. 8.
30. Fenrick, *supra* note 27, Margin No. 10.

properly investigated and fairly tried, instead of condoning sham investigations or show trials.[31]

In conclusion, it appears that in the event *inter alia* that the aforementioned decisive criterion of the factual or legal ability to exercise control cannot be proven in criminal proceedings, subsequently the subordinate accused cannot invoke the defense of superior orders. In such a situation it cannot be claimed that the subordinate could reasonably rely on the particular order, when this absence of the element of control regarding the "commander" in question was obvious.

### 2.2.2   Superior responsibility and imputed liability

The doctrine of command responsibility, as further developed by the ICTY and ICTR inclines to "imputed liability," this being reflected in Art. 7 (3) of the ICTY Statute and Art. 6 (3) of the ICTR Statute, whereby the commander is held criminally liable for a subordinate's unlawful conduct, which is not based on the commander's order, due to failure to act.[32] In the *Celebići* case, the ICTY stated—although the Tribunal used the term "vicarious liability"—that the basis of this doctrine is indeed not vicarious liability.[33] Although the mere existence of the element of authority over subordinates, both *de jure* and *de facto*, suffices as to the qualification of being a "superior" under Art. 7 (3) of the ICTY Statute,[34] the mere fact that a commanding officer is in a position of authority does not, according to ICL, *eo ipso* incur criminal responsibility. An opposite view would introduce in fact the burden of vicarious or strict liability, which contravenes the principle of individual culpability in ICL.[35]

### 2.2.3   Interaction of superior orders and duress

Interestingly, the *Erdemović* case dealt also with the defense of obedience to superior orders. The Trial Chamber of the ICTY noted that "( . . . ) *when it assesses the objective and subjective elements characterizing duress or the state of necessity, it is incumbent on the Trial Chamber to examine whether the accused in his situation did not have the duty to disobey, whether he had the*

---

31.   Fenrick. *supra* note 27, Margin No. 14.

32.   *See* M. Cherif Bassiouni & P. Manikas, *supra* note 2, at 345; *see* also *Aleksovski* Judgment, para. 67.

33.   *See Celebići* Decision, *supra* note 21, para. 675; Bantekas, *supra* note 19, at 577.

34.   Bantekas, *supra* note 19, at 579.

35.   *See infra* section 5.

*moral choice to do so or to try to do so,"*[36] leading this Tribunal to a "rigorous and restrictive approach" with regard to duress. As Blakesley stresses, this moral choice aspect confuses the concept of superior orders unjustly with duress.[37] The Tribunal explicitly rules that *"the order of a superior must, however, also be examined in the light of the related issue of duress."*[38] Duress is, however—it cannot be emphasized enough—not a form of superior orders, although it may be involved in many situations in which superior orders are raised as a defense.[39] Duress, as a separate, independent defense, confronts the accused with an excruciatingly difficult moral choice, whereas the defense of superior orders is not based on the confrontation with an extreme difficult moral choice, but rather founded upon the notion that in a command structure soldiers must obey their superiors.[40] It seems judicially incorrect to uphold the suggestion, as evidenced by the Trial Chamber, that if a superior order defense is denied, the defense of duress is likewise untenable. The discrepancy in such a perception is that compulsion, empowered by superior authority, is easily considered the main, or even the sole, source of duress. The external pressure as prerequisite for duress can, however, be embodied by several other causes, e.g. sexual abuse by fellow soldiers. This incorrect perception can thus possibly lead to an unjustified rejection of the defense of duress.[41]

Judge Cassese, in his Separate and Dissenting Opinion to the *Erdemović* decision of the Appeals Chamber, observes that in the case law in ICL duress is commonly raised in conjunction with superior orders.[42] As rightly pointed out in this Opinion, no necessary juridical relationship exists between these two defenses. Superior orders *"may be issued without being accompanied by* any *threats to life or limb."*[43] Cassese illustrates the independence of these two defenses by referring to the rule that, if the superior order is manifestly illegal under international law, the subordinate has the legal obligation to refuse to obey the order. If, however, such

---

36. *Erdemović* Judgment, *supra* note 8, para. 19.

37. Christopher L. Blakesley *Atrocity and Its Prosecution: The Ad Hoc Tribunals for the Former Yugoslavia and Rwanda*, in THE LAW OF WAR CRIMES 219 (Timothy L.H. McCormack and Gerry J. Simpson, eds., 1997); *see* also Harmen van der Wilt, in I ANNOTATED LEADING CASES OF INTERNATIONAL CRIMINAL TRIBUNALS 535 (1999).

38. *See* Sentencing judgment, *Prosecutor v. Erdemović*, *supra* note 8, para. 54.

39. Blakesley, *supra* note 37, at 220.

40. Blakesley, *supra* note 37, at 220; *see* also the *Llandovery Castle* case, Judgment of 1922, Leipzig Court, Am. Journal International Law, 708 (1922); *See* also *U.S. v. Calley*, 46 C.M.R. 1131 (1971).

41. *See* also H. Van der Wilt, *supra* note 37, at 535.

42. *See* Separate and Dissenting Opinion of Judge Cassese to *Prosecutor v. Erdemović*, Appeals Chamber Decision dd. 7 October 1997, Case No. IT-96-22-A, para. 15.

43. Cassese, *supra* note 42.

refusal culminates in an order which is reiterated under a threat to life or limb, *"then the defense of duress may be raised, and superior orders lose any legal relevance. Equally, duress may be raised entirely independently of superior orders, for example where the threat issues from a fellow serviceman."* Therefore Cassese concludes that, where duress is raised in conjunction with manifestly unlawful superior orders, the accused may only have a defense if he first refused to obey the unlawful order, and then only carried in out after a threat to life or limb. This observation of Cassese underlines the autonomy of both duress and superior orders, as already discussed in Chapter II above.

In recognition of the doctrinal distinction between duress and superior orders, which distinction is in fact neglected by the ICTY, the Tribunal should differentiate by accused and not adopt a general, overall concept in which these defenses *a priori* are, *de facto*, excluded from international criminal proceedings. In the next sections we will assess the five supportive arguments as to the principle of adjudicatory differentiability regarding these two defenses.

## 3  THE PRINCIPLES OF LEGALITY AND THE *RATIONAE MATERIAE* OF SUPRANATIONAL DEFENSES

The principles of legality require that there be no crime without a law (*nullum crimen sine lege* or *sine jure*), no punishment without a law (*nulla poena sine lege*), and no *ex post facto* application of laws.[44] These principles are deemed part of fundamental justice because they protect against potential judicial abuse and arbitrary application of the law, fundamental considerations also applying to general parts of ICL.[45] It is thus important to recognize that these principles of legality also affect the legitimacy of the submitted defenses and subsequently the adjudication of international tribunals hereto. This relates to the first argument for the admissibility of duress and superior orders as complete defenses to war crimes.

It goes without saying that as an integral part of the aforementioned principles of legality the requirement of procedural fairness also emerges, which subsequently is connected to the possibility of recourse to defenses to war crimes accusations.[46] The substance of war crimes has to be free from prejudices and selective application of ICL; rather ICL has to

---

44.  M. Cherif Bassiouni, *The Sources and Content of International Criminal Law: A Theoretical Framework*, in I INTERNATIONAL CRIMINAL LAW 33 (M. Cherif Bassiouni, ed., 1999).

45.  *See* Bassiouni, *supra* note 44, 1999, at 33.

46.  *See* Gerry J. Simpson, *War Crimes: A Critical Introduction*, in THE LAW OF WAR CRIMES 11 (Timothy L.H. McCormack & Gerry J. Simpson, eds. 1997).

endorse, in order to maintain the highest standards of justice and moral-ity,[47] a fair application of its rules to individual defendants, this being an important element of the principles of legality.[48] Supportive to this approach is the fact that the principles of legality in ICL are *sui generis:* "*They must balance the needs of justice for the world community and fairness for the accused in the context of the rule of law.*"[49] In achieving this balance in ICL, according to Bassiouni and Manikas, "( . . . ) *various factors must be taken into account,*"[50] which factors, from the perspective of the aforemen-tioned Rule of law, certainly include a fair application of legal defenses without *eo ipso* being *de facto* excluded from the ICL adjudicatory process.

Questions of legality have especially arisen in connection with the two most common substantive defenses to war crimes indictments: superior orders and duress. From the perspective of the aforementioned principles of legality, the Nuremberg War Tribunal jurisprudence related to these defenses, encompassing a general decree that these defenses were not available to the defendants—is questionable.[51] "*A system that,*" as stated by Simpson, "*denies either of these defenses' applicability may well successfully convict more 'war criminals' but there are costs to justice and order in such an approach.*"[52] Undoubtedly, the defenses of superior orders and duress incite a conflict between the principle of (procedural) legality in conjunc-tion with procedural fairness to the accused on the one hand and military discipline and criminal liability on the other. Military discipline implies a concept of military obedience (not to question military orders) whereas the law of war imposes an obligation to question those very same orders as to crimes against humanity.[53] ICL has tried to resolve this dilemma by virtue of establishing a distinction between "knowing" and "they had rea-son to know" standards in relation to reasonable orders and clearly aber-rant orders, which presupposes the presence of some notion of reasonableness or moral choice in wartime situations.[54] This is also exem-plified by Article 28 in conjunction with Article 33 of the ICC Statute.

---

47. *See* Speech by Judge Louise Arbour, Chief Prosecutor of the ICTY and ICTR, to the ISISC Meeting on Comparative Criminal Justice System dd. 18 December 1997, "The Development of a Coherent System of Rules of International Criminal Procedure Tribunals," at 1 and 12.

48. Simpson, *supra* note 46, at 11.

49. *See* M. Cherif Bassiouni & P. Manikas, *supra* note 2, at 268.

50. Bassiouni & Manikas, *supra* note 2, at 268.

51. *See* Simpson, *supra* note 46, at 14; superior orders were only admitted as a mitigating factor to punishment but were not adopted as a full defense.

52. Simpson, *supra* note 46, at 14.

53. *See* the above discussed decision by the Trial Chamber dd. 29 November 1996, *Prosecutor v. Erdemović, supra* note 8.

54. Simpson, *supra* note 46, at 14.

## 4    THE CONCEPT OF JUSTIFICATIONS AND EXCUSES

It is remarkable that international criminal tribunals are not inclined to differentiate, on the basis of both the Common Law and Civil law systems implemented, the doctrinal distinction between legal defenses as justifications on the one hand and as excuses on the other hand, as elaborated in Chapter I above. In the event of a justification, an otherwise criminal offence is transformed into a justified act. This occurs *inter alia* with regard to the defense of self-defense; an act arising from self-defense is considered to be juridically justified since the legal community *"positively approves of it."*[55] In the event of an excuses the otherwise criminal act remains unlawful or unjustified, since the community disapproves of it but thinks it is not right to treat it as a crime and therefore the defendant ought to bear, by virtue of factual or juridical reasons, no criminal liability.[56] The rationale of an excuse can be based on mistake of fact or law as well as on the premise that criminal law *"is not the law regulating decoration of heroism."*[57] This is the position adopted with regard to the defense of duress, in which event the particular criminal offence remains illegal though the accused is exculpated, because the law cannot uphold criminal responsibility at all costs, especially not in situations of extreme mental stress resulting from external pressure whereby it would be unreasonable to demand compliance with the law.

Notwithstanding a clear rejection of obedience to superior orders as an absolute *justificatory* defense for an accused acting under military authority in armed conflict, this substantive defense to war crimes by virtue of a legal excuse ought to be maintained.[58] As to duress, Dinstein's opinion that *"the correct approach is that no degree of duress or necessity may justify murder, let alone genocide,"*[59] is only legitimate as to duress being a justification, but cannot be recommended when the defense of duress is to be qualified as merely an excuse.[60]

Moreover, in order to adopt absolute excuses in regard to war crimes, two particular circumstances are complementary to the rationale of the defenses of superior orders and duress. The first emerges from the military structure encompassing the concept that, according to military law,

---

55.    JOHN SMITH AND BRIAN HOGAN, CRIMINAL LAW 193 (1996).

56.    *See* for this distinction: Smith and Hogan, *supra* note 55, at 193.

57.    *See* Mordechai Kremnitzer, *The World Community as an International Legislator in Competition with National Legislators*, in PRINCIPLES AND PROCEDURES FOR A NEW TRANSNATIONAL CRIMINAL LAW 345 (1992).

58.    *See* also Kremnitzer, *supra* note 57, at 345.

59.    Yoram Dinstein, *International Criminal Law*, 20 ISRAEL LAW REVIEW 235 (1985).

60.    *See* also Kremnitzer, *supra* note 57, at 345.

a subordinate is criminally liable for not obeying lawfully given orders of superiors. The second is that, especially in wartime, the subordinate is often not in a position to assess the lawfulness (either factual or legal) of the order in question, so that in principle recourse has to be made on the submitted orders. From this perspective Kremnitzer raises the question "( . . . ) *whether or not the special and unique nature of army structure and military discipline necessitates a specific defense.*"[61] It is noteworthy, however, that in the application of Article 4 (2) of the Control Council Law Number 10, the Nuremberg International Military Tribunal (IMT) in the *High Command* case interpreted this provision, notwithstanding its strict rewording or draft, teleologically; only compliance with superior orders as a justification is excluded by the IMT, leaving thus the possibility open that an accused can invoke this defense as an excuse because of excusable ignorance of the illegality of the ordered act, as well as the fact that a subordinate under the prevailing circumstances has the right to assume that the superior orders were lawful.[62] This is certainly also the view of the drafters of the ICC. The defense of Article 33 (1) can never *justify* a behavior by a subordinate corresponding to a legal order to commit any of the crimes punishable under international law, but can at the utmost only excuse this person. In the latter situation, the defense of Article 33 is applicable not by itself, *"but when the conditions come close to other defenses like duress or coercion."* Only then can criminal responsibility under the Statute be excluded.[63] Although the drafters of the ICC failed to make a clear distinction between justifications and excuses, the wording of Article 33 (1), namely *"shall not relieve that person of criminal responsibility,"* reads without doubt as *excuse.* From this perspective the drafters seem to have paid attention to Article 2(3) of the Torture Convention of 1984, which provides that superior orders may not be invoked as a justification for torture.

In the controversy surrounding the defenses of superior orders and duress, several scholars endorse the view that these defenses in the context of excuses should be available, even regarding war crimes litigation.[64] It should be noted that duress and superior orders were both recognized as mitigators at the Nuremberg Trial, although literally excluded from the London Charter. Apart from the fact that the acceptance under the ICC Statute of a mitigative result of the defenses of Articles 28, 31 and 33 already implies *a de facto* recognition of the existence of an excuse, Green

---

61. Kremnitzer, *supra* note 57, at 345, especially note 31.

62. *See* also Dinstein, *supra* note 59, at 210; *German High Command* Trial (U.S. Military Tribunal, Nuremberg, 1948), 15 I.L.R. 376.

63. Otto Triffterer, *Article 33, Margin No. 12*, in COMMENTARY ON THE ROME STATUTE (Otto Triffterer, ed., 1999).

64. *See* Kremnitzer, *supra* note 57; M. CHERIF BASSIOUNI, CRIMES AGAINST HUMANITY IN ICL 437 (1992); Leslie C. Green, *Drazen Erdemović: The International Criminal Tribunal for the Former Yugoslavia in Action*, 10, LJIL 369–370 (1997).

provides a further strong argument on this subject: "*While one may under-stand the reasons for the Tribunal (the ICTY; GJK) considering that the plea of superior orders as a mitigating factor is only one of many factors to be assessed, it is not quite so clear why the idea that 'a crime against humanity' is so sub-stantially different from a similar crime—murder—under 'ordinary law,' and should in any way alter the validity of the defenses available to an accused.*"[65] In fact, Green advocates the principle of equal application of the law—emerg-ing from the principles of legality—by reasoning that although "( . . . ) *there is some substance to the argument that if the plea of duress under orders is adequate for murder under an ordinary system of criminal law, the same should prevail regardless of the system of law* (including ICL; GJK) *that is being applied.*" In addition, this scholar poses the question if it "( . . . ) *really affects the person of the accused and the validity of his defense that 'humanity as a whole' might consider its interests to have been affected?*"[66] Green's answer clearly recog-nizes the reality of warfare by saying that "*in any case, given the facts it is well-nigh impossible to assume that Erdemović ever had 'humanity' in mind at any time during his service or his participation in the shooting.*"[67] International war crimes litigation may only be justified when they take place in con-ditions of fairness and when they are legitimized by high standards of jus-tice and morality rather than political utility or expediency.[68] This high adjudicatory standard is also expressed by the significant decision of pros-ecution of war criminals and crimes against humanity rendered by the Supreme Court of Canada March 1994 in the *R.v. Finta* case.[69] On August 18, 1988, Imre Finta was indicted by the Attorney General of Canada and charged with kidnapping, illegal confinement, robbery and manslaugh-ter of 8.,617 Hungarian Jews, crimes allegedly having been committed in Hungary in 1944 when Finta was an officer in the Hungarian Gendarmerie who collaborated with the German SS. The indictment, added to the above mentioned crimes, constituted crimes against human-ity and war crimes, since Finta was alleged to have been the senior officer of the Gendarmerie at the Szeged "concentration center" (where the Hungarian Jews of that city were assembled before being sent by train to the concentration camps) with effective control over this center. The majority of the Supreme Court held, in dismissing the appeal against the initial acquittal of Finta, that it was not sufficient for the prosecution to establish the *mens rea* for the charged Canadian Criminal Code offences, such as manslaughter, but that an additional element of inhumanity had to be proven by the Prosecution, i.e. the proof that the accused knew that his or her actions were inhumane or constituted war crimes. Although the

---

65. Green, *supra* note 64, at 369.
66. Green, *supra* note 64, at 369–370.
67. Green, *supra* note 64, at 370.
68. Simpson, *supra* note 46, at 30.
69. 28 C.R. (4th) 265, S.C.C. 1994.

outcome of the Finta case can be questioned, this case demonstrates the approach that obedience to superior orders and the defense of duress against war crimes are as such valid and absolute defenses for an accused acting under military command in the event the accused had no moral choice but to follow the order, even—depending on the facts—where the order was manifestly unlawful.[70]

Therefore the view of Bassiouni—that in the event the subordinate had no moral choice with respect to obeying or refusing to obey the particular order, the defense of superior orders is available to the accused, and likewise if the subordinate is *"coerced or compelled to carry out the order,"* the norms of the defense of duress should apply—is judicially more acceptable than the hereinafter described absolutist approach, which *ab initio* excludes every defense of superior orders and duress to war crimes.[71]

The requirements of international criminal justice and the principles of legality include, as can be concluded hereto, the admissibility of superior orders and duress as absolute defenses to war crimes.[72]

## 5   THE PRINCIPLE OF INDIVIDUALITY AND *MENS REA*: INDUCTIVE METHOD

In addition to the arguments deduced from the principles of legality, a second main argument arises as to the extension of the scope of defenses of superior orders and duress to war crimes indictments, i.e. the argument embedded in the principle of individuality, which is related to the concept of *mens rea*. This principle implies that ICL must not only comport with international human rights protection of the accused but also that adjudication must focus on the individual merits of the case and the person of the accused. In the light of the controversy between the utilitarian versus absolutist doctrines, this principle may be defined. This controversy was examined in the above-mentioned *Erdemović* case of the ICTY.[73] Erdemović was a Croat and a soldier in the 10th Sabotage Detachment of the Bosnian Serb Army, indicted with the charge of having directly

---

70.   *See* for this case also Sharon A. Williams, *Laudable Principles Lacking Application: The Prosecution of War Criminals in Canada*, in THE LAW OF WAR CRIMES 164–170 (Timothy L.H. McCormack & Gerry J. Simpson, eds., 1997).

71.   *See* Bassiouni & Manikas, *supra* note 2, at 408; *see* also Section 10 of the Israeli Nazis and Nazi Collaborations (Punishment) Law, 1950, wherein the defense of duress is—as a reason for acquittal—provided for, with regard to war crimes, crimes against humanity and crimes against the Jewish people.

72.   C.L. Blakesley, *supra* note 37, at 212.

73.   *Prosecutor v. Drazen Erdemović*, Sentencing Judgment, Case No. IT-96-22-1, 29 November 1996; discussed by Leslie C. Green, *Drazen Erdemović, The ICTY in Action*, 10 LJIL 363–381 (1997).

participated as a member of a firing squad in the murder of Bosnian Moslem refugees who had taken shelter in the Srebrenica "safe area." Erdemović pleaded guilty to the crimes against humanity charge, whereas the Trial Chamber dismissed the charges as to violation of the laws or customs of war. The accused, Erdemović, stated during the proceedings that he never willingly participated in the firing squad and was sorry for the murdered Moslem refugees. Although he did not explicitly invoke the defense of duress, he asserted that he was compelled or forced to shoot the Moslem refugees, being forced to choose between his life and that of the Moslems, which was sustained by the statement of Erdemović that he was injured by a member of the participating sabotage unit. It is noteworthy that the Prosecutor's Brief on Aggravating and Mitigating Factors[74] mentions that the acting of Erdemović under orders encompassed coercive elements because *"his low rank ( . . . ) at the time of commission of the offences suggests a* greater pressure (my emphasis; GJK) *on him than on one holding a higher rank."* The Trial Chamber, however, did not accept the defense of duress, other than as a mitigative factor. It thus rejected the *utilitarian* approach—derived from the famous *Masetti* case decided by the Court of Assize in *L'Aquila*[75]—which allows, under certain circumstances, a duress defense with regard to crimes against humanity in the event the charged fact would have occurred anyway, i.e. irrespective of the will of the accused, and the participation in the criminal act enabled the saving of the life of the accused or his/her relative, whereas the *absolutist* doctrine opposes every killing of innocent people even under duress.[76] It is clear that in an area of law so thoroughly politicized, culturally freighted and passionately punitive as war crimes, there is need for even greater protections for the accused[77] and individual assessment instead of law-making based on fixed and strict doctrinal standards, an assessment which should be abstracted from the particular merits of the case as well as from the subjective conception of the accused in question as a "human being." In face of the ICC Statute, it should be noted that its drafters seem to endorse an intertwining between subjective and objective methods of law finding. Article 31 (1)(d), the provision on duress, it attempts *"to find a line in-between: in objective terms it is not required that the person concerned in fact avoids the greater harm by his criminal conduct, but in subjective terms how he must intend to do so."*[78] This view leaves the Court

---

74.  Case No. IT-96-22-1, 11 November 1996, at 3.

75.  *See* Joint Separate Opinion of Judges MacDonald and Vohrah to the *Erdemović* judgment, *infra* note 68, para. 79.

76.  *See* for the former, utilitarian, approach: Diss. Op. of Judge Casesse regarding the *Erdemović* case; *see* for the latter, absolute, doctrine: Joint Separate Opinion of the Judges MacDonald and Vohrah concerning the *Erdemović* case.

77.  Simpson, *supra* note 46, at 15.

78.  *See* Albin Eser, *Article 31, Margin No. 40*, in COMMENTARY ON THE ROME STATUTE (Otto Triffterer, ed., 1999).

open to perform law making on the basis of the inductive method, which also stems from its Article 31 (2), referring to *"the case before it."*

In conclusion it can be asserted that the principle of individuality ensures the susceptibility of ICL with regard to the acceptance of duress and superior orders related to war crimes as being absolute defenses. It is perhaps necessary to observe that the ICTY and ICTR on the one hand entrench the notion of individual culpability for international crime,[79] whereas on the other hand this notion is not endorsed with regard to the legal defenses in question. This contradiction should be eliminated in ICL. Moreover, the approach of the ICTY regarding such legal defenses as duress and superior orders contravenes the attitude of the Tribunals in respect to the doctrine of the "presumption of knowledge" in the area of superior responsibility. It is remarkable that the ICTY in the *Celebići* judgment, rejected the "must have known standard" adopted by the *Yamashita* judgment and the U.S. Military Tribunal in the *Hostage* case which standard implies that crimes committed by soldiers under command of a single superior are *prima facie* evidence of that person's liability. Although this is in fact a presumption of knowledge, the ICTY fails to advance it on the basis that it does not emerge from international criminal law.[80] Confronted with the explicit reference to this presumption in the *High Command* Case,[81] the ICTY held that the *High Command* Tribunal decided *"by striking a balance between the extent of the atrocities and the lack of communications."*[82] Clearly, the Tribunal is inclined to evaluate law making in this realm on the basis of the principle of individuality. It is somewhat ambiguous to abstain from application of this principle when it relates to the defenses of duress and superior orders to war crimes. This approach seems inconsistent considering the position taken by the ICTY in both the *Aleksovski* and *Celebići* cases with respect to the third element of superior responsibility,[83] where the Tribunal held that *"a superior should be held responsible for failing to take such measures that are within his material position,"* emphasizing that *"such a material responsibility must not be considered* abstractly *but must be evaluated on a* case-by-case basis *depending on the circumstances"* (emphasis added; GJK).[84] It seems inappropriate that the Tribunal diverges in its determination of the applicability of legal defenses to war crimes. For the Tribunal, criminal (superior) responsibility pursuant

---

79. *See* also Timothy L.H. McCormack & Gerry J. Simpson, *Preface in* THE LAW OF WAR CRIMES XXII (1997).

80. *See* also ICTY Trial Chamber Judgment dd. 25 June 1999, *Prosecutor v. Z. Aleksovski*, para. 79–80.

81. *See supra* note 15.

82. *See* Bantekas, *supra* note 19, at 589; *Celebići* decision, *supra* note 21, para. 385.

83. The element that the superior did not take all the necessary and reasonable measures to prevent the crime; *see*, e.g., Aleksovski case, o.c. para. 69.

84. *See Aleksovski* Judgment, o.c. para. 81.

to Art. 7 (1) of the ICTY Statute is not an automatic fact, but rather *"merits consideration against the background of the factual circumstances."*[85] This approach calls for equal application of the associated doctrines of defenses of superior orders and duress. Supportive to this approach is the view, initially asserted by Lauterpacht in 1944 and in 1965 amplified by Dinstein, that the concept of obedience to superior orders should be viewed as part of the *mental* element of the crime and not as a separate defense as such. The concept of superior orders should, pursuant to this standard, be assessed on the basis of *"general principles of criminal law, namely as an element in ascertaining the existence of* mens rea *as a condition of accountability."*[86] The multiplicity of factual and legal sources makes it difficult to ascertain the overall scope and legal standards of defenses to war crimes, so that the only appropriate means of ascertaining them is by way of an *inductive* law-making method on a case-by-case basis.

In this connection it may be appropriate to recognize, as a starting point, the defense of superior orders in accordance with a similar provision envisaged by Art. 32 (2) of the Canadian Criminal Code, which states: *"Everyone who is bound by military law to obey the command of his superior officer is* (excused; GJK) *in obeying any command given by his superior officer ( . . . )* unless the order is manifestly unlawful" (emphasis added, GJK).[87]


## 6    THE PRINCIPLE OF EQUAL APPLICATION AS TO LEGAL DEFENSES

The ambiguity in recognizing superior orders and duress as absolute defenses to ICL litigation, especially to war crimes, is apparently not inflicted by ICL upon the doctrine of self-defense. Pursuant to Art. 31 (1) (c) of the ICC Statute, the defense of self-defense in ICL is applicable even when invoked against war crimes, as opposed to the defenses of superior orders and duress. Close reading of Article 31 (1) of the ICC Statute teaches that self-defense is in fact subject to *an excuse, although by nature justificatory;* Article 31 provides namely for the possibility that *"a person shall not be criminally responsible ( . . . ),"* notwithstanding the fact that it is questionable whether the committing of a war crime based on the concept of self defense affects the requirement of proportionality, and whether it can be accepted as an excuse. Article 31 (1) (c) expressly extends the right

---

85.  *See Aleksovski* Decision, o.c. para. 65.

86.  Hersch Lauterpacht, *The Law of Nations and the Punishment of War Criminals,* 21 BRITISH YEARBOOK OF INTERNATIONAL LAW 58, 87 (1944); Yoram Dinstein, *The Defense of Obedience to Superior Orders,* in INTERNATIONAL LAW 5–20 (1965).

87.  *See* also Leslie C. Green, *Superior Orders and Command Responsibility,* 27 THE CANADIAN YEARBOOK OF INTERNATIONAL LAW 167 (1989). *See* also the 1956 US Army Field Manual 27–10, 501, para. 509.

of self-defense to war crimes and legitimizes a proportionate defense of the accused *pro se*, or of another person or property essential to survival of people or essential for accomplishing a military mission against an imminent and unlawful use of force.

In order to develop a methodical and systematic uniform judicial framework of ICL, and to ensure the principle of equal application of ICL[88] from both material and procedural perspectives, this ambiguity should be lifted by means of including, as well as self-defense, superior orders and duress as absolute defenses to war crimes. The juridical criticism of the self-defense provision in the ICC Statute as such will not be discussed here, but considered in Chapter VI. Before turning to the juridical consequences of the principles for the application of the defenses of duress and superior orders in the realm of multinational peacekeeping and enforcement operations, two other arguments are of interest for the articulation of these defenses.

## 7  ABSENCE OF A SPECIFIC RULE OF ICL; PREVALENCE OF THE GENERAL RULE ON DURESS IN CASE OF KILLING

The reality is that for the reasons set out in the Joint Separate Opinion of Judge MacDonald and Judge Vohrah (discussed in Chapter II above), as well as in the Separate and Dissenting Opinion of Judge Li, the majority of the Appeals Chamber in the *Erdemović* case found that duress does not afford a complete defense to a soldier charged with a crime against humanity and/or a war crime involving the killing of innocent human beings.[89]

In my opinion, this view of the Appeals Chamber is neither logically nor legally consistent. On the one hand, the majority of the Appeals Chamber recognizes that no customary international rule can be derived on the question of duress as a defense to the killing of innocent persons, and that it is likewise clear from the different positions of the principle legal systems of the world that there is no consistent, concrete rule which answers hereon.[90] On the other hand, the Appeals Chamber excludes duress as a complete defense to war crimes *"bearing in mind the specific context in which the international Tribunal was established ( . . . )."*[91]

---

88. *See* for this principle of Public International Law: IAN BROWNLIE, THE RULE OF LAW IN INTERNATIONAL AFFAIRS 214 (1998).

89. *See Prosecutor v. Erdemović*, Appeals Chamber Decision dated 7 October 1997, Case No. IT-96-22-A, para. 19.

90. *See* paras 46 et seq. and 72 of the Joint Separate Opinion of Judges McDonald and Vohrah in conjunction with para.19 of the Appeals Chamber Decision in the *Erdemović* case, o.c.

91. Para. 72 of the Joint Separate Opinion of Judges McDonald and Vohrah.

From this perspective it can be held with Judge Cassese that *"After finding that no specific international rule has evolved on the question of whether duress affords a complete defense to the killing of innocent persons, the majority (of the Appeals Chamber; GJK) should have drawn the only conclusion imposed by law and logic, namely that the general rule on duress should apply—subject, of course, to the necessary requirements."*[92] This implies that the common law approach to duress in case of killing (i.e. an exclusion of this defense) should not prevail in ICL and cannot be upheld in ICL. This opinion of Judge Cassese produces therefore a fourth argument to accept duress as a complete defense against international crimes, including war crimes. As argued by the latter author, if no exception to a general rule can be proved, in logic the general rule prevails, so in law, when no special rule is available to govern a particular topic of ICL, recourse to the general rule in order to regulate that specific topic can be made. It can be held that this general rule on duress encompasses in principle the admissibility of this defense in case of killing, presupposing four strict conditions are met, which conditions are deduced from the relevant and *"almost unanimous"* case law of civil as well as common law systems, namely:

    i.   the act charged was done under an immediate threat of severe and irreparable harm to life or limb;

    ii.   there was no adequate means of averting such evil;

    iii.  the crime committed was not disproportionate to the evil threatened (this would, for example, occur in case of killing in order to avert an assault). In other words, in order not to be disproportionate, the crime committed under duress must be, on balance, the lesser of two evils; and

    iv.  the situation leading to duress must not have been voluntarily brought about by the person coerced.[93]

In the realm of IHL in conjunction with war situations, the importance of the fourth requisite is clearly illuminated. A considerable amount of case law on IHL is available emphasizing that duress or necessity cannot excuse from criminal responsibility the person who intends to avail himself of such defense if he freely and knowingly chose to become a member of a unit, organization or group which institutionally commits actions contrary to IHL.[94] From this principle it emerges that members of peacekeep-

---

92.  *See* para. 11 of the Separate and Dissenting Opinion of Judge Cassese.

93.  Para. 16 of the Separate and Dissenting Opinion of Judge Cassese, o.c.

94.  *See* para. 17 of the Separate and Dissenting Opinion of Judge Cassese, o.c.; *see*, e.g., The Trial of Otto Ohlendorf et al. (*Einsatzgruppen* case) in Trials of War Criminals before the Nurernberg Military Tribunals under Control Council Law No. 10, Vol. IV; *see* also Trial of Erhard Milch (the *Milch* case) o.c., Vol. III at 964.

ing or peace-enforcement forces, since they are not institutionally intent to undermine norms of IHL, comply with this fourth requirement.

In conclusion, the fourth argument against the approach of the Appeals Chamber of the ICTY rejecting duress as absolute defense against the killing of innocent persons stems from the non-existence of a specific rule of international law in this area and the fact that ICL does not uphold the common-law approach to duress in case of killing.

## 8 DURESS AS A DEFENSE TO WAR CRIMES: FREE WILL AND POLICY CONSIDERATIONS

The final argument on the subject can again be derived from the expert opinion of the former President of the ICTY, Judge Cassese. As expressed in the Joint Separate Opinion of Judges McDonald and Vohrah to the *Erdemović* decision of the Appeals Chamber of the ICTY, the English common law rule is that duress forms no defense to murder.[95] This rejection of duress as a defense to murder is based on two assumptions:

a. According to English common law, duress does not destroy free will. In other words, it does not negate *mens rea* or the voluntariness of the *actus reus* nor the *mens rea*; and

b. acceptance of duress as a defense to murder would be contrary to the moral dimension in law, i.e., upholding the sanctity of human life and the protection thereof as the highest duty of the law.[96]

It is a weakness of the policy-oriented approach of the Appeals Chamber of the ICTY that the implementation of the English common law doctrine on duress, introduced through concept of free will, is not presented with clarity. It appears to be unrelated to the psychological notion of human free will, what is still considered to be the most accurate one.[97] According to this notion, free will can be described as *"an emotional impulse or urge, stemming from a human self-being, directed to or focused on a freely chosen goal, accompanied by the consciousness that this goal is to be reached through one's own free activity."*[98] It is more enlightening to examine what

---

95. *See* para. 70 of this Joint Separate Opinion, wherein it is referred to the decision of the House of Lords in *R. v. Howe and others*, 1987, 1 ALL ER 771.

96. *See* para. 70 of the Joint Separate Opinion of Judges McDonald and Vohrah, o.c.

97. *See* HANS KELSEN, HAUPTPROBLEME DER STAATSRECHTSLEHRE 108 (1945); H.J. VAN EIKEMA HOMMES, DE ELEMENTAIRE GRONDBEGRIPPEN DER RECHTSWETEN-SCHAP 239 (1983).

98. Van Eikema Hommes, *supra* note 97.

this notion has to say about free will than it is to study a legal policy view. The perception of free will according to this psychological viewpoint, although still problematical with regard to the interpretation of elements such as "a freely chosen goal," indicates that in the event of duress no absolute free will appears. It makes no good sense to propound that an accused, acting under duress, is easily able to carry out his emotional impulse, focused on a freely chosen goal synchronic to his free activity. To the extent that policy-orientation would allow overriding the existing legal and psychological principles, which constitute after all the best evidence of community values, it must be rejected. Leaving aside the contestability of the first presumption above,[99] the criticism of Cassese in rejecting the second assumption merits serious consideration. His argument transposes the basic principles of ICL, so that a complete citation is appropriate:

> "( . . . ) *The majority of the Appeals Chamber has embarked upon a detailed investigation of practical policy considerations and has concluded by upholding policy considerations substantially based on English law. I submit that this examination is extraneous to the task of our Tribunal. This International Tribunal is called upon to apply international law, in particular our Statute and principles and rules of international humanitarian law and international criminal law. Our International Tribunal is a court of law; it is bound only by international law. It should therefore refrain from engaging in meta-legal analyses. In addition, it should refrain from relying exclusively on notions, policy considerations or the philosophical underpinnings of common law countries, while disregarding those of civil law countries or other systems of law. What is even more important, a policy-oriented approach in the area of criminal law runs contrary to the fundamental customary principle* nullum crimen sine lege. *On the strength of international principles and rules my conclusions on duress differ widely from those of the majority of the Appeals Chamber ( . . . )."*[100]

Therefore, this view of Cassese is—as fifth argument—in line with the acceptance of duress as complete defense in case of killing or even war crimes.

---

99.   *See* further Chapter VIII, *infra*.

100.   *See* para. 11 (ii) of the Separate and Dissenting Opinion of Judge Cassese to the *Erdemović* Decision of the Appeals Chamber, o.c.

## 9  CONCURRENCE OF THE DEFENSE OF SUPERIOR ORDERS AND SUPRANATIONAL MANDATES AS TO MULTINATIONAL PEACEKEEPING AND ENFORCEMENT OPERATIONS.

We have thus far observed that the adjudicatory assessment of duress and superior orders to war crimes should include the principles of legality, individuality and uniformity.

How are these principles to apply in the context of military assignments or mandates imposed by international organizations such as the UN or NATO? This question was addressed by a Military Court at Brussels in the controversial *Marchal* Case. That case concerned the killing of ten Belgian para-commandos (blue helmets) assigned to the UNAMIR (United Nations Intervention Mission in Rwanda, a peace keeping force) on the 7th of April 1994, during a massacre in the military camp at Kigali (Rwanda). The noteworthy factor is that, in 1996, the commanding officer of these Belgian soldiers (part of the Belgian battalion), Colonel Marchal, assigned with maintaining the security of the Belgium UNAMIR military personal at Kigali, was, under Belgian criminal law, charged by the Attorney-General at Brussels of having negligently caused this death due to absence of adequate precautionary measures. Moreover, Col. Marchal was deemed to have (reasonably) known that Rwandan paramilitaries (*"Interhamwe"*) intended to assassinate Belgian soldiers in order to force their withdrawal and subsequent continuance of the internal (tribal) war. According to the particular UN Mandate (i.e., UN Resolution dated 5 October 1993), the aim of the UNAMIR mission was firstly to ensure the security of Kigali, especially within the demilitarized zone (based on the peace agreement between the Republic of Rwanda and the Rwanda Patriotic Movement) whereby the UNAMIR forces were, by virtue of the UNAMIR rules of engagement, attributed with limited (in reality poor) powers to act with force in self-defense only when compelled to hand over their weapons. Secondly, their aim was to secure the safety of prominent Rwandan politicians, i.e., Rwanda's Prime Minister.

The Military Court, faced with compliance of the accused to national criminal (Belgian) law on the one hand and compliance to international customary law, i.e., the UN Mandate in question and UN rules of engagement on the other hand, attached priority to the strict fulfillment of the UN Mandate. According to the Court, the 7 April 1996 order of General Dallaire, Chief Commander of UNAMIR, to Colonel Marchal, commander of the UNAMIR Kigali sector, to ensure a military escort of the Prime Minister, was thus legitimate. Since the defendant was not in a legal or factual position to question the legitimacy of the political aspect of the Mandate and escort assignment,[101] the refusal of said UN-authorized

---

101. *See* Judgment rendered on 4 July 1996 of the Military Court of Justice at

order would be a military criminal offense. In addition, the Court took into account that Colonel Marchal reasonably could not have foreseen the severe violation of the Geneva Conventions conducted by the Rwandan militia, since the Belgian para-commandos escorting the Prime Minister surrendered to the militia but were nevertheless killed. The Court implicitly expresses the view that both UN-mandatory rules and military rules of engagement apply during international peacekeeping, peace-enforcement and general enforcement operations; and although the particular military commander must comply with national military penal law, he or she can prevail over these national rules and officiate as a basis for the defense of superior orders.[102]

When we consider that rules of engagement are directives issued by a competent authority (i.e., the UN) the control military forces, specifying the circumstances and the limitations under which the UN or other (inter) national military forces will engage in the use of force or will initiate and/or continue combat operations, and that they also reflect principles of international, national and customary law, the Court's primacy as to the international UN mandate and UN rules of engagement is tenable. Faced with these rules of engagement, invoked by the defendant Marchal, the Court determines their consistency and concludes that because of their clearness with regard to the use of force by means of self-defense by UNAMIR, no causation exists between the practical application of these rules and the massacre of the ten UN soldiers. The Court's decision hereto is one of the first judicial rulings whereby the prominent legal status of the (UN) rules of engagement are assessed and perform the superior orders test in ICL. This interplay between UN peacekeeping rules and ICL or domestic criminal law at the international level forms, I believe, the most suitable approach to doctrine of superior orders, considering the nature of these rules, adjusted especially for UN military personnel. This test in no way widens the scope of the defense of superior orders, since it follows the established principle of international law of command responsibility through the concept of control,[103] This concept is envisaged by the "Standing Rules of Engagement for UN Forces" (peace enforcement) of the United Nations, wherein it is noted: *"Issued as prohibitions, they (these rules; GJK) are orders not to take certain specific actions. Issued as permissions, they are guidance to commanders ( . . . )."*[104] Despite the adjudicatory (lawmaking) freedom of international criminal tribunals, the validity of superior orders and duress as complete defenses to international crimes, including war crimes, based on reliance on these rules of engagement, can

---

Brussels, No. 13 R.G. 1996, *Le Ministere Public v. L.M.G.M. Marchal.*
    102. In my opinion this *a fortiori* applies to duress.
    103. *See* for this latter concept: Bantekas, *supra* note 19, at 594.
    104. *See* the UN Peace Enforcement Rules of Engagement, at 2.

under these circumstances not be expelled from the ICL legal framework. The *Marchal* case teaches that the principles of legality are to be extended to compliance with such rules of military commanders. Their decisive and exonerative power has, in each case, to be determined on its own merits by the impartial criminal courts. Only such a non-absolutist approach can strengthen the ICL—and international criminal justice system.

## 10    THE CONCEPT OF INDIVIDUAL SELF-DEFENSE IN UN AND NATO MILITARY OPERATIONS

### 10.1 Introduction

The final topic of this chapter involves a closely related area, namely the doctrine of self-defense by individuals, emerging in the course of multinational military operations, conducted by *inter alia* UN or NATO. Although international criminal responsibility of States and individuals are two distinct, non-interchangeable concepts, there are judicial interrelations. This also counts for the subsequent concepts of self-defense, i.e., the presence of the right to self-defense by individual military personnel during peace-keeping and peace enforcement operations on the one hand, pursuant to the particular multinational rules of engagement (hereinafter ROE), and the right of self-defense by individuals in ICL as analyzed in the previous sections. Although these ROE, as will be noticed in the next chapter, are meant to be in fact part of *jus in bello*, their contents are from a comparative view important, in order to analyze possible common principles with self-defense in ICL. The relevance of an analysis of these ROE appear in the face of the absence of clear norms ruling self-defense (by individual military personnel of a certain State) in case of absence of UN authorization, i.e. Article 51 UN Charter situations. Moreover, this relevance appears in the realm of forcible humanitarian operations, such as the Kosovo war. It is my opinion that the underlying principles of these ROE can serve as normative guidelines in these kinds of situations. There is in fact a certain similarity between the *jus in bello*, on the one hand, and the law of self-defense in criminal law, on the other. Both set rules for conduct that is basically illegal by indicating ultimate juridical limits of the use of force.

### 10.2 The concept of self-defense in multinational ROE of UN and NATO

The literature on the concept of individual self-defense with regard to multinational military operations is poor.[105] Evidence and articulation

---

105.   *See*, e.g., the (unpublished) work of G.S. Holder, Rear Admiral, U.S. Navy,

of this concept emanates primarily from the particular multinational ROE themselves. From an analysis of these ROE emerges the following overall view.

## 10.3  Use of force during multinational operations

As observed in the foregoing sections of this chapter, international law as well as ICL recognizes the right to use force in self-defense. Because the use of force carries the risk of causing or incurring injury, death and damage, legal authorities, such as the UN, NATO or coalition governments, must provide clear direction regarding the level of force necessary to accomplish an assigned mission within specified limits. Here, a tension emerges between principles of ICL and international humanitarian law on the one hand, and military politics on the other. Therefore, utmost care must be exercised when coordinating the efforts of multinational forces to ensure that differing views and interpretations among the multinational nations comprising the force are clearly enunciated and addressed.[106]

Whether in self-defense or in furtherance of mission accomplishment during peacetime operations or during armed conflict, use force is not unlimited. Close reading of the UN as well as NATO ROE teaches that the principles of proportionality and military necessity and the laws of armed conflict must be adhered to at all times, as observed in section 3 above.

On this point these ROE seem to comply with rules of customary international law on the topic of self-defense by States pursuant to Article 51 of the UN Charter. Article 51 makes no mention of limits to the actual amount of force used in self-defense. Customary international law requires that a State does not go beyond the limited purpose of protecting its rights, and uses no more force than necessary to do so.[107] This principle has often been referred to as the requirement of proportionality.

The law of armed conflict is, according several international conventions, not intended to inhibit commanders in the accomplishment of their mission, but to:

1.  protect combatants and non-combatants from unnecessary suffering;
2.  protect property of historic, religious or humanitarian value and the environment from unnecessary destruction; and

---

*Use of Force During Multinational Maritime Operations*, Revision 6, 20 September 1997, Chapter III, Section 2, although its elaboration on this topic is modest.

106.  *See* Holder, *supra* note 105, at 3–1.

107.  *See* TIMOTHY L.H. MCCORMACK, SELF-DEFENSE IN INTERNATIONAL LAW, THE ISRAELI RAID ON THE IRAQI NUCLEAR REACTOR 276–277 (1996).

3.  facilitate the restoration of peace upon the conclusion of the conflict.

The use of force through the concept of individual self-defense in NATO or UN ROE must administer all these different interests. This forms an important difference with self-defense in ICL. In the latter field, the law has only to deal with two interests, i.e. the international community and the interest of the individual, which is a less difficult task.

## 10.4  Use of force and the spectrum of conflict

The *spectrum of conflict* ranges from peacetime to *armed conflict*. Within this continuum, there are a variety of possible missions and associated legal underpinnings that will affect any direction issued for use of force. This section will focus mainly on the situation of peacekeeping and peace-enforcement operations, since during these kind of operations, the use of force is limited to self-defense and, as specifically authorized by a competent authority, to mission accomplishment.[108] In the context of peacekeeping or peace enforcement operations, use of force direction for an international operation draws its authority from each contributing nation and, consequently, any such direction must consider both each member nation's domestic law and the requirements of international law. The mechanism used to control this kind of force is the concept of *rules of engagement (ROE)*. These are based on the unique requirements and objectives of each mission (mission accomplishment) and the long-recognized right of self-defense. Use of force direction would normally consist of general instructions and definitions and a range of specific authorizations or restrictions (called supplementary measures) that multinational commanders may use to direct, control and order the use of force to achieve an assigned mission in support of broad strategic interests and objectives.[109]

---

108. Holder, *supra* note 105, at 3–3.
109. The US Navy is governed by the Chairman of the Joint Chiefs of Staff's Standing Rules of Engagement (the CJCS SROE). The SROE "( . . . ) *provide implementation guidance on the inherent right and obligation of self-defense and the application of force for mission accomplishment.*" All multinational forces, including those of the US, involved in multinational operations must consult with their governments to ensure that proposed coalition ROE are consistent with their own domestic law and policy.

## 10.5 Nature of multinational rules of engagement (ROE)

According to the submitted definition of the UN and NATO, ROE are (as described clearly by Holder): *"directives issued by competent military authority that delineate the circumstances and limitations under which military forces initiate and/or continue the use of force. ROE consist of (1) guidance on self-defense and (2) directions and orders regarding the positioning of units and the use of force by military forces for mission accomplishment, during domestic and international operations in peacetime, periods of tension and armed conflict. They constitute lawful commands and are designed to remove any legal or semantic ambiguity that could lead a commander to violate national policy by inadvertently under-reacting or overreacting to an action by foreign forces. While national policy decisions deal broadly with "what, where, when and why" force will be used, operational ROE directives deal with the specifics of "how, when and where" force will be implemented. ROE generally confine themselves to when force is allowable or authorized, and to what extent it may be used to accomplish the mission. ROE are applicable to situations ranging from peacetime operations to armed conflict. Because they reflect deeply held national policies and norms regarding use of force, developing and implementing ROE is one of the most complex and difficult aspects of establishing and maintaining an effective and cohesive multinational force."*[110]

## 10.6 ROE principles as to self-defense by individuals

The following concepts, which are common to use of force in multinational operations, are fundamental to understanding the application of ROE. These concepts or principles can be derived from the Multinational ROE of UN and NATO.

*The spectrum of conflict*

The spectrum of conflict, as discussed before, is particularly important when determining the legal basis for ROE to be applicable to an operation. When considering the use of military force, the appropriate ROE authorizations will often depend on where the crisis or emergency event falls within the spectrum of conflict. If the operation will take place in a relatively peaceful environment where there is no immediate threat to the multinational force, ROE may be quite restrictive. If however, the operation will occur in an active war zone or when the risk of hostilities is high, then, according the UN and NATO ROE, it may be appropriate to authorize considerably more extensive application of the ROE to defend the force, and if required, enforce the mandate. This forms in fact a derivative

---

110.  Holder, *supra* note 105, at 3–5.

of the principle of *reasonableness*, which enables ICL to a likewise variable application of individual self-defense, on a case-by-case basis.

## Minimum force

*Minimum force* is the least amount of force reasonably necessary to counter a *hostile act* or demonstration of *hostile intent* to ensure the continued safety of applicable multinational forces, personnel or property while pursuing mission accomplishment. Depending upon the circumstances, *minimum force* may include use of *deadly force* or destruction of an opposing force where such action is the only prudent means by which a *hostile act* or demonstration of *hostile intent* can be prevented or terminated, or the mission accomplished.

## Non-deadly force

The second principle emerging from the UN and NATO ROE forms the element of *non-deadly force*. This includes any physical means of forcing compliance that does not reasonably pose a risk of death or grievous bodily harm to the individual against whom the force is directed.[111] This is usually achieved through the use of physical force short of the use of firearms or other deadly weapons. Examples include pushing and lesser forms of striking or hitting, and physically or mechanically restraining persons. Tear gas and warning shots are considered *non-deadly force*, even though the latter activity involves the use of firearms.

## Deadly force

As to the third principle, *deadly force*, this implies a level of force which is intended or is likely to cause death or grievous bodily harm regardless of whether death or grievous bodily harm actually results. This is the ultimate degree of force.

## Hostile act

The forth principle forms a clear difference as to individual self-defense in ICL. This element consists of the definition of *hostile act*, according the UN and NATO ROE meaning an attack or other use of force against a national force, personnel, ships, aircraft, equipment or property assigned to an multinational operation. For certain operations, this definition may be expanded to include an attack on designated allies, non-military personnel, objects, sites, platforms and/or materiel. Such a wide scope is neither envisioned in domestic law nor in ICL regarding individual self-defense.

---

111. "Minimum force" is designed to avoid death or serious bodily harm. However, any use of force can possibly result in loss of life. Consequently, "minimum force" is not synonymous with "non-deadly force."

*Demonstration of hostile intent*

The fifth principle relates to the element of *hostile intent*, equally appearing to be an extension of the self-defense notion in ICL. According to UN and NATO ROE, under certain circumstances, armed force may be used preemptively to protect against the threat of imminent use of force against national ships, aircraft, equipment or property. For certain operations, this definition may be expanded to include the protection of designated allies, non-military personnel, and other foreign military personnel, objects, sites, platforms, and/or materiel. Although precise criteria can be established for identifying a *hostile act*, it is more difficult to recognize a demonstration of *hostile intent*, in which case greater amplification may be required depending on the anticipated operational context. Such amplification must take into account that a determination that *hostile intent* exists must be based on convincing evidence and requires a reasonable belief that the use of force by the opposition is *imminent* and the necessity for a unit to use force is instant and overwhelming, and there is no choice or means for deliberation. Thus a reasonable belief is necessary before justifying the use of any force in response, which reasonable belief forms a parallel as to the principle of reasonableness hereto in ICL. Furthermore, the extent of reaction permitted in the face of a *hostile act* or demonstration of *hostile intent* must be clearly understood in terms of the proportionality and duration of force in response. Thus, when designing ROE to support multinational operations, the criteria for what constitutes a *hostile act* or the demonstration of *hostile intent* must be clearly enunciated.[112]

## 10.7 Controlling the use of force and (individual) self-defense through multinational ROE

As stated by Holder, analyzing multinational ROE, *"when national or alliance interests are involved, governments may authorize the use of military force, up to and including deadly force, as a means to maintain peace, deter aggression, control conflict or return to a state of peace. The military, as an element of national power, enable these objectives to be met. However, because use of force can lead to damaged property, destruction of natural resources, injury and loss of human lives, governments must establish mechanisms that authorize the force necessary to accomplish an assigned mission within specified limits."*[113] The submitted ROE enable governments to achieve this by authorizing specific use of force directives or ROE itself. These written directives are, according to Holder, broadly based on two concepts, namely *self-defense* and *mission accomplishment*. In this chapter, only the former concept draws

---

112. *See* Holder, *supra* note 105, at 3–6.
113. *Ibid.*

major attention. In multinational operations, the right of self-defense involves:

1. national self-defense;
2. collective self-defense;
3. unit/individual self-defense; and
4. defense of the mandate.[114]

From these connected variations, only the categories (3) and (4) are a corollary of the doctrine of individual self-defense in ICL. With regard to category (3) similarities to the latter doctrine are visible. This category refers to the act of defending one's unit, other national elements of an authorized multinational force or one's self, against a *hostile act* or demonstration of *hostile intent*. The right of personal/unit self defense does not change from mission to mission. The ROE require no special authority for individual and unit self-defense. International law recognizes the authority to use appropriate force in self defense, up to and including *deadly force* in the context of *jus in bello*, i.e. when members of peacekeeping forces are subject to imminent threat or attack by belligerent parties. When self defense is used, the UN and NATO ROE eliminate the following criteria:

*Application of self-defense*

Because of different legal regimes underpinning international operations, there may be differences in the application of self defense. During international operations, a multinational force may be operating under various strategic directives, including special UN Security Council Resolutions, where the use of force in self defense and defense of others may provide for a much wider latitude of actions than allowed under domestic laws. Such directives notwithstanding, the right of unit/individual self defense does not require special authorization.

*Actions in self-defense*

Without assuming unacceptable risk, according the submitted ROE, multinational commanders should make every effort to control a situation without the use of force. When time and conditions permit, the potentially hostile force should be warned of the situation and further warned that self-defensive action will be taken as necessary. When in the context of peacekeeping operations a self-defense situation occurs, use of force

---

114. Not all nations recognize defense of the mandate as a separate category of self-defense. Many nations would consider that defense of the mandate, as defined in this publication, is a form of collective or unit self-defense. Defense of the mandate should not be confused with either enforcement of the mandate or mission accomplishment.

must be timely, but it must be preceded by a clear recognition that hostility is occurring or is imminent. In exercising the right of self-defense, a commander must identify the presence of an immediate and compelling need to use force. If the responsible commander identifies that action must be taken in self-defense, the following elements apply.[115]

1. Necessity: An attack is occurring (*hostile act*) or about to occur (demonstration of *hostile intent*).
2. Proportionality: This means that a response commensurate with the perception of the level of the threat is justified. The force used must be reasonable in degree, intensity, and duration, based on all facts known to the commander at the time, to decisively counter the *hostile act* or demonstration of *hostile intent* and to ensure the continued safety of the force.

*Anticipatory self-defense*

Multinational forces, pursuing their task of peacekeeping or peace enforcement, are not required by international law to be attacked before they are authorized to respond with *deadly force*. In the foregoing it was observed that this principle also is endorsed in domestic criminal law as well as ICL. Under certain circumstances, which should be designated in the ROE, force up to and including *deadly force* may be used preemptively to protect forces or other designated personnel, against the threat of *imminent attack* (i.e., the demonstration of *hostile intent*). The ROE indicate, however, that there must be however, a reasonable belief by the on-scene commander that the use of force by an opponent is imminent and the requirement for assigned units to use force is instant and overwhelming.[116] It appears to me that this element reveals the only subjective touchstone in the ROE regarding the interpretation of self-defense,

*The right to hold position*

The last criterion indicates, like common law, no requirement to retreat in order to avoid situations that justify the use of force in self defense. This notion accords clearly with self-defense in common law. Nonetheless, where retreat is a practical alternative, Holder argues that it sometimes may be the most reasonable way to avoid injury and preserve personnel and material assets to continue with the mission. If the attacker

---

115. Not all states share identical conceptions of the acts or indicators which trigger a right to self-defense. Consequently, members of a multinational force should take care to advise the other members of the multinational force, and especially, the multinational force commander (MFC), of national policies and assumptions in this regard.

116. Holder, *supra* note 105, at 3–10.

is known or can be identified, an alternative response may possibly be initiated later with less danger.[117]

## 10.8 Summary and overview

The concept of self-defense by individual military personnel pursuant to the submitted UN or NATO ROE tends to neglect—because of adherence to strict principles, comparable to the approach in civil law systems—the role of the subjective element, as strongly represented by American law.[118] This observance is not surprising because the purpose of these ROE is *"the authorization for or limits on the use of force during military operations,"*[119] these rules being defined as *"( . . . ) directives to military forces (including individuals) that define the circumstances, conditions, degree, and manner in which force, or actions which might be construed as provocative, may or may not, be applied. ROE are not used to assign tasks or give tactical instructions. With the exception of self-defense, during peacetime and operations prior to a declaration of counter aggression, ROE provide the sole authority to NATO forces to use force. Following a declaration of counter aggression, ROE generally limit the otherwise lawful use of force."*[120] It is apparent that resort to self-defense by military personnel during multinational military operations amounts to mainly objective and strict criteria, in contrast to, generally speaking, this concept in domestic criminal law and ICL.

It is evident that the purpose and definition of self defense in UN and NATO ROE, inclines to a more objective adjudicatory scope, rather than a subjective assessment. This distinction is closely connected to the kind of self defense derived from governmental or international institutional powers, which needs *"limiting and guidance"* in order to avoid abuse of powers by States. Nevertheless, a synthesis of the concept of individual self-defense in ICL and that of the unit or individual self-defense endorsed in multinational ROE by UN or NATO is visible. Examples of those parallels are the *"rule of non-retreat,"* and the major principle of *reasonableness* with its exponent, i.e., the principle of proportionality. The consequential findings of this Chapter hereto are that the aforementioned concepts are mainly governed by much of the same principles and norms. A careful comparison reveals that it actually is also here the *rule of law*, which rules the two submitted concepts of self-defense. Although the doctrine of self-defense by individuals in ICL seems to encompass a more sophisticated as well as more individualized concept than the notion of the self-defense in

---

117.  *Ibid*.
118.  *See* Chapter III, *infra*.
119.  *See* Part 1 of NATO ROE, MC 362, 3rd Draft of February 1998.
120.  *Ibid*.

ROE, the latter legal standard relates more to the protection of State or institutional interests. Exemplary therefore is the reference in the NATO ROE, MC 362, to the concept of individual self-defense as *"the use of such necessary and proportional force, including deadly force,* to defend NATO forces and personnel *against attack or an imminent attack* (emphasis added)," in which definition the element of attack is similarly described as *"the use of force against NATO forces and personnel."*[121]

## 11   NECESSITY AND PREVENTION OF CRIME: MINDFUL DEFENSES IN THE REALM OF MULTINATIONAL MILITARY OPERATIONS

### 11.1 Introduction

There are two further aspects of the subject of defenses related to the regulation of armed conflicts that are certainly worthy of separate treatment. Although, as demonstrated in Chapter III, the defenses of necessity and prevention of crime in ICL can be adopted on the basis of comparative criminal law, international developments connect this category of defenses also to current customary (military) international law. These defenses can acquire this separate identity as a distinct category of international defenses in customary international law, especially because the standard of reasonableness in assessing the defense of prevention of crime should *"take account of the* nature of the crisis (emphasis added) *in which the necessity to use force arises for, in circumstances of great stress, even the reasonable man cannot be expected to judge the minimum degree of force required to nicety."*[122]

In this section, a special kind of crisis will be assessed, namely the increasing phenomenon of peacekeeping and peace enforcement operations by multinational organizations, such as UN and NATO, in which context the fundamental question is addressed whether individual soldiers, participating in these forces, can rely, under prevailing circumstances, upon these defenses. These defenses can have a significant function in the tension between military obedience and compliance with human rights protection. From this perspective the defenses of necessity and prevention of crime counterbalance the doctrines of command responsibility and superior orders. One should keep in mind that the defense of superior orders does not have, to state with Paust, its true basis in equity, but rather in a concept of protecting soldiers from criminal prosecution in group action or chain action situations, when the lower ranking soldier does not possess the requisite criminal mind or criminal culpabil-

---

121. *See* part II (6) of the NATO ROE, MC 362, 3rd Draft.
122. Smith and Hogan, *supra* note 55, at 262.

ity, and has thus its true base in *mens rea* (knew) or dangerous character (should have known).[123] It is consistent with this view of endorsing morality and *mens rea* regarding individual soldiers that legal instruments to suppress illegal military conduct are designed.

## 11.2 Necessity and prevention of crime: limiting military obedience and the basis for military peace and law enforcement

In the system of protecting human rights, the doctrine of legal defenses has scarcely been used at all. It has been assessed that multinational peace-keeping and peace enforcement forces are attributed with an important responsibility in maintenance of the law of wars and human rights, or in other words the prevention of war crimes. Their legal instruments are, apart from the ROE, either quite limited in scope or inappropriately used, as exemplified by *inter alia* the above-illustrated cases of the Belgian Colonel Marchal in Rwanda and the Dutch Lieutenant-Colonel Karremans in Srebrenica.

It is therefore the opinion of the present writer that, more than has been the case, individual soldiers of all ranks participating in these forces need to be encouraged to take such protective measures and, where necessary, to be provided with legal powers which enable them to act in compliance with the law of wars and conventions without fear of being prosecuted by military authorities pursuant to military (law) obedience and disciplinary provisions.

In this context, one possibility to be considered is the establishment for the members of these forces, of a system of protective legal defenses, such as the above-illustrated defenses of necessity and prevention of crime. It must be recognized, however, that the sensitivity of much multinational military operations is such that individual interpretative powers for soldiers must be limited in scope.

Not only all States but also individual members of multinational military operations have a measure of responsibility for ensuring compliance with the law of war and human rights conventions. Individual responsibility for superiors arises also from Articles 82, 83, and 87 of Additional Protocol I to the Geneva Conventions. Article 87 provides that *"in order to prevent and suppress breaches High Contracting Parties and Parties to the conflict shall require that, commensurate with their level of responsibility, commanders ensure that members of the armed forces under their command are aware of their obligations under the Conventions and this Protocol."*

---

123. *See* Jordan J. Paust, *Superior Orders and Command Responsibility*, in I International Criminal Law 225 (M. Cherif Bassiouni, ed., 1999).

While it may be perhaps too extensive to read this provision as enabling, under certain circumstances and under the protection of the legal defenses of necessity and prevention of crime, individual soldiers to intervene in order to prevent or remedy violations of the laws of war and human rights, it denotes at least exonerative norms. Moreover, when acting to endorse these laws, it denotes the standing of effective defenses. There can be little question that otherwise a soldier cannot struggle to comply with these laws when left no legal choice but to obey the military disciplinary and penal laws.

Having drawn attention to these principles, also indirectly laid down in Additional Protocol I to the Geneva Conventions and Human Rights Conventions, from the point of view of limiting or preventing violations of the laws of wars and human rights provisions it is worth looking at some practical consequences of this view. Chapter IV above described, the Belgian domestic criminal case against Colonel Marchal, the force commander of the UN Belgian peacekeeping contingent of UNAMIR during the Rwanda civil war in April 1994,in which a UN Force Commander was charged with involuntary manslaughter of members of this UN Belgian contingent since, as was asserted, he failed to act, being superior, in securing the safety of his UN personnel, and also failed to act in self defense. Apart from laying down the principle of compliance to the UN Mandate in question, and the consequent acquittal by the Belgian Military Penal Court on the 4th July 1996, the *Marchal* case reveals an unsatisfactory outcome in its implications concerning compliance with the laws of war and international human rights law. In that case, the Military Court was faced with a severe violation of common Article 3 of the Geneva Conventions, because the ten Belgian para-commandos or "Blue helmets," being members of a UN multinational force, are to be considered *"persons taking no active part in hostilities,"* envisioned by common Article 3. Commenting on this incident and leaving for the moment consideration of compliance to UN Mandates and ROE, it becomes apparent that in the event Colonel Marchal, supposing it were actually possible, had ordered to defend and fire on the belligerent attackers, he could have resorted to the defense of necessity (i.e., the saving of ten innocent UN soldiers outweighing resort to deadly force) or prevention of crime (or self-defense) when criminally charged with manslaughter with infringement of the UN Mandate.

Having thus seen the consequences of strict adherence to military obedience without independent attachment to contemporary international (human rights) law principles, it is perhaps appropriate to be aware that—considering the recent and revealing testimonies before the ICTY in April 2000 of Dutch officers participating in the aforementioned UN-Dutch battalion in Srebrenica—the incident at the Srebrenica enclave in Bosnia Herzegovina, where the UN-Dutch battalion under the force command of Lieutenant-Colonel Karremans was engaged, could have been avoided only if the force commander attained to forcible intervention (even outside the UN Mandate) based upon the legal defense of necessity or prevention of crime.[124]

## 11.3 Summary

In fine, perhaps it might be suggested that the time is ripe for a further effort to draw up an agreed code or codification to endorse, in certain extreme circumstances, these defenses as applicable to the forces of multinational military peacekeeping or peace enforcement forces in order to bridge the tension between military disciplinary (penal) law on the one hand, and international human rights law and IHL on the other. Provided that all the legal requisite elements on the two submitted defenses are fulfilled, and presupposing that these defenses are advanced to charges in ICL cases like those of Colonel Marchal, this approach may secure a further inducement to both States and individual military persons to comply with the laws of war, human rights protection and the achievement of the purposes of IHL.

The law-making process of national and international courts, can perhaps, in the realm of the maintenance of international law, be matched by appropriate law enforcement through these defenses. The most important weakness, as observed by Greenwood, in the laws of war today lies not in their substance but in their implementation.[125] To that end, the defenses of necessity and prevention of crime can improve the achievement of humanitarian goals as well as compliance with, and enforcement of, human rights law.

## 12 CONCLUDING REMARKS: THE PRINCIPLES OF REASONABLENESS, FAIRNESS AND GOOD FAITH

It is evident, as analyzed in this chapter, that the *"rigorous and restrictive"* approach of the *ad hoc* War Crimes Tribunals, the ICTY and ICTR, towards the admissibility of legal defenses pose several judicial difficulties. It is arguable that this present approach contravenes the minimum standards of protection for an accused person in international human

---

124. Presupposing that this unit was equipped with sufficient weaponry and ammunition, which is disputed by testimony by Dutchbat officers before the ICTY in April 2000.

125. *See* CHRISTOPHER GREENWOOD, INTERNATIONAL HUMANITARIAN LAW AND THE LAW OF WARS, PRELIMINARY REPORT FOR THE CENTENNIAL COMMEMORATION OF THE FIRST HAGUE PEACE CONFERENCE 1899, 79, 189 (1998).

rights law, enshrined by the principles of legality and derivative standards of individuality and equal application of the law. It may well be that the present attitude and jurisprudence of the *ad hoc* Tribunals are being perceived as effective in gaining custody of and prosecuting perpetrators of war crimes. This perceived success, however, must comport with the international human rights of the accused. Policy considerations—such as those embodied in the English common law doctrine of duress—about the expediency and effectiveness of international criminal tribunals cannot be invoked to the detriment of the submitted principles; nor can the mere absence, for now, of a specific international rule on the admissibility of duress in case of killing of innocent people. War crimes tribunals and ICL litigation must be vindicated by the rule of law, which, as observed in this study, incorporates a fair implementation and assessment of legal defenses to these crimes. The policy needs of justice for the world community misses its educational function when it facilitates a concession towards the overall principle of ICL, i.e., the fairness of international criminal litigation. Admittedly, *"the choice of any legal standard is ultimately a matter of legal policy."*[126] Thus, the standard of the superior orders defense as an *objective* one, i.e., the ordinary reasonable person having the subordinate's knowledge of the facts and operating under like circumstances, would produce a different outcome than if a *subjective* test which relies on actual personal knowledge were applied, whether the subordinate is with or without conscious wrongdoing.[127] A more flexible and conclusive criterion is that of the application of the principles of *reasonableness* and *fairness* as well as *good faith*. The defenses of duress and superior orders to war crimes may be invoked if it would be unreasonable to require resistance against the particular coercive element, or if the subordinate acted in good faith, i.e., if the subordinate did not know and could not reasonably have been expected to know that the act ordered was unlawful. This approach requires law finding by means of an *inductive* method, instead of pursuing a deductive, normative approach, with its rigid reliance on dogmatic principles of proportionality and subsidiarity which govern the admissibility of legal defenses. While this inductive method is essentially concerned with "the law of the case," it should be extended to the regulation of armed conflicts, from which regulation the defenses of necessity and prevention of crime arise. It is to be considered positive that the drafters of the ICC seem to support such an inductive method, as shown by Article 31 (2) of the Statute.

---

126. Bassiouni & Manikas, *supra* note 2, at 345.
127. This choice as to objective or subjective determination of guilt also entails the doctrine of command responsibility; *See* Bassiouni & Manikas, *supra* note 2, at 345.

# CHAPTER VI

## SELF-DEFENSE BY STATES AND INDIVIDUALS
## IN THE LAW OF WAR

## 1 INTRODUCTION

The theme of this chapter embodies a highly legal provenance, since, as stated by Shaw, *"The rules governing resort to force form a central element within international law and, together with other principles such as territorial sovereignty and the independence and equality of states, provide the framework for international order."*[1] This especially applies to the Post Cold War Era.

Throughout the Cold War, characterized by paralysis of the UN Security Council (hereinafter: SC), the UN Charter's explicit exceptions to the prohibition of the use of force became more important than the collective security provisions of Chapter VII, notably Articles 39, 41 and 42.[2] Despite the original expectations of the drafters of the UN Charter, according to MacCormack the SC was prevented from fulfilling the role envisioned for it in the maintenance of international peace and security, at least for the first 45 years of its history. Assessment of the explicit exceptions to the general prohibition of the use of force in the UN Charter teaches that in fact Article 51, endorsing the *"inherent right of self defense,"* is the only *"( . . . ) on-going exception permitting unilateral action by a state without prior authorization by the SC,"*[3] thus resulting in an increasing recourse to Article 51 to justify forceful unilateral action by States in the period 1945–1990.[4] A clear example hereof forms the forcible unilateral action conducted by Israel on the 7th June 1981 by bombing "Osiraq"—the French supplied Iraqi nuclear reactor at Baghdad—pursuant to the pre-existing customary international law right to resort to force in anticipatory self-defense,[5]

---

1. MALCOLM N. SHAW, INTERNATIONAL LAW 777 (1997).
2. *See* TIMOTHY L.H. MCCORMACK, SELF-DEFENSE IN INTERNATIONAL LAW, THE ISRAELI RAID ON THE IRAQI NUCLEAR REACTOR 9 (1996).
3. McCormack, *supra* note 2, at 9.
4. McCormack, *supra* note 2.
5. *See* for this latter form: Shaw, *supra* note 1, at 789–791; Gerardus G.J.

which is typical in case law for the Cold War era.[6] MacCormack observes that from 1990 a much greater compliance to *collective* action through the powers of the SC based on Articles 41 and 42 of the UN Charter exists.[7] The *first* question to be addressed in this chapter, dealt with in section 2, is whether this is a correct analysis. Subsequently, the *second* question is whether collective forcible action without authorization from the SC is in accordance with public international law, especially in the context of the Kosovo intervention. This question will be considered in section 3. The *third* question—examined in section 4—assesses the current scope of the right of self-defense in international law, including an additional legal argument on behalf of the acceptance of humanitarian forcible intervention. In this context, section 6, describing the exact nature of self-defense, will provide a further argument. In section 5 this Chapter will examine a possible relationship between these recent developments regarding the international (collective) right of self-defense of states on the one hand and the individual right of self-defense by persons under International Criminal Law (hereinafter ICL) on the other. Contrary to the Statutes of the *ad hoc* Tribunals of the ICTY and ICTR, which are silent on this defense, the Rome Statute of the ICC ensures such an individual the right to self-defense based on obviously similar criteria to the right of self-defense by States. Because both forms of self-defense feature in the realm of international law, it is important to analyze parallels as to the underlying legal and moral principles. This analysis can perhaps be very helpful as to the identification and acceptance of the (as will be observed) conceptual change of the use of force by States after the Cold War. The value of the latter comparison can itself be provided with a theoretical basis. This consists of the reference to the policy elements in the use of force system (by States) in the UN Charter, as described by the International Law Commission, noting that "( . . . ) *it is obvious that only in relatively recent times ( . . . ) the international legal order did adopt a concept of self-defense that, in certain essential aspects, is entirely comparable to that normally employed in* national legal systems (emphasis added; GJK)."[8] Based upon this observation, the judicial dialogue between self-defense by States and individual (private) self-defense in international law seems clear and comprehensive; an interpretive connection between these two concepts of self-defense clearly exists and is therefore worthy of debate.

---

Knoops, *Interstatelijk Noodweerrecht: disculpatiegrond voor internationaalrechtelijke onrechtmatige daad*, 43 NEDERLANDS JURISTENBLAD 2018 (1999).

    6.   *See* extensively: McCormack, *supra* note 2, at 10, *et seq.*

    7.   *See* McCormack, *supra* note 2, at 10.

    8.   *See* Reports of the International Law Commission to the General Assembly on the Work of the Thirty-Second Session, International Law Commission, Yearbook 1980, II, at 52.

## 2  THE USE OF FORCE BY STATES AND THE NEW CONCEPT OF "FORCIBLE HUMANITARIAN INTERVENTION"

It is necessary to turn first to the legal theory propounded by the literature indicating that after the Cold War, the concept of collective forcible intervention by authority of the UN SC, pursuant to Articles 41 and 42 of the UN Charter, was invoked more extensively. This assumption must be read together with the fact that the system of the UN Charter represents the normal elements of a *public order system*, that is to say, a centralized authority with *prima facie* a monopoly of the use of force and a restrictive regime of self-help by individual States.[9] Consequently, forcible intervention is, as advocated by the literature, only permissible if authorized by the SC.[10]

First of all, the assertion that after the Cold War recourse to authorization by the SC would be more willingly conducted, seems to be incorrect, since international law after 1995 reveals apparent exceptions to this assumption. Serious efforts to develop some form of collective intervention began soon after the end of the Cold War, when (as Henkin stated), it ceased to be hopeless to pursue collective intervention by authority of the UN Security Council.[11] The Security Council-authorized military interventions for humanitarian purposes in Iraq and Somalia in 1991 and 1992 were in fact justified by the responsibility of the SC under Chapters VI and VII of the Charter, because international peace and security were considered to be threatened by concomitant war crimes, massive human rights violations and other crimes against humanity, even if unrelated to war.[12] The Kosovo intervention, based on humanitarian reasons, was conducted without leave or authorization from the SC. Like the situation that led to the Iraq and Somalia military interventions, the Kosovo crisis surely threatened international peace and security, as was shown by the SC in several prior resolutions.[13] However, NATO's Kosovo intervention clearly exemplifies *a new* concept of the use of force by States or international organizations, such as NATO and the UN, in international law; that is to say, a new form of legal order at the entrance of the new millennium,

---

9.  *See* IAN BROWNLIE, THE RULE OF LAW IN INTERNATIONAL AFFAIRS 195 (1998).

10.  *See* also Jorrie Duursma, *Justifying Nato's Use of Force in Kosovo?* 12 LJIL 287–295 (1999).

11.  Louis Henkin, *Kosovo and the Law of Humanitarian Intervention*, in Editorial Comments: Nato's Kosovo Intervention, 93 THE AMERICAN JOURNAL OF INTERNATIONAL LAW 825 (1999).

12.  *See* Henkin, *supra* note 11, at 825, emphasizing that those interventions were thus not justified as "humanitarian," a term as such unknown in the UN Charter.

13.  *See* Resolutions 1160 (March 31, 1998), 1199 (September 23, 1998) and 1203 (October 24, 1998); *See* Henkin, *supra* note 11.

namely the use of forcible humanitarian intervention pursuant to an extension of the doctrine of the use of force or self-defense by States, despite the absence of authorization of the SC.

The *rationale* of this new use of force concept seems obvious. Even after the Cold War, both historical and political considerations rendered unanimity by the permanent members in support of military action, especially in the Balkans, highly unlikely. This resulted in NATO's decision not to ask for authorization regarding the Kosovo intervention, an action preferable to having it frustrated by veto. The latter situation might have complicated diplomatic efforts to address the Kosovo crisis and would have consequently rendered military intervention politically even more difficult.[14] The fact that the NATO action in Kosovo gained ultimately the support of the SC (twelve out of fifteen members of the SC voted to reject the Russian resolution of March 26, 1999, to declare the action unlawful and to direct its termination), suggested the SC's implicit approval of this NATO intervention, but did not change this plausible fear.[15]

In conclusion, compliance with the powers of the SC is no longer a specific feature of the use of force by States after the Cold War. Although the history of the use of force during the Cold War provides examples of forcible humanitarian intervention without authorization from the competent UN organs, such as, *inter alia*, the 1983 intervention in Grenada by a joint task force composed of troops of the US and member States of the Organization of Eastern Caribbean States,[16] this use of force by States after the Cold War is validated by the increasing importance of human rights ad its *jus cogens* dimension.[17]

## 3    THE USE OF FORCE BY STATES AND THE RULE OF LAW

### 3.1  Introduction

As to the second question of this chapter—the (non-) justificatory or exculpatory character of the use of force by States without authorization of the SC or legal basis in the UN Charter—the legal regime of the UN Charter includes various vulnerable areas. The justification that this legal regime ensures an *"inherent"* right to resort to the use of force in the course of a *"humanitarian intervention"* presupposes the validity of two underlying premises; *first*, that the threat or use of force by individual States pro-

---

14.  *See* Henkin, *supra* note 11, at 825.

15.  Henkin, *supra* note 11, at 826.

16.  *See* for this case: W.D. Verwey, *Humanitarian Intervention*, in THE CURRENT LEGAL REGULATION OF THE USE OF FORCE 57–78 (Antonio Cassese, ed., 1986).

17.  *See* Knoops, *supra* note 5, at 2019.

hibited as a principle of Article 2 (4) of the UN Charter has a *contextual* not an *absolute* character, and thus implicitly allows for exceptions additional to those explicitly enumerated in Articles 42, 51 and 107; and *second*, that forcible humanitarian intervention embodies one of these contextual exceptions.[18]

## 3.2 Contextual or absolutist approach?

As Schachter observes, summarizing the submitted doctrine clearly: *"No United Nations resolution has supported* (explicitly; GJK) *the right of a State to intervene on humanitarian grounds with armed troops in a state that has not consented to such intervention. Nor is there evidence of State practice and related* opinio juris *on a scale sufficient to support a humanitarian exception to the general prohibition against non-defensive use of force."*[19] Arising from this point is the central question as to the contextual or absolutist interpretation of the present legal regime. The controversy in this area is clearly exemplified by the Kosovo crisis; on the one hand the *absolutist* approach refers to the international legal regime which clearly intends to restrict the resort to self-help and also the resort to different, restrictive, forms of armed intervention and reprisal,[20] whereas on the other hand the *contextual* approach challenges the values of democracy, human rights or dignity and the rule of law in the view of the particular facts of the event.[21] No doubt the international legal regime on the use of force by States, interpreted in the absolutist way, will always entail problems of application, and rules alone, however carefully formulated, will not induce States to behave in a civilized way.[22] Moreover, and more importantly, the absolutist approach bears a major threat to the legal regime relating to the use of force by States themselves, i.e., the danger of dogmatic, unreasonable rigidity, to the detriment of international law-making on a case-by-case basis. Therefore, the *contextual* approach, resorting to the exercise of due diligence regarding the particular circumstances surrounding the event in question with respect to judicial reasoning on the individual merits of the event, is more appropriate. In this sense it endorses refinement of international positive law. Since it has long been recognized that judicial

---

18. *See* Verwey, *supra* note 16, at 57.

19. OSCAR SCHACHTER, INTERNATIONAL LAW IN THEORY AND PRACTICE, 178 GENERAL COURSE IN PUBLIC INTERNATIONAL LAW 124 (1982–V).

20. *See* Brownlie, *supra* note 9, at 209–210.

21. *See* NATO Statement "The Situation in and around Kosovo," issued at the Extraordinary Ministerial Meeting of the North Atlantic Council held at NATO Headquarters, Brussels, on the 12th April 1999, at 1. No. 1; http://www.nato.int/docu/pr/1999/p.990, 51e htm.

22. *See* Brownlie, *supra* note 9, at 210.

activity involves law-making and a range of choices beyond *"a single model of law-finding"* (as is the case with regard to the absolutist model), and the rule of law implies much more than the mere application of the existing legal norms but must also involve an assessment of the quality of the legal norms (i.e., the norms governing the use of force by States), the contextual model provides a more sophisticated framework of the concept of the law in general and that ruling the use of force specifically.[23] Moreover, the contextual model counters one of the major disadvantages of the present absolutist legal regime regarding the use of force by States, i.e., the threat due to the appearance of new practices. This threat, emerging in the last decade in the sphere of exterminating people by political regimes allegedly with State protection but using in fact no less than discriminative or racist motives, has arisen in the face of *"the highly selective application"* of sanctions and resolutions by the Security Council with regard to resort to force by individual States.[24] This threat can lead to the *"result that the penalty-free delinquent (State) is tempted to argue that the inaction of the Council is evidence of the legality of its actions."*[25] This aforementioned threat is not encouraged in the realm of the contextual model, wherein resort to the use of force by States or coalitions, by virtue of humanitarian intervention to protect the lives and dignity of people, is endorsed.

In conclusion it must be evident that the legal regime of the use of force, by States or international organizations, or in the name of self-defense, has to adopt the contextual model of law finding. This assertion involves the implementation of the rule of law and subsequently results in the legitimacy of exceptions to the current doctrine, i.e., exceptions to the absolutist view on the use of force envisioned by the UN Charter. The rule of law embodies much more than, as observed, the application of the existing legal norms.

### 3.3 Forcible humanitarian intervention as contextual exception

The next question worthy of debate is whether, apart from a justification to resort to armed force in this area based on ethical or moral grounds—which doesn't change the contravention of current international law—contemporary international law entails parameters that might lead to a *"gradual legitimization of forcible humanitarian countermeasures by a group of States* (or international organization; GJK) *outside any authorization by the*

---

23.   *See* Brownlie, *supra* note 9, at 1–3, concerning the function of law in the international community.

24.   Brownlie, *supra* note 9, at 210; *see*, e.g., the forcible intervention of Russia in Tsjetsjenia.

25.   *See* Brownlie, *supra* note 9, at 210.

*Security Council"* in a particular situation.[26] The starting point must be that the UN Charter's prohibition of humanitarian intervention addressed to individual States equally applies to several States acting together, as well as in the context of an international organization, outside authorization of the SC.[27]

The contextual model relates to various sets of contingencies with distinct elements of liberalness as a result of the *inductive* method of law finding. Cassese seeks reliance on a more flexible and contextual concept of the use of force by States, analyzing the following six *"basic premises or roots"* of humanitarian intervention, such as in the Kosovo conflict, in the international legal community,[28] which can be summarized as follows:

1. The truism that nowadays human rights protection is no longer of exclusive concern to the particular state but affects the world community as a whole. The latter aspect is also evidenced by the *jus cogens* character of (most) human rights law.[29]

2. The vast majority of States and authoritative writers now recognize that the fundamental principles of human rights form part of customary or general international law. In 1970, the ICJ rendered the judgment in the *Barcelona Traction* case, referring to obligations *ergo omnes* in contemporary international law, ruling that these included *"the principles and rules concerning the basic rights of the human person, including protection from slavery and racial discrimination."*[30] Consequently, states both within and without the scope of an international organization have to be endowed with powers to ensure this respect.

3. Cassese further points to the emerging development in international law encompassing the fact that *"large-scale and systematic atrocities may give rise to an aggravated form of State responsibility, to which other States or international organizations may be entitled to respond by resorting to countermeasures other than those contemplated for delictual responsibility."*[31]

4. A subsequent emerging tendency in international law is the increasing receptiveness of the international community to intervene in internal conflicts, where human rights atrocities are conducted. This was shown by several precedents such as

---

26. *See* Antonio Cassese, *Ex Iniuria ius oritur: Are We Moving Towards International Legitimation of Forcible Humanitarian Countermeasures in The World Community*, 10 EUROPEAN JOURNAL OF INTERNATIONAL LAW 3 (1998).

27. *See* Henkin, *supra* note 11, at 826.

28. *See* Cassese, *supra* note 26, at 3–4.

29. *See* Shaw, *supra* note 1; Brownlie, *supra* note 9, at 65–78.

30. ICJ Reports, 1970, at 3.

31. Cassese, *supra* note 26, at 3.

the UN interventions in Iraq to protect the human rights of Iraqi Kurds in the north and Iraqi Shiites in the south (1991–1992), in Somalia in 1992 to prevent atrocities, in Bosnia and Herzegovina (1992–1995), and in Rwanda in 1994 to stop the Tutsi's genocide.

5.  Though a minority, some are proposing the legality of humanitarian intervention to restore peace.[32]

6.  The international community has revealed a consciousness that *"under certain exceptional circumstances, where atrocities reach such a large scale as to shock the conscience of all human beings and indeed jeopardize international stability, forcible protection of human rights may need to outweigh the necessity to avoid"* the use of force.[33]

In addition to Cassese's six *"basic premises or roots,"* a *seventh* premise can be conceded, i.e., the notion that the collective character of the intervening international organization or group of States provides sufficient safeguards against abuse of powers by a single State which is pursuing egoistic national or improper interests, presupposing that interventions can be (even *post factum*) monitored by international organs such as the SC.[34] In face of these parameters or roots, humanitarian intervention as contextual exception regarding the prohibition of the use of force is tenable, when used with considerable caution.

### 3.4 Legal requirements of humanitarian forcible intervention as contextual exception

After setting forth the general premises or roots as to the aforementioned exception, it is necessary to turn to the legal conditions of applying this exception, considering the factual and legal complexities presented by the distinct (political and military) situations arising in practice. In particular, six criteria can be indicated as to the contextual basis of the legal justification and application of this exception, when any authorization of the SC is absent. Here also Cassese provides guidance, analyzing as follows:[35]

*"(i) gross and egregious breaches of human rights involving loss of life of hundreds or thousands of innocent people, and amounting to crimes*

---

32.  *See* also Henkin, *supra* note 11, at 826.
33.  *See* Cassese, *supra* note 26, at 4.
34.  *See* Henkin, *supra* note 11, at 826.
35.  *See* Cassese, *supra* note 26, at 4.

*against humanity, are carried out in the territory of a sovereign state, either by the central governmental authorities or with their connivance and support, or because the total collapse of such authorities cannot impede those atrocities;*

*(ii) if the crimes against humanity result from anarchy in a sovereign state, proof is necessary that the central authorities are utterly unable to put an end to those crimes, while at the same time refusing to call upon or to allow other states or international organizations to enter the territory to assist in terminating the crimes. If, on the contrary, such crimes are the work of the central authorities, it must be shown that those authorities have consistently withheld their cooperation from the United Nations or other international organizations, or have systematically refused to comply with appeals, recommendations or decisions of such organizations;*

*(iii) the Security Council is unable to take any coercive action to stop the massacres because of disagreement among the Permanent Members or because one or more of them exercises its veto power. Consequently, the Security Council either refrains from any action or only confines itself to deploring or condemning the massacres, plus possibly terming the situation a threat to the peace;*

*(iv) all peaceful avenues which may be explored consistent with the urgency of the situation to achieve a solution based on negotiation, discussion and any other means short of force have been exhausted, notwithstanding which, no solution can be agreed upon by the parties to the conflict;*

*(v) a group of states (neither a single hegemonic Power, however strong its military, political and economic authority, nor such a Power with the support of a client state or an ally) decides to try to halt the atrocities, with the support or at least the non-opposition of the majority of Member States of the UN;*

*(vi) armed force is exclusively used for the limited purpose of stopping the atrocities and restoring respect for human rights, not for any goal going beyond this limited purpose. Consequently, the use of force must be discontinued as soon as this purpose is attained. Moreover, it is axiomatic that use of force should be commensurate with and proportionate to the human rights exigencies on the ground. The more urgent the situation of killings and atrocities, the more intensive and immediate may be the military response thereto. Conversely, military action would not be warranted in the case of a crisis which is slowly unfolding and which still presents avenues for diplomatic resolution aside from armed confrontation."*

In fact, the requirements ad 2,3,4 and 6 represent the requisite conditions in international law of *necessity, proportionality* and *immediacy,* also to be fulfilled with regard to individual self-defense.[36] It is noteworthy that Cassese concludes that in the Kosovo war NATO met these six conditions, notwithstanding his remark that (according to the absolutist doctrine) its intervention remained unlawful.[37] A decisive criterion as to the contextual exception is the argument that the international community cannot refrain from intervention when large numbers of innocent lives can be saved in circumstances of gross oppression by a state of its people.[38] Supportive of this view is also the study of the Canadian scholar Francis Abiew, in which he remarks that, notwithstanding the viewpoint that humanitarian intervention cannot be legal, justifiable, or permissible, there is a growing international concern for the protection of human rights and the right of intervention towards those ends, or for some, an obligation to intervene when violations reach a stage that incite the outrage of the international community.[39] This element also applies to individual self-defense in criminal law, as will be observed in section 5. As observed by Abiew, a notable shift in the context of the evolution of the doctrine and practice of humanitarian intervention seems to be under way, emphasizing that, at present, humanitarian intervention has gained wide support in the international community. Such intervention though, in support of human rights is grounded, however, in the premise that it is the interests of humanity at large that are at stake, and not the interests of any particular state or group of states. This development especially seems to be justified, since from a legal perspective the internationalization of human rights points to holding governments accountable for gross and systematic violations.[40]

### 3.5 Conclusion

*"Perhaps the Kosovo intervention sets a precedent for the development of new international law to protect human rights,"* observed Charney, adding that *"perhaps the example of Kosovo may stipulate the development of a new* Rule of Law (emphasis added; GJK) *that permits intervention by regional organizations to stop these crimes without the Security Council's authorization, while*

---

36.   *See* for these conditions: YORAM DINSTEIN, WAR, AGGRESSION AND SELF-DEFENSE 202–212 and 221–229 (1988).

37.   Cassese, *supra* note 26, at 5.

38.   *See* also Shaw, *supra* note 1, at 802–803.

39.   *See* FRANCIS K. ABIEW, THE EVOLUTION OF THE DOCTRINE AND PRACTICE OF HUMANITARIAN INTERVENTION, Preface (1999).

40.   *See* Abiew, *supra* note 39, at 278.

*limiting the risks of abuse and escalation,"* being thus the task for the future.[41] The evolution of a new rule of law is not incompatible with the decision of the ICJ in the merits phase of the *Nicaragua* case, wherein the Court applied the criterion of *opinio juris.*[42]

It can be conceded that, with regard to the matter of proof of *opinio juris,* the Court's requirement of evidence of express consent to the relevant norms is unusually rigorous.[43] This is especially true since, in the *North Sea* cases, the ICJ referred to the *"emergent rules of customary international law,"*[44] a formulation, which indicates a rather flexible approach to the criterion of *opinio juris.*[45] The jurisprudence of the ICJ shows a certain willingness to adhere to the existence of an *opinio juris* on the basis of evidence of a general practice or *consensus in the literature.*[46] The latter element of *opinio juris*—the writings of scholars[47]—produces an argument in favor of the acceptance of a new rule of law regarding forcible humanitarian intervention by States (without Chapter VII authorization) as being, in particular, exceptional and contextual circumstances, fully justified. To quote Shaw: *"( . . . ) it is possible that such a right* (to an outside forcible humanitarian intervention; GJK) *might evolve in cases of extreme humanitarian need."*[48] Specific doctrinal sources do appear, as observed, hereto.

## 4. THE CONCEPT OF ANTICIPATORY SELF-DEFENSE AS A CONTEXTUAL ELEMENT OF HUMANITARIAN INTERVENTION

A particular argument in favor of the conclusion drawn in section 3.5 above seems to be the concept of anticipatory or preemptive self-defense. When assessing the legitimacy of a specific intervention, reference can be made to this concept as one of the contextual and constituting elements of such an intervention. Charney has expressed the more or less interchangeable character of forcible humanitarian intervention on the one hand and anticipatory self-defense on the other hand in this way: *"In fact, the Kosovo intervention reflects the problems of an undeveloped rule of law in a morally dangerous situation. It was actually an anticipatory humanitarian*

---

41. *See* Jonathan I. Charney, *Anticipatory Humanitarian Intervention in Kosovo,* in Editorial Comments: NATO's Kosovo Intervention, 93 THE AMERICAN JOURNAL OF INTERNATIONAL LAW 841 (1999).
42. ICJ Reports, 1986, at 92–97.
43. *See* Brownlie, *supra* note 9, at 23.
44. ICJ Reports, 1969, at 39 and at 40.
45. Brownlie, *supra* note 9, at 21.
46. *See* also Brownlie, *supra* note 9, at 21; Shaw, *supra* note 1, at 803.
47. Also referred to by the ICJ in the *Nottebohm* case, second phase, ICJ Reports, 1955, at 4 and 22.
48. Shaw, *supra* note 1, at 803.

*intervention, based on past actions of the FRY regime and future risks.*"[49] A further necessary preliminary is to ask whether the right to anticipatory self-defense for states actually is part of customary international law. Essential here are both several precedents set out in international law—e.g. the preemptive strikes of Israel in 1967 conducted against its Arab neighbors, not condemned by the UN in its debates thereon[50]—as well as the jurisprudence of the ICJ. This Court in the *Nicaragua* case left open the matter of the lawfulness of anticipatory self-defense by States.[51] Therefore, according to current customary international law, a forcible response of (a group of) state(s) to an imminent threat of armed attack is, under some circumstances, to be allowed, Much will depend upon the characterization of the threat and the nature of the (requisitely proportionate) response.[52] Moreover, Article 51 of the UN Charter does not exclude anticipatory self-defense.[53] Consequently, since it is *"universally accepted today that it is not lawful to resort to force merely to save nationals abroad,"* even by means of preemptive self-defense,[54] this is equally applicable to the saving of people of the delinquent state itself. In this context, it is a striking fact that the drafters of the UN Charter did not intend to restrict the pre-existing right of self-defense. In the *travaux préparatoires* of Article 2 (4) it was explicitly stated that the right of self-defense, as it existed in customary international law at the time, was not to be excluded by the general proscription of the use of force.[55] The legislative history of Article 51 also reveals an explicit recognition of the pre-existing or anticipatory right of self-defense. The wording of this Article, causing much controversy, is *"a classic example of the pressure for political compromise to make the entire document acceptable overriding the need for precise draftsmanship in a specific provision."*[56] In this context it is also to be recalled that Article 51 cannot be interpreted in isolation from the overall scheme to maintain international peace and security, a conclusion which stems as well from Article 31 of the Vienna Convention on the Law of Treaties.[57]

---

49.  Charney, *supra* note 41, at 841.
50.  *See* Shaw, *supra* note 1, at 789.
51.  ICJ Reports, 1986, at 14, 103; *see* for this opinion also McCormack, *supra* note 2, at 141.
52.  Shaw, *supra* note 1, at 790.
53.  *See* McCormack, *supra* note 2, at 138.
54.  *See* Shaw, *supra* note 1, at 793, where several precedents hereof are described.
55.  *See* Doc. 810, I/1/30, Report of the 12th Meeting of Committee I/1, UN (1945), Vol. 6, 342; Doc. 739, I/1/A/19 (a), UN (1945), Vol. 6, 717, at 720; Doc. 784, I/1/27, Vol. 6, 331, at 334; *See* also McCormack, *supra* note 2, at 139.
56.  McCormack, *supra* note 2.
57.  *See* McCormack, *supra* note 2, at 144.

In sum, against the background of the observation that Article 51 of the UN Charter includes the customary international law right of anticipatory self-defense—to be assessed in each particular situation—forcible humanitarian intervention can be an appropriate application of this form of self-defense by States.

It must, however, be clarified whether protection of the lives of citizens of other countries than the intervening states falls within the scope of anticipatory self-defense. This element involves the requirement of valid *"necessity"* and is the derived criterion of the *"severity of the threat"* as to the legitimacy of the use of force in self-defense. In principle, a state can only use force in self-defense to protect its fundamental *national* security.[58] In determining the substantive, defensible rights for which force in self-defense is justified, it is *opinio juris* hereto that *"surely a fundamental right is the right to use force to guarantee the preservation of the lives of the citizens of the claimant state in situations where there is an intention to kill or seriously injure them."*[59] It would be incompatible with the nature of the Charter—maintenance of international peace and security—and rather anomalous to restrict these defensible rights to only nationals and not citizens of the delinquent State. An analogous argument can be derived from ICL. Self-defense by individuals in ICL is not limited to their own lives or health, but can entail also the lives and health of other persons.

## 5    EXCULPATION BY INDIVIDUAL SELF-DEFENSE IN ICL: SYNCHRONIC AND SUPPORTIVE DEVELOPMENTS AFTER 1990

### 5.1 Introduction

It is tempting to see a synchronic development in public and private self-defense since the Cold War. Recent ICL developments suggest such a parallel. As observed in Chapter IV above, Article 31 (1) (c) of the 1998 Rome Statute of the ICC, provides that a person shall not be criminally responsible if, at the time of that person's conduct *"the person acts reasonably to defend himself or herself or another person or,* in the case of war crimes (emphasis added; GJK) *property which is essential for the survival of the person ( . . . ) against an imminent and unlawful use of force in a manner proportionate to the degree of danger to the person or the other person or property protected."*

For present purposes, the essence of this definition consists of three elements:

---

58.  *See* McCormack, *supra* note 2, at 263.
59.  McCormack, *supra* note 2, at 265.

1. The defense of self-defense (by persons) under the ICC Statute is not excluded in the event that the accused is charged with a war crime. This implies that self-defense under the Statute constitutes a highly profound and elementary right of the accused, which view strengthens the previous extensive interpretation of the right of self-defense by States.

2. Secondly, the element of *"an imminent and unlawful use of force"* indisputably constitutes self-defense by virtue of anticipatory self-defense. This view is justified by the rationale that it would be unrealistic and unjustified to require that a defending person must actually wait until the attack has occurred before being entitled to respond with self-defense.[60]

3. Finally, it must be self-evident that the legal regime of the use of force in self-defense by states has to enshrine the element *"or another person"* as a *"defensible"* object or subject matter.

It is in the context of these three elements that a legal interaction between the judicial development of self-defense by States and private self-defense exists.

## 5.2 ICL and the inclusion or exclusion of individual self-defense to war crimes

As to the primary question whether a plea of self-defense is to be admitted to a war crimes indictment or whether this defense contravenes the nature of war crimes, the decision of *United States v. Krupp* is of particular interest, as already observed in Chapter IV above. The admissibility of this defense before war crimes tribunals was in fact accepted by the International Military Tribunal (hereinafter IMT). In the case of *US v. Krupp*, the Court implied that it would accept a defense of self-defense, defined as executing *"the repulse of a wrong"* and even a defense of necessity that is *"the invasion of a right."* The inclusion, however, of the plea of self-defense before a war crimes tribunal is also clearly expressed in the literature. *"(It) may be successfully put forward in war crimes trials in much the same circumstances as in trials held under municipal law."*[61] This extensive view on the legitimacy of the concept of private self-defense in international law—contrary, e.g., to the defenses of duress and superior orders—is also supported by more recent literature, especially in the recognition in public international law that an individual defending the State is not

---

60. *See* also for states: McCormack, *supra* note 2, at 265 and 268.
61. *See* INTERNATIONAL CRIMINAL LAW, CASES AND MATERIALS 1389 (Jordan J. Paust and M. Cherif Bassiouni et.al., eds., 1996).

required to actually wait until its citizens are killed before being entitled to use force. The rationale of the admissibility of private self-defense is *"that it would be inhuman to ask people to abstain from such action when it is necessary, because defending oneself against an illegal attack, is the most natural thing to do, so that the right of self-defense (of an individual) ( . . . ) is therefore an inherent right of a human being."*[62] The literature provides a very persuasive example of this view: a State does not have the right to kill its prisoners of war, even if they endanger the success of a military mission. But why should a guard of a POW camp not be entitled to defend himself against an attack by prisoners of war on his person?[63] In sum, it can be accepted that the right of self-defense of individual persons, by its nature, exists in customary ICL even with regard to war crimes, being recognized by Article 31 (1)(c) of the Rome Statute of the ICC. There is good reason to believe that Article 31 (1)(c) fails to be considered as a substantive indicator that private self-defense in ICL has an extensive scope, since other individual defenses, such as superior orders, are excluded in the ICC Statute.[64] Since both the constituent elements of the right to use force in self-defense of States and the right of self-defense by individuals are, as earlier observed, comparable, as a consequence this independent and exclusive character—the latter a right in ICL (as opposed to other private defenses)—can have supportive value as to the aforementioned extensive and contextual interpretation of the use of force by States in self-defense. The fact, however, that a State may legitimately use force in self-defense does not automatically imply that its military personnel, agents or other nationals are endowed with the private right to use force in self-defense and are therefore allowed to commit, under this shield, international crimes. The concept of individual criminal and command responsibility must be assessed independently from the use of force by a State.

## 6    THE CONTEXTUAL MODEL AND THE SUBJECTIVE NATURE OF SELF-DEFENSE

Another feature of the development of the doctrine of the use of force by States since the Cold War, and another argument in favor of the application of the contextual model, emphasizes the *subjective* element of self-defense. It is of interest to note that this subjective element was in fact envisioned in the Kosovo intervention, where no advance authorization

---

62.   *See* Nico Keyzer, *Self-Defense in the Statute of Rome*, unpublished, at 5.
63.   The example is described by C. NILL-THEOBALD, DEFENSES BEI KRIEGSVER-BRECHEN 197, 363 (1998).
64.   *See* Article 33 (1)(2) ICC Statute; *see* also, e.g., Articles 7 (3) and 6 (3) respectively of the ICTY and ICTR Statutes.

of the SC was obtained. This subjective element implies that, by nature, the decision to resort to force in self-defense is a subjective one.[65] While the assessment of the constitutive elements of self-defense refers to *objective* measures, such as the principles of proportionality and subsidiarity, it is for the individual State and, in ICL, the individual person, facing an emergency situation, to decide that it (he or she) must resort to force to defend itself or him (her) self. Article 51 refers to the right of self-defense as an *"interim privilege."*[66] The Charter recognizes the right of an individual State to use force in self-defense: *"( . . . ) until the Security Council has taken the measures necessary to maintain international peace and security. Measures taken by Members in the exercise of this right of self-defense shall be immediately reported to the Security Council and not in any way affect the authority and responsibility of the Security Council under the present Charter to take at any time such action as it deems necessary in order to maintain or restore international peace and security."*

Therefore, despite the fact that Article 51 reserves the authority of the Security Council to intervene at any stage after action has been taken in self-defense, it is clear that the *initial* decision to resort to force is made by the State itself.[67] It is of considerable importance to distinguish between the establishment of the initial decision to resort to the use of force by the individual State(s) on the one hand, and its submission to legal control and analysis on the other. The fact that this initial decision is made by the State itself does not put that use of force beyond the law.[68] Consequently it must be accepted that the use of force in self-defense by States (and *a fortiori* by individual persons) on the one hand can be evaluated retrospectively (based on the aforementioned objective criteria), though, on the other hand, this retrospective evaluation should be conducted with considerable caution since a legal approach, (and immediate control), dictates a reference to the subjective context of the very moment, that is to say, the necessity of self-defense and the purposive context which it presents.[69] The bombing of a bridge by NATO in Kosovo, killing several citizens, invoked strong criticism based on an objective, retrospective adjudication by the international community. This tendency shows too little consideration of the subjective nature of self-defense, and its inevitably subjective appreciation of the factual situation at the very moment of deciding to act in self-defense.[70] When, e.g., a State itself has *"a good reason"* to believe that a threat of nuclear attack genuinely exists, international law cannot pre-

---

65. *See* McCormack, *supra* note 2, at 259.
66. McCormack, *supra* note 2.
67. *See* McCormack, *supra* note 2, at 260.
68. *See* McCormack, *supra* note 2, at 260.
69. *See* also Brownlie, *supra* note 9, at 204.
70. *See* also William J. Fenrick, *Attacking the Enemy Civilian as a Punishable Offence*, 7 Duke Journal of Comparative & International Law 542–544 (1999).

clude a state from acting in self-defense. This was the case in the 1981 Israeli attack on the Iraqi Nuclear reactor, which attack was legitimately conducted on the basis of anticipatory self-defense.[71] However, like the adjudicatory control of the use of force in self-defense by individual persons, a more or less independent assessment of the evidence alleged to justify the action of the State in question must be part of the control mechanism of the legal regime. At Nuremberg, Germany's argument that it alone could determine the conditions justifying force in self-defense was rejected.[72] The Military Tribunal found that the right to make the decision to resort to force does not relieve the claimant State of the responsibility to justify its use of force to the international community after the action has commenced.[73] Since the factual and contextual element hereto must be primarily decisive for the claimant State—whether or whether not to decide if it has any choice but to use force in self-defense[74]—it is difficult to understand how any other but a subjective approach is tenable. MacCormack has expressed the *"subjective"* doctrine in this way: *"There may be situations in which a state believes that its fundamental security is threatened without an attack actually having been launched against it. If the threatened state uses force before an attack has commenced, it is obviously more difficult for that state to show that its claim to be acting in self-defense is not a spurious one than for a state responding to an actual armed attack. But if a state can substantiate its claim that it needed to use force to defend itself against the threat it faced, its claim should not fail simply because the actual attack has not yet begun."*[75]

The development of the legal regime regarding the use of force by States since the Cold War teaches that the international community appears to be more conscious of the *subjective* nature of the concept of self-defense by States. Especially in the area of human rights atrocities, recourse to this subjective nature to legitimize an extensive interpretation of self-defense and the use of force is visible and tends to be primary. The Kosovo intervention provides a clear example of this shift from a purely *objective* to, an at least partly *subjective* view of self-defense. An explanation may entail the failure of the SC to authorize and impose strong measures in the face of gross human rights abuses, as well as the prospects of vetoes by members of the SC to prevent authorization of unilateral or regional (NATO) enforcement or the use of force.[76] The analogy

---

71. *See* Mc Cormack, *supra* note 2, at 268; 258–302.

72. *See* II Trials of War Criminals before the Nuremberg Military Tribunals, 1946, 207.

73. *Ibid.*

74. *See* also Secretary Kellogg's opinion hereto; McCormack, *supra* note 2, at 261.

75. McCormack, *supra* note 2, at 261.

76. *See* Gerardus G.J. Knoops, *supra* note 5, at 2018, and Christine M. Chinkin, *Kosovo: A Good or Bad War*, in *Editorial Comments* ( . . . ), *supra* note 41, at 842–843.

with self-defense by individuals in ICL is also present. This account of the current subjective pattern of self-defense consequently focuses upon the prominent role of the contextual approach and supplies an additional argument to endorse this approach, rather than a strict absolutist view of the use of force by States.

## 7   CONCLUSIONS AND SUMMARY

It must be emphasized that *"the Rule of Law is not a purely* legal *artifact, since it involves elements derived from political science, constitutional theory, and historical experience,"* and moreover, *"it cannot be reduced to a few simple formulations (but) ( . . . ) involves a series of conjointly applicable principles or desiderata."*[77] First of all, the rule of law is a practical and contextual concept, not restrained by dogmatic and absolutist restrictions. The determination of the phenomenon of the use of force by States since the Cold War exemplifies the tendency from an absolutist model to a more flexible and contextual interpretation of the legal regime regarding this topic, wherein the subjective nature of self-defense is more respected. Evaluating the application of the use of force by States since the Cold War in terms of the rule of law, it can be observed that the advancing development of standards of human rights as *jus cogens* and *ergo omnes* obligations of States[78] have penetrated the sphere of this legal topic, the use of force by States, to a considerable degree. The many examples of humanitarian intervention with absence of SC authorization, such as the Kosovo war, form clear exponents of this tendency. Analogous to the increasing synthesis of human rights protection and the doctrine of State (criminal) responsibility (also regarding the treatment of aliens),[79] it can be conceded that humanitarian forcible intervention by States, even absent authorization of the SC, is both a legally and an ethically tenable result. In the event of two conflicting principles of *jus cogens* (on the one hand the prohibition of using force against other States and on the other the right to internal self-determination of people and the prohibition of annihilating a people), it is defensible that the latter principle(s) should prevail.[80] The extension of the concept of individual self-defense to war crimes is also, as observed in this study, supportive of this evolution. This view, however, is bound to have certain limits and depends on the exceptional circumstances of each event. In dealing with this issue, only an

---

77.  *See* Brownlie, *supra* note 9, at 213.

78.  *See Barcelona Traction* Case, ICJ Reports 1970.

79.  Brownlie, *supra* note 9, at 73.

80.  *See* Knoops *supra* note 5, at 2019; *see* also IAN BROWNLIE, PRINCIPLES OF PUBLIC INTERNATIONAL LAW 515 (1990).

*inductive* law-finding method, similar to the assessment of the individual right to self-defense, is appropriate.

The main feature of the development of the concept of the use of force by States since the Cold War is the increasing support in international law and the international community that, in particular instances, resorting to forcible humanitarian intervention, absent authorization by the SC, seems appropriate. Cassese summarizes this development as follows: *"This particular instance of breach of international law may gradually lead to the crystallization of a general rule of international law authorizing armed countermeasures for the exclusive purpose of putting an end to large-scale atrocities amounting to crimes against humanity and constituting a threat to the peace."*[81] However, to quote Cassese, *"such a rule, should it eventually evolve in the world community, would constitute an exception to the UN Charter system of collective enforcement based on the authorization of the Security Council. In other words, it would amount to an exception similar to that laid down in Article 51 of the Charter (self defense)."*

Here, a parallel between the use of force and self-defense—the latter as an additional basis for forcible humanitarian intervention—is visible:

> *"In the case of self-defense unilateral resort to armed violence is justified by the need to repel an instant and overwhelming aggression which leaves no choice of means and no moment for deliberation. In the case of forcible countermeasures to prevent crimes against humanity, unilateral resort to force (i.e. resort force outside an authorization of the SC) would be warranted by the need to terminate violations of human rights so grave as to pose a threat to international peace, under circumstances where there would exist no alternative means to put a stop to such violations."*[82]

In this chapter, it is submitted that the contextual exception to the prohibition of the use of force by States has several traits in common, and must fulfill at least the following requirements:

i.   The exception must be justified by very special and unique circumstances;
ii.  the exception must always constitute an *extrema ratio*;
iii. it must be strictly limited to the purpose of stopping the aggression of the atrocities;
iv.  it must be strictly proportionate to the need to attain this goal; and

---

81. *See* Cassese, *supra* note 26, at 6.
82. Cassese, *supra* note 26.

v.   it must yield to collective enforcement under United Nations
authority as soon as possible.[83]

These criteria indicate already that possible resort to armed countermeasures, in the area of protection of human rights, even under the aforementioned strict conditions, should therefore be used with great
circumspection by the particular States. Especially, these States should take
into account the reaction of the international community, as well as
whether the matter is being brought to the forum of the General Assembly,
or, as was the case in the Kosovo crisis, the absence of such a meeting.

It is, to quote Cassese, the task of international lawyers *"to pinpoint
the evolving trends as they emerge in the world community, while at the same
time keeping a watchful eye on the actual behavior of States."*[84]

## 8   CRITICAL REMARKS OR QUESTIONS

The Kosovo intervention shows that the international community
continues to script international law, even when it has to be done to the
detriment of the "ancient" legal regime of the UN Charter and its doctrine
before 1990, i.e., during the Cold War. It can certainly be concluded that a
"post-Charter" international law has evolved, as also evidenced by actions
in Iraq, Somalia and Haiti.

At the same time, the commitment to human rights that humanitarian
intervention supposedly entails does not mean equality of rights world-
wide. The human rights of some people seem to be more worth protecting
than those of others. Military intervention on behalf of the victims of
human rights abuses has not occurred in, *inter alia*, Sudan, Afghanistan,
Ethiopia, or Rwanda.

All these incidents seem to undermine the Charter on an *ad hoc* selective
basis without providing clear articulation of the underlying legal principles
or even assurance of future acceptance by those who currently espouse
them. From this perspective the criteria of Cassese are worth elaborating
on. The case of Kosovo highlights the continuing controversy between
human rights and legal reality. International lawyers must formulate ways
in which this can be bridged. These may include, as suggested by Abiew,
the establishment of a comprehensive framework of general principles or
statements to guide the UN in deciding when a domestic human rights situation or internal conflict warrants action by the Security Council, regional
organization or a collectivity of states, together with acknowledgment by
the international community as a whole.[85]

---

83.  Cassese, *supra* note 26.
84.  Cassese, *supra* note 26.
85.  *See* Abiew, *supra* note 39, at 280.

# CHAPTER VII

## CONTEMPORARY AND NEW TECHNICAL ISSUES OF INTERNATIONAL CRIMINAL LAW DEFENSES

### 1   INTRODUCTION: THE INDIVIDUAL AS A SUBJECT OF INTERNATIONAL LAW ENSURING PROCEDURAL RIGHTS

From the vast array of practices with regard to the international rights and duties of the individual under customary and treaty law, it is clearly demonstrated that individuals are, besides objects, also subjects of international law, concludes Shaw.[1] As far as obligations are concerned, public international law has imposed direct criminal responsibility upon individuals in certain events, e.g., in cases of piracy, slavery, crimes against the laws and customs of war, genocide and apartheid.[2] The principle of individual criminal responsibility under ICL, and the ability of ICL to directly enforce this principle without going through the mediation of States, is now *opinio juris*.[3] Shaw argues that the only context in which the individual as such has full procedural capacity is within the sphere of international criminal responsibility for war crimes and crimes against humanity.[4] This demonstrates that the qualification of individuals as subjects of public international law supervenes or prevails. An analysis of the ICTY and ICTR Statutes, as well as the Rules of Procedure and Evidence of the ICTY of 1994, reveals that they endorse certain rights of the individual—the accused—which are independent from the prior consent of States.[5]

There can therefore be little question that the implementation of these rights is based upon the recognition of the individual as a subject (in at

---

1.   MALCOLM N. SHAW, INTERNATIONAL LAW 190 (1997).

2.   IAN BROWNLIE, THE RULE OF LAW IN INTERNATIONAL AFFAIRS 48 (1998).

3.   *See* M. Cherif Bassiouni, *The Sources and Theory of International Criminal Law*, in I INTERNATIONAL CRIMINAL LAW 23 (M. Cherif Bassiouni, ed., 1999); Farhad Malekian, *International Criminal Responsibility* in I INTERNATIONAL CRIMINAL LAW 157 (M. Cherif Bassiouni, ed., 1999).

4.   *See* Art. 5, resp. Art. 3 of ICTY and ICTR Statutes.

5.   *See*, e.g., Art. 21 resp. 20 of the mentioned Statutes.

least a procedural capacity) of public international law. This chapter will focus on the procedural context of defenses to international criminal litigation from the perspective of the accused as a subject of international law. Furthermore, since interdisciplinary processes master contemporary ICL—making it a new and complex discipline, as noted in Chapter III above—this Chapter also looks into current developments on new technical issues, including the application of genetic defenses by those entrusted with international criminal litigation and law-finding.

## 2    THE PROCEDURAL ROLE OF THE PRINCIPLE OF FAIRNESS

The rules of procedure and evidence, as Bassiouni observes, which have been developed by the ICTY and ICTR, as well as those of the ICC, are based on general principles of procedural law which emerge from the laws and practices of the world's major criminal justice systems as well as the rules of procedure and evidence which are embodied in international and regional conventions.[6] These rules are thus an exponent of convergence or concurrency of international, regional and national judicial norms *"that represent contemporary standards of procedural due process."*[7] It is tenable that the principle of due process and fair trial has evolved to a *jus cogens* norm of international criminal law as such, endorsed by international conventions and municipal systems.[8]

This main procedural principle in international criminal litigation, in which the influence of the rule of law can be observed, is evidenced in Art. 21 sub 2 of the Statute of the International Tribunal for the Former Yugoslavia and Art. 20 sub 2 of the Statute of the International Tribunal for Rwanda, referring to the entitlement of the accused to *"a fair ( . . . ) hearing."* Procedural due process norms envisaged by Part 6 of the ICC Statute, especially Articles 63 (trial in the presence of the accused), 66 (presumption of innocence), and 67 (rights of the accused), are direct exponents of various legal systems and international conventions, such as the ICCPR and ECHR. The principle of fairness in international criminal litigation constitutes therefore an *erga omnes* obligation in international criminal law, validated by the emerging international normative rule enhancing *"( . . . ) a universal sense of fairness which is finding its way into codes of regional and global standards and into the practice and jurisprudence of international institutions."*[9] The rights of the accused to a fair trial, envis-

---

6.    *See* M. Cherif Bassiouni, *supra* note 3, at 109.

7.    M. Cherif Bassiouni, *supra* note 3, at 109–110.

8.    *See*, e.g., Art. 6 Section 1 of European Convention on Human Rights, Art. 14 Section 1 of the ICCPR.

9.    THOMAS M. FRANCK, FAIRNESS IN INTERNATIONAL LAW AND INSTITUTIONS 85 (1995).

aged in Art. 21 of the ICTY Statute are expressed in several rules. One of these is the more general Rule 95 of the ICTY-rules of Procedure and Evidence, prohibiting admission of evidence that is *"obtained by methods which cast substantial doubt on its reliability or if its admission is antithetical to, and would seriously damage, the integrity of the proceedings,"* which rule was amended at the fifth plenary session in January 1995 *"to broaden the rights of suspects and accused persons."*[10] Although the Trial Chamber is, according to Rule 89A, not bound by national rules of evidence, it will refuse to admit evidence, no matter how probative, if obtained by improper, i.e., unfair methods.[11] Clearly the purpose of the ICTY and ICTR Rules are to ensure, as Rule 95 shows, fair procedural rights to the accused. Although the test of Rule 95 seems very high or strenuous and therefore does act, *prima vista*, to *"bind the ICTY to internationally recognized human rights standards,"*[12] the Trial Chamber in the Tadić witness protection case[13] acknowledged that Article 21 of the Statute provides minimum judicial guarantees to which all defendants are entitled and reflects the internationally recognized standards of due process as set forth in Article 14 of the ICCPR. Moreover, the Trial Chamber emphasized that accused persons before the ICTY are deemed to have greater rights than under the ICCPR,[14] although on the other hand it attributes to itself full independence and authority to determine when and how it wants to comply with the ICCPR rights.[15] Another component of the procedural dimension of the fair trial notion, endorsed by the ICTY Rules of Procedure and Evidence, is Rule 89 (D), which provides that the Trial Chamber may exclude evidence if its probative value is substantially outweighed by the need to ensure a fair trial.

## 3   THE PRINCIPLES OF FAIRNESS BEFORE THE ICTY

### 3.1 Introduction

It is important that the ICTY Rules of Evidence and Procedure (hereinafter the Rules) *"( . . . ) be perceived as effective in gaining custody of and prosecuting perpetrators of war crimes in an efficient manner that comports with*

---

10.  *See* JOHN R.W.D. JONES, THE PRACTICE OF THE INTERNATIONAL CRIMINAL TRIBUNALS FOR THE FORMER YUGOSLAVIA AND RWANDA 311 (1998).

11.  *See* also Jones, *supra* note 10, at 311.

12.  *See* James Sloan, *The ICTY and Fair Trial Rights: A Closer Look*, 9 LJIL 483 (1996).

13.  Case No. IT-94-I-T, 10 August 1995.

14.  *See* Para. 25 of the *Tadić* Witness Protection decision, o.c.

15.  *See* Sloan, *supra* note 12, at 488.

*international human rights protection afforded those accused,"*[16] since they will have an impact on the development not only of international justice but also of the international legal community and system.[17] The Rules fulfill this condition and ensure a fair trial, evidenced by the following principles, standards and provisions, which can be divided into four categories:

1. Fair trial and Art. 14 ICCPR (3.2 *infra*)
2. Fair trial and equality of arms (3.3 *infra*)
3. Fair trial and the principle of non-discriminatory protection (3.4 *infra*)
4. Fair trial and moral integrity (3.5 *infra*).

### 3.2 Fair trial and the threshold of Article 14 ICCPR

In its first Annual Report, the Tribunal noted that its Statute incorporates all the fundamental guarantees of a fair and expeditious trial that are enshrined in international instruments for the protection of human rights and, more specifically, in Article 14 of the ICCPR, the all-important provision designed in particular to safeguard the basic rights of the accused. These rights, as stated by the Tribunal, have been restated in Article 21 of the Tribunal's Statute.

Close reading of the Statute shows that it is intended to go beyond the fair trial threshold of Article 14 of the ICCPR, as shown by Article 18 Section 3 of the Statute, which endorses rights, based on the principle of fair trial, relating to the pretrial phase. These include the provision of fundamental safeguards for persons who are not yet *"accused"* but only *"suspects,"* such as, *inter alia*, the right to legal counsel during police questioning or investigation. The Trial Chamber's decision in the *Mucić* case is a vivid example of the serious application by the ICTY of the principle of fair trial enshrined in Article 18, since it excluded from the evidence the Austrian police Statement of the accused Mucić obtained in violation of Article 18.[18]

---

16. *See* Christopher L. Blakesley, *Atrocity and its Prosecution: The Ad Hoc Tribunals for the Former Yugoslavia and Rwanda*, in The Law of War Crimes 211 (Timothy L.H. McCormack & Gerry J. Simpson, eds., 1997).

17. *See also* Blakesley, *supra* note 16, at 227.

18. *See* Decision of 2 September 1997 on the defense Motion to Exclude Evidence, *Prosecutor v. Z. Mucić*, Case No. IT-96-21-T; Goran K. Sluyter, *Recht op aanwezigheid van raadsman tijdens politieverhoor*, 23 NJCM-Bulletin 80–87 (1998).

## 3.3 Fair trial and equality of arms

The Tribunal's Rules reaffirm and even expand these above discussed safeguards for both the suspect (Rules 42–45) and the accused (Rules 62, 63, 65–68, and 72). It is clear that these Rules advocate the principle of due process of law and enumerate several guarantees ensuring fundamental fairness and substantial justice. This is also expressed by the implementation of the sub-principle of *"equality of arms,"*[19] whereby the accuser and accused are equal in procedural perspective. This approach is clearly endorsed by Rules 66–68 concerning the rights of the Prosecutor; Rule 42 concerning the right to legal counsel at the expense of the ICTY; Rule 78 regarding the right to a public hearing, with an exception in both Rules 53 (b) and 79; Rule 85 with respect to the accused's right to test the prosecution's evidence and present evidence on his own behalf; Rules 62 and 87 endorsing the presumption of innocence; Rule 90 regarding the right to be protected against self-incrimination; and finally Rule 87 (a) and (b) in regard to the requirement that guilt must be proven beyond reasonable doubt.[20]

Furthermore, Rule 98 is also considered a component of *"equality of arms,"* this being evidenced by Trial Chamber I of the ICTR in the *Akayesu* case,[21] which, in conjunction with Rule 89, was relied upon to order the prosecutor to submit *"( . . . ) all written witness statements already made available by her to the Defense Counsel in this case."*[22]

The aforementioned leads logically to Rules 66 and 67. The old Rule 66 (A) was amended at the Fifth Plenary Session to introduce certain time limits within which the Prosecutor must disclose to the defense the supporting material which accompanied the indictment and witness statements in order to *"broaden the rights of suspects and accused persons."*[23] Rule 66 (A) contains a *"continuing obligation"* of the Prosecutor to disclose all statements that it has in its possession as well as prosecution witnesses.[24] It is noteworthy, that unlike the prosecution, the defense is under Rule 67–(A) (i) not obliged to disclose the names of its witnesses.[25] The absence

---

19.  This sub-principle is derived from the principle of fair trial.

20.  *See* for the latter condition: Renee C. Pruitt, *Guilt by Majority in the ICTY: Does This Meet the Standard of Beyond Reasonable Doubt?* 10 LJIL 557–578 (1997); *See* also Jones, *supra* note 10, at 292.

21.  Case No. ICTR-96-4-T.

22.  Decision by the Tribunal on its request to the Prosecutor to submit the written witness statements, 28 January 1997.

23.  *See* Jones, *supra* note 10, at 231.

24.  *See* ICTY, Trial Chamber II, Decision 26 September 1996, in *Delalić at al.*, IT-96-21-T, para. 4 and Trial Chamber I, Decision 27 January 1997, in the *Blaškić* case, IT-95-14-T, paras. 35–39.

25.  *See* also *Delalić et al.*, IT-96-21-PT decision TC II, 21 February 1997, paras. 10–11.

of a general reciprocal obligation on the defense hereto shows that the Rules go even beyond a protective shield by means of fair trial on behalf of the defense.[26]

## 3.4 Fair trial and principles of nondiscriminatory protection

Another sub-principle, deduced from the main principle of fair trial, is indicated by Article 21 Section 1 of the Statute, i.e., the nondiscriminatory protection and application of the law which is fundamental to human rights protection in international criminal law.[27]

This nondiscriminatory protection is clearly reflected in Rule 85, the presentation of evidence.[28] Although Article 21 (e) does not provide for the right to cross-examine witnesses, this right is explicitly viewed by Rule 85(b) and Rule 7 (e), preserving the right of cross examination during depositions, to be limited only by Article 22 and Rule 96 in cases of sexual assault.

This sub-principle is also envisaged by paragraph 4(A) and (F) of Article 21, which ensure the accused's right to be promptly informed in understandable language, subsequently implemented through Rule 42 (A) (ii) providing a right to free assistance of an interpreter and Rule 62 (ii), also a Rule designed to guarantee and implement this right.[29] In interpreting the term *"promptly"* in Article 21 (4) (A), Rule 62 is helpful, stating that *"upon his transfer to the seat of the Tribunal, the accused shall be brought before a Trial Chamber without delay."*

In addition, paragraph 4 (b) of Article 21, providing the accused the right to have adequate time and facilities to prepare a defense, ensures the equality of the accused in regard to the substantive investigative powers of the prosecution.[30] It is from this perspective that Rule 97, preserving the lawyer-client privilege, must be read.

## 3.5 Fair trial and moral integrity of the criminal justice process

The notion of fair trial refers, finally, also to the moral integrity of international criminal proceedings since "( . . . ) *the Rules* (of ICTY; GJK)

---

26. *See* also Jones, *supra* note 10, at 237.

27. *See* M. CHERIF BASSIOUNI AND PETER MANIKAS, THE LAW OF THE ICTY 959 (1996), especially note 176 regarding other human rights instruments.

28. Both prosecution and defense are entitled to call witnesses and present evidence and are empowered to the right of direct and cross-examination.

29. *See* Bassiouni and Manikas, *supra* note 27, at 962 and 970.

30. *See* also Michail Wladimiroff, *The Assignment of Defense Counsel before the ICTR*, 12 LJIL 2 (1999).

*must work, and should not become an unwieldy obstacle to the achievement of international criminal justice," "( . . . ) not become a reflection of the political compromises between seemingly competing national approaches,"* and *"uphold the highest standards of criminal justice and fairness."*[31]

The drafters of the Rules intended to develop this moral standard by virtue of Rule 95. This Rule was amended at the fifth plenary session in January 1995 *"to broaden the rights of suspects and accused persons."*[32] The previous Rule 95 contained a sanction for *"evidence obtained directly or indirectly by means which constitute a serious violation of internationally protected human rights,"* whereas the revised Rule 95 expands that concept to include evidence *"obtained by methods which cast substantial doubt on its reliability"* or the admission of which is *"antithetical to, and would seriously damage, the* integrity *of the proceedings"* (emphasis added: GJK). Rule 95 is a mandatory rule of exclusion and, since it applies only to the gathering of evidence, it does not cover instances where the accused has been brought before the Tribunal because of serious violations of internationally protected human rights. Exclusion appears to require a finding that the evidence was obtained by means contrary to internationally protected human rights.[33] Although Rule 95 offers no guidance as to what evidence gathering methods would damage the integrity of the proceedings,[34] it is obvious that the drafters of the Rules were well aware that the Tribunal is obliged to endorse the *"highest standards of criminal justice and fairness."*

These morally *"highest standards"* are also endorsed by Rule 92—a rule which is consistent with Rule 95—ensuring a mandatory exclusion where the accused's confession is obtained involuntarily.[35] The phrase *"free and voluntary"* should be read to mean that the confession was given without mental or physical coercion. The *rationale* hereof is evident: any confession that is coerced in any way should be considered not only unreliable but, more importantly, as having been obtained by methods that, if this evidence was admitted, would damage the *integrity,* and thus the *"highest standards,"* of criminal justice in the ICTY.[36]

---

31. *See* speech by Judge Louise Arbour, Chief Prosecutor of the ICTY and ICTR to the ISISC meeting on Comparative Criminal Justice System dd. 18 December 1997, *"The development of a coherent system of Rules of International Criminal Procedure Tribunals,"* at 1 and 12.

32. *See* J.R.W.D. Jones, *supra* note 10, at 311; *see* also separate opinion Judge Sidhwa by Rajic Rule 61 Decision, IT-95-12-R 61, 13 September 1996.

33. *See* Bassiouni & Manikas, *supra* note 27, at 952.

34. Bassiouni & Manikas, *supra* note 27, at 952–953.

35. *See* also Bassiouni & Manikas, *supra* note 27, at 945.

36. *See* Bassiouni & Manikas, *supra* note 27, at 946.

## 3.6 Conclusion

International criminal lawyers with trial experience should not be left *"with a sense of frustration from the rules,"*[37] since, as has been pointed out above, these Rules ensure for their clients a fair trial. Moreover, reason for frustration is unfounded since the question whether the Rules ensure a fair trial is closely connected with the application of Article 31(1) of the Vienna Convention on the Law of Treaties, and also expressed in the Joint and Separate Opinion of the Judges MacDonald and Vohrah in the *Joseph Kanyabashi v. Prosecutor* case.[38] Both the contextual and teleological elements, endorsed by Article 31 (1) of the Vienna Convention, require that the provisions of the Rules *"( . . . ) be construed in the light of the object of the Statute to ensure a fair and expeditious trial"* whereby *"in the search for procedures to expedite trials, the requirement of fairness must not be sacrificed ( . . . )."*[39]

## 4   THE PRINCIPLE OF FAIRNESS AND DEFENSES

From the foregoing it goes without saying that, as already emphasized in Chapters III and IV above, the principle of procedural fairness must be implemented more intensely to apply (also) to the admissibility of defenses.

Moreover, it cannot be denied that, besides inspiring the key Articles 20 and 21 of the ICTY in regard to the principle of procedural fairness, monistic municipal law systems also determine the judicial validity of criminal trials mainly regarding the element of "fair trial."[40] It is therefore fair to subject international criminal law to analysis in terms of the judicial values of domestic systems. As Brownlie observes: *"Indeed ( . . . ) the procedural standards prevalent in International Tribunals as an aspect of general principles of law demonstrate that domestic law standards, adopted as paradigms or ideals, have penetrated the sphere of international law to a considerable degree."*[41]

---

37.   Daniel D. Ntanda Nsereko, *Rules of Procedure and Evidence of the ICTY*, 5 CRIMINAL LAW FORUM 554 (1994).

38.   Case No. ICTR-96-15-A, 3 June 1999, at para. 15: recourse by analogy is appropriate to Article 31 (1) Vienna Convention in interpreting the provisions of the Statute; *see* also Guest Lecture of Judge P. Robinson, Ensuring Fair and Expeditious Trials at the ICTY, 30 September 1999, at 3–4.

39.   *See* Robinson, *supra* note 38, Art 44.

40.   *See* the self-executing norm of article 6 section 1 of the European Convention on Human Rights, which is directly, vertically, applicable in most European national legal systems, e.g., The Netherlands, Belgium and France.

41.   Brownlie, *supra* note 2, at 213.

Thus, developing and determining the procedural aspects of defenses to international litigation entails the elaboration of a substantial standard of procedural fairness in a more sophisticated sense than the *ad hoc* Tribunals make it appear.

Special attention must be given to Rule 67 (A)(ii) of the Rules of Procedure and Evidence of the ICTY, i.e. the defense's obligation to notify the Prosecutor of its intent to offer the defense of alibi as well as any special defense, including that of diminished or lack of mental responsibility. Notwithstanding the fact that it is clear from the text of Rule 67 (A)(i) that the *defense* is not obliged to disclose the names of its witnesses in advance to the Prosecution, there exists in fact a reciprocal obligation on the defense to give notice to the Prosecution of these alibi and special defenses. This was confirmed by the case law of the ICTY, especially the decision rendered on 21 February 1997 in *Delalić et al.* by Trial Chamber II, ruling *inter alia "The trial chamber accepts the submission of the defense that under the Rules there is no general reciprocal obligation on the defense to give notice to the prosecution of the witnesses it intends to call at trial. Sub-Rule 67 (A)(ii), however, imposes such an obligation upon the defense when it intends to offer a defense of alibi or any other special defense, including that of diminished or lack of mental responsibility."*[42] A notice of intent to offer a defense of diminished or lack of mental responsibility was filed before the ICTY by the accused Esad Landzo in *Delalić et al.*[43] It is noteworthy that Rule 67 (A)(ii)(b) suggests the possibility of invoking special defenses other than those regarding diminished or lack of mental responsibility, such as the above-described neurobiological and toxicological defenses.

## 5 ADMISSIBILITY AND BURDEN OF PROOF

The first effective manifestation of the principle of procedural fairness in regard to defenses consists in the inclusion of admissibility of defenses and the subsequent crystallization of the burden of proof criteria.

It is a general principle of criminal law that a person may not be convicted of crime unless the prosecution have proved beyond reasonable doubt both:

a.   that he/she has caused a certain event or that responsibility is to be attributed to him/her for the existence of a certain state of affairs, which is forbidden by criminal law, and,

---

42.   *See* Case No. IT-96-21-PT, at 10.

43.   *See* Notice of the defense to the Prosecutor pursuant to Rule 67 (A)(ii)(b) of the Rules of Procedure and Evidence, 15 November 1996, case No. IT-96-21-T.

    b.   that he/she had a defined state of mind in relation to the causing of the event or the existence of the state of affairs, which event—or state of affairs—is mentioned as the *actus reus* and which state of mind is named the *mens rea* of the crime.[44]

The provisions of the two *ad hoc* Tribunals[45] and the Rome Statute of the ICC presently endorse this view. Pursuant to Art. 66 section 2 of the latter statute, the onus is on the Prosecutor to prove guilt of the accused, while Art. 66 section 3 ensures that in order to convict the accused the Court must be convinced (by the prosecution) of the guilt of the accused beyond reasonable doubt. Although the ICC Statute, like the European Court of Human Rights, does not enshrine a clear interpretative rule of this criterion, general principles of law suggest that *"evidence on sentencing be established on a balance of probabilities, with the burden to prove mitigating or aggravating factors resting on the defense and the prosecution respectively."*[46] Likewise, Articles 20 and 21 of the two *ad hoc* Tribunals do not clarify the requisite standard of proof. They merely provide that *"all persons shall be equal before the International Tribunal and that the accused shall be presumed innocent until proved guilty according to the provisions of the present statute ( . . . )."* The *ad hoc* Tribunals therefore do not indicate the standard of proof required to maintain the presumption of innocence in the face of prosecution. The ICTY Rules of Procedure and Evidence, written and adopted by the ICTY judges, elaborate hereto on the Statute, upholding in Rule 87 that the Trial Chamber shall deliberate in private and a finding of guilt only may be reached when a majority of the Chamber is satisfied that *"( . . . ) guilt has been proved beyond reasonable doubt."* Notwithstanding the disposition of *"proof beyond reasonable doubt,"* this provision again does not entail a clear definition of reasonable doubt. Even after proposals to define this notion,[47] the ICTY declined to accept any form of definition, obviously concluding that law practice can function better without any description of *"reasonable doubt."* Law making, in the end, is no scientific matter.[48] In practice the *ad hoc* Tribunals ensure indeed a standard of proof *"beyond a reasonable doubt,"* reflecting in its Rules of Procedure many features of the British and American common law system, wherein this stan-

---

44.  *See* JOHN SMITH & BRIAN HOGAN, CRIMINAL LAW 29 (1996).

45.  *See* Art. 87 (A) of the rules of procedure and evidence of the ICTY and Article 14 of the Statute of the ICTR.

46.  William A. Schabas, *Article 66, Margin No. 13*, in COMMENTARY ON THE ROME STATUTE (Otto Triffterer, ed., 1999).

47.  *See* the proposal of the American Bar Association; R.C. Pruitt, *supra* note 20, at 559.

48.  *See* also Pruitt, *supra* note 20, at 559.

dard is endorsed.[49] In the *Delalić* case, the Trial Chamber of the ICTY adopted a common law definition on this subject by ruling: *"a reasonable doubt is a doubt which the particular jury entertains in the circumstances."*[50] In fact, this means the existence of doubt that is founded in reason,[51] which implies a rather subjective element. Therefore, within the ICTY and ICTR framework of guaranteeing the rights of the accused to a fair trial, the burden rests squarely on the Prosecutor to prove guilt beyond a reasonable doubt, and clearly the accused must never be required to discharge a similar onus with respect to establishing his or her innocence, which equally applies to the establishing of defenses.[52]

This concept could imply that, e.g., when a soldier in an armed conflict kills a civilian—that is, if he has caused an *actus reus*—it is doubtful that he can be convicted for murder if there is a reasonable possibility that the killing was accidental, since it has not been proved beyond reasonable doubt that the soldier had the requisite mental element. Schabas asserts that *"the presumption of innocence may be breached where an accused person is required to produce evidence to counter the charge, even in the absence of any direct evidence of guilt,"* pointing to the example of the possession of recently stolen goods, in which event the accused bears a *"reverse onus"* of proof.[53] It has to be emphasized, however, that the ICC Statute provides for no exceptions to the general principle of the presumption of innocence. On the other hand, the European Court of Human Rights has decided already that reverse onus provisions are not *per se* contrary to this presumption unless they go beyond reasonable limits in the context of the nature of the case and the rights of the defense.[54] Article 67 (1)(i) of the ICC Statute seems to enlarge the scope of this presumption since it allows no *"reversal of the burden of proof or any onus of rebuttal."* Because the European Convention does not have such an extensive clause, it is questionable if any rebuttal within the system of the ICC would be considered legitimate, based upon European jurisprudence. Future development of this topic will show the exact meaning of Article 66 in conjunction with Article 67 (1)(i).

Regarding defenses, however, according to both common and civil law systems, the defendant bears only a preponderance of evidence, i.e. the necessity to introduce a "beginning of evidence" of all the constituent elements of the defense, whereupon it is up to the prosecution to establish

---

49.  *See* also Jan M. Sjöcrona, *The ICTY: Some Introductory Remarks from a Defense Point of View,* 8 LJIL 468 (1995).

50.  *Prosecutor versus Delalić et al.,* o.c.

51.  Schabas, *supra* note 46, Margin No. 25.

52.  *See* L. Arbour, *supra* note 31, at 8 and 11.

53.  Schabas, *supra* note 46, Margin No. 18.

54.  Schabas, *supra* note 46, Margin No. 22; *see* also Judgment EHRM, in: *Salabiaku versus France,* Series A. NO. 141-A of 7 October 1988, para. 28.

proof that one of those constituents did not apply. The major difference with respect to the onus of proof of the prosecution is that a defendant fulfils the "burden of proof," underlying a defense, on a balance of probabilities—the same standard as that of a plaintiff in a civil action—without the requirement of proving beyond reasonable doubt.[55]

Analogous to Rule 68 regarding defenses to war crimes, the requirement of presenting a *prima facie* case is to be considered the maximum condition. The test to be applied for discovery under Rule 68 is that the defense must present a *prima facie* case, which makes probable the exculpatory nature of the materials sought.[56] The M'Naghten Rules provide, with regard to the defense of mental insanity, *"that every man is presumed to be sane, and to possess a sufficient degree of reason to be responsible for his crimes, until the contrary be proved to the jury's satisfaction: and that to establish a defense on the ground of insanity, it must be clearly proved, etc."*[57] This principle can equally be applied to the other legal defenses discussed in this study.

## 6    THE RIGHTS OF EFFECTIVE PARTICIPATION AND LEGAL REPRESENTATION: INDEPENDENT SAFEGUARDS OF FAIR TRIAL UNDER ARTICLE 6(1) ECHR AND ARTICLE 21(2) OF THE ICTY STATUTE

### 6.1 Introduction

*"When the ICTY and the ICTR were set up, little attention was paid to the role of defense counsel in the effectuation of the defendants rights"*[58]—a remark equally applicable to the International Criminal Court (hereinafter ICC) in which Statute the defense counsel is only mentioned in four articles.[59] This is, as stated by Wladimiroff,[60] indeed *"( . . . ) surprising given the considerable influence on the way rights of the defendant are applied in the framework of both ad hoc Tribunals."* The same is true for the European Convention on Human Rights (ECHR), which refers only in Article 6 section 3 to the role of Defense Counsel in criminal litigation. This seems equally surprising, since Article 6 is a derivative of the rule of law referred to in the Preamble of the European Convention, a rule which is supposed to protect

---

55. Smith and Hogan, *supra* note 44, at 30.
56. *See* Decision on the production of Discovery Materials, rendered by Trial Chamber I, in the *Blaškić* case dd. 27 January 1997, Case No. IT-95-14-T, para. 49.
57. *See* Smith and Hogan, *supra* note 44, at 211.
58. *See* M. Wladimiroff, *supra* note 30, at 2.
59. *See* articles 48, 55, 65 and 67 of the ICC Statute.
60. Wladimiroff, *supra* note 30, at 2.

the accused against abuse of governmental powers.[61] An aspect of these safeguards is the attribution to a defendant of effective defense rights, under which lies the right to legal assistance. In both common law and civil law systems, defense counsel does not only, to a certain extent, exercise the defendant's rights but is also attributed with its own independent rights to ensure an adequate effectuation of the defendant's defense. The question arises whether non-violative endorsement of the right of legal representation in international criminal cases, ensured by Article 6 (3)(c) of the European Convention and Article 21 (4)(d) of the ICTY Statute, depends on how the accused was able to facilitate his or her own defense (counsel).

The European Court on Human Rights (hereinafter the Court), in the *Stanford v. the UK* judgment, pursued the principle of effective participation, making this an integral part of the overall principle of fair trial, envisaged by Article 6 section 1 of the ECHR.[62]

While it is clear that both the sub-principle of effective participation of the accused in a criminal trial and that of effective legal assistance have attained the status of principles of general international (human rights) law,[63] it is still unclear as to whether, and the extent to which, a connection exists between, on the one hand, the principle of an effective participation, as embedded in the overall principle of fair trial by virtue of Article 6 section 1 ECHR, and the right to legal assistance pursuant to Article 6 (3)(c) ECHR on the other hand. The debate in this section will focus upon this question.

It is well known that the ECHR in the *Stanford* judgment indicated a rather strict approach to the question whether absence of effective participation by the accused as such implies a violation of Article 6 (1) of the ECHR when the requisite effective legal representation pursuant to Article 6 (3)(c) of the ECHR is fulfilled.

A recently rendered judgment of the ECHR in the highly sensitive case of *T. and V. versus UK* raises the question as to whether the Court is inclined to stipulate that, even if the principle of effective legal assistance is maintained, the notion of fair trial can be infringed due to the absence of effective participation of the accused.[64] After assessing this question on

---

61. *See*, e.g., ECHR dated 20 November 1989, *Kostovski versus the Netherlands* Series A 166.

62. *See Stanford v. the United Kingdom*, judgment ECHR dated 23 February 1994, Series A No. 282–A, para. 26.

63. The following ECHR judgments attest to this: *Stanford v. UK* judgment resp. Campbell and Fell, judgments 28 June 1984, Publ. ECHR Series A Vol. 80, para. 48; *S. v. Switzerland* 28 November 1991, Series A 220 Pakelli, 25 April 1983, Series A Vol. 64, para. 31.

64. Judgment European Court, dated 16 December 1999, Application No. 24724/94; besides this item another seven interesting judicial and human rights

the basis of the aforementioned case law of the ECHR and several other arguments illustrated in subsections 2–5, this section will examine in subsection 6 further recent developments regarding the right of legal assistance in the jurisprudence of ECHR as well as other international Tribunals such as the ICTY and ICTR. An increasingly important aspect of this right is the question whether effective legal assistance during investigative criminal proceedings is a prerequisite to the right of a fair trial.

Finally, the question whether the principle of effective participation appears in other areas will be examined in subsection 7.

## 6.2 Previous case law

As observed in the introduction to this section above, the articulation of the principle of effective participation in criminal proceedings is one thing; the procedural implications and connections of this principle with regard to the concept of legal representation pursuant to Article 6 (3)(c) ECHR is quite another. Before turning to the latter key question, it is necessary to determine how the principle of effective participation is embodied in the jurisprudence of the ECHR.

The question of how to assess the scope of the defense rights under Article 6 section 1 of the Convention was raised and answered clearly in the *Stanford* case, where the Court ruled that "( . . . ) *Article 6, read as a whole, guarantees the right of an accused to* participate effectively *(emphasis added; GJK) in a criminal trial.*"[65] The *Stanford* case shows the following relevant facts. The applicant, Mr. Bryan Stanford, was committed for trial by jury at the Crown Court in Norwich on seven counts arising out of his relationship with a young girl. The counts included indecent assault, two counts of rape, and unlawful sexual intercourse. The trial before a High Court judge and a jury lasted six working days, and throughout the trial Mr. Stanford sat in a glass-fronted dock and was represented by a solicitor and a counsel highly experienced in criminal law. After having been found guilty of several counts, including indecent assault and one count of rape, Mr. Stanford was sentenced to a total of ten years imprisonment. It is noteworthy that during the trial evidence was given by, among others, the then 15-year old Miss M., the alleged victim of the offenses, as well as her mother and sister. While giving evidence the judge directed Miss M. to move closer to him and the jury since it was difficult to hear her. After refusal of two requests for leave of appeal to the Court of Appeal, based on being unable to hear the original proceedings as the acoustics in

---

questions were answered by the Court; they are however outside the subject matter of this study.

65.   *Stanford v. United Kingdom*, o.c. para. 26.

the court had been inadequate, Mr. Stanford was denied an appeal to the House of Lords. Mr. Stanford also complained to the Solicitors' Complaints Bureau about the solicitors' alleged failure to take action with regard to his difficulties in hearing the evidence. However, at no time during the trial did the applicant or his lawyers make any complaint to the court or to any of its officials concerning the claim that he could not hear the proceedings.

On 8 January 1990, Mr. Stanford lodged his application with the Commission. The application was based upon violation of the fair trial principle pursuant to article 6 (1) of the ECHR, positing that he could not hear the proceedings which resulted in his conviction. The Commission declared Mr. Stanford's complaint admissible, whereupon, in its report of 21 October 1992, the Commission concluded, with eleven to seven votes, that there had been no violation of Article 6 (1).

Mr. Stanford subsequently complained to the ECHR for not having received a fair trial. Since he had been unable to hear the proceedings, he was therefore not a fully informed party to the counsel's decisions on the conduct of his case and, in fact, was deprived of an effective participation in his trial(s). Mr. Stanford further submitted that the responsibility of the British Government was at stake. The ECHR held unanimously that no breach of Article 6 (1) had occurred in Mr. Stanford's case by the United Kingdom to ensure a fair trial.

In the crucial paragraphs 27–30, it is stressed that the Government cannot normally be held responsible for the actions or decisions of the lawyer of the accused, who in Mr. Stanford's case—having lengthy experience in criminal litigation—chose for tactical reasons to remain silent about the acoustic difficulties; nor were there any indications established that Mr. Stanford disagreed with this decision. In view of the Court, the Government is obliged to intervene only in the event of a manifest and sufficiently indicated failure by the counsel to provide "effective representation," a situation which did not occur in Mr. Stanford's case.[66]

The Court has traditionally attributed an important weight and a subsequent high level of legal protection to the principle of a fair trial to ensure that the proper balance between the means necessary to protect democracy and the demands of the protection of individual rights are maintained.[67] Therefore the Court consistently considers, *proprio motu*, the criminal proceedings "as a whole" in order to ascertain, as a matter of its

---

66. *See* para. 28; *see* also *Imbrioscia v. Switzerland*, ECHR judgment, 24 November 1993, Series A No. 275, para. 14.

67. *See inter alia Kostovski v. The Netherlands*, judgment of 20 November 1989, Series A, Vol. 166 para. 44; *Delcourt* judgment of 17 January 1970, Series A, No. 11, para. 25.

judicial and interpretive task, *"whether the proceedings in their entirety, as well as the way in which evidence was taken, were fair."*[68]

Close reading of the *Stanford* judgment of the Court leads already to the conclusion that the Court is not inclined to a restrictive approach on the concept of "effective participation." In response to the assertion of the UK Government—supported by the European Commission in its report of 21 October 1992—that its *"responsibility was not otherwise engaged since neither the applicant nor his lawyers complained or made any representation to the court about the applicant's hearing difficulties,"*[69] the Court noted that the principle of effective participation *"( . . . ) includes,* inter alia (emphasis added; GJK), *not only his right to be present, but also to hear and follow the proceedings,"* which rights, according to the Court, *"( . . . ) are implicit in the very notion of an adversarial procedure ( . . . )."*[70] The conclusion must be that the concept of effective participation embodies various unlimited procedural aspects, which together determine the right of effective participation. Violation of one of these can already constitute a breach of Article 6 (1). The Court is inclined to adopt State responsibility hereto only to the extent that the Government cannot normally be held responsible for the actions or decisions of an accused's lawyer, but is only obliged to intervene in the event of "manifest" failure by counsel to provide "effective representation."[71] The principle of fair trial thus reflects also, to a certain extent, in addition to the obligation to promote effective *participation* of the accused, the State's responsibility to ensure an effective *legal representation*. Yet in the *Stanford* case the Court concluded that there had been no violation of the principle of fair trial ensured by Article 6 Section 1, since— notwithstanding the State's own responsibility for securing the right of the accused to an appropriate participation in his criminal trial, i.e., ensuring good acoustics in the courtroom—the accused was *"ably defended by his counsel and ( . . . ) the trial judges ( . . . ) reflected the evidence presented to the court."*[72]

---

68. *See* para. 24 of the *Stanford* decision, o.c., wherein the Court also referred to its judgment in the *Edwards v. UK* case of 16 December 1992, Series A, No. 247–B, para. 34.

69. Mr. Stanford claimed that as a result of not being able to hear the proceedings he was not a fully informed party to counsel's decisions on the conduct of his case and thus deprived of a fair trial.

70. *See* para. 26.

71. *See* para. 28.

72. *See* para. 30.

## 6.3 The case of *T. and V. v. the United Kingdom:* adoption of another view on the principle of "effective participation"?

An additional finding of particular interest in this realm was the following remark in the dissenting opinion of Mr. Bustill of the European Commission regarding the Stanford judgment: *"A fair hearing does not simply mean that an accused is entitled to be heard; it also means that he must be able to conduct an effective defense."*

The *Stanford* judgment of the ECHR raises the question whether the presence of experienced legal assistance as such constitutes an "effective defense" or "effective participation" and excludes a defense as to a violation of the principle of fair trial. The real issue at stake in the Stanford case was whether the fulfillment of the principle of fair trial could be decided on the basis of an acceptance of the general theory of delegation. In other words, is a mere delegation of an accused's right to understand and follow the criminal proceedings to the representing counsel sufficient to constitute a fair trial? Contrary to the opinion of the ECHR, the joint dissenting opinion by three European Commission members expressed as a matter of guidance that *"an accused's right to understand the proceedings implied from his right to be present cannot be satisfied by the mere fact that his counsel alone could follow the proceedings."*[73] Whereas the ECHR in the Stanford judgment seems to adhere to this concept of delegation, the concept may be subject to restrictions. Such a restriction recently appeared in the judgment of the ECHR in the *T. and V. v. United Kingdom* case.

The *T. and V. v. UK* case resembles the *Stanford* case in several respects. Again the Governmental authorities asserted that the applicant was "represented by highly experienced leading counsel."[74] There were, however, some differences between the two cases, which are perhaps explanatory for the submitted restriction in the latter. The applicants T. and V. were arrested on 12 February 1993. At that time T. was only ten years old. After playing truant from school, he abducted a two year old boy from a shopping precinct, took him on a journey of over two miles, subsequently battered this boy to death and left him on a railway line to be run over by a train. The trial which took place over three weeks in November 1993, in public, before a judge and twelve jurors, was conducted with the formality of an adult criminal trial, although modified to a certain extent in view of the defendant's age. This was evidenced by the fact that T. and V. were seated next to social workers in a specially raised dock, the defendant's parents and lawyers were positioned near them, the hearing times were

---

73. *See* Joint Dissenting Opinion of Mr. Loucaides, Gozubuyuk and Rozakis of the European Commission in the *Stanford* case, concluding that Mr. Stanford was deprived of a fair hearing.

74. *See* para. 81.

shortened to reflect the schooldays, a ten-minute interval was taken every hour, and finally during adjournments the defendants were allowed to spend time with their parents and social workers in a play area.

It should be added that, in order to understand judgment, the Court was privy to the existence of a report dated 5 November 1993 of Dr. Eileen Vizard, a consultant child and adolescent psychiatrist, who was originally instructed by T.'s solicitors. She concluded that T. showed signs of post-traumatic stress disorder, involving *inter alia* a constant preoccupation with the alleged events, which disorder, combined with the lack of any therapeutic work since the offence,[75] had limited *"his ability to instruct his lawyers and testify adequately in his own defense.*[76] Moreover, the Court, in the *T. and V. v. UK* case, stresses that the applicant himself *"( . . . ) in his memorial states due to the conditions in which he was put on trial, was unable to follow the trial or take decisions in his own best interests."*[77]

This distinctive feature of the *T. and V. v. UK* case culminates in a breach of Article 6 section 1 of the Convention since, according to the Court, *"in such circumstances the Court does not consider that it was sufficient for the purposes of Article 6 § 1 that the applicant was represented by skilled and experienced lawyers"*[78] and therefore T. was unable *"to participate effectively in the criminal proceedings against him ( . . . )."*[79]

In the light of the *Stanford* judgment by the ECHR, no revolutionary conclusions can be deduced from the recent case law of the ECHR regarding the (exclusionary) role of the aforementioned concept of counsel delegation on the principle of fair trial. Obviously, the specific circumstances of the *T .and V. v. UK* case—particularly the minor status of the defendants—amounted to the interpretation of the principle of "effective participation" as being incompatible with the concept, as illustrated in the *Stanford* case, of attribution or delegation of defense rights from defendant to legal counsel. Yet the Court's judgment in the *T. and V. v. UK* case can undoubtedly be read as an endorsement of the relativity of the latter concept.

In the *T. and V. v. UK* case the Court clearly indicates that the presence of experienced and effective legal assistance as such is not a sufficient basis or guarantee for the establishment of a fair trial, even in the absence of a specific complaint before the domestic fora based upon a breach of the effective participation rule. Thus the ECHR inclines to differentiate between determinative factors as to the right of a fair trial enshrined by Article 6 (1) ECHR in conjunction with the principle of effective partici-

---

75. T. was detained during trial.

76. *See* para. 87.

77. *See* para. 87; the opposite situation occurred in the Stanford case where neither the defense nor applicant raised this argument before the trial judge.

78. *See* para. 88.

79. *See* para. 89; decision made by sixteen votes to one.

pation on the one hand and the principle of legal assistance pursuant to Article 6 (3)(c) ECHR on the other hand. These factors as a whole constitute an "effective defense."

Concluding the case law analysis, based upon the two judgments illustrated, there can be no question that the right of effective participation by an accused in a criminal trial is not confined to the presence of legal assistance pursuant to Article 6 (3) (c) of the Convention. The former right inheres in all defendants, irrespective of the way they were represented by counsel. It is against this background that the Court does not adopt the view of Judge Baka in his dissenting opinion, which asserted that *"in terms of fairness of criminal proceedings, it is rather illusory to expect that a child of this age could give any legally relevant instruction to his or her lawyer in order to facilitate his or her defense."*

### 6.4 The origin of effective participation in the right to adversarial proceedings; distinction from effective legal assistance

Earlier in this study, the conjunction between the principle of fair trial and that of effective participation—the latter being a derivative of the former—was stressed. The independence of the principle of effective participation as to the provision of Article 6–(3) (c) of the European Convention stems from an additional argument, i.e., the principle of "adversarial proceedings." This principle is embodied in article 6 (1),[80] whereas the latter provision of Article 6(3)(c) is an exponent of the principle of equality of arms, likewise embedded in Article 6(1) of the Convention.[81]

That the right to effective participation of an accused in his or her criminal trial is generally seen by the ECHR as an aspect of the right to an adversarial proceeding emerges from the case law of the Court. The following decisions attest to this:

1. *Mantovanelli versus France,*[82] wherein the Court ruled that the applicants were not able to comment *effectively* on the main piece of evidence (an expert report) and therefore the proceedings were not fair since *de facto* they did not comply with the adversarial principle enshrined in Article 6 (1). In its judgment on this topic, the Court states in para 33:

   *"What is essential is that the parties should be able to participate properly in the proceedings before the Tribunal"*

---

80. *See* ECHR of 28 August, 1991, *Brandstetter versus Austria*, Series A 211.
81. *See* ECHR of 30 October 1991, *Borgers versus Belgium*, Series A214–B.
82. Judgment ECHR of 18 March 1997, ECHR Reports 1997–II 425.

2.   *Krcmar versus Czech Republic*,[83] regarding a civil action of Krcmar. This domestic case was decided by the Constitutional Court in the Czech Republic based on new documents which this Court *proprio motu* obtained, absent notification nor having revealed the contents of this new evidence to the parties to the dispute. The Court concluded unanimously to a breach of Article 6 (1), expressing that the right to adversarial proceedings involves the ability of the parties to become familiar with the submitted evidence, enabling them to effectively and adequately respond to the existence, contents and authenticity of this specific material.

Thus the fact that the principle of effective participation is related to the right to adversarial proceedings, contrary to the provision of Article 6 (3)(c) of the Convention, precludes already the assumption that effective legal assistance, enshrined in the latter provision, implies the presence of effective participation by the accused in his or her criminal case.

## 6.5  Effective participation: further independent assessment based upon functional or teleological interpretation

The final argument for the aforementioned conclusion stems from the functional scope of the principle of effective participation itself. Article 6 is one of the most important articles of the Convention.[84] In the *Golder* case,[85] the Court promoted a wide interpretation of Article 6, holding the right of access to a court inherent to the rights stated by Article 6 Section 1. In reaching this conclusion, the Court adopted the interpretive principles as set forth in the 1969 Vienna Convention on the Law of Treaties, especially the general rule, envisaged by article 31 of this Convention, providing that a treaty shall be interpreted both in *"good faith"* and *"in the light of its object and purpose."*[86] The susceptibility of the ECHR to these interpretive rules enables the Court to apply, in particular circumstances, a *functional and teleological interpretation* of article 6 of the Convention.[87]

---

83.   Judgment ECHR of 3 March 2000, NJB 2000 No. 18.

84.   *See* the ECHR judgment in the *Golder vs. UK* case of 21 February 1975, Series A, Vol. 18, at 6.

85.   *See* note 27 *supra*.

86.   *See* paras. 29 and 30 of the *Golder* case; the European Court thus expanded its interpretative boundaries within the primacy of the rule of law as such; *see* also F. Matscher, *Methods of Interpretation of the Convention*, in THE EUROPEAN SYSTEM FOR THE PROTECTION OF HUMAN RIGHTS 65 (McDonald et al., eds., 1995).

87.   *See* Matscher, *supra* note 86, at 66; the ICJ submitted this interpretation

When addressing the merits of the *T. and V. v. UK* case, the Court avowedly followed this dynamic method of *functional or teleological interpretation*, which is in the present case justified because of the special status of the accused. Closely connected to this method is the underlying principle of the ECHR that, in case of doubt, an interpretation should be endorsed which *"leads to effective protection (effet utile) of the individual rights."*[88] The decision of the ECHR in the *T. and V. v. UK* case seems to justify the conclusion that, in the field of juveniles such as applicant T., the Court is inclined to apply the method of functional interpretation, thus endorsing the aforementioned principle of effective protection.

This is exemplified in paragraph 83 of its judgment, which reads as follows:

> *"The Court notes that Article 6, read as a whole, guarantees the right of an accused to participate effectively in his criminal trial ( . . . ). It has not until the present time been called upon to consider how this Article 6 § 1 guarantee applies to criminal proceedings against children, and in particular whether procedures which are generally considered to safeguard the rights of adults on trial, such as publicity, should be abrogated in respect of children in order to promote their understanding and participation (see the* Nortier v. the Netherlands *judgment of 24 August 1993, Series A no. 267, and particularly the separate opinions thereto)."*

Thus the Court, after reaffirming that Article 6, read as a whole, guarantees the right of an accused to participate effectively in his criminal trial, subsequently determines the *subject matter*—in the light of the specific concept of criminal proceedings against children—as an *autonomous* interpretive phenomenon, as opposed to the general safeguards attending the rights of adults on trial.[89]

The cited *"effet utile"* approach finds expression in the extension to children's criminal trials, notwithstanding the Courts ruling that trials on criminal charges of children, even one as young as Applicant T., as such do not violate the fair trial guarantees under Article 6 Section 1.[90] The functional margin of interpretation granted by the Court is formulated by means of a minimum sub-rule, emerging from Article 6, which reads as follows:

> *"( . . . ) it is essential that a child charged with an offence is dealt with in a manner which takes full account of his age, level of maturity and*

---

method also several times in regard to interpretation of the UN Charter; *see*, e.g., the *Certain Expenses* Case.

88. *See* Matscher, *supra* note 86, at 67 and, e.g., the *Artico* judgment of the European Court of 13 May 1980, Series A, No. 37, para. 33.

89. *See* para. 83.

90. *See* para. 84.

*intellectual and emotional capacities, and that steps are taken to promote his ability to understand and participate in the proceedings.*"[91]

This functional margin of interpretation for States is, according to the Court, submitted to the following guidelines:

1. The obligation of national authorities to conduct criminal proceedings in such a way as to reduce as far as possible the feelings of the accused young child with respect to intimidation and inhibition, an obligation which complies to the *"international tendency towards protection of the privacy of child defendants"*; and

2. the obligation of States to accommodate this kind of trial to *"the age and other characteristics of the child and circumstances surrounding the criminal proceedings."*[92]

Since the judicial authorities of the United Kingdom, in the opinion of the Court, failed to fulfill these obligations in the case of T., it is of no surprise that subsequently Article 6 was considered to be violated.[93]

It is therefore noteworthy that the Court, following its earlier expressed concept that the *"convention is a living instrument which ( . . . ) must be interpreted in the light of present-day conditions,"*[94] expands the scope of Article 6 section 1 to the constantly changing developments in, not only international law, but also international society and human rights Law. An international court cannot neglect today's intellectual concepts or ideologies. This judgment of the Court in the *T. and V. v. UK* case is a vivid example of these law-making aspirations of this international tribunal. Moreover, it is a clear example of the submitted independence of the concept of effective participation, irrespective of the way legal assistance was conducted in a particular case.

## 6.6 The right to legal assistance in the jurisprudence of the ICTY and ICTR

It is remarkable that, in the development of the jurisprudence of both the *ad hoc* war crimes tribunals (ICTY and ICTR), the right to legal assistance was adhered to as an *absolute* right in the realm of fairness as well as

---

91. *See* para 84.
92. *See* para. 85.
93. *See* for the Court's factual reasoning leading to this opinion: para. 86.
94. *See* judgment ECHR in the *Tyrer* case, 25 February 1978, Series A, No. 26, para. 31; *See* also Matscher, *supra* note 86, at 68–69.

of the validity of submitted evidence. Moreover, to no extent was this right interpreted functionally—contrary to the right of effective participation by the ECHR—nor was it subject to relativity. As with Article 6 Section 1 of the ECHR, Articles 18 (3) and 20 of the Statute of ICTY encompass the principle of fair trial, whereas the Rules of Procedure and Evidence of the ICTY (hereinafter the Rules), drafted by its judges, ensure in Rule 42 the rights of the accused during investigation.[95]

Although the minimum guarantees for a fair trial, endorsed by these Statutes and Rules, are based on those of the ICCPR and resemble those of both the African Charter on Human and Peoples' Rights and ECHR,[96] the principle of effective participation in international criminal litigation as such is not envisaged by the ICTY or ICTR Statutes and Rules. However, in its judgment in the *Mucić* Case of 2 September 1997, Trial Chamber II of the ICTY,[97] applied the concept of "effective defense" in international criminal litigation. Compared to the aforementioned case law of the European Court, the ICTY seems to endorse a broader and more abstract concept of *the right to legal assistance*. However, the ICTY arrives at this interpretation on the basis of exactly the same case law of the European Court.

The *erga omnes* character of Human Rights obligations encompasses also the principle of a fair trial. From the view of the principles of legality and the need for implementation of erga omnes obligations into the framework of International Criminal Law, a comparative exercise to the case law of the ICTY is appropriate.

The starting point of the *Mucić* case is the arrest of the accused Mucić, one of four defendants in the *Celebići* case, charged with severe human rights atrocities allegedly committed in the Celebići camp under Mucić's command by subordinates, in Vienna on 18 March 1996. After the defense lodged a motion, based on ICTY Rules 89 D and 95,[98] to exclude from evidence all the statements made to Officers of the Austrian Police Force in Vienna by the accused Mucić, directly after his arrest on 18 March 1996, the ICTY concluded that Mucić's first police interview could not pass the test under Article 18 of its Statute and both Rules 42 and 95 which are read by the Tribunal jointly.[99] The Yugoslavia Tribunal, faced with the Austrian legal provision precluding the right of suspect to counsel during

---

95. Rule 42 provides *inter alia* for the right to assistance of counsel of the accused's choice also during investigative questioning.

96. *See* also M. Wladimiroff, *supra* note 30, at 4.

97. Decision of 2 September 1997 on the Defense Motion to Exclude Evidence, *Prosecutor v. Z. Mucić*, Case No. IT-96-21-T.

98. Providing that evidence can be excluded the probative value of which is substantially outweighed by the need to ensure a fair trail, or obtained by means contrary to internationally protected human rights.

99. *See* para. 44.

questioning, clearly follows the line of reasoning of the European Court as adhered to in its 1993 judgment in the *Imbroscia v. Switzerland* case, where the Court held that Article 6(3)(c)—which is equivalent to Article 18 of the ICTY Statute—applies also to *pre-trial* proceedings, emphasizing that in the latter case "( . . . ) *the European Commission on Human Rights, during the stage of the proceedings before it, stated that Article 6 (3)(C) gives the Accused the right to assistance and support by a lawyer throughout the proceedings. To curtail this right during investigation proceedings may influence the material position of the defense at the trial and therefore also the outcome of the proceedings.*[100] The same line of reasoning emerges as to the Tribunal's compliance with the European Court's judgment in the *Campbell and Fell v. UK* case,[101] from which case law the Tribunal deduced an important requisite of international criminal law, encompassing the rule that "( . . . ) *in the (criminal) proceedings taken as a whole, an accused person* effectively *(emphasis added GJK) had the benefit of legal assistance as required by Article 6(3)(c) of the Convention.*"[102] The Tribunal was inclined to follow hereto an uncompromising line; even if it conceded that the Austrian provision restricting the right to counsel is within Article 6(3)(c) as interpreted, this approach is "*inconsistent with the unfettered right to counsel in Article 18(3) and sub rule 42 (A)(i).*"[103]

The position articulated by the ICTY is rather progressive, not to say relatively lenient, considering the judgment of the European Court in the *John Murray v. UK* case.[104] The *Murray* ruling abstains from a pronunciation on the question whether the right of the presence of counsel during questioning of the accused by the police is envisaged by Article 6 (3) (c) of the ECHR, and consequently this judgment does not adopt an *absolute* right to be assisted by counsel of the defendant's choice during police investigation. A closer look at the European Court's decision in the *Murray* case suggests that it advances a concept in which a restriction of the submitted right to counsel assistance *eo ipso* does not violate the ECHR, assuming that the criminal proceedings "*as a whole*" were fair.[105]

At the outset it can therefore be presumed that the European Court, elaborating on its present case law, probably would not have concluded Article 6 of its Convention to be violated in the *Mucić* scenario of the ICTY. After all Mucić, directly after his arrest (unlike Mr. Murray) was allowed to invoke legal assistance.[106]

---

100. *See* para. 50 of the *Mucić* decision, NJCM Bulletin, Vol. 23 (1998), No. 1, at 80.
101. Judgment dd. 25 March 1992, Series A. 233.
102. *See* para. 51.
103. *See* para. 51 of the *Mucić* decision.
104. Judgment of 8 February 1996, Series A, No. 593, especially at para. 69.
105. *See Murray* judgment, o.c. at para. 63.
106. *See* also commentary of Goran K. Sluiter, *supra* note 18, at 85.

Turning to the main subject of this Chapter, it is clear that, opposed to the European Court's approach, the ICTY envisions a more abstract interpretation of the principle of "effective participation" and legal assistance; the mere absence of counsel during police questioning already can violate ICTY Rules 42 and 95, thus leading to exclusion of evidence,[107] whereas in the view voiced by the European Court such an alleged infringement has to be assessed *in concreto* and based on the factual proceedings read "as a whole."

The articulation of the principle of effective defense under the ICC Statute is likewise of importance. Hall observes that *"in a significant advance in the protection of suspects over previous international instruments, the ICTY and ICTR Rules both prohibit questioning of a suspect in the absence of counsel unless the suspect has voluntarily waived that right,"* and that *"Article 55 para. 2(d) of the Rome Statute includes the same prohibition as in these rules, although it does not contain the express prohibition in these rules on continuing questioning of a suspect who, after a previous waiver, subsequently expresses the desire for counsel."*[108] In effect, however, this provision implies the same guarantee as envisioned by the ICTY and ICTR Rules.

## 6.7 Implementation of the principle of effective participation in a broader perspective

While the aforementioned judgments of the Court in both the *Stanford* and *T. and V. v. UK* case undeniably seek to strengthen the defendant's position, in the presence or need of the principle of *"equality of arms,"* it is interesting to see whether the principle of effective participation in the case law of the Court takes effect in other defense areas.

The evolution of recent case law of the Court inclines indeed to an effective protection of human rights in various other defense topics. One of the most striking examples thereto forms the Court's position towards anonymous witnesses. Its position hereto is clear; that in this defense area, *"human rights are a shield against the almighty State ( . . . )."*[109] This is reflected by the latest judgments of the Court governing the admissibility of evidence based on anonymous witnesses, i.e. its decision in the *Van Mechelen et al.* case,[110] which followed earlier case

---

107. *See* also Sluiter, *supra* note 18, at 87.

108. Christopher K. Hall, *Article 55, Margin No. 15* in COMMENTARY ON THE ROME STATUTE (Otto Triffterer, ed., 1999).

109. RICK LAWSON, OUT OF CONTROL: STATE RESPONSIBILITY AND HUMAN RIGHTS 1 (1998).

110. Judgment dd. 23 April 1997, Reports of Judgments and Decisions, 1997–III; *See* also Dutch Jurisprudence (NJ) 1997, No. 635, with commentary of Prof. Dr G. Knigge.

law.[111] For present purposes paragraphs 54 and 62 of the *Van Mechelen* judgment draw our attention:

(para. 54)   *"However, if the anonymity of prosecution witnesses is maintained, the defense will be faced with difficulties which criminal
proceedings should not normally involve. Accordingly, the Court
has recognized that in such cases Article 6, paragraph 1, taken
together with Article 6 paragraph 3 (d) of the Convention requires
that the handicaps under which the defense labors be sufficiently
counterbalanced by the procedures followed by the judicial authorities (ibid. p. 471, paragraph 72)."*

(para. 62)   *"( . . . ) However these measures cannot be considered a proper
substitute for the possibility of the defense to question the witnesses in their presence and make their own judgment as to their
demeanor and reliability. It thus cannot be said that the handicaps
under which the defense labored were counterbalanced by the
above procedures."*

These rulings of the Court illustrate that the principle of effective participation, as derivative of the right to adversarial proceedings, is not
restricted to mere procedural subjects. It also affects material aspects, such
as the admissibility of anonymous witnesses. The Court's *rationale* hereto,
i.e., *"( . . . ) the place that the right to a fair administration of justice holds in a
democratic society, any measures restricting the rights of the defense should be
strictly necessary"* (emphasis added; GJK),[112] seems to be an application *in
concreto* of the principle of "effective participation."

In conclusion, the anonymous witnesses case law seems to be well in
line with that of the Court's adjudication on the latter concept, submitted
in the *Stanford* and *T. and V. v. UK* rulings.

## 6.8 Conclusions

A first conclusion to be drawn from the above is that the case law of
the European Court regarding the judicial developments of international
criminal tribunals such as the ICTY and ICTR can and actually has served
as a laboratory for the development of the principle of fair trial and its
subsequent sub-principle of *"effective participation"* regarding the accused
and counsel. The outcome seems favorable; notwithstanding criticism on
this point,[113] the case law of the ICTY—hereto influenced by the European

---

111.  *See* judgment of the Court 26 March 1996, in *Doorson v. The Netherlands,*
1996–II, at 446.

112.  *See* para. 58 of the *Van Mechelen* decision.

113.  *See* Sluiter, *supra* note 18, at 87.

Court—has substantially improved, resulting in a deviation from its previous point of view as shown by the *Tadić* decision of 10 August 1995.[114] In this case the Tribunal was not inclined to apply unconditionally interpretive arguments regarding the rights of the accused (faced with protected witnesses one of whom was anonymous) derived from the European Court's case law. In view of the progressive *Mucić* ruling, the reservation in the *Tadić* decision as to the Strasbourg case law seems to be even more substantive. The judicial incongruence between these two adjudicatory moments (i.e., in the cases of *Mucić* and *Tadić*) and allowance to derogation *"from recognized procedural guarantees"*[115] is evidenced by, first, the Trial Chamber's remark in the latter decision that *"( . . . ) As such, the interpretation given by other judicial bodies to Article 14 of the ICCPR and Article 6 of the ECHR is only of* limited relevance (emphasis added; GJK) *in applying the provisions of the Statute and Rules of the International Tribunal, as these bodies interpret their provisions in the context of their legal framework, which do not contain the same considerations,"*[116] and, second, the Tribunal's observation in *paragraph 28* that *"the interpretations of Article 6 of the ECHR by the European Court of Human Rights are meant to apply to ordinary criminal ( . . . ) adjudications."* At the time of the *Tadić* decision, the ICTY was even willing to compare its adjudicatory scope with that of a "Military Tribunal" and consequently limit defense rights.[117] How "present-day" conditions can change, even from the perspective of an international criminal tribunal!

Having said that, both the Strasbourg case law and the jurisprudence of the ICTY give firm indications that in domestic criminal proceedings as well as in International Criminal litigation, the sub-principle of "effective participation" must be endorsed and secured in a *non-restrictive* manner, this in order to protect the defense rights *functionally*. Moreover, this sub-principle should be situated in the context of *present-day conditions* related to the principle of individuality.

To reinforce the "achievement of International criminal justice," this approach seems to be more appropriate than a concept whereby rules become a reflection of legal policy or political compromises.[118] It must be recalled that international law encompasses the highest moral and legal standards, which have to be even higher in respect to trials of criminal offences of the most serious kind, where *"nothing less than the most exacting standard of evidence* (i.e., of human rights; GJK) *is required."*[119]

---

114. Case No. IT-94-1-T, para. 28.
115. *See* para. 61, *Tadić* judgment.
116. *See* para. 27, *Tadić* judgment.
117. *See* para. 28, *Tadić* judgment of 10 August 1995; *see* also Sluiter, *supra* note 18, at 85.
118. *See* also Speech by Judge L. Arbour, *supra* note 31, at 12.
119. *See Mucić* judgment of the ICTY, o.c. at para. 41.

## 7   CONTEMPORARY SCIENTIFIC METHODS FOR ESTABLISHING DEFENSES

### 7.1 The present method for judging duress

Although duress cannot be qualified as a mental or affective disorder, it requires a causal relationship with a certain mental state. The defense of duress can succeed only in the event of an external (and personalized) unexpected pressure (an event from outside the actor) producing a particular inner mental pressure or mental compulsion, which affects the freedom to act according to one's own (free) will. Therefore, in the event of duress one cannot say that the acting of the defendant is not voluntary and not intended. When the defendant is required to kill an innocent person, in an objective sense he has a choice between either defeating the threat or threatening circumstance or risking a conviction for murder and life imprisonment if he does not defy the threat. The essence of duress is that the alternative to commit the crime may have been so exceedingly unattractive that no reasonable person would have chosen it; but *de facto* there was a choice. It is more appropriate to describe the act committed under duress as "morally involuntary," the "involuntariness" being judged on the basis of society's expectation of appropriate and normal resistance to mental pressure.[120]

One of the main criteria in both continental and common law to determine the defense of duress is therefore the so-called "objective standard," meaning that only in the event that even a person of good will and reasonable fortitude might have chosen to do the "criminal" act and have been "overborne" by the threat can the defense succeed. If the prosecution can prove that the defendant would have done the same act even if the threat had not been made, it is likely that the defense of duress will fail.[121]

In the 1987 *Howe* case the (objective) duress standard was emphasized by the House of Lords when they judged that the defense of duress fails if the prosecution proves that a person of reasonable firmness sharing the characteristics of the defendant would not have given way to the threats as did the defendant.[122]

This objective duress standard, given the reference to the specific characteristics of the defendant, implies both a subjective component (i.e., the mental resistance of the particular defendant involved) and also a nexus with neural science.

---

120.  Smith and Hogan, *supra* note 44, at 238.
121.  Smith and Hogan, *supra* note 44, at 239.
122.  Smith and Hogan, *supra* note 44, at 245.

It must be stressed that, considering the fact that duress is a legal defense because threats of immediate death or serious personal violence so great as to overbear the ordinary powers of human resistance should be accepted as a justification for otherwise criminal acts, the input of neurobiology herein seems to be important. The overbearing of the ordinary powers of human resistance can originate from neurobiological and genetic aspects. The present legal view concerning duress, that behavior and the power of human (mental) resistance is determined by the character of the defendant (heredity) and environment, seems to be too restricted.

## 7.2 Neurobiological view on mental resistance or mental compulsion

The central thesis of modern neural science is that all behavior is a reflection of brain function. Also the human mind itself is considered to be a compilation of functions carried out by the brain.[123] Considering also the fact that the brain evolves not only relatively simple motor behaviors such as walking and breathing but also affective and cognitive behaviors like feeling and thinking, it can be concluded that human mental resistance or mental compulsion (two main elements of duress) are also reflections of brain function. Indeed, as recent studies observe, mental functions can be allocated to particular regions of the brain.[124] The mental compulsion underlying duress can involve several mental functions and may include such affects as anger, jealousy, fear, hate, or grievance.

Although the causes of duress are extremely complex and usually result from the interaction of a number of different variables, of which the neurobiological component is only one,[125] observations made by modern neural science indicate that a causal relationship between duress and neurobiological predisposition might be stronger than accepted until now. Several arguments justify this conclusion.

First of all, observations made as early as 1981 suggest that boys and men are more likely than girls and women not only to act aggressively, but also to imagine themselves responding with aggressive behavior to conflict situations.[126] Observations made by Reinisch presented the view that verbal estimates of aggressive response are enhanced in males and females by prenatal exposure to synthetic progestins with androgenic potential.[127] The fact

---

123. ERIC KANDEL, PRINCIPLES OF NEURAL SCIENCE 5 (1993).

124. Kandel, *supra* note 123, at 12.

125. GERARDUS G.J. KNOOPS, PSYCHISCHE OVERMACHT EN RECHTSVINDING (Transl.: Duress and finding law) (1998).

126. We know that a defense of duress arises often based on such a conflict situation; Knoops, *supra* note 125.

127. J.M. Reinisch, *Prenatal Exposure to Synthetic Progestins Increases Potential for Aggression in Humans*, 211 SCIENCE 1171–1173 (1981).

of the observed influence of hormones during gestation on later aggressive responses in humans, suggesting that differences in the frequency of
aggressive behavior between males and females as well as individual differences may be related to natural variations in hormone levels prior to
birth,[128] collaborates the thesis of influence of neurobiological components
on duress. This idea is reinforced by the observation that males are
exposed more to duress offences (i.e., criminal behavior originating from
a duress situation) than females. My thesis[129] suggested that in the evaluated 32 cases of (potential) duress, about 70 percent of the defendants
were males.

Secondly, human resistance can be influenced by impulse control.
Recent studies on specific genes that predispose to psychiatric illness have
taught us that certain genes can cause a decrease of impulse control. It has
now, for example, been observed that Wolfram Syndrome, an autosomal
recessive disorder (characterized by the occurrence of neurological, psychiatric and behavioral abnormalities such as violent assaultative behavior) is caused by a gene on the short arm of chromosome 4 p, and that
these observations show that heterozygous carriers of the disease gene are
26-fold more likely to require psychiatric hospitalization for depression
and other behavioral disturbances than non-carriers.[130] Because of the fact
that poor impulse control is one of the characteristics of the Wolfram
Syndrome and decreased impulse control can be one of the underlying
factors that code for mental compulsion, genetic involvement in duress is
likely. This plausible synthesis between duress and genetics shows the
necessity of molecular-genetic diagnostic research in each criminal case
when the defense of duress is raised. In addition to this necessity, neuro-
chemical study implies that specific neuronal systems in the central nervous system that synthesize, store and release norepinephrine, acetylcholine,
dopamine and serotonin are differently engaged and suggest that the
release of norepinephrine facilitates, sometimes even triggers, the expression of affective aggression.[131] This implies that specific neuronal pathways and processes can influence the occurrence of a mental compulsion
creating a situation of duress.

Neurobiological research also suggests that abnormalities in the
brain's serotonergic functioning predispose individuals to impulsive
aggressive behavior rather than nonimpulsive, premeditated aggressive

---

128. Reinisch, *supra* note 127.

129. Knoops, *supra* note 125.

130. R.G.Swift, M.H.Polymerpoulos, R. Torres, & M. Swift, *Predisposition of
Wolfram Syndrome heterozygotes to psychiatric illness*, 3 MOLECULAR PSYCHIATRY 68–91
(1998).

131. M.Goldstein, *Brain Research and Violent Behaviour*, 30 ARCHIVES NEUROL-
OGY 13 (1994).

behaviors.[132] In addition, a study by Coccaro indicates that reduced central 5-HT post-synaptic receptor function in the limbic-hypothalamic system is associated with a trait dysregulation of impulse control, the presence of which enhances the likelihood of self- and/or other-directed aggressive behavior, given appropriate environmental triggers.[133] Therefore an important neurobiological correlation with respect to duress as an impulsive acting out is likely.

In the third place a neurobiological basis of duress can be deduced from recent studies with respect to neurophysiological effects of stereotaxic bilateral amygdalotomy for intractable aggression. These observations suggest that the amygdala is important for associating stressful stimuli with an autonomic arousal response and also indicate that both the amygdala and orbitofrontal (limbic) frontal cortex play a role in the distributed neural systems that underlie emotion.[134] Previous studies indicated that electrical stimulation of the amygdala could lead to the appearance of defensive behavior in humans.[135] With regard to the stress component of duress, and also the fact that emotion is a main underlying base for this defense, a clear link between these neurobiological findings (neural systems) and duress is likely.

The last argument for a neurobiological component with respect to duress is provided by a study revealing that affective and predatory offenders differ in terms of the regulatory cortical control they exert over such impulses. While predatory violent offenders have sufficient left prefrontal functioning to modulate such aggressive behavior so as to bully and manipulate others to achieve desired goals, affectively violent offenders, this study indicates, lack this prefrontal modulatory control over their impulses, resulting in more unbridled, deregulated, aggressive outbursts.[136]

Current neural science offers the notion that all behavior is determined by the functioning of the brain, and also that brain functioning, in turn, is the product of interactions between genetic and developmental

---

132. Richard Kavoussi & Ph. Armstead, Emil F. Coccaro, *The neurobiology of impulsive aggression*, 20 THE PSYCHIATRIC CLINICS OF NORTH AMERICA 395–403 (1997).

133. E.F.Coccaro, *Impulsive aggression and central serotonergic system function in humans: an example of a dimensional brain-behavior relationship*, 7 INTERNATIONAL CLINICAL PSYCHOPHARMACOLOGY 3–12 (1992).

134. G.P.Lee, A. Bechara, R. Adolphs, J. Arena, K.J. Meador, D.W. Loring, & J.R. Smith, *Clinical and Physiological Effects of Stereotaxic Bilateral Amygdalotomy for Intractable Aggression*, 10 JOURNAL OF NEUROPSYCHIATRY 413–420 (1998).

135. Goldstein, *supra* note 131, at 25.

136. Adrian Raine, J. Reid Melog, Susan Bihrle, Jackie Stoddard, Lori LaCasse, & Monte S. Buchsbaum, *Reduced Prefrontal and Increased Sub cortical Brain Functioning Assessed Using Position Emission Tomography in Predatory and Affective Murderers*, 16 BEHAVIOURAL SCIENCE AND THE LAW 319–332 (1998).

processes on the one hand, and environmental factors (e.g., learning) on the other. Thus, insofar as duress (being a product of human behavior) is a reduction of the functioning of the human brain, genetic processes are likely to also provide a part of the foundation for duress and should be part of the adjudication method covering this area.

## 7.3 Direct genetic influences on duress?

In criminal law practice, the element of *mens rea* is, improperly, not associated with genetic aspects. Indirect evidence for a relationship between the mental element of a crime and genetic components comes, e.g., from studies on brain research and violent behavior.[137] From studies on this subject made before 1974, Goldstein concluded that genetic factors play at least some role in human aggression, although these studies (on both humans and animals) emphasize the strong interaction between the social environment and the genetic makeup. It is therefore not possible to separate the genetic contribution to aggression in humans from environmental influences. The interesting question is whether there exists such a direct genetic contribution to duress.

Positive arguments therefore can be derived from several observations:

First of all, an argument may be derived from the involvement of genetics in stress. The mesocortical system in the brain (projecting to the prefrontal cortex, which is involved in temporal organization of behavior and social behavior) is important in the normal response of stress. Thus reduced function in this system can be caused by gene defects and subsequently increase the vulnerability of a person to stress.[138] In turn, stress is one of the factors that alter gene expression. It is therefore likely that duress as "criminal" behavior contains a genetic component.

According to the aforementioned Goldstein study, (affective) self-defense can include an element of aggression in which genetic factors interact with the social environment. Although there are several legal differences between self-defense and the defense of duress, it is not unlikely (but without further survey too early to conclude) when an aggressive element would be involved in duress "crimes."[139] Studies corroborating the existence of a genetic contribution to aggression are therefore relevant for this legal phenomenon.

---

137. Goldstein, *supra* note 131, 1974.

138. D.R. Weinberger, *Implications of normal brain development for the patho-genesis of schizophrenia*, 44 ARCHIVES GENERAL PSYCHIATRY 660–669 (1987); Kandel, *supra* note 123, at 865 and 1028.

139. Knoops, *supra* note 125.

In the third place, there is the more general conclusion based on twin studies indicating that aggression and violent behavior may both have a strong genetic component.[140] It has to be noted that genetic factors involved in violent and aggressive behavior are polygenetic and involve a number of neurobiological processes. Also indications have been established that specific neurotransmitters exist that may be responsible for aggressive behavior.[141]

Finally, a number of studies conducted in the last two decades show that both genetic and hereditary bases for aggression (also originating from effects resulting in affective offences) are likely. In 1997 Coccaro conducted a study to determine the degree of genetic and environmental influences on assessments of aggression and irritability in male subjects.[142] Data from monozygotic 182 and 118 dizygotic twin pairs were available and analyzed using model-fitting procedures. Three of four BDHI subclasses demonstrated significant heritability of non-additive nature: 40% for indirect assault, 37% for irritability, and 28% for verbal assault. Additive genetic variance accounted for 47% of the individual differences for direct assault. Non-shared, but not shared, environmental influences contributed to explaining the variance in the model, with estimates ranging from 53% (direct assault) to 72% (verbal assault). Because some of these BDHI scales have been shown to correlate with indices of central serotonin function, it is possible that impulsive aggression, as reflected by these scales, is heritable in men.[143]

Despite these arguments, it has to be noted that the impact of neurobiological influences on crimes committed in duress is a complex one, depending on various social, environmental and cellular circumstances.[144]

## 7.4 Genetic defenses to international crimes?

### 7.4.1 An aggressive component in affective offences: genes for aggression?

It must be emphasized that a genetic factor only implies an increased risk element, the development of aggression, and that many other factors

---

140. Remi J. Cadoret, Leslie D. Leve, & Eric Devor, *Genetics of Aggressive and Violent Behaviour*, 20 THE PSYCHIATRIC CLINICS OF NORTH AMERICA 301–322 (1997).

141. Cadoret, *supra* note 140.

142. Emil F. Coccaro, C.S. Bergeman, R.J. Kavoussi, & A.D. Seroczynski, *Heritability of aggression and irritability: a twin study of the Buss-Durkee aggression scales in adult male subjects*, 1 BIOL PSYCHIATRY 273–284 (1997).

143. Coccaro, *supra* note 142.

144. STEVEN ROSE, LIFELINES, BIOLOGY, FREEDOM, DETERMINISM (1992).

are involved.[145] Raine indicates that when early neuromotor deficits and negative family factors cluster together, individuals are particularly likely to become criminal and violent compared with those with only poverty or only obstetric risk factors.[146] In Raine's research the biosocial group with the combined risk factors accounted for 70% of all crimes committed in the entire sample. Another factor can be deduced from research by Neugebauer, who presented data that suggest that severe nutritional insults (malnutrition) to the developing brain *in utero* increase the risk of antisocial behaviors in offspring.[147] Only an indirect relationship seems to exist between testosterone level and human aggression, and an additional Y chromosome (Klinefelter Syndrome or testicular dysgenesis) in men is not linked to violent criminal behavior.[148] Despite the difficulties encountered while searching for a direct relationship between human aggression and testosterone levels, several studies indicate the existence of such a relationship between testosterone and defensive aggression in non-primates. In addition, the relationship between aggression and testosterone is well established in primates.[149]

### 7.4.2    Molecular genetics of affective crimes

Although there is no evidence for the existence of one "aggression gene," genetic factors predisposing to aggressive and violent behavior do seem to exist.[150] They appear to act only in an oligenetic and/or polygenetic way, i.e., the genetic factors involve some or many loci that act in concert and that are embedded in complex developmental pathways involving various neurotransmitter systems.[151] As Alper points out, only in very few cases is a particular form of abnormal behavior known to be

---

145. JONATHAN GLOVER, THE IMPLICATIONS FOR RESPONSIBILITY OF POSSIBLE GENETIC FACTORS IN THE EXPLANATION OF VIOLENCE 194, 237–247 (1996).

146. Adrian Raine, P. Brennan, B. Mednick, S.A. Mednick, *High Rates of Violence, Crime, Academic Problems and Behavioural Problems in Males with both early neuromotor deficits and unstable family environments*, 53 ARCH GEN. PSYCHIATRY 544–549 (1996).

147. R. Neugebauer, H.W. Hoek, E. Susser, *Prenatal Exposure to Wartime Famine and Development of Antisocial Personality Disorder in Early Adulthood*, 282 JAMA 455–462 (1999).

148. D. Nelkin & L. Tancredi, *Dangerous Diagnostics: The Social Power of Personality*, 72 SOCIAL PSYCHOLOGY 207–217 (1994).

149. D.J. Albert, M.L. Walsh, R.H. Jerik, *Aggression in Humans: What is its biological foundation?*, 17 NEUROSCIENCE AND BEHAVIORAL REVIEWS 405–425 (1993).

150. DEAN HAMER & PETER COPELAND, LIVING WITH OUR GENES (1998).

151. Cadoret, *supra* note 140.

caused by an alteration in one single gene.[152] However, it is a known fact that both gluttony and morbid obesity can be caused by genetic mutations. However, Alper argues that none of these two diseases, nor any other genetic diseases known to affect behavior, result in criminal behavior. However, if we consider the existence of self-mutilation as a form of self-aggression, the importance of genes in aggression is obvious. In addition, the observation of Brunner *et al.* that characteristic behavioral phenotypes, including aggressive outbursts, can be related to isolated MAO-A gene deficiency (see below), is of importance here.[153] Moreover, Manuck *et al.* have recently found that persons possessing one of the two alleles of a intronic polymorphism in the TPH gene (the A218 C U allele) scored significantly higher when aggression and propensity to unprovoked anger were measured.[154] These persons were more likely to report expressing their anger outwardly than individuals homozygous for the alternate L allele. These findings may reflect a genetic correlate of normative variability in aggression and anger-related traits of personality.[155] In their study they note that these data are the first to show the possible association of a genetic polymorphism with variability in aggressive disposition.

An example of identifying a specific gene or genes associated with the abnormal or even criminal behavior of (a) human being(s) based on family studies is the above-mentioned Dutch study on a family with X-linked nondysmorphic borderline mental retardation, caused by a genetic defect on chromosome Xp11–21, a primary defect in the structural gene for mono-amine oxidase-A (MAO-A). MAO is a mitochondrial enzyme required for the metabolism of several neurotransmitters, including dopamine, noradrenaline and serotonin. There are two MAO isozymes, i.e., MAO-A and MAO-B.[156] Affected males in this family showed a tendency to aggressive outbursts of some sort, usually with little or no provocation. Also sexually aberrant behavior, like grasping or holding of female relatives, and even (attempted) rape and arson were recorded. The conclusion, drawn from these data, that excessive amounts of neurotransmitters, such as dopamine or serotonin, might be responsible for criminal behavior and/or that these data should imply the existence of a "gene for aggression," would, however, as Alper pointed out, be "an overinterpretation

---

152. Joseph S. Alper, *Genes, Free Will and Criminal Responsibility*, 46 Soc. Sci. Med 1599–1611 (1998).

153. Han G. Brunner *et al. Borderline Mental Retardation with Prominent Behavioral Disturbance: Phenotype Genetic cocalization and Evidence for Disturbed Monoamine Metabolism.* 52 American Journal Human Genetics 1032–1039 (1998).

154. Stephen B. Manuck *et al., Aggression and Anger-Related Traits Associated with Polymorphism of the Tryptophan Hydroxylase Gene*, 45 Society of Biological Psychiatry 603–614 (1999).

155. Kavoussi, *supra* note 132.

156. H.G. Brunner, *supra* note 153, at 155–167.

of that study." It appears that a direct relationship between abnormal behavior and a specific gene becomes less apparent when widely differing types of behavior occur, such as the ones described in the above mentioned Dutch study. Secondly, a complete loss of MAO-A function in an individual may cause negative effects of many different aspects of human brain function and behavior. Lastly, a causal relationship between the altered MAO-A gene and criminal behavior would become more probable when every subject with this altered gene would engage in the same type of criminal acts, independent of the social context, which was not the case. Although the Brunner *et al.* study of 1996 does not fulfill these criteria, it certainly reinforces the possible importance of the genetic background for criminal behavior.

### 7.4.3   Genetic defenses and (international) affective crimes

In criminal law, as observed, the individual and his or her criminal responsibility is to be judged upon; although the defendant stands trial not as a member of a group, judicial decision making depends often on precedents and is in this sense, like medicine, based on information—on the compilation of defendants or court cases, from which compilation future decisions are deduced. However, scientific evidence in both disciplines can only be deduced from investigating groups. The introduction of the analysis of human molecular-genetic influences on behavior in criminal law is the acknowledgement of this concept of individuality. Genetics can advance our understanding, and that of criminal courts, regarding particular affective crimes. Human behavior is of course too complex to be understood only at the genetic level of explanation.[157] For example, genetic defects in dopamine receptor genes are likely to play an important role in the cause of pathological gambling, but the presented studies indicate that pathological gambling is a multifaceted disorder, caused in part by genetic and in part by environmental factors, the genetic part being polygenic in nature.[158] This seems to be a judicial explanation for the very restrictive attitude of criminal courts to accept neurobiological defenses. For criminal courts the acceptance of neurobiological predispositions as factors in the explanation of criminal behavior is, moreover, controversial because of the alleged (legal) consequence that this would lead to the elimination of "free will" and the element of *mens rea*, i.e., criminal responsibility. This perception misjudges the fact that genetic reductionism —in which concept behavior is the result of a single or few gene(s) with-

---

157. Alper, *supra* note 152.
158. D.E. Comings, *The Molecular Genetics of Pathological Gambling*, 3 THE INTERNATIONAL JOURNAL OF NEUROPSYCHIATRIC MEDICINE 20–37 (1998).

out interference of the cellular and social environment—is not considered a realistic concept in the neurobiological literature either. Judicial reluctance to admit genetic influences on human behavior seems therefore to be based upon a misinterpretation of the current neuroscientific literature.[159]

## 7.5 Summary and conclusions

The complexity of neurogenetics appears from observations that one single gene may be involved in many cellular processes and that multiple genes are involved in one particular behavior. With respect to the admissibility of genetic defenses in ICL, this topic is even more complex when considering the longitudinal data analysis of Miles and Carey, which study suggests that in youth genes and environment equally promote similarity among relatives, whereas in adults the influence of the environment is negligible but that of heritability increases.[160] The hypothesis of age-dependent influences of genes on human aggression, with the genetic influence increasing in later ages while in juvenile violent behavior the environmental factors dominate, makes clear that genetic defenses must be considered cautiously. However, their admissibility should be beyond discussion. Law practise has proven that neurobiology is of great relevance in our understanding of behavior, particularly in order to obtain an answer to the question of how crimes against humanity can take place.

Although current law practice *ipso facto* does not advocate the existence *per se* of a connection between neuroscientific developments and criminal law, neurobiological aspects definitely play an important role in the manifestation of a "criminal" offence committed in duress, considering the fact that mental resistance and mental compulsion are the essentials of duress.

Despite the fact that the exact relationship of certain genetic input on duress has not yet been specifically researched, such a relationship is realistic. On the basis of the present neural scientific view, it is important not only to investigate this (possible) relationship further, but also to recognize the relevance of neural science for the (legal) analysis of a defense of duress. The interaction between neurobiology and the study of duress presents a challenge in both (international) criminal law and neural science. It is therefore useful to introduce neural scientists as expert witnesses (more often than presently occurs) with respect to the admissibility

---

159. Gerardus G.J. Knoops, *Nieuwe visie op opzet en toerekeningsvatbaarheid*, 22 ADVOCATENBLAD 1125–1127 (1999).

160. D.R. Miles and G. Carey, *Genetic and Environmental Architecture of Human Aggression*, 72 JOURNAL OF PERSONALITY AND SOCIAL PSYCHOLOGY 207–217 (1997).

of a duress-defense in the realm of ICL and international criminal litigation, especially since the Rome Statute of the ICC explicitly allows for the application of special defenses, thus leaving open genetic or neurobiological defenses.

## 8   EXPANSION OF SCIENTIFIC EXPERT WITNESSES REGARDING INTERNATIONAL CRIMINAL DEFENSES

Traditionally the role of expert witnesses with clinical expertise in both common law and civil law criminal proceedings in regard to defenses is limited to the domain of the mental insanity plea.[161] This mere context is without doubt too narrow and rigid an angle of investigation. From this several arguments emerge.

First of all, a close reading of *inter alia* the Rules of Procedure and Evidence of the ICTY contravene such a restrictive role. Rule 90 (D) mentions expert witnesses, but nowhere do the Rules explain the proper use of expert witnesses. The role of experts, though, may be significant, not only in cases of rape and sexual assault, which may require expert medical testimony, but also in criminal cases requiring expert psychiatric, religious and cultural expert testimony.[162] Although this study does not deal with the law of evidence in ICL, it cannot be doubted that current scientific knowledge of expert witnesses can have considerable repercussions on proceedings before international criminal tribunals. In the last few years a technique known as DNA fingerprinting has emerged, which has turned out to be indispensable for these proceedings. This technique provides, to all intents and purposes, for indisputably accurate evidence of identity by means of a comparison of samples of organic material taken from a person. In the realm of criminal law defenses, it can also provide, by comparison of samples from a putative assailant and self-defender, equally indisputable evidence of the factual validity of self-defense. The need for conceiving expert witness testimony within a broader scope of defenses in ICL is therefore significant. One must be constantly aware that—given the availability of, *inter alia*, DNA fingerprinting techniques—*"elimination of the innocent is no less important."*[163] This legitimating the introduction of expert witnesses before international criminal courts to reveal more infor-

---

161.   *See*, e.g., Smith and Hogan, *supra* note 44, at 197–216; regarding civil law systems *see* Knoops, *supra* note 125, at 180–188; Gerardus G.J. Knoops, *De positie van de forensisch psychiater en psycholoog in relatie tot strafuitsluitingsgronden*, 28 TRIAS (Faculty Journal of the Legal Faculty of the University of Leiden) 2–3, 16 (2000).

162.   *See* M. Cherif Bassiouni & P. Manikas, *supra* note 27, at 606.

163.   Robin M. White and Jeremy J.D. Greenwood, *DNA Fingerprinting and the Law*, 51 THE MODERN LAW REVIEW 149 (1988).

mation about the factual validity of certain criminal law defenses such as self-defense, superior orders, and duress. A final argument to progress with this concept on expert testimony in ICL is debated already in Chapter III above; genetic and neurotoxicological knowledge enables criminal courts to adjudicate upon subsequent defenses more accurately.

Secondly, according to Bassiouni and Manikas, certain (standard) procedures must be adopted hereto to ensure fairness.[164] Part of this principle of fairness, described earlier in this chapter, forms, without doubt, the right of the defendant to establish his legal defense, as set out in Chapter II above, with reliance on respective expert witnesses. Therefore, endorsing the principles of fairness, due process and equality of arms in the context of legal defenses, is without sense or substance when efficient provisions and possibilities to invoke expert witnesses are not present.

Thirdly, expert witnesses can contribute to the process of fair trial from the perspective of the judiciary, since the purpose of their role in Court is to "*supply knowledge that will aid the judge or jury in reaching a final determination*" of either the evidence or admissibility of defenses.[165] It is against this background that reliance on expert witnesses in ICL validates an additional higher standard of justice. In fact, the legal system, as stated by Loftus, "*is better suited to modulating evidence once it is offered than to dredging it up in the first place. Put another way, the mechanism for gathering information is not as well developed as is the mechanism for controlling information.*"[166] The latter aspect especially counts for the evidence-obtaining possibilities of the ICTY and ICTR, since they are not attributed with their own law enforcement entities. The major development in the United States in the last two decades regarding the use of expert witnesses in criminal Courts, in the context of adversarial proceedings, shows that ICL should welcome a contribution of (these kind of) expert witnesses and even "( . . . ) *should welcome a disagreement between experts (in Court) because in the long run we will all benefit from it.*"[167] To a considerable degree the quality of ICL itself can improve through it. In the procedural context of ICL litigation, however, one must keep in mind that, as ruled by Trial Chamber II of the ICTY in *Delalić et al.*, "( . . . ) *an expert witness is one specially skilled in the field of knowledge about which he is required to testify. The question of whether a person is an expert is one of law for the determination of the Trial Chamber.*"[168] This definition exhibits a substantial safeguard as to

---

164. *Ibid.*, which authors refer to the Articles 36 and 39 of the Rules of Procedure of the Inter American Human Rights Court.

165. *See* also Elisabeth F. Loftus, *Ten Years in the life of an Expert Witness*, 10 LAW AND HUMAN BEHAVIOR 245 (1986).

166. *Ibid.*

167. Loftus, *supra* note 165, at 259; *see* also at 260–261.

168. *See* Decision on the Motion by the Prosecution to allow the investigators to follow the Trial during the testimonies of witnesses, rendered by Trial

achieving a high standard of law finding. It may be recalled that, to quote Robinson regarding the role of the bioscientific expert, "*the tasks of a forensic ( . . . ) specialist are to conduct examinations of the physical evidence ( . . . ) and convey these results to the trier of fact, the judge and jury. In doing so he/she will have to defend his/her professional opinions without* bias or becoming an advocate for the client" (emphasis added), since "*the goal of forensic medicine is for the specialist to be a participant, a witness, an expert, whose primary function is* to assist the legal system in determining the causation of a disease process and the assignment of fault" (emphasis added).[169] The value of this theory is in accordance with the mainly adversarial structure of the proceedings before the *ad hoc* Tribunals and ICC. It also acts as authorization to clarify, in certain situations, the admissibility of special defenses such as those described in this Chapter.

In the context of raising defenses to international crimes, expert witness testimony other than to support a mental insanity defense can indeed be relevant. As regards the limits of this kind of expert witness testimony, the Appeals Chamber of the ICTY submitted several criteria in *Prosecutor v. Erdemović*. In pursuance of Rule 115 of the Rules of Procedure and Evidence, the appellant addressed to the Appeals Chamber two requests to obtain additional evidence to support his assertion of acting under duress or extreme necessity,[170] namely to:

1.  appoint a distinguished professor of ethics to submit a scientific opinion and position regarding the possibility of the moral choice of an ordinary soldier who is faced with committing a crime when following the orders of a superior in time of war; and
2.  receive an additional mental evaluation by the same panel of experts which conducted psychological examination prior to the sentencing hearing, this time on the question of the mental condition of the accused Erdemović at the time the offence was committed. The Appeals Chamber, though rejecting these requests, set out two important instructions for the defense regarding the question of the relevancy of defense-related expert witness testimony. These can both be found in paragraph 15 of the Appeals Chamber's decision:

---

Chamber II in *Delalić et al.*, Case No. IT-96-21-T, on 20 March 1997, para. 10; *See* also Jones, *supra* note 132, at 304.

169. F.R. Robinson, *The Bioscientist as an expert witness*, 37 VETERINARY AND HUMAN TOXICOLOGY 5 (1995).

170. *See Prosecutor v. Erdemović*, Decision Appeals Chamber dd 7 October 1999, Case No. IT-96-22-A, paras. 11 and 14.

a. First, the Court ruled that *"in any event, if the defense believed that the evidence was of assistance to its case, it should have brought this evidence to the attention of the Trial Chamber for the purposes of the Sentencing Hearing,"* since the appeals process of the ICTY *"is not designed for the purpose of allowing parties to remedy their own failings or oversights during trial or sentencing."* The defendant must address the Court a request for expert witness testimony for the purpose of establishing legal defenses at a pre-trial stage. Before the ICTY, this is in fact in accordance with Rule 67(A)(ii)(b) of its Rules of Procedure and Evidence.

b. A second requisite seems to emerge from the Appeals Chamber's sentence in paragraph 15 where it is said that *"the appellant has filed no affidavit or other material to indicate the substance of any statement which either 'the distinguished professor of ethics' or the panel of experts would present to the Appeals Chamber."* This remark clearly amounts to some form of "preponderance of evidence," bearing on the defendant in the sense of addressing to the Court relevant facts to establish the substance of a particular expert witness testimony. From this perspective, it goes without saying that a simple reference to *"a distinguished professor of ethics who shall give a scientific opinion and position regarding the possibility of the moral choice of an ordinary soldier"* in order to invoke the defense of duress or superior orders, does not suffice. Such an expert witness testimony would only merit a defense of necessity or superior orders since moral choice, as observed earlier, is not a constituent element of duress. Duress, as described in Chapter III above, is the acting under a threat from a third person of severe and irreparable harm to life or limb. From a juridical perspective, the defense of necessity also covers situations other than those where one is faced with threats or compulsion of a third party, e.g. the situation where a person in extremity of hunger kills another person to survive. Thus necessity covers a broader area than duress, although not encompassing threats to life and limb emanating from persons.[171]

With regard to the decision of the Appeals Chamber in the *Erdemović* case, it can thus be concluded, as a general procedural rule of ICL, that

---

171. *See* para. 14 of Separate and Dissenting Opinion of Judge Cassese to the Appeals Chambers Decision in *Prosecutor v. Erdemović*, o.c.

expert witness testimony can enable an international criminal tribunal to obtain a clear picture of the admissibility or tenability of defenses to war crimes or other international crimes. The relevance, however, of such evidence must be highlighted by the defense itself at an early stage of the criminal proceedings, and concrete material should be submitted which enables the Court to appreciate this relevancy.

The ICC Statute manifests a significant advance in the expansion of the role of expert witness testimony or assistance on behalf of the defense. This is perhaps most clearly recognized in Article 56(2)(c) of the ICC Statute, in which the Pre-Trial Chamber is required to ensure measures in particular to protect the rights of the defense. These measures may include, *inter alia*, "*appointing an expert to assist.*" As illustrated by Guariglia, "*the Pre-Trial Chamber could authorize under subparagraph (c) that an expert proposed by the defense be also appointed to assist ( . . . ).*" This author rightly emphasizes that "*this paragraph does not include a* numerus clausus *of available measures*" since it ends in paragraph 2 (f) with an open-ended clause that empowers the Pre-Trial Chamber to create new measures.[172] Subparagraph 2 (c) thus establishes the procedural and unique opportunity for the defense to endorse, at an early stage of the criminal proceedings, the participation of expert witnesses for the purpose of constituting certain defenses.

Generally, (to cite Jakobs and Sprangers), the position of the defense with respect to forensic expertise is not equal to that of the prosecution, which has all the resources at its disposal. Since the need for counter-expertise in ICL is not limited to certain areas of expertise, it is important that the costs of counter-expertise requested by the defense are regulated in such a way that either the State or the international organization responsible for establishing a specific criminal tribunal bears these costs.[173]

It is of course important to focus upon the role of the defense lawyer before international criminal tribunals. It would be hard to do justice to this view on the use of expert witnesses absent, as will be elaborated on in Chapter VIII, an active and initiating role of defense counsel. Robinson propounds this role, affirming that "( . . . ) *the task of the (defense counsel) is to obscure, ignore or subjugate the positive facts of the opposition and to emphasize the positive aspects for his side of the question* (to the expert in Court; GJK)."[174] This requisite active role also emerges from the principle that the ICL proceedings be adversarial; both parties must be given the opportunity to have knowledge of and comment on the observations filed and the

---

172. Fabricio Guariglia, Article 56, Margin No. 8, in COMMENTARY ON THE ROME STATUTE (Otto Trifferer, ed., 1999)

173. Livia E.M.P. Jakobs and Wim J.J.M. Sprangers, *A European View on Forensic Expertise and Counter-Expertise,* in HARMONISATION IN FORENSIC EXPERTISE 223 (Johannes F. Nijboer & Wim J.J.M. Sprangers, eds., 2000).

174. Robinson, *supra* note 169, at 31.

evidence adduced by the other party. This activity stems also from the principle that the parties in ICL be provided with the opportunity to confront expert evidence on an equal basis.[175] Therefore defense lawyers in ICL must ensure the active and critical attitude towards the quality of forensic expertise.[176] This is especially important in war crimes cases before international tribunals such as ICTY and ICTR, since in those systems no forensic institutes are established or appointed yet to guide scientific expertise, or to act as institutional counter-expertise on behalf of the defense.

## 9 RAISING INTERNATIONAL CRIMINAL LAW DEFENSES FOR MITIGATING PURPOSES

International criminal law has rarely accorded more than summary considerations to the impact of international criminal law defenses to sentencing, that is to say, to their role as mitigating factors in the determination of sentence. According to Schabas *"in the relatively limited practice of international tribunals, although the judgments are relatively rich in substantive law considerations, the sanction imposed often appears to be little more than an afterthought."*[177] This final paragraph considers therefore the relationship between international criminal law defenses and international sentencing, a more procedural aspect of these defences. As opposed to aggravating factors—which were obvious—the judgments at Nuremberg and Tokyo and of the various national military tribunals addressed themselves, in fixing sentence, above all upon mitigating factors.[178] For example, international law consistently refuses the defense of superior orders, but allows it in mitigation of sentence. As a general rule defenses that are rejected by the trial court—such as necessity, duress, voluntary intoxication, insanity and self-defense—may still be relevant in mitigation, evidenced by the judgment of the Appeals Chamber of the ICTY in *Erdemovic v. Prosecutor* of 7 October 1997, which recognized the admissibility of duress, not as a defense, but as a mitigating factor to a charge of war crimes or crimes against humanity. Remarkable is that, although admissible in theory, in practice the Nuremberg Tribunal systematically dismissed the argument of superior orders in mitigation, whereas superior orders was viewed as

---

175. Petra van Kampen, *Confronting Expert Evidence under the European Convention*, in HARMONISATION IN FORENSIC EXPERTISE 210 (Johannes F. Nijboer & Wim J.J.M. Sprangers eds., 2000).

176. *See* Jakobs and Sprangers, *supra* note 173, at 229.

177. William A. Schabas, *International Sentencing: From Leipzig (1923) to Arusha (1996)*, in III INTERNATIONAL CRIMINAL LAW 171 (M.Cherif Bassiouni, ed., 1999).

178. *See* Schabas, *supra* note 177, at 180.

a mitigating circumstance by the British Military Tribunal in the *Peleus* case, which brought a reduced sentence of fifteen years imprisonment.[179] Similarly, the United States Military Tribunal sentenced Wilhelm von Leeb in the *High Command Trial*, to the very light sentence of three years in prison, because no evidence was available of criminal orders signed by him. The Court applied the excuse of superior orders not as a defense but as a factor in mitigation of punishment.[180] The issue of superior orders was indeed central to the sentencing debate before the ICTY in the *Erdemovic* case. After considering the fact that the IMT had not accepted superior orders as a mitigating factor in the case of the major war criminals, the Trial Chamber considered that *"(. . .) the precedent setting value of the judgment in this respect is diminished for low ranking accused."*[181] As the Trial Chamber observed, it is not sufficient to establish a subordinate position; the accused must demonstrate that superior orders did in fact influence his or her behavior: *"if the order had no influence on the unlawful behavior because the accused was already prepared to carry it out, no such mitigating circumstances can be said to exist."*[182] The Trial Chamber seems to accept, in paragraph 54, as principle of international criminal law that *"a man who does things only under threats may well ask for greater mercy than one who does things* con amore." In the specifics of the *Erdemovic* case, the Trial Chamber found insufficient evidence to accept the duress argument, although it accepted as relevant the fact that the offender had followed orders and that he held a subordinate position in the military hierarchy.[183]

During the drafting of the Statute of the ICTY, the Committee of French Jurists considered the matter of mitigating and aggravating factors and urged respect for *"the fundamental principles of proportionality and individualization,"* and suggested that the ICTY in sentencing could consider, *inter alia*, the intention, premeditation, motives and goals of the perpetrator, as well as his state of mind, in addition to the personality of the offender including his background.[184] Similar suggestions were made by the United States with respect to the Rules of Procedure and Evidence of the ICTY, underscoring the individual circumstances of the accused in reaching sentence. In the *Erdemovic* case, the Trial Chamber continues therefore saying that *"in general, national criminal practice in this respect authorizes taking into consideration any grounds of defense which might have been rejected as grounds for exculpating the accused."*[185]

---

179. *See United Kingdom v. Eck et al.*, (1947).
180. *See United States of America v. Von Leeb* (1948).
181. *See* para. 51 of *Prosecutor v. Erdemovic*.
182. *See* para. 53.
183. *See* paras. 91–95.
184. *See* letter of 10 February 1993 from the Permanent Representative of France to the UN, UN Doc S/25266, paras. 129–131.
185. *See* para. 48.

War crimes tribunals have also taken into account efforts by an accused to reduce suffering of the victims, evidenced for instance in the *Hostage* case, where the tribunal found that the accused Ernst Dehner had attempted to apply the actual rules of warfare and not Nazi deviations from them. The Court concluded that such examples of conscientious efforts to comply with correct procedure warrant mitigation of punishment.[186] With respect to the charges of war crimes, the case law of these tribunals as well as the ICTY and ICTR has therefore developed mitigating norms which can be qualified as rules of international sentencing. Among these sentencing denominators a wide range of possibilities emerge. In the *Erdemovic* case, the Trial Chamber gave weight in mitigation to the relatively young age of the accused and his family status (recent common law marriage, two-year old child), whereas in the *Tadic* case the ICTY took into account his age as well as the effect of the length of the sentence on his family and his indigence as mitigating factors.[187] Notwithstanding the fact that the Rules of the *ad hoc* tribunals do not provide for the relevancy of raising international criminal law defenses in mitigation, they do not exclude this possibility. Article 101 (b)(ii) of these Rules specifically contemplates significant cooperation with the prosecution as a mitigating factor in sentencing. This provision apparently leaves other mitigating elements open.

Finding an appropriate balance between international sentences that fit the horror of human rights atrocities and ultimately endorse a model of enlightened criminal policy with pursuing international criminal law defenses, is the challenge that confronts the judges at The Hague and Arusha and in future those of the ICC. Despite their antagonistic nature, international criminal law defenses can, in any event, be perceived as mitigating elements to express the human view of sentencing.

---

186. *See* for this case law further Schabas, *supra* note 177, at 186–187.

187. *See Prosecutor v. Tadic*, Sentencing Judgment Trial Chamber 14 July 1997, Case No. IT-96-22-T, paras. 62–63.

# CHAPTER VIII

# A NEW CONCEPT OF INTERNATIONAL DUE PROCESS

## 1 THE INTERNATIONAL RULE OF LAW

While ICL itself is difficult to define, it can be more appropriate to consider it as a "concept of law," i.e., embodying its own characteristics and its own integrity, expressing thus the fact that ICL is relative to the constantly moving legal and social order of the international community. Notwithstanding the fact, as noted in Chapter VII above, that certain due process protections have been incorporated into ICL, the latter discipline purports to present higher legal values, as evidenced by *inter alia* the contemporary genesis of the concept *obligatio erga omnes* for *jus cogens* crimes found in the ICJ's advisory opinion on *Reservations to the Convention on the Prevention and Punishment of Genocide* and the ICJ's *South West Africa cases*.[1] Based upon my observations in the previous chapters, the evolution of an international due process norm *sui generis* seems to be well in line with these developments. The consequence is that this norm rises to the level of a "peremptory norm." The value of such a norm is, at least in principle, of the same dignity as the concept of *jus cogens* norms, since the principle of due process embodies today a universally accepted notion.

The study of defenses to international criminal litigation cannot ignore the impact of the international rule of law. The appearance of certain defenses in international tribunal statutes are inevitably exponents of the present public order system and meant to enforce the principle of fair trial before international tribunals. The moral purpose of the United Nations, from which international organizations as well as both *ad hoc* International Tribunals[2] and the International Court of Justice emerge, was in fact the promotion of the rule of law in international relations.[3] The rule of law, in its turn, is—like the concept of human rights—*"closely allied with ethics and morality."*[4]

---

1. *See* 1951 ICJ Reports 15 (May 28) resp. 1963 ICJ Reports 319 (December 21).
2. *See* Resolutions 808 (1993) and 955 (1994) of the Security Council.
3. IAN BROWNLIE, THE RULE OF LAW IN INTERNATIONAL AFFAIRS 1 (1998).
4. *See* MALCOLM N. SHAW, INTERNATIONAL LAW 197 (1997).

The perception of defenses in international criminal affairs as being expressions of the moral dimension of international law governs the link with the international rule of law in this field. An evaluation of the rule of law with respect to these defenses is also appropriate because "( . . . ) *the rule of law is much more than the application of the existing legal norms, but must involve an assessment of the quality of the legal norms.*"[5] Assessing of the quality of international criminal proceedings is a main goal of public international law. From this perception the subsequent recognition of defenses to international criminal litigation should be based upon the rule of law. The purpose of this Chapter is to investigate whether the entry of the international rule of law can serve as a norm or international legal source to determine defenses before international war crimes tribunals.

Brownlie proposes five elements as an epitome of the rule of law as a practical concept. The second key element constituting the rule of law mentioned by this author is that *"the law itself must conform to certain standards of justice both substantial and procedural,"* while the fifth key element is that *"all legal persons are subject to rules of law which are applied on the basis of equality."*[6] In the sphere of international defenses, this second criterion of the rule of law—that the law itself should be exercised in accordance with certain standards of justice, both substantial and procedural—is of particular relevance. What is, or should be, the practical effect of this notion with regard to defenses on the international plane? It is a striking fact that in his guest lecture *"Ensuring Fair and Expeditious Trials at the ICTY,"* held on the occasion of the start of the LLM Public International law program of the University of Leiden on 30 September 1999, the honorable judge of the Yugoslavia Tribunal, P. Robinson, emphasized in analyzing the jurisprudence of the *ad hoc* Tribunals, that *"of significance is the finding in these dicta (referring to the decisions of the ICTY-Tribunal in* Kanyabashi *and* Aleksovski*) that one of the objects, if not the fundamental object, of the Statute and Rules (of the ad hoc Tribunals) is achieving a fair and expeditions trial,"* thus adverting to the notion that *"( . . . ) Trial Chambers have on occasion highlighted the achievement of a fair and expeditious trial as the fundamental purpose of the Statute and Rules."*[7]

This fundamental object and purpose of the *ad hoc* Tribunals—to ensure that trials are fair and expeditious—is stated in Article 20 (1) of the ICTY-Statute, obligating the Trial Chambers to *"ensure that a trial is fair and expeditious, and that proceedings are conducted in accordance with the Rules of*

---

5.	I. Brownlie, *supra* note 3, at 1.
6.	I. Brownlie, *supra* note 3, at 213–214.
7.	"Ensuring Fair and Expeditious Trials at the ICTY," Guest Lecture Opening Academy Year LLM Public International Law, University of Leiden, 30.09.1999. at 6–7.

*Procedure and Evidence, with full respect for the rights of the accused and due regard for the protection of victims and witnesses.*"[8]

The overarching requirement of fairness involves acceptance of the rule of law as prominent directory in regard to the admissibility, compatibility and judgment of defenses to international criminal litigation. Tribunals can therefore not act arbitrarily nor absolutely[9] concerning these defenses, but must adhere to the principle that certain standards of both procedural and substantial fairness require no discretionary powers as to whether a certain defense can be invoked or is to be admissible or not. In principle a defendant cannot *a priori* be restrained from presenting a certain defense. Such is actually the case in Art. 33 of the Rome Statute of the International Criminal Court. In this context it is to be recalled that Article 20 of the ICTY Statute provides that international criminal proceedings are conducted "( . . . ) *with* full (emphasis added) *respect for the rights of the accused ( . . . )."*

The conclusion must therefore be that international defenses to international criminal litigation should not be subject to the determination of political or otherwise discretionary compatibility, with the nature of international crimes at stake. It can be asserted that such compatibility with regard to defenses is not in accordance with the principle of substantial and procedural fairness imposed by the rule of law. This view is actually expressly envisaged by the Appeals Chamber of the ICTY in the *Tadić* case, where the Court declared: *"An examination of the Statute of the International Tribunal and of the Rules of Procedure and Evidence adopted pursuant to that Statute leads to the conclusion that it has been established in accordance with the rule of law. The fair trial guarantees in Article 14 of the ICCPR have been adopted almost verbatim in Article 21 of the Statute. Other fair trial guarantees appear in the Statute and the Rules of Procedure and Evidence. For example, Article 13, Paragraph 1, of the Statute ensures the high moral character, impartiality, integrity and competence of the judges of the International Tribunal, while various other provisions in the Rules ensure equality of arms and fair trial."*[10]

This refers explicitly not only to the rule of law but also to high moral character, a concept also encompassed by Rule 95 of the ICTY, which excludes evidence when obtained by methods contradictory to *inter alia* the *integrity* of the proceedings. The practice of the ICTY, using its Rules of Procedure and Evidence, has already shown that it is possible to create an

---

8.   *See* also in this respect both the Appeals Chamber of the ICTY in the *Joseph Kanyabashi v. the Prosecutor* case and the decision of the ICTY in the case *Erdemović v. Prosecutor*, No. IT 96-22-A, 7 October 1999, which held that recourse by analogy is appropriate to Article 31 (1) of the Vienna Convention on the Law of Treaties in interpreting the provisions of the Statute

9.   *See* Chapter III *infra*.

10.   Case No. IT-94-I-T, Decision on the Defense Motion for Interlocutory Appeal on Jurisdiction, 2 October 1995, para. 46.

international criminal procedure and court that functions in conformity *"with the highest standards of international human rights law."*[11] These standards should ensure also the rights of the accused to invoke defenses abstracted from an absolutist approach.[12] In ICL, the prosecution of war crimes and crimes against humanity must be not simply a matter of the application of law and justice. It is likewise important that—considering the described framework of fair trial and equality of arms—the international legal community provides the defense in international criminal cases with necessary procedural instruments, such as access to expert witnesses, investigative powers and budgets, to effectively implement and practice criminal law defenses before international tribunals; otherwise the law in this area is worthless. Providing these means effectively forms a definite part of a norm of international due process. Such a norm stems also from the European Court's case law, concerning the role of expert witnesses in relation to the right to a fair trial. From the *Bönisch v. Austria* and *the Brandstetter v. Austria* cases as well as the case of *Mantovanelli v. France*, it can be derived that the European Court conducts a double test designed to ensure that criminal proceedings as regards expert evidence are fair.[13] The first requisite of the Court is that domestic courts in any event ensure that both parties are able to have knowledge of, and freedom to comment at trial, on the evidence adduced by the opposing party. Secondly, domestic courts have an obligation to ensure that the defendant has the opportunity to secure the attendance and examination of experts and witnesses on his or her behalf under the same conditions as the prosecution, under circumstances dictating the need to appoint counter-experts on an equal footing.[14] These two requirements indicated by the European Court's case law ascertain the existence of a norm of international due process, the implementation of which is the responsibility of the international legal community. To embellish this norm, a uniform protocol, containing standard procedures for both defense and prosecution in international criminal cases as regards the admissibility of evidence or defenses, is advisable. Alignment with the *'reasonableness of interest'* criterion rendered by the Dutch Supreme Court in the *Dev Sol* case embodies a practical guideline. In 1996, the Dutch Supreme Court—faced with the interpretation of the words *"documents of the case record"*—held, in the spirit of the *Edwards* decision of the European Court, that the record of the

---

11.   H. Ascepsio, *the Rules of Procedure and Evidence of the ICTY*, 9 LJIL, 1996, at 478.

12.   *See* Chapter IV, *infra*.

13.   *Bönisch*, ECHR 6 May 1985, Series A, 92; *Brandstetter*, ECHR 28 August 1991, Series A. 221; *Mantovanelli*, ECHR 18 March 1997.

14.   *See* also Petra van Kampen, *Confronting Expert Evidence under the European Convention*, in Harmonisation in Forensic Expertise 201 (Johannes F. Nijboer & Wim J.J.M Sprangers, eds., 2000).

case should include and disclose to the defense documents that may *reasonably* be of interest, *in either a disculpatory or an exculpatory way*.[15] In effect, this criterion implies that—although the prosecution may have knowledge or more documents than those disclosed to the defense—the right to a fair trial is violated in case of withholding evidence against the defendant, which evidence the prosecutor unjustly considers not to be of reasonable interest.[16] International due process requires therefore equality in knowing what reasonably bears relevance to deciding the criminal case. The common law concept of due process of law, as understood in the Courts of Common Pleas up until the 1600, referred to procedural laws in existence prior to the trial.[17] Since language guaranteeing procedures established by law in the criminal process is found in ninety-two national constitutions, translating the concept of due process of law to an international level is not without difficulties.[18] When following the approach, however, that the very term *"international due process of law,"* similar to the Fifth and Fourteenth Amendments of the United States Constitution, is not an explicit right but represents rather a conceptual framework or approach to the conduct of criminal proceedings,[19] one can administer and foster a concept of international due process; that is to say, a conceptual approach to the conduct of international criminal proceedings of such a level of generality that it embodies all the ingredients discussed above and ensures the effectiveness of the defense including legal defenses. The emergence of concerns about the rights of alleged war criminals with regard to the application of legal defenses confronts us with several implications of this concept of international due process, especially concerning the scope of legal defenses to war crimes, discussed hereinafter.

## 2   INTERNATIONAL DUE PROCESS: BOTH PRINCIPLE AND CORNERSTONE FOR INTERNATIONAL CRIMINAL LAW DEFENSES

First of all, the character of the term *"international due process of law,"* not as an explicit right but rather as a conceptual framework, includes the recognition of this concept as a judicial *principle*. The correlation to the term *"principle"*—as opposed to the qualification as a *"rule"*—is not without

---

15. *See Edwards v. United Kingdom*, ECHR 16 December 1992, Series A, 247–B; *Dev Sol*, Dutch Supreme Court 7 May 1996, NJ 1996, 687.

16. *See* P. Van Kampen, *supra* note 14, at 203.

17. *See* M. Cherif Bassiouni, *Human Rights in the Context of Criminal Justice: Identifying International Procedural Protections and Equivalent Protections in National Constitutions*, 3 DUKE JOURNAL OF COMPARATIVE & INTERNATIONAL LAW 272 (1993).

18. *See* M. Cherif Bassiouni, *supra* note 17, at 272–273.

19. M. Cherif Bassiouni, *supra* note 17, at 273–274.

consequences. The concept of rights, observes Dworkin,[20] and particularly the concept of rights against the government or international legal community, has its most natural use when a political society is divided. This especially applies with respect to the rights of defendants to, e.g., war crimes, crimes against humanity, and other human rights atrocities. When one accepts the view that legal defenses to war crimes in fact emerge from the principle of procedural fairness, this fairness being part of the concept of international due process, it is thus not appropriate to speak of a *rule*. Rules merely determine and dictate a particular result, and when a contrary result is reached, the rule is abandoned or changed. *Principles*, however do not work that way; they incline a decision one way, though not conclusively, and they survive intact when they do not prevail in a certain case.[21] ICL is the *resultant* of a constant dialogue between rules, prohibitions and principles, such as the principle of fairness, leaving it from case to case to determine how open the decision will be. Like common Law, ICL cannot work from pre-established truths of universal and inflexible validity to conclusions derived from them deductively. Its method for decision-making is *inductive*, i.e., it draws its generalizations from particulars. The rules and principles of case law have never been treated as final truths but as working hypotheses, continually re-tested in the international and domestic courts. Cardozo refers to the following interaction: *"Every new case is an experiment; and if the accepted rule which seems applicable yields a result which is felt to be unjust, the rule is reconsidered. It may not be modified at once, for the attempt to do absolute justice in every single case would make the development and maintenance of general rules impossible; but if a rule continues to work injustice, it will eventually be reformulated. The principles themselves are continually re-tested; for if the rules derived from a principle do not work well, the principle itself must ultimately be re-examined."*[22] This view implies that in certain events principles can prevail over a particular rule, and are especially able to derogate as to a prohibition. Ensuring the concept of international due process of law as a new *"norm"* of ICL necessarily means that the exonerative effect in certain events of legal defenses to international (war) crimes must be accepted.

---

20. RONALD DWORKIN, TAKING RIGHTS SERIOUSLY 184 (1977).
21. *See* Dworkin, *supra* note 20, at 35.
22. *See* BENJAMIN N. CARDOZO, THE NATURE OF THE JUDICIAL PROCESS 23 (1921).

## 3    THE POSITION OF THE DEFENSE LAWYER IN ICL AS PART OF INTERNATIONAL DUE PROCESS

### 3.1 Introduction

The previous section calls also for an illumination of the role of the defense lawyer engaged with defendants accused of serious breaches of ICL or international crimes as a constitutive element of international due process. The role of defense lawyers and prosecutors in criminal cases is misunderstood by much of the public, even the well-informed public. In fact, many lawyers have little real understanding of what advocates are expected to do in a "hotly contested criminal trial," observes Dershowitz.[23] In particular in regard to the defense of war criminals and defendants accused of crimes against humanity and standing trial before international tribunals, the apprehensions are understandable.

The most common complaint about criminal defense lawyers is that they distort the truth.[24] The discovery of historical or scientific truths is hardly, however, to be determined in a criminal trial. The requisite "proof beyond reasonable doubt"—the degree of evidence required in the statutes of both ICTY, ICTR and ICC—already implies that a criminal inquiry is not basically a search for *objective* and verifiable truth, replicable to historic and scientific tests.[25] Although (objective) truth was and is certainly one important goal of both the post World War II international criminal trials and, at present, the *ad hoc* Tribunals, it is not the only goal. While in an international criminal trial one is generally dealing with a decision that must be delivered under conditions of uncertainty,[26] the standard of proof required before the *ad hoc* Tribunals is that of "beyond reasonable doubt." If, for example this standard would be "a preponderance of the evidence," as in a civil case, "( . . . ) *there would be a smaller risk of factual errors that result in freeing guilty persons, but a far greater risk of factual errors that result in convicting the innocent.*"[27] The reason for permitting a lower standard of proof in civil cases is that the risk of error on each side is equal and the rule of law does not prefer one type of error above another. In

---

23.    ALAN M. DERSHOWITZ, REASONABLE DOUBTS, THE O.J. SIMPSON CASE AND THE CRIMINAL JUSTICE SYSTEM 157 (1996).

24.    *See* also Dershowitz, *supra* note 23, at 166. Of particular concern is the misapprehension of both the nature of an international criminal litigation and the impact of the rule of law on the functioning of the defense.

25.    Dershowitz, *supra* note 23, at 37.

26.    *See*, e.g., the decision of the Israeli Courts in the *Demjanjuk* trial regarding whether the accused was or was not the alleged camp-guard "Iwan."

27.    Justice J. Harlan, concurring opinion in *re Winship*, 397, US 358, 371 (1970).

criminal cases, however, the rule of law ensures preference for the type of error under which a possibly guilty defendant would go free for the type of error under which a factually innocent defendant would be imprisoned or even executed.[28] So it is evident that another purpose of international criminal trials is to contribute fairness and equality of arms to the principle of due process, as now embodied in international covenants.[29] In addition to the requirement in international criminal litigation of "proof beyond reasonable doubt," there are various other legal barriers to absolute, objective truth that have been deliberately built in. This is envisioned in the process of the present *ad hoc* Tribunals to serve other functions. For example, the exclusion from evidence of a coerced confession may produce falsity in a case where the confession, although coerced, is nonetheless true and can be independently corroborated. It is therefore applicable that Rule 92, in connection with Rule 63, of the 1994 Rules of Procedure of Evidence of the ICTY includes certain requirements in order to accept a confession by the accused. This also accounts for Article 21 section 4 (g) of the 1993 Statute of the ICTY, providing that the accused shall be entitled not to be compelled to testify against himself or to confess guilt. The adversarial procedural system of both the ICTY and ICTR, expressed *inter alia* in Rule 90 sub a of the 1994 Rules of Procedure of Evidence of the ICTY, is also exemplary for this concept. These barriers can be justified as perhaps contributing to the search for truth in the long run, while probably sacrificing truth in a particular case. In any event, they preserve and maintain the integrity and fairness of the international criminal law system, thus reflecting a balance among often-inconsistent goals which include truth, privacy, fairness, finality, and equality.[30] It is the primary task of the defense lawyer to safeguard this important set of values and, within his or her ethical rules and means, to protect mainly the principle of equality of arms.

### 3.2 Statutory international defense assignments and the rule of law

Both the Statutes of the *ad hoc* Tribunals and the ICC Statute entail the provision[31] not only to conduct the defense through legal assistance of the accused's choosing but also to be entitled *"to raise defenses and to present other evidence admissible ( . . . )."*[32] To this extent, these statutes are clearly influenced by the International Covenant on Civil and Political Rights and

---

28.  *See* also Dershowitz, *supra* note 23, at 41.
29.  *See* also Chapter VII, *infra*.
30.  Dershowitz, *supra* note 23, at 42.
31.  *See* Art. 67, section 1 (b and d).
32.  *See* Art., 67 section 1 (e) of the ICC Statute.

the European Convention on Human Rights, which latter instrument ensures in Art. 14 or Art. 6 (1)(3) the same provision. Therefore, a statutory or international conventional task is imposed upon a defense attorney to raise defenses, and in doing so he or she actually contributes to the preservation of a system of international justice that ought to exclude conviction of the innocent. In this context, it must be noted that the Drafters of the ICTY Rules of Evidence opted for the common law litigation model between two parties—a contest between two professional attorneys, i.e., the defense and the prosecution—and implemented principles mostly from common law jurisdiction.[33] In this system, the prosecution has no *obligation* to actively seek exculpatory evidence, which is rather the responsibility of the defense. The ICTY proceedings deviate on this point crucially from civil law jurisdictions, where the discovery obligation must be conducted also on behalf of the defense by the prosecution body. This imposes on the defense attorney acting before the two *ad hoc* Tribunals an even more important task: to equalize the inculpatory investigative powers of the prosecution.[34] By contrast, the Rome Statute of the ICC provides for a duty of the prosecution to investigate both incriminating and exonerating evidence equally and tends therefore to a civil law approach.[35] But even in the latter situation, the defense lawyer is essential to control the prosecution's exonerative task. It is much in dispute, in the past and the present, if special defenses to international criminal litigation can, legally or morally, be based on new scientific observations regarding genetic or neurobiological aspects of human behavior leading to possible exonerative legal decisions. This applies especially to indictments to war crimes and crimes against humanity, genocide and torture. Chapters III and VII above showed the opposite, however. Notwithstanding the understandable reluctance of the international (legal) community to embrace the admissibility of these kinds of defenses,[36] the following remarks should be made.

---

33. *See* Vladimir Tochilovsky, *Rules of Procedure for the International Criminal Court: Problems to address in light of the experience of the Ad hoc Tribunals*, XLVI NILR 345 (1999).

34. The ICTY, however, stressed in its decision of 21 September 1998, *Prosecutor v. Kupreskič et al.*, that the task of the prosecutor as an organ of international criminal justice is not simply to secure a conviction, but also to discover the truth by gathering inculpatory and exculpatory evidence, no. IT-95-16-T at 3.

35. *See* Rule 54 of the ICC Statute, although not enhancing an *obligation* of the prosecution to investigate for the defense; *See* also Tochilovskyu, *supra* note 33, at 350.

36. *See* also the remarks of Prof. Dr. C.J.R. Dugard regarding political criminal cases before international tribunals in *Een Internationale balie bij het Internationale Strafhof*, 1 ADVOCATENBLAD 17–18 (2000).

1.  First of all, science is morally neutral, since it endorses an objective view of the physical part of the world and its natural forces. In this sense, it does not deal with moral good and evil or with ethical questions. Therefore, scientific achievements—in this instance regard to neurogenetical or neurotoxicological observations—are neither the basis nor the code for moral doctrine.[37] New developments in neurobiological science show that the human brain is a dynamic system of inseparable, interacting and integral components. ICL can therefore no longer perceive an accused as *an object*, independent from these processes, not inextricably linked to these scientific processes. In this context, as expressed in Chapter VII above, defense lawyers in ICL affairs must ensure their active and critical attitude towards the quality of forensic expertise.

2.  Secondly, according to constitutions, domestic legal systems and the Statutes of the *ad hoc* Tribunals, the defense counsel is not supposed to defend the contested international crime itself, but only the *judicial process*. The starting point for the defense lawyer must thus be the induction, within his/her ethical limits, of "the reasonable doubt" notion. Therefore, for the defense lawyer in international criminal affairs, the judicial and ethical freedom to deliberately obstruct the judicial process of fact finding at the detriment of the prosecution and international courts would contradict the rule of law. There is no question that this rule of law governs the behavior of *all* legal participants of ICL including the activities of the defense. In this respect, the defense lawyer is charged both with his/her own responsibility as well as the rule of law, according to which he/she cannot act as a *"hiding place"* for the accused. In other words, the defense counsel cannot move as a functional and protective mechanism, with all means for the accused, in this sense. The liberal and dialectal dimensions of the task or role of the defense lawyer in international criminal cases and his/her legal solidarity towards the accused reaches its limit, which the defense lawyer cannot cross.[38] From this outset, it may be said that the approach of Dershowitz, asserting that *"when defense attorneys represent guilty clients ( . . . ) their responsibility is to try, by all fair and ethical means,* to prevent *the truth about their client's guilt from*

---

37. *See* MENACHEM M. SCHNEERSON, TOWARD A MEANINGFUL LIFE 189 (1995).

38. *See* also P. Mout, *Korte Notities over de Raadsman in Strafzaken*, in NAAR EER EN GEWETEN 388, 383–391 (Liber Amicorum J. Remmelink 1987).

*emerging"* and failure to do so *"is malpractice"*[39] seems to me a judicial and ethical path too far taken. A different matter is the feature of *independence* of the defense lawyer before international tribunals. This implies, first, that he or she is not independent from his or her client; secondly, that with respect to an accused who pleads not guilty but whom the defense lawyer knows from the inner circle is in fact guilty, that in these situations the defense entails the duty to test the evidence against the accused by the Court, not to mix it with attacking evidence.

In the adversarial system—a feature of the trial stage of the ICTY and ICTR—it is the defense's obligation to produce counterbalancing evidence. Contrary to the civil law system, the accused is not an *object* of investigation but rather a party equal to the other party, the prosecution. From this dogmatic distinction between these two jurisdictions, it emerges that the defense counsel, in an adversarial system, bears its own responsibility, thus having legal duty to counterbalance the evidence to a charge presented by the prosecution. Therefore within such a system it is not only allowed but also obligatory for the defense counsel—even in the event of an actually guilty client who pleads not guilty—to *test* the incriminating evidence, within the legal and ethical codes, without *attacking* this material by illegal means. The evidence criterion of *"reasonable doubt,"* upheld by the International Criminal Court, is also supportive of this view. The implication is that this role of the defense also involves the forwarding of legal defenses. Otherwise, his or her obligation to employ his or her juridical expertise unreservedly for the benefit of his client, entailing the maximal exploitation of possibilities of defense afforded by law,[40] would be meaningless.

## 3.3 International political defense borders

The task of the defense lawyer is a subtle one; it is surely a matter of appropriate defense to achieve a diversion or distinction between the inner feelings of the defense lawyer regarding the person of the accused or the alleged international crime and his/her external juridical behavior before the international courts. This dialectical tension arises especially in

---

39. Dershowitz, *supra* note 23, at 166.
40. *See* Michail Wladimiroff, *The Assignment of Defense Counsel Before the International Criminal Tribunal for Rwanda*, 12 LJIL 2 (1999).

the realm of the defense of political international crimes, such as a defense of defendants charged with international crimes such as terrorism or hijacking, based on political motives. Although it seems inevitable that the defense lawyer in these kinds of international criminal cases elucidates on the (non-) political motives of the accused in order to provoke a court decision in favor of the accused[41] or to mitigate the sentence, the task or role of the defense hereto cannot serve as purely supportive to the illegal distortion of the international legal community. On the contrary, it can only configure within the legal boundaries of this system.[42] However, the international legal system permits the defense to try to persuade the (international) courts to review either their previous rulings on the legitimacy of statutory elements regarding, *inter alia*, the requisite elements of such international crimes as genocide, torture and sexual assault, or to a restrictive or extensive interpretation of international covenants in favor of the accused. Ultimately, the international criminal defense attorney can make a significant contribution to defining the limits of current ICL norms.[43]

In fact, the international legal system[44] prescribes that this approach shall be endorsed by the defense by lawful and ethical means. This element is well exemplified in defending an international crime committed by an accused who raises the political offence exception. It is well accepted that the defense ensures that the extradition court will be called upon for a judgment on this exception by establishing relevant circumstances sustaining this exception in concrete cases.[45]

### 3.4 International code of conduct for defense and prosecution: sequel to international due process

The basis for a norm of international due process can be reinforced and expanded by addressing an overarching framework of ethical rules for both defense and prosecution in order to protect the integrity of the

---

41.  *E.g.*, in extradition cases regarding the political offense exception; *see*, e.g., Article 3(1)(2) of the European Convention on Extradition dd. 13 December 1957.

42.  *See* also Mout, *supra* note 38, at 389.

43.  *See* also *"Position paper of ICDAA on defence independence before the International Criminal Court,"* in: Proposal for the establishment of an Independent Office of the Defence (ICDAA), June 21, 1998, published in ICDAA Annual Report 1998–1999.

44.  *See* the conditions on the defense rights in the Statutes of ICTY, ICTR and ICC.

45.  *See* also *Regina v. Ex Parte Pinochet*, available at: <http.www.parliament.thestatione . . . 199899/ldjudgmt/jd990324/pinol.htm>; *see* for the element of jus cogens: the opinion of Lord Browne-Wilkinson, in the "Torture section."

international criminal process. ICL does not yet provide clear and general standards of ethical behavior as regards the role of the international criminal defense lawyer and prosecution. Apart from the aforementioned boundaries, ICL may stipulate that a defense lawyer will practice with due diligence based on his/her own professional responsibility. The principles of "due process" and "fairness" applied in ICL rule out totalitarian control of the exercise of defense activities. Otherwise the defendant's elementary right to be represented by a defense of his/her own choice will become meaningless.[46] In this way the international rule of law in ICL will prevail and be protected. Political and public attention focuses, as stated by Wladimiroff, primarily on the vigorous prosecution of alleged war criminals, while it is equally important to remember that professional defense of the accused is vital to the legal and political legitimacy of any efforts to extend the rule of law internationally. The principle of the rule of law within the criminal justice system, as this author continues, does not only depend on the way in which investigative, prosecutorial and adjudicatory institutions fulfill their duties, but also on the proper fulfillment by defense counsel of their duties. On the one hand we can endorse the same conclusion, as drawn by this author: *"A full and fair defense is an essential element of any claim to conduct a fair trial and enforce the rule of law."*[47] On the other hand, it is the obligation of the defense lawyer in international criminal cases, as an *"Officer of the Court,"* to endorse this rule of law, contributing to the establishment of this new norm of international due process. Indeed one can assert with Shabuddeen that *"the Court (The ICJ: GJK) does not have a monopoly over the guardianship of the rule of law in international relations; that is the responsibility of all actors (emphasis added) in the field."*[48] Including the field of international criminal law.

A sequel to this new norm of international due process is undoubtly the formulation of a code of conduct for international criminal defense lawyers acting before international criminal tribunals. Apart from the imperative of certain professional requirements, pursuant to Rules 44 (A) and 45 of the ICTY Rules of Procedure and Evidence, ethical standards can no longer be excluded from the field of ICL. The European Community Code of Conduct for Lawyers of 28 October 1988 demonstrates a precedent hereof, although it lacks any specific regulations for criminal defense attorneys, let alone for ICL. From 1997, the ICTY Registrar recognized the relevancy of a specific code of conduct for international criminal defense attorneys by promulgating a so-called *"Code of Professional Conduct*

---

46. *See* for this right: Rule 42(A)(i) and (B) of the ICTY Rules of Procedure and Evidence; Article 55(2)(c) (d) and 67 (1)(b) ICC Statute.

47. M. Wladimiroff, *supra* note 40.

48. M. Shahabuddeen, *The World Court at the Turn of the Century*, in THE INTERNATIONAL COURT OF JUSTICE 8 (A.S. Muller, et al., eds., 1997).

*for Defence Counsel Appearing before the International Tribunal."*[49] Analogous
to the latter Code of Professional Conduct, it seems imperative that synchronic with the establishment of the ICC—and in addition to the proposed creation of an Office of the defense similar to the Office of the
Prosecution, to assist defense counsel practicing before the ICC[50]—a *"Code
of Professional and Ethical Conduct for Defense Counsel appearing before the
ICC"* has to be enacted. Not only would such a code of conduct contribute
to the development of an ICL norm of international due process, but it
would also ensure a defense independency, advocated by the ICDAA,[51]
as well as create proper ethical thresholds. The principle of reciprocity
implies that, in the light of the second element of the international rule of
law as to ensuring that alleged war criminals are granted the right to a
fair trial and requiring fairness from the side of the prosecution, the
defense has to maintain the same fairness and legal dignity. In this context, Articles 5 and 6 of the aforementioned Code of Professional Conduct
for Defense Counsel appearing before the International Tribunal can serve
as a model of draftsmanship and a starting point for a framework for a
similar ICC Code, regulating international due process unilaterally.
Articles 3, 5 and 6 of the ICTY Code of Conduct lay down significant provisions governing ethical conduct for defense attorneys within the framework of the ICTY. Accordingly, in addition to Article 3, which points out
that *"the general purpose of this Code is to provide for standards of conduct on
the part of Counsel which are appropriate in the interests of the fair and proper
administration of justice,"* Articles 5 and 6 read:

Article 5—Competence and Independence
In providing representation to a Client, Counsel must:
a. act with competence, skill, care, honesty and loyalty;
b. exercise independent professional judgement and render
   open and honest advice;
c. never be influenced by improper or patently dishonest behaviour on the part of a client;
d. preserve their own integrity and that of the legal profession
   as a whole;
e. never permit their independence, integrity and standards to
   be compromised by external pressures.
Article 6—Diligence
Counsel must represent a Client diligently in order to protect the
Client's best interests. ( . . . )

49. *See* http://www.un.org/icty/basic/counsel/IT125.htm, which code
entered into force on 12 June 1997.
50. *See* Proposal for the establishment of an Independant Office of the
Defense, *supra* note 43.
51. *See* Proposal, *supra* note 43.

Conversely, the principle of international due process must place significant emphasis on fundamental ethical guidelines for the role of the prosecutor within the system of ICL. Already in 1990 this important facet of ICL was formulated. At that time the UN Congress on the Prevention of Crime and the Treatment of Offenders adopted specific Guidelines on the Role of Prosecutors. The main section of these guidelines is the one which is titled Role in Criminal Proceedings, which role is defined herein and contains a nonexhaustive list of the following ethical rules:

( ... )

10. The office of prosecutors shall be strictly separated from judicial functions.
11. Prosecutors shall perform an active role in criminal proceedings, including institution of prosecution and, where authorized by law or consistent with local practice, in the investigation of crime, supervision over the legality of these investigations, supervision of the execution of court decisions and the exercise of other functions as representatives of the public interest.
12. Prosecutors shall, in accordance with the law, perform their duties fairly, consistently and expediously, and respect and protect human dignity and uphold human rights, thus contributing to ensuring due process and the smooth functioning of the criminal justice system.
13. In the performance of their duties, prosecutors shall:
    a. Carry out their functions impartially and avoid all political, social, religious, racial, cultural, sexual or any other kind of discrimination;
    b. Protect the public interest, act with objectivity, take proper account of the position of the suspect and the victim, and pay attention to all relevant circumstances, irrespective of whether they are to the advantage or disadvantage of the suspect;
    c. Keep matters in their possession confidential, unless the performance of duty or the needs of justice require otherwise;
    d. Consider the views and concerns of victims when their personal interests are affected and ensure that victims are informed of their rights in accordance with the Declaration of Basic Principles of Justice for Victims of Crime and Abuse of Power.
14. Prosecutors shall not initiate or continue prosecution, or shall make every effort to stay proceedings, when an impartial investigation shows the charge to be unfounded.

15. Prosecutors shall give due attention to the prosecution of crimes committed by public officials, particularly corruption, abuse of power, grave violations of human rights and other crimes recognized by international law and, where authorized by law or local practice, the investigation of such offenses.

16. When prosecutors come into the possession of evidence against suspects that they know or believe on reasonable grounds was obtained trough recourse to unlawful methods, which constitute a grave violation to the suspect's human rights, especially involving torture or cruel, inhuman or degrading treatment or punishment, or other abuses of human rights, they shall refuse to use such evidence against anyone other than those who used such methods, or inform the court accordingly, and shall take all necessary steps to ensure that those responsible for using such methods are brought to justice.

17. In countries where prosecutors are vested with discretionary functions, the law or published rules or regulations shall provide guidelines to enhance fairness and consistency of approach in taking decisions in the prosecution process, including institution of waiver of prosecution.

( . . . ) (Observance of these Guidelines)

23. Prosecutors shall respect the present Guidelines. They shall also, to the best of their capability, prevent and actively oppose any violations thereof.

Such a description of the Role of the Prosecution in ICL in general must be encouraged. Considering that the concept of international due process will be (or perhaps is) consolidated into the system of ICL, the implementation and codification of an overall code of conduct for ICL counsel as well as prosecution constitutes an essential foundation for the international rule of law. The aforementioned Codes of Conduct of ICTY regarding the defense, and United Nations regarding the prosecution encourage a progressive development of the moral and legal dignity of ICL. There is yet no provision in the Statute of the ICC that specifically details how the law of professional conduct should be regulated with respect to defense counsel and prosecution appearing before that Court. The international legal community should carry out further inductive investigations in order to subject defense counsel and prosecution's trial attorneys to the same set of ethical rules.[52] For now, with regard to a future

---

52. *See* Michael Bohlander, *International Criminal Defence Ethics:The Law of Professional Conduct for Defence Counsel Appearing Before International Criminal Tribunals,* 1 SAN DIEGO INTERNATIONAL LAW JOURNAL 98 (2000).

ICC-Code of Professional Conduct, it can be concluded that, as Bohlander points out, *"a common code of ethical conduct for both defence counsel and prosecutors is also imaginable, albeit with some specifications because defence counsel and prosecutor duties differ in some respects."*[53] Undoubtedly, following Article 19 of the ICTY Code of Professional Conduct for Defense Counsel, such an ICC-Code should prevail in any conflict between it and a national code of professional conduct. Indeed, international due process has to voice the general maxim that international legal practitioners must maintain a high standard of professional conduct; they must act honestly, fairly, skillfully, diligently, and courageously. Furthermore they have an overriding duty to defend their client's interests, subject to the limitation that they must not act dishonestly or improperly prejudice the administration of justice.[54]

## 3.5 Towards a new perception of the position of the international criminal defense counsel: implications of his or her role in ensuring legal defenses

The aforesaid leads to some important implications as regards the position and role of the international criminal defense counsel in proceedings before the international criminal tribunals. Guaranteeing the accused the right to counsel *"in the determinations of any criminal charge against him,"* ensured by *inter alia* Article 14 (3)(d) of the ICCPR, is one element. Another is the fact that this right axiomatically necessitates that both the international community and international criminal courts are free from bias or prejudice with regard to the important and at the same time antagonistic role of the international criminal defense counsel in the maintenance of the international rule of law.[55] Remarkably, although this protection against bias or prejudice seems implicit and obvious, the statutes of the various international criminal tribunals fail to reaffirm the important role of defense counsel in the maintenance of the international rule of law which, as Dugard observes, *"inevitably ( . . . ) creates the impression that defense council are not a primary concern of those responsible for the establishment of these courts, nor central to their concept of a fair trial."*[56] Indeed, it seems an underestimation of the role of the international criminal defense

---

53. *See* Bohlander, *supra* note 52.

54. *See* Bohlander, *supra* note 52, at 91.

55. *See* M. Cherif Bassiouni, *Human Rights in the Context of Criminal Justice: Identifying International Procedural Protections and Equivalent Protections in National Constitutions*, 3 DUKE JOURNAL OF COMPARATIVE & INTERNATIONAL LAW 270 (1993).

56. John Dugard, *Independent Defence Before the ICC: The Role of Lawyers Before International Courts*, in AN INDEPENDENT DEFENCE BEFORE THE INTERNATIONAL CRIMINAL COURT 22 (Hans Bevers & Chantal Joubert, eds., 2000).

counsel to realize that the constitutional framework of international criminal tribunals—including the Nuremberg Charter, with its detailed provisions on the role of the prosecutor with little on defense counsel, the ICTY and ICTR Statutes, and even the ICC Statute which includes only an acknowledgment of the accused's right to counsel—"( . . . ) *devotes so little attention to defense lawyers, despite the fact that their role in securing a fair trial is crucial.*"[57] Since it is still important that the general public must be educated to understand the important role of defense counsel,[58] not only in domestic but especially in international criminal trials, this might best be done by means of more expressive provisions or texts in the statutes of international criminal tribunals, such as a provision that *"the role of defense counsel is to defend and promote the defense interests of his client with due regard to the ethical, professional rules binding upon him as a lawyer."* To that end, a general statement or directive that is brought to the attention of the international community is also desirable. With regard to this educational element, a primary and important argument understanding of criminal law defenses before war crimes tribunals should illuminate more intensively the role of the international criminal defense counterpart, i.e., the role of the prosecutor in international criminal trials. The role of the latter person or institute in these trials—"to prosecute not persecute," meaning that "the prosecutor must adopt an evenhanded and fair approach,"[59]—sheds light on the fact that the defense counsel must be able to exploit all possibilities of defense accorded or afforded by law to the utmost extent. Whereas the prosecutor in international criminal litigation must do her or his best to secure a prosecution (not conviction), and this must not be done at the expense of fairness, consequently the international criminal law system, by nature, focuses on a full and fair defense and legal defenses. In other words, the position of the prosecution in ICL provides for, not only a vital position of defense counsel as such, but also for extensive defense responsibilities and possibilities within the international criminal justice system, including effective remedies to lodge legal defenses. These remedies can also be deduced from Article 21 of the *UN Basic Principles on the Role of Lawyers*. By emphasizing and accentuating the role of the prosecution in this way, more understanding of both the vital role of defense counsel in ICL—playing an important part in promoting and extending the international rule of law—and the legal as well as the political legitimacy of effectuating criminal law defenses in this kind of trial is encouraged. Understanding the right of representation by counsel at each important stage of criminal proceedings in this way as paramount to the concept of due process—i.e., as the essential right to pursue a fair trial,

57.  Dugard, *supra* note 56, at 22.
58.  Dugard, *supra* note 56, at 23.
59.  Dugard, *supra* note 56, at 21.

endorsing the rule of law—cannot only redress the "educational" imbalance within the international community, but also channel the conduct of international criminal defense counsel more uniformly. To me, the following principles of conduct for international criminal defense attorneys (in relation to lodging legal defenses) are paramount to the concept of due process:

1. Lawyers shall at all times maintain the honour and dignity of their profession as essential agents of the administration of justice.[60]
2. Defense counsel must defend and promote the defense interests of his client, with due regard to ethical, professional rules binding upon him as a lawyer. In protecting the rights of their clients and in promoting the cause of justice, defense counsel shall seek to uphold human rights and fundamental freedoms recognized by national and international law and shall at all times act freely and diligently in accordance with the law and recognized standards and ethics of the legal profession.[61]
3. Within this primary rule, defense counsel in ICL must, where legally possible, lodge or raise criminal law defenses with due diligence.
4. Defense counsel in ICL should be independent, not only of the prosecution, but also of the accused's political accomplices.[62] Although the defense counsel must understand, and to a certain extent be able to empathize with, the accused's position, and recognize his duty to act as confidant, he or she cannot totally identify with the accused's views and must avoid such identification to all costs.[63] The understanding, as independent counsel, of the political motivation and ethnic loyalties of the accused is one thing; it is another thing, to cite Dugard, to seek to promote a cause or ethnic group.
5. Defense counsel in ICL must act as legal interpreter both to the other parties in the proceedings and to the defendant. To that end he must explain the law and criminal justice system to the defendant, advising him "( . . . ) *on the options open to him in the conducting of his defense*" and advising him on *"the*

---

60. *See* Article 12 of the UN Basic Principles on the Role of Lawyers.

61. *See* Dugard, *supra* note 56, at 23; *see* also Article 14 of the UN Basic Principles on the Role of Lawyers.

62. Dugard, *supra* note 56, at 24.

63. *See* Michail Wladimiroff, *Position of the defence: the role of defence counsel before the ICTY and the ICTR*, in AN INDEPENDENT DEFENCE BEFORE THE INTERNATIONAL CRIMINAL COURT 36 (Hans Bevers & Chantal Joubert, eds., 2000); *see* also Dugard, *supra* note 56, at 23.

*wisest course to pursue,"* but ultimately leaving decisions of
this kind to the accused.[64] In the realm of legal defenses in
ICL, the defense counsel should provide—both for the defendant and, in court, the other participants—a clear explanation
of the impact and consequences of these defenses, when
available or occurring.

6.  Defense counsel in ICL must secure and prevent infringe-
    ments of the substantive and procedural rights of the defen-
    dant. This implies that he or she is obliged *"to strive to achieve
    the most favourable outcome"* for the defendant, and is also "( . . . )
    *obliged to employ his juridical expertise unreservedly for the bene-
    fit of his client."*[65] This perception includes the lodging of crim-
    inal law defenses before international criminal tribunals
    within the appropriate legal merits.

The perception of the role of the international criminal defense counsel performing before international criminal tribunals investigated in this
section is derived primarily from concordance with the role of its judicial
counterpart, i.e., the prosecutor, and of the concept of international due
process of law. ICL should further expand this perception and strengthen
the validity of this new perception, to corroborate the emergence of the
described concept of international due process. With regard to criminal
law defenses in ICL, the divergence between the domestic application
of these defenses—as pointed out in Chapter I above—can be deduced
"( . . . ) *in promoting a greater understanding of the role of defense lawyers before
the ICC as they play an important part in promoting the Rule of Law,"* for which
promotion, according to Dugard, *"there seems to be some urgency."*[66] To me,
this urgency in promoting this kind of greater understanding especially
applies to international criminal defense lawyers themselves; their own
awareness of their task, role, ethical and legal attitude, as well as their professional susceptibility towards legal defenses as analyzed in previous
chapters, is crucial to make this concept of international due process work
effectively. Indeed, for this reason it would be feasible to enact an international code of conduct applicable to both defense and prosecution with
the aforesaid contents as proposed in subsection 3.4 above.[67] At the end
of the day, a code of professional conduct (for the ICC), jointly developed
and applied by both prosecution and defense will, as well as ensuring this

---

64. Dugard, *supra* note 56, at 23.
65. Wladimiroff, *supra* note 63, at 36.
66. Dugard, *supra* note 56, at 25.
67. *See* for such a common code: Wladimiroff, *supra* note 62 at 42; Elise
Groulx, *A Strong Defence before the International Criminal Court,* in AN INDEPENDENT
DEFENCE BEFORE THE INTERNATIONAL CRIMINAL COURT 15–16 (Hans Bevers &
Chantal Joubert, eds., 2000).

concept of international due process, will endorse and increase *"the chances that all parties, including the groups supporting the accused war criminals, will accept both the trial process and the ultimate verdicts."*[68] Last but not least, the international community can itself comply with the outcome of these trials and the legitimacy of lodging legal defenses to war crimes charges.

## 4 TOWARDS AN INDUCTIVE LAW FINDING METHOD REGARDING INTERNATIONAL CRIMINAL LAW DEFENSES

### 4.1 Introduction

In their note on case preparation for the ICTY, Bergsma and Keegan remark, from the perspective of the Prosecution, that the process of collecting evidence includes *inter alia "the intents, behavior and* personality (my emphasis: GJK) *of the alleged perpetrator ( . . . )."*[69] The principle of individuality, emerging from this view, constitutes also one important aspect of the rule of law in international criminal litigation. The central devices of the rule of law are legal rules that prohibit certain options of official behavior or that mandate certain kinds of official action which may be more or less "open textured."[70]

Allen observes that some areas of legal regulation are of a nature that makes creation of formal rules unfeasible, in which case resort to broad guidelines for official action or less formal modes of control is more appropriate.[71] The question arises (already discussed in Chapters III and IV above and to be resolved in this paragraph) if the proclamation of general criteria or rules can have any determinative value in regard to the adjudication of legal defenses.

### 4.2 Prevalence of the law of the case

The maintenance of the principle that legal rules must always comply with the power of the concrete case and, if existing, be applied with the greatest possible clarity,[72] already calls for a factual and inductive attitude towards their application. Precisely because a strict and dogmatic approach to legal defenses can obstruct a concrete outcome of criminal

---

68. Groulx, *supra* note 67, at 18.
69. M. Bergsma & M. Keegan, *A note on case preparation for the ICTY*, at 5.
70. *See* FRANCIS A. ALLEN, THE HABITS OF LEGALITY 20 (1996).
71. Allen, *supra* note 70, at 20.
72. *See* Allen, *supra* note 70, at 21.

cases that may be thought to produce a wiser, functional, or more just result, the absence of strict conditions for defenses seems to better accommodate the nature of judicial thinking and law making. Therefore the aspect of functionality contradicts the determinative value of hard conditions to legal defenses.

A second contradictory argument can be deduced from the ever existing tension between *"rules and aspirations for individual justice,"* described by Allen, who notes that this tension can be identified even in substantive criminal law, the domain in which the case for general rules of certain application is considered to be the strongest.[73] Even here, to continue with the same authority, *"the unique facts of the particular situation may condition the generality of rules,"* referring not only to the concept of criminal negligence (which has never been fully defined) but also to the defense of the "lesser evil." The latter aspect is articulated in several domestic statutory forms: valid disobedience of penal commands regarding *ad hoc* determinations by courts implies that the accused's failures to comply produces lesser evils than would have been created had the law been obeyed,[74] which seems equivalent to the defense of necessity. The same is true with respect to other legal defenses. It is obvious to me that the concept of individualized scrutiny of the Courts with respect to legal defenses to international litigation can better safeguard a more humane, ingenious and sensitive International Criminal law system. It must be stressed, however, that this approach can never be meant to sacrifice the international rule of law. It is therefore important to be aware that a normative framework remains essential to endorse legality, equity and non-abuse of powers. Because defenses in (international) criminal law involve a combination of law and facts, ICL—which especially applies to the Yugoslavia and Rwanda Tribunals considering their current attitude—must pay more attention to the law of the case. The facts of a particular case are *stricto sensu* the basis of a legal defense. It cannot be denied, however, that in some cases the facts prevail more intensely over the law than in other cases, due to the presentation of the facts by both the defense and prosecution. In these cases, the qualification of a "law of the case" seems justified. The multiplicity of applicable legal sources to the concept of criminal law defenses—evidentiary for the complexity of the multidisciplinary nature of defenses—also argues for the need for a more preponderant position of the law of the case. This qualification relates to common law, which system does not work from pre-established truths of universal and inflexible validity to conclusions derived from them deductively. The nature and method of its judicial process is inductive, i.e. drawing its gen-

---

73. Allen, *supra* note 70, at 21.
74. Allen, *supra* note 70, at 22.

eralizations from particulars or particular facts.[75] For Benjamin Cardozo, describing this nature or method, *"every new case is an experiment"* and *"if the accepted rule which seems applicable yields a result which is felt to be unjust, the rule is reconsidered."* Similarly, according to Cardozo, *"the principles themselves are continually restested; for if the rules derived from a principle do not work well, the principle itself must ultimately be re-examined."* Consequently, a judgment of an international criminal tribunal related to such a "law of the case" does not necessarily apply to a similar defense in an other case. To this extent, ICL cannot utilize a uniform and general approach the absolutist view on criminal law defenses, which excludes *ab initio* a criminal defense from the arena of an international criminal court. Following general principles of international law, by nature the absolute approach regarding criminal law defenses cannot *"be so extremely specific and precise as to afford certainty of the law and at the same time be broad and general enough to allow for the growth and evolution of international law."*[76] The tension of law and facts has become particularly evident in the application of criminal law defenses to war crimes charges. Since there is little consensus about the legal processes and methods of applying these defenses—evidenced through the various decisions of international criminal tribunals over recent decades—the legitimacy of the adjudication process for criminal law defenses to international crimes may be found elsewhere than in positive texts, i.e., in the law of the case. In the antagonistic area of these defenses one has to accept that sometimes the facts condition the law, as opposed to the law conditioning the facts. Especially when no simple uniform method to be applied exists, elaboration on the "law of the case"—i.e., the facts—provides a more determinative outcome than reliance on positive textbooks. At the same time, this approach prevents in fact rigid adherence to precedents that may impact on future cases, as so feared by "real" politicians. The approach of the law of the case injects also a dynamic element into ICL which takes into account, *inter alia*, the military background of the defendant with respect to defenses such as superior orders and duress. The prevalence of the law of the case prevents—as observed in Chapter II above with regard to superior orders—a static application of (archaic) norms and legal methods *"to what is admittedly an evolving legal process designed to frame or regulate the dynamic exigencies and needs of a community of nations with changing interests and mutable goals and objectives."*[77]

---

75. *See* BENJAMIN N. CARDOZO, THE NATURE OF THE JUDICIAL PROCESS 22–23 (1974).

76. M. Cherif. Bassiouni, *A Functional Approach to General Principles of International Law*, 11 MICH. J. INT'L. L. 776 (1990).

77. *See* M. Cherif. Bassiouni, *supra* note 76, at 777.

## 4.3 Conclusion: exclusion of a general rule of non-application of certain international defenses

As a consolidation, it can therefore be concluded that it would be wrong to endorse, within the system of ICL, any *a priori* elimination of criminal law defenses from the arena of international crimes, including crimes against humanity. To neglect this notion is to negate the value not only of *"the law of facts"* but also of the principle of fair trial and equality of arms which must be maintained especially as regards severe charges such as crimes against humanity. ICL clearly needs no absolutist approach with respect to international criminal law defenses. What is left is only an application of these defenses on a purely factual basis. In my view it is not according to the nature of the process of judicial law making and thinking to accept, as a principle, some kind of general rule of non-applicability of certain defenses as such, e.g. the defense of duress or superior orders. The exclusion as to a defense to international crimes of the "act of State" doctrine, obedience to national law and the immunity of heads of State and diplomats, seems, contrary to the aforementioned defenses, justified because of the involvement of the State as such in these crimes.[78] When qualified not as justifications but only as possible *excuses*, the defenses of duress, necessity or superior orders do not undermine the gravity of certain international crimes.[79]

The more *nuanced approach*, mentioned in the introductory chapter of this study and analyzed and concluded in this study, surely accords more with elementary principles of ICL: that is, the various principles of legality described in Chapter III above as well as the *rule of law* itself and its substantive exponents envisaged by the principles of fairness and reasonableness. Only an *inductive* method of law-finding in this antagonistic area (*vide* Chapter III above) as well as a *contextual model* (*vide* Chapter VI above) as opposed to an absolutist model, can balance the need to prosecute human atrocities with *"limiting and guidance"* of governmental powers to accord with high standards of justice, morality and fair trial.[80] Only in this way can the rights of the accused—provided for in Article 67 of the ICC Statute and in this context exemplified by Article 67 (1)(e), which ensures that *"the accused shall also be entitled to raise defenses ( . . . )"*—be endorsed. In the sphere of defenses in ICL, a rejection of the absolutist

---

78. *See* Yoram Dinstein, *International Criminal Law*, 20 ISRAEL LAW REVIEW 238–240 (1985). Mordechai Kremnitzer, *The World Community as an International Legislator in Competition with National Legislators*, in PRINCIPLES AND PROCEDURES FOR A NEW TRANSNATIONAL CRIMINAL LAW 345 (A. Eser & O. Lagodny eds., 1992).

79. *See* also Kremnitzer, *supra* note 78, at 345.

80. *See* also for these methods regarding legal defenses: GERARDUS G.J. KNOOPS, PSYCHISCHE OVERMACHT EN RECHTSVINDING (1998).

approach to defenses is now formalized in Article 31 (2) of the ICC Statute, which reads: *"The Court shall determine the applicability of the grounds for excluding criminal responsibility provided for in the Statute to the case before it."* Article 31 of the ICC Statute is well in line with the common law proposition of a rather broad and undifferentiated concept of criminal law defenses.[81] The genesis of this Article takes consciously into account "the law of the case." Assessing exclusionary grounds implies more than a rigid application of the law, requiring reference to and understanding of the individual merits and character of the case and the alleged crime. This view receives affirmation in this provision. At the same time, Article 32 (2), by means of the phrase *"provided for in this Statute,"* widens the scope of the determinative powers of the ICC to exonerative norms other than those enumerated in Article 31(1).[82]

Governmental powers also should, in the course of multinational military operations (as observed in Chapters IV and V above) maintain the highest standards of justice and ethics, for the prevalence they bear in legal responsibility for their actions. This view depends for its success on the formulation of the opening statement of Justice Robert Jackson at the Nuremberg Trials, which vividly clarified the pitfalls of the absolutist approach to criminal law defenses in ICL by saying that *"we never (must) forget that the record on which we judge these defendants today is the record on which history will judge us tomorrow. To pass these defendants a poisoned chalice is to put it to our lips as well. We must summon such detachment and intellectual integrity to our task that this trial will commend itself to posterity as fulfilling humanity's aspirations to do justice."* It is in the spirit of this notion that this thesis closes as it opened, with the words of Chaim Herzog, saying *"I always believed with unquestioning faith that the State of Israel must base its existence on strong foundations if it wishes to live and thrive as a unique, ethical society."*[83] Let us hope that all States endeavor to establish and sustain such strong foundations by means of the unique international rule of law and the progression of international due process, which norms must be maintained not only by governments, to provide the necessary procedural instruments to endorse the submitted criminal law defenses in ICL, but also by international criminal defense lawyers and prosecutors. *"That is why one can dream."*[84]

---

81. Albin Eser, *Article 31, Margin 2*, in COMMENTARY ON THE ROME STATUTE (O. Triffterer, ed., 1999).
82. *See* A. Eser, *supra* note 81, Margin No. 44.
83. CHAIM HERZOG, LIVING HISTORY 425 (1996).
84. *Ibid.*

# INDEX

# BIOGRAPHICAL NOTE

*Geert-Jan (Alexander) G.J. Knoops,* born 10 June 1960, Eindhoven (Netherlands), graduated from the Law School of the University of Tilburg in 1986 and specialized in international criminal law at Utrecht University. In 1998 he obtained his Ph.D. degree at Leiden University with the thesis "Duress and Law-Finding," a subject on the use of forensic psychiatry or neurobiology in both national and international criminal law. The thesis also contained several sections on comparative criminal law.

A member of the Dutch Bar, the author has practiced law in the Netherlands since 1987. He is currently senior partner of the Amsterdam law firm Korvinus & Knoops, working in the field of international criminal and extradition law; he also practices before the Dutch Supreme Court. The author has been counsel in eleven proceedings before the European Court of Human Rights at Strasbourg.

After graduating from the LL.M. programme at Leiden University on 14th July 2000 (Public International Law and International Criminal Law Specialization), he began this book. He was registered on the list of the ICTY as defense counsel in September 2000. On the first of December 2000, the author was admitted to the list of defense counsel of the ICTR.

As Captain (Reserve) of the Royal Netherlands Marine Corps, the author has attended, as legal military advisor, several Navy and NATO exercises throughout the world.

Dr. Knoops' articles on international criminal law, as well as on neurobiological subjects in relation to international criminal law, have been published in various legal journals.

# PRINCIPAL PUBLICATIONS OF GEERT-JAN G.J. KNOOPS

Psychische overmacht en rechtsvinding, een onderzoek naar de straf-rechtelijke, forensisch-psychiatrisch en psychologische grenzen van psychische overmacht (Dissertation). S. Gouda Quint-Deventer. Brouwer en Zoon, Deventer (1998).

*Het EVRM en de Internationale Overdracht van Gevonniste Personen*, 3 ADVO-CATENBLAD 133–138 (1999).

*Neurogenetica in het Strafrecht; nieuwe visie op opzet en toerekeningsvat-baarheid*, 22 ADVOCATENBLAD 1125–1127 (1999).

*De Lockerbie-Affaire: transponering van internationaalrechtelijke staat-saansprakelijkheid naar nationale jurisdictie. No hiding place for the State?*, 29 DELIKT & DELINKWENT 601–613 (1999).

*Interstatelijk Noodweerrecht: disculpatiegrond voor internationaalrechtelijke onrechtmatige daad*, 43 NEDERLANDS JURISTENBLAD 2016–2021 (1999).

*De positie van de Forensisch psychiater en psychologie in relatie tot strafuit-sluitingsgronden*, 3 TRIAS 2–3, 16 (2000).

*T.B.S. en straftoemeting: Van reparatie naar revalidatie of rehabilitatie?*, 2 TREMA Straftoemetingsbulletin 50–53 (2000).

*Neurobiological Causes of Affective Crimes: Explanatory Powers of Neurogenetics*, INTERNATIONAL JOURNAL OF LAW AND PSYCHIATRY (G.G.J Knoops & D.F Swaab 2000), submitted.

*Extraterritorial and exonerative application of the use of force during maritime law enforcement operating on the high seas*, LEIDEN JOURNAL OF INTERNA-TIONAL LAW (2000), submitted.